Health in the Highlands

Health in the Highlands

INDIGENOUS HEALING AND SCIENTIFIC MEDICINE IN GUATEMALA AND ECUADOR

David Carey Jr.

Foreword by Jeremy A. Greene

UNIVERSITY OF CALIFORNIA PRESS

University of California Press
Oakland, California

Library of Congress Cataloging-in-Publication Data

Names: Carey, David, Jr., 1967- author. | Greene, Jeremy A., 1974- writer
   of foreword.
Title: Health in the highlands : indigenous healing and scientific medicine in
   Guatemala and Ecuador / David Carey Jr. ; foreword by Jeremy A. Greene.
Description: Oakland, California : University of California Press, [2023] |
   Includes bibliographical references and index.
Identifiers: LCCN 2022049620 (print) | LCCN 2022049621 (ebook) |
   ISBN 9780520344785 (cloth) | ISBN 9780520344792 (paperback) | ISBN
   9780520975682 (ebook)
Subjects: LCSH: Traditional medicine—Guatemala—History—20th century. |
   Traditional medicine—Ecuador—History—20th century. | Medical
   care—Guatemala—History—20th century. | Medical care—Ecuador—
   History—20th century.
Classification: LCC GR880 .C325 2023 (print) | LCC GR880 (ebook) |
   DDC 362.109728105/2—dc23/eng/20221216
LC record available at https://lccn.loc.gov/2022049620
LC ebook record available at https://lccn.loc.gov/2022049621

Manufactured in the United States of America

32 31 30 29 28 27 26 25 24 23
10 9 8 7 6 5 4 3 2 1

To the memory of my mother Margot, suegro Steverino, and uncle Steve, who all passed away while I was writing this book.

CONTENTS

ILLUSTRATIONS

MAPS

FIGURES

FOREWORD

There is no separating health from politics. The history of Latin America—especially in the early twentieth century, especially in its multiple entanglements with *gringoísmo*—is especially rich in examples of this. One needs only to recall the role of yellow fever in justifying US engagements in Cuba and the Panama Canal at the turn of the twentieth century, or the role of malaria in justifying new forms of anti-Indigenous assimilationist politics in Mexico under the auspices of the Rockefeller Foundation a few decades later, to witness how health and politics are deeply entwined on both micro and macro scales. And yet the history of Latin America is also full of attempts to deemphasize the politics of health in favor of more comforting geographical or social-scientific narratives that explain away the political economy of health and disease as natural or inevitable.

Perhaps the most pernicious of these exculpatory narratives is the recurrent naturalization of steep health disparities between Indigenous peoples and Criollo/Ladino/mestizo populations that can be found within every state in the Americas. Vast differences in maternal and infant mortality and fatalities from non-communicable and infectious diseases have repeatedly been explained away through tropes of inherent geographical differences on the one hand or cultural differences on the other. Yet as David Carey Jr. shows in this important book, these differences are overwhelmingly the result of social and structural forces—racism, dispossession, unequal citizenship—whose legacies we continue to live with today.

For the most part, late twentieth and early twenty-first century medicine and public health have learned to decry biological racism—even if new forms continue to emerge each year. But *cultural* difference remains a common retreat for even the liberal-minded to redirect blame for the perpetuation of health disparities on those who suffer the most from them. Over the past century, many historians, sociologists, and anthropologists have perpetuated this belief as well. In the culturalist model of disease disparity—long favored by official publications of the Pan-American Health Organization (formerly the Pan-American Sanitary Bureau) and the World Health Organization— the pluralism of health care encompassing home remedies, traditional herbalists, and spiritual healers was often depicted as a distraction from meaningful engagement with scientific medicine. This distraction is then thought to have fatal consequences when meaningful biomedical interventions (such as antibiotics and vaccines) are eschewed. In this model, cultural difference—here read as a static, timeless traditional health system—is remade as the leading barrier to acceptance of modern, effective clinical and public health interventions for Indigenous populations.

Observing in 1997 that similar narratives were used to explain the disparities in tuberculosis outcomes between Mayan communities in Chiapas compared to Blanco-Mestizo populations elsewhere in Mexico, the late anthropologist and infectious disease physician Paul Farmer pointed out that it was all too easy to blame health disparities on cultural differences. Yet the links themselves, when examined closer, were specious and threadbare—and covered up other, more important differences in political economy that all too often played a determining role in producing health outcomes. "In medical anthropology," Farmer continued, "often enough *culture* is held up as the determinant variable. Surely these immodest claims of causality amount to inadequate phenomenology and are underpinned by inadequate social theory. Because culture is merely one of several potentially important factors, anthropologists and other researchers who cite cognitivist 'cultural' explanations for the poor health of the poor have been the object of legitimate critiques." If one looks beyond convenient explanations of cultural difference, one sees a more powerful map of political economy and lack of access behind what is painted as lack of knowledge or poor choice. "Throughout the world," he concluded, "those least likely to comply are those least able to comply."

I remember reading these words the summer of 1997, before starting my first year of medical school that fall. Farmer's approach to social medicine was the reason I enrolled, and I was fortunate enough to be mentored by him first as a clinician, then as an anthropologist and then as a historian. As a medical student, intern, and resident, I worked with Farmer and other physician-scholars on health equity projects with ethnographic components to understand health disparities among Aymara-speaking populations in the Andean highlands of Bolivia and in Mayan populations in the Sierra Madre of Chiapas, Mexico. Aymaran residents in the shantytowns of La Paz who had stopped taking their tuberculosis treatments were often dismissed by providers as being poorly-educated in the ways of scientific medicine, or castigated for pursuing treatments with local herbalists and spiritual healers instead of their prescribed antibiotics. But all of the Aymara who let me follow along as an ethnographer in their daily lives could recite with great precision the role of Koch's bacilli and antituberculosis chemotherapy in determining tuberculosis outcomes. They were very clear that their use of Aymara healing practices did not interfere at all with their understanding of the etiology and treatment of tuberculosis. What interfered, instead, was the inability to comply with the extensive fiscal and temporal demands of treatment while also holding down a job in a vulnerable labor market. Several Mayan residents living in remote villages along the southern Sierra Madre suffering from treatable bacterial and parasitic diseases pointed to the well-painted but shuttered health clinic in their town and the empty shelves of the local pharmacy, even as the metropolitan physicians responsible for staffing them blamed poor health outcomes on the backwardness and ignorance of the people they were failing to serve. While La Paz and Chiapas may be worlds apart in terms of their physical geography, infectious disease epidemiology, and chronology of settler colonialism, independence, and revolution, the prevalence of culturalist explanations for Indigenous health disparities shared common roots—as did the overall refusal by those responsible for the health of the public to acknowledge the structural violence and ongoing political economy as important determinants of health disparities past, present, and future.

Carey's book starts with this problem and works backwards to move forwards. He uses the tools of the social historian to extend a historical dynamism and range that restores to Indigenous actors the agency and history that our self-serving narratives of cultural difference elide. Comparing two very different Indigenous contexts in South and Central America—one Andean, one Mayan—he works through neglected records of Latin American state reckonings with disparities in health and diseases between Indigenous and Mestizo/Ladino/Criollo populations in Ecuador and Guatemala. In the process, he recreates a vernacular of how physicians and public health officials in both locales wielded their authority in describing health differences to create self-satisfying narratives about cultural determinants of health, and then used them to justify further forms of structural dispossession which, paradoxically, augmented disparities in health. But if the stories of medicine, public health, and Indigenous health disparities have similarities, the two states are not the same. Throughout the early twentieth century, political positioning of Indigenous rights and Indigenous health played out differently in these locales, with quite different outcomes. It is here that the connected—not merely comparative—history that Carey recounts allows the reader to understand not only the plurality of paths not taken, but also just how much agency and potential still resides in the possibility for meaningful interventions to achieve health equity in the present day.

So, too, with the possibility for restoring agency and plurality in our understanding of the complex landscape of healthcare which Indigenous peoples face in both one-on-one clinical encounters and in the face of massive public health interventions like COVID-19 vaccination in the present day. The Kaqchikel and Kichwa actors whose traces Carey teases from the state archives did not perceive a stark choice between "scientific medicine" on the one hand and "traditional medicine" on the other, no matter how much Ecuadorian physicians, Guatemalan public health officials, or traveling representatives of the Rockefeller Foundation may have liked to portray it that way. From the very beginning of the introductory chapter, through to the end of the coda, Indigenous Americans seeking health care in the twentieth century faced a range of choices and demonstrated practical savvy. They demanded access and equity in receiving the benefits of biomedicine as well as the freedom to benefit from traditional birth attendants and the grounded use of *remedias caseras*, *naturistas*, and other *curanderos*.

In recent years, the Pan-American Health Organization has promoted a more syncretic approach to intercultural primary health care and integrated health systems, recognizing that the ability of Indigenous peoples to move back and forth across a number of healing frameworks and practices is crucial to the success of future health systems and public health efforts moving forward. That the existence of Indigenous healing practices and healers could be an asset to public health efforts, rather than a distraction or competition. That disparities in access to key economic, political, medical, and public health resources—seen so dramatically in the present COVID-19 pandemic—is as much or more of a determinant of disparities in health outcomes as any simple clash between traditional Indigenous healing and modern scientific medicine.

Health in the Highlands shows this has always been the case.

Jeremy A. Greene
Baltimore, MD
August 27, 2022

ACKNOWLEDGMENTS

Without supportive colleagues and friends, generous institutions, and a loving, adventurous family, this book would not have been possible. Gracious scholars of Ecuador welcomed a neophyte: Chad Black, Ronn Pineo, Nicola Foote, Marc Becker, Betsy Konefal, and especially Kim Clark, who patiently answered my many queries about Ecuadoran archives, indigenous peoples, and history. Historians of medicine also shared their expertise: Steve Palmer, Gabriela Soto Laveaga, Graciela Espinosa, Adam Warren, and Pablo Gómez. Jeremy Greene and Elizabeth O'Brien twice invited me to present works in progress at the Johns Hopkins University History of Medicine seminars. Their feedback, and that of their colleagues, enriched this monograph considerably.

Kim Clark, Elizabeth O'Brien, Sarah Foss, and two anonymous reviewers at the University of California Press all read earlier versions of this manuscript in its entirety. Their comments, suggestions, and critiques significantly improved it. Dillon Vrana, Gema Klopp-Santamaría, Allen Wells, Jeremy Greene, Randy Packard, Martha Few, Matt Mulcahy, Betsy Schmidt, and Steve Palmer did the same with the chapters they read. Thanks, too, to the editors of *Environmental History*, *American Historical Review*, and *Mesoamérica*, which published pieces I wrote—and, with their permission, have drawn on here—along the way. Janice Jaffee, Ixnal Ambrocia Cuma Chávez, and Ixq'anil Judie Maxwell helped me to understand nuances of translation in Spanish and Kaqchikel. At the University of Southern Maine Osher Map Library, Matthew Edney, Louis Miller, and Libby Bischof all provided invaluable assistance in locating maps for this book.

More archivists than I can list in Guatemala, Ecuador, and the United States listened closely to my questions and guided me toward invaluable sources. Rocío Bedón made the Museo de Medicina feel like a second home and quickly became a trusted friend in Ecuador. At the Archivo General de Centroamérica (AGCA), former director Anna Carla Ericastilla and her staff were similarly welcoming. Ilonka Matute, at the Biblioteca Nacional de Guatemala (BNG), and María Eugenia Gordillo, at the Hermeroteca Nacional de Guatemala (HNG), graciously allowed me to research newspaper, rare books, and other collections. The Biblioteca del Ministro de Salud archivist was also especially helpful. RAC's talented staff helped me hone my research questions, identified and retrieved relevant materials, and facilitated permission to publish photographs in this book.

When Loyola University Maryland hired me in 2014, they offered a research grant that was untethered to a narrative, which allowed me to conduct research in Ecuador—a place I had long hoped to compare to Guatemala because of their similarly significant indigenous populations and diverse ecologies. That support, and a subsequent Hanway Faculty Scholar in Global Studies fellowship (2015–18), facilitated research at the Archivo Nacional de Ecuador and Museo de Medicina in Quito and numerous archives in Guatemala (AGCA, Academia de Geografía e Historia de Guatemala, Biblioteca del Ministerio de Salud, BNG, HNG, Centro de Investigaciones Regionales de Mesoamérica). Doehler Chair funds supported two research trips to the Rockefeller Archive Center in Sleepy Hollow, New York. An American Philosophical Society grant allowed a return trip to conduct archival research in Quito in 2017. A 2018 Loyola Center for Humanities National Endowment for the Humanities summer research grant afforded another round of research in Guatemala. A 2019–20 John Simon Guggenheim Foundation Fellowship allowed me to finish the research and draft much of the manuscript.

Additionally, Loyola supports regular Writing Retreats for Faculty that have deepened and broadened my writing community, propelling this project forward and helping me learn from and with my colleagues. Other Loyola faculty, along with students and staff, also contributed to this book with their insightful questions and keen comments during public presentations of the research as part of my Doehler Chair opportunities. The outstanding undergraduate student Maeve Hill populated the bibliography.

A special thanks to Kate Marshall at the University of California Press, who believed in this project when it was still only a concept, displayed monumental patience as my research and writing slowly unfolded, and was ready to talk it all through with me at various stages—including over many coffees at the American Historical Association and Latin American Studies Association conferences. Thanks also to her talented colleagues, including Enrique Ochoa-Kaup, Jeff Anderson, and Chad Attenborough. The manuscript's final transformation came about with help from developmental editor Megan Pugh, whose feedback ranged from structural to sentence level.

My wife Sarah and our daughters Ava and Kate have been my bedrock. Their patience, understanding, and curiosity buoy me. During three magical summers, we explored Ecuador along with my nephew Stephen Rothrock and Guatemala with Stephen's sister Ellie, my sister-in-law Becky O'Connor, and her daughter Keegan. I owe them all a huge debt for their sense of adventure and willingness to *aguantar* my stories about the past. Although I am sure her sole goal was to stay up past her bedtime, Kate regularly plied me for "bedtime stories from the archives," while Ava embraced every new adventure, from the highlands of Guatemala and Ecuador to the Galapagos Islands. Sarah enriched everything, from the routines of daily life to the unexpected, at home and in the many places this project has led us: Antigua, Quito, Austin, San Francisco, and New Orleans. I have asked too much of her, yet she manages simultaneously to be there for me and our daughters, and to pursue her own profession and passions. She is a brilliant, soulful, and warmhearted role model for Ava and Kate and an inspiration for me.

A NOTE ON SOURCES, METHODOLOGY, AND EVIDENCE

Histories of medicine often are informed by exceptional moments or flash-points rather than everyday life. If we are fortunate, illness marks an anomaly; we seldom take (and almost never make) note of when we or others are feeling well. Despite their extraordinary nature, records of health crises go beyond mere descriptions of chaotic or exceptional events to offer insights into people's everyday experiences with illness and healing. Medicine and health are not merely moments of epidemics and death, but also waking, eating, moving, and breathing. Even epidemics sometimes pass without scholarly note.[1] Because archival records tend to capture more sensational than mundane events, evidence of persecuted *empíricos* (untrained practitioners) outweighs descriptions of sanctioned ones.

Archives are replete with silences, but they become particularly deafening around the intersections of indigeneity, modernization, and medicine in nations committed to advancing scientific medicine in ways that disparage indigenous healing and hygiene practices. Building off of Marcos Cueto's and Steven Palmer's lament that archives penned, organized, and maintained by Hispanics offer scant evidence of indigenous notions concerning medicine and disease,[2] I examine two countries—Ecuador and Guatemala—with such large indigenous populations that their erasure from national archives is not possible.

Focusing on language and wording can reveal how *indígenas* (indigenous people) responded to state-sanctioned medical knowledge.[3] Language and orthography matter. As such, close attention to malleable transnational terms and local details is crucial. Some Spanish words change meaning from Guatemala to Ecuador. In Guatemala, *jefe político* is a governor whereas in Ecuador the term denotes a municipal official. Public health offices were named Servicio de Sanidad in Ecuador and Salubridad Pública in Guatemala.

Similarly, the term *indio* is a racist epithet in Guatemala whereas it holds little denigration in Ecuador. I use indígena when referring to indigenous people, unless documents state otherwise, in which case I adhere to scribes' word choices. Orthography too shifts. When I quote a document, I stay true to contemporary scribes' choices of Cakchiquel and Quichua. Otherwise, I adhere to the standardized spelling of Kaqchikel and Kichwa. I occasionally use the term Maya to refer to the broader group of Guatemalan indígenas comprised of twenty-one different linguistic and ethnic groups. But that term seldom appears in archival documents from the first half of the twentieth century.

Conducting archival research across three countries is daunting, but to facilitate ongoing transnational analysis, I interleaved short research trips (one to three weeks) in each location instead of completing research in one country before moving on to another. That approach also served me well within each country. My findings at one archive informed my subsequent research at other archives. The overarching goal and arguments largely remained the same, but the organic process of relating research findings in one archive to those in another deepened my sense of the historical actors, events, and processes.

As is true in Guatemalan archives, Ecuadorian archives only parsimoniously divulge indigenous perspectives on topics surrounding public health, medicine, and healing. Fewer indigenous perspectives still were forthcoming at the Rockefeller Archive Center (RAC) in Sleepy Hollow, New York. The sparse appearance of indigenous and other poor and working-class people in the archives resulted in a book primarily populated by middle-class and elite medical professionals and government officials, but wherever possible, I highlight marginalized voices.

Their omission of some vital details notwithstanding, Guatemalan, Ecuadorian, and Rockefeller Foundation (RF) archives document public health ambiguities. Archival evidence generated by the very authorities who contrasted clean, modern, and scientific medicine against dirty, backwards, and indigenous practices argues against those categories by revealing the complexity, dynamism, and heterogeneity of health, illness, and healthcare in early-twentieth-century Guatemala and Ecuador. The rhetoric of scientific medicine's supremacy and discourse denigrating indígenas and their healing practices often gave way to more nuanced observations whereby authorities and medical professionals recognized indígenas' contributions to public health and the legitimacy of *curanderos* (traditional healers). Archival documents reveal the give and take between indigenous and scientific medicine and between indígenas and state-sanctioned public health endeavors. The vibrancy of scientific, indigenous, Hispanic, and hybrid healthcare demonstrates that the diffusion of medical knowledge was seldom spontaneous or universal, but rather disseminated through social networks, guided by financial considerations, and tied to differential patterns of exposure and invisibility.[4] Alongside (and often contravening) medical professionals and public health institutions, unofficial health care practitioners, indigenous and other ethnic communities, and marginalized patients helped to construct heterogeneous medical systems that varied as they adapted to local needs.[5]

To detect indigenous residents' responses to epidemics and to access curanderos' and empíricos' perspectives, I tap court records, municipal reports, petitions, letters, and newspapers. As historian Charles Rosenberg demonstrates in his study of cholera in nineteenth-century New York City, epidemics and responses to them produce social, moral, and political responses traceable through newspapers and archives.[6] Tracking such signals as they emerge in twentieth-century Ecuadorian and Guatemalan public health campaigns facilitates analyzing the contingent role that engaging indígenas played in health care systems. Although archival holdings in Guatemala and Ecuador are different, they both contain evidence of how scientific and indigenous healing cultures coalesced and clashed.

By reading against the grain of historical documents for evidence of how ethnicity and race shaped perceptions of healing, hygiene, and public health, I build on the work of historians of Latin American medicine like Pablo Gómez and Martha Few who demonstrate respectively how race and ethnicity informed and influenced "multiple coexistent popular healing traditions" and the equally diverse practices of learned or "enlightened" medicine.[7] Gómez and Few interrogate such archival sources as inquisition records, medical manuals, vaccination censuses, and correspondence to demonstrate how Afro-Caribbean and indigenous healers and patients influenced colonial medicine. But while this method is more accessible in their periods of study—the sixteenth, seventeenth, and eighteenth centuries—few scholars have applied that approach to postcolonial Latin America.[8] As was true in colonial Central America and the Caribbean, assumptions about racial and ethnic hierarchies saturated early-twentieth-century scientific medicine and public health initiatives.[9]

At times my ignorance nearly derailed the project. As scribes and legislators described clothing prohibited for street and market vendors with words like *follón* and *centro*, I did not comprehend that they denoted the traditional wide skirt worn by indigenous women. In 1926, Ecuadoran legislators passed laws prohibiting milk, meat, bread and other food vendors from wearing a follón or centro.[10] Until Dr. Rocío Bedón at the Museo de Medicina explained those terms to me, I did not recognize the racial and ethnic contours of those laws. Anticipating such blind spots in my knowledge, I concurrently expanded my historiographical knowledge of the RF, medicine, and Ecuador. I approached archival research and historiographical reading as symbiotic processes, which helped me to both narrow my focus on certain topics and broaden my efforts where I lacked content and context. Yet not all of this contextual knowledge fit into the narrative. Because of the wide empirical and analytical net cast in this book, I often keep context succinct.

Evidence of complex and contradictory approaches to scientific medicine abound in Guatemalan, Ecuadorian, and RF archives that were organized, in part, to capture the unitary power of modern medicine. Those archival sources almost invariably push readers toward *ladino* (non-indigenous), *blanco-mestizo* (white-mixed race), or US technocratic perspectives steeped in scientific medicine. By critically reading such hegemonic narratives, I demonstrate scientific medicine's variability and inability to dominate popular healing. Although sources produced by nonindigenous scribes at best approximate indígenas' thoughts about illness, well-being, epidemics, healing, and medicine, some eyewitness accounts of indigenous participation in public health campaigns and initiative in others reveal indigenous public health practices and responses to epidemics. Latin American historians of medicine have expertly analyzed syncretism in the region, but often with static, structuralist portrayals of scientific medicine that in reality could be as dynamic as popular healing. As much as Latin American authorities and medical professionals and RF representatives portrayed scientific medicine as coherent and unified, scholars have demonstrated how social diversity, regional variation, and resource deprivation alter how scientific medicine is practiced in different places, cultures, and times.[11] A multiplicity of medicines—scientific, folk, indigenous, African, hybrid—characterized health care in Ecuador and Guatemala.

For historians interested in transnational research on medicine, philanthropy, agriculture, and a host of other topics, RAC provides an excellent launching pad. For historians of medicine, the Museo de Medicina (MM) in Quito, Ecuador offers a plethora of sources (archival, material, and visual) for the twentieth century. MM's digitized index for the Sanidad and Asistencia Pública collections facilitated locating correspondence between public health officials, medical professionals, municipal authorities, and international experts and voyeurs. Although largely muted in the Sanidad collection, indígenas emerge with strong voices in the Asistencia Pública collection, particularly in correspondence between officials who oversaw the hacienda system fueled by *huasipungueros* (resident farm laborers). Scholars interested in earlier centuries can consult the Archivo Nacional de Ecuador (ANE), located across the park, which reveals the complex relationship between traditional and scientific medicine in a turn-of-the-century hospital where curanderos also practiced.

Although Guatemala does not boast an archive dedicated to medicine, the Archivo General de Centroamérica (AGCA) in Guatemala City offers a rich repository of material for the colonial and postcolonial periods. AGCA has catalogued the colonial collection of interest to historians of medicine in Central America. Access to the national period continues to grow as archivists develop finding guides. Fortunately, much of the material related to Guatemala City's hospitals and the nation's public health is indexed digitally (though few of the documents have themselves been digitized). Twentieth-century correspondence between the Director of the General Hospital in Guatemala City, indigenous patients and family members, municipal mayors, doctors, dictators, presidents, police chiefs, military surgeons, and prison wardens all open windows into how access to health care revealed power relations and ethnic and class privileges. Since the *legajos* (bundles) are thick and seldom organized, the AGCA's limit of ten requests per day was rarely constraining. In separate rooms, the AGCA holds Annual Reports from the *Gobernación* (Government) that contained sections on public health and the Ministry of Health (after 1932) and the *Boletín Sanitario de Guatemala* (1927–1945). Those sources provide insights into government-sanctioned public health campaigns.

The archive and library of the Academia de Geografía e Historia de Guatemala (AGHG) has the *Boletín Sanitario de Guatemala*, *Revista Militar*, *Revista Agricola*, and Government and Public Health *Memorias*. In turn, the Biblioteca del Ministerio de Salud has nearly a full run of *Memorias de Sanidad* and other twentieth-century public health publications.

Although I stretch my analysis from the late nineteenth century to the mid-twentieth century, the temporal focus from 1913–45 tracks RF public health engagement in the region. By 1945, the RF was transitioning from public health to agricultural development. I incorporate the RF in my study not because of its dominance in the region (often it was peripheral and ineffective), but rather because of the insight gained by analyzing the role of an international public health actor that operated in both nations to varying degrees. Since Ecuador and Guatemala seldom interacted with each other formally or informally, the RF serves as a linchpin between the two nations and offers a different window into indigenous-state relations and racist thought.

The material culture of archives conveys power. Whereas the correspondence coming from the governor's office, presidential palace, and elite Guatemalans was almost invariably typed, responses from municipal councils and local residents were handwritten by the same person, suggesting municipalities could not afford their own scribe, let alone a typewriter. Such gradations in resources correlated with a hierarchy of power. (In an exception to that rule, elite Ecuadorians sometimes penned instead of typed their letters in the first half of the twentieth century.) Attuned to such manifestations of power differentials, scholars can deepen their analysis and contextualization of archival silences.

Unfortunately, reliable data on diseases and epidemics in Guatemala and Ecuador is scant—making the reconstruction of demographic health trends elusive and complicated.[12] Prior to 1900, Ecuadorian authorities tallied malaria under "other fevers" rather than separately, partly because its symptoms were not easily distinguished from other diseases.[13] In 1914 Dr. Carlos A. Miño, the Sanidad (Public Health Office) Subdirector in Quito, lamented that even after the 1900 Law of Civil Registry mandated all deaths be recorded with the state (rather than the Catholic church), the lack of scientific basis in determining the cause of death rendered statistics useless.[14] Even when reporting diseases was mandated by law and crucial to stemming epidemics, some medical practitioners failed to do so. Such was the case during a 1913 dysentery and 1915 typhoid outbreak in Guayaquil.[15] In the 1920s, Ecuadorian authorities persecuted a medical student for illegally practicing medicine because he failed to report typhoid cases he treated.[16]

Guatemalan public health and RF officials similarly insisted rural data was useless. In 1916, RF director of Guatemala Alvin Struse explained why they could not determine indigenous subjects' ages or even names, let alone other crucial data related to their health: "The field men cannot make this accurate Age Census, and they acquire the habit of bad guessing, which is unscientific, and small inaccuracies make all the statistics absolutely worthless."[17] His agency's track record was no better. In his research on Central America and the Caribbean, historian Steven Palmer concluded RF data were "far from accurate."[18] After failing to collect data on illness, birth, and death rates from the Northwestern (and predominantly indigenous) departments of Quetzaltenango, Huehuetenango, Quiche, Totonicapan, and San Marcos a decade and a half later, the regional health inspector explained in 1933, "It was impossible for me. I unfortunately collided with the insurmountable difficulty of the data from those offices having no practical value, the majority of diagnoses are from indigenous empíricos for whom 'mal de ojo' [evil eye] is the cause of the death toll, which makes any scientific control impossible."[19] According to El Quiche governor Rogelio Morales it was not simply indigenous curanderos who incorrectly attributed causes of deaths: "Assistant councilors are completely ignorant of the true causes of death, they have no medical preparation or principles and from that it is impossible to get exact statistics on the diseases that cause deaths."[20] According to Morales's contemporary Dr. Federico Castellanos, assistant councilors recorded any lethal fever as malaria.[21] Yet even those with medical training were prone to mistakes that corrupted data so extensively as to make it useless. Responding to a June 1945 typhus outbreak in rural Huehuetenango, the head of the Typhus Commission Dr. Isidro Cabrera had to dismiss the physician's assistant because of so "many anomalies ... problems and errors ... disorder."[22] Some authorities deployed data deficiencies for political expediency. Based on Cabrera's report, the Director of Public Health insisted typhus cases had not increased but "notably diminished."[23] Palmer concedes, "Between the whim, fudging, and error of inspectors, nurses, and microscopists and the taxonomical challenges of the ethnic groups, the data collected was far from reliable."[24] Although such shortcomings undermined my efforts to analyze broader trends as they related to epidemics and public health, the archives contain rich evidence of how epidemics and disease shaped individual, national, and international relations.

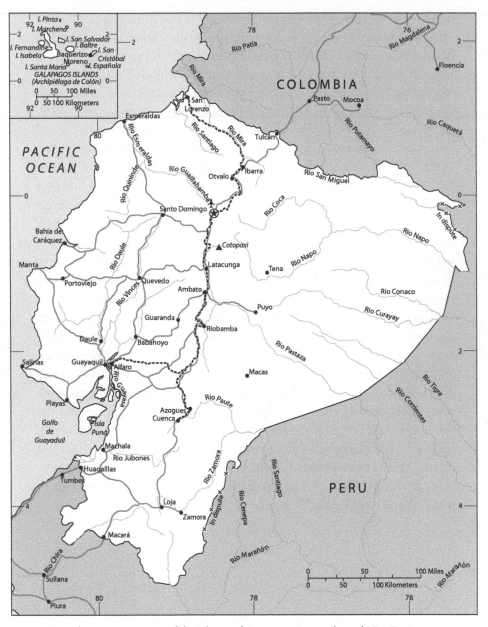

MAP I. Ecuador, 1976. Courtesy of the Library of Congress, Geography and Map Division.

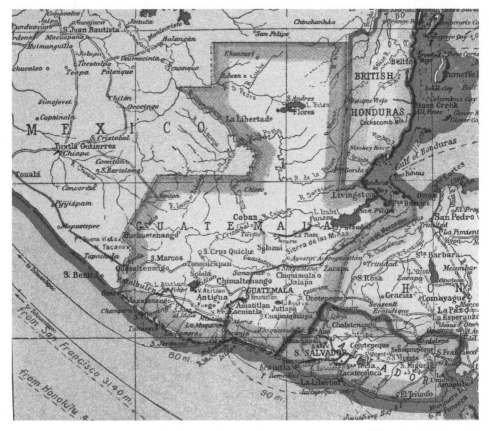

MAP 2. Guatemala, 1922. Detail of map of Central America in *Harmworth's Atlas of the World*. Courtesy of the Osher Map Library, University of Southern Maine.

ABBREVIATIONS

FEI   Federación Ecuatoriana de Indios (Ecuadorian Federation of Indians)

IING   Instituto Indigenista Nacional de Guatemala (National Indigenist Institute of Guatemala)

LNHO   League of Nations Health Organization

MM   Museo de Medicina

PAHO   Pan American Health Organization

PASB   Pan American Sanitary Bureau

RF   Rockefeller Foundation

UFCO   United Fruit Company

USPHS   United States Public Health Service

INTRODUCTION

————

Disease, Healing, and Medicine in
Indigenous Highlands

ON AUGUST 31, 1942, two Kaqchikel Maya men from the rural highland town of San Juan Comalapa, Alberto Calí Cuzal and Cipriano Chovix Chalí, traveled some seventy kilometers to Guatemala City. They hoped to access free expert healthcare at the publicly-funded General Hospital. Since neither spoke Spanish, they carried letters written by a scribe who explained their symptoms. Work and even relaxation had become excruciating for both because of pain in the abdomen (Cuzal) and lung (Chalí). Chalí could barely eat and suffered headaches. He had consulted a doctor in the department capital of Chimaltenango, but reported that medication "had no effect on him."[1] Now, both men appealed to leading authorities of scientific medicine in Guatemala. "I urgently beg [you] . . . to present me with a cure or an indication of what I should do to end my suffering," Cuzal implored the hospital director.[2]

There is no archival evidence of what response or treatment Chalí and Cuzal received. But the letters' existence suggests that the hospital deemed them valuable enough to save, so the Kaqchikel men likely got, at the very least, some form of attention. The social interactions they had in the hospital, as well as their own notions of illness and healing, would have shaped their decisions around whether to pursue whatever potential cures may have been recommended to them.

Indígenas (indigenous people) across Latin America commonly consulted diverse practitioners while pursuing healthcare, whose hybrid forms included scientific, indigenous, Afro-descendant, folk, traditional, and other medicines.[3] By the time Chalí and Cuzal travelled to the hospital, they probably would have already consulted indigenous *curanderos* (traditional healers), whom the Guatemalan government tended to portray, with both condescension and racism, as retrograde. But indígenas were also embracing modernity, understood as a set of technological, social, and cultural changes catalyzed by capitalism and science.[4] And they consulted doctors in urban hospitals enough to suggest they were ready to claim their rights to healthcare,[5] even though they faced considerable obstacles along the way.[6]

Some two thousand kilometers to the southeast, in Ecuador, Andean indígenas were up against similar challenges. A few years later, in June of 1945, the regional director for the north-central highlands of Ecuador, Dr. Enrique Garcés, travelled from Quito to Otavalo, a busy market town with a strong indigenous presence, to deliver a speech about typhus in Kichwa. His trip, part of a larger public health effort to disseminate information about disease, diet, and hygiene to rural indígenas,[7] built on a legacy of communication between politically active indígenas in the region and colonial and national governments.[8] It was also in keeping with a pattern in which, again and again, Ecuadorian government and health officials showed more respect to indígenas and their health practices than did their Guatemalan counterparts.

The differences in indigenous healthcare in each country were shaped, in part, by difference in government. Guatemala was a dictatorship. Since the 1871 Liberal Revolution, it had been ruled largely by caudillos whose administrations dispossessed indigenous land and conscripted indigenous labor to expand Guatemala's agro-export economy. A functional legal system notwithstanding, a general disinterest in hearing from anyone who was not at the top of the hierarchy permeated Guatemalan political and social life, and meant that indigenous participation in public health initiatives was more or less foreclosed. Ecuador, on the other hand—while still authoritarian—had at least a semblance of representative governance, and it often encouraged indigenous participation in civic life. Although few indígenas could vote, they held a moderate demographic influence, comprising 25 to 40 percent of the population in the early to mid-twentieth century, and a burgeoning indigenous movement in the 1930s and 1940s led to increasing autonomy.[9] Indígenas seldom threatened political power, but the government encouraged Ecuadorian medical professionals to approach them with cultural sensitivity, which helped make for better results in their healthcare.

Yet a close reading of Garcés's speech reminds us that in Ecuador, too, racism endured. "In your language ... I come again to teach you how you should live and how you can guard against this illness that is in your land," he said. "You call it fever, we know it as Typhus," the speech continued, suggesting that these differences were not just in perception, but in expertise: the indigenous audience might "call" the disease by its symptom, but scientists "know" about the facts. He blamed the disease's spread on indigenous life-styles, asserting that "everywhere people live untidy [and in] grubby [sur-roundings] they contract it and die."[10] Subtly and explicitly, Garcés advanced medical science and discounted indigenous healing. By distinguishing tax-onomies that fit state-sanctioned scientific medicine, he minimized indige-nous knowledge.

During the first half of the twentieth century, encounters like these between indigenous Ecuadorians and Guatemalans and medical profession-als took place in greater numbers than ever before. And they were enabled by desires for both humanitarianism and social control.[11] The Rockefeller Foundation (RF), then one of the most significant international public health organizations, was working to mitigate disease and improve public health in both countries until the late 1940s, when it shifted its focus prima-rily to agricultural development.[12] Healthy workers were good for US com-panies relying on local labor. For their part, Ecuadorian and Guatemalan officials, too, wanted to solve real health problems, from plagues to infant mortality. Yet they also railed against—and even penalized—indigenous modes of healing and well-being. During early-twentieth-century nation-building periods, for example, officials in Guatemala and Ecuador outlawed indigenous bathing and funerary rituals, respectively, for fear they spread deadly germs. These longstanding practices were part of dynamic, holistic approaches to health that took into account an individual's psychological, emotional, and physical well-being.[13] Attacking them meant attacking indig-enous worldviews, histories, sense of place, and communities.

Racist thought shaped the public health initiatives in both countries.[14] With nineteenth- and early-twentieth-century citizenship in Latin America reserved for those who elites deemed capable of participating in civic life—urban, cosmopolitan Hispanic citizens—indígenas and their healing prac-tices tended to be relegated to society's margins.[15] In Guatemala, a relatively united oligarchy exploited indígenas singlemindedly, and eugenicists demanded indigenous assimilation. Convinced indígenas and their culture undermined the nation's march toward progress, economic and political elites coercively extracted indigenous labor and dispossessed indigenous land. Ecuador followed eugenicist thinking as well, but framed its efforts as attempts to improve a national (rather than solely indigenous) race. In con-trast to Guatemala, Ecuadorian officials did not demand assimilation and sometimes corrected for such overreach, which facilitated conditions whereby indígenas could embrace public health and health care initiatives without fear of surrendering their ethnicity. Moreover, divisions among political and economic elites in Ecuador created openings in which indígenas could advance their agendas and mitigate some of the structural racism they faced. RF representatives acted in kind, advancing notions about indígenas in Guatemala that often mirrored racist thought there, but seldom denigrating indígenas in Ecuador where they enjoyed greater respect.

Yet influence acted in multiple directions, such that—during an epoch of intense nationalism and modernization—indígenas and their healers shaped the evolution of healthcare and public health programs in both countries. With their consistent and robust demand for curanderos, indígenas ensured medical science never monopolized healthcare in either country.[16] In turn, indigenous midwives who taught their natal care techniques and knowledge to interested doctors injected indigenous expertise into gynecological care. Even when their states did not recognize them as citizens, indigenous men and women claimed medical citizenship, the right to public health initiatives and healthcare.[17] And while medical science became increasingly powerful and orthodox, it did not fully edge out the knowledges and remedies on offer—sometimes thriving—among *empíricos* (who learned through experience rather than formal medical training), curanderos and indígenas. The contact, conflict, and collaboration of the era led to new forms of syncretism, too.

RACE RELATIONS, RACIALIZATION, AND INDIGENEITY

Unlike other Latin American nations such as Costa Rica, Chile, and Argentina, postcolonial Guatemala and Ecuador both had and continue to have large indigenous populations. Mexico and Peru also had significant indigenous populations, but as colonial hubs and postcolonial capitalist centers of modernization, they attracted numerous foreign entrepreneurs, diplomats, interlopers, and later, attention from historians. In contrast, Guatemala and Ecuador saw less in-migration and, with notable exceptions, have been less extensively chronicled.[18] As importantly, Ecuador and Guatemala represent different, albeit sometimes overlapping, elite approaches to indigeneity which both shaped and were shaped by the history of public health. Taken together, they can help us elucidate connections between imperialism, public health, state and non-state actors, and constructions of race and racism.

Recognizing that ethnic identities are created, contested, and reinvented, for the purposes of this study, the term "indígena" hews closely to its use in archival documents, from which it is difficult to know how scribes and observers defined indigeneity. Most likely clothing, language, footwear (or a lack thereof), diet, and other outward ethnic markers served to distinguish indigenous from nonindigenous people (contravening postmodern scholars' discouragement of defining indigenous people by discrete cultural, traditional, linguistic, or historical traits).[19] Archival materials shed little light on how actors came to define indígenas and even less on how indígenas defined themselves. While the 1896 Ecuadorian constitution referred to natives as the "indigenous race" (*raza indígena*) the 1906 constitution referred to them as the "Indian race" (*raza india*).[20] When scribes denote ethnicity explicitly, I identify people as such. Elsewhere I attempt to ascertain ethnicity, being transparent about how fraught that process is. While my focus is on indígenas living in rural highland communities, there is broad variety within that category: Guatemala is home to more than twenty different Maya linguistic groups; in Ecuador, regional differences distinguish Kichwa speakers in the Andes mountains, various Amazonian tribes, and a few indigenous groups along the coast.[21]

In both Ecuador and Guatemala, indígenas occupy similar places in racial hierarchies shaped by conquest, colonization, and slavery. Although the racial order has varied over time, its broad contours have remained consistent: lighter-skinned citizens have enjoyed more social, political, economic, and political privileges than their darker-skinned counterparts. In Ecuador, whites have persisted atop the social structure followed by *blanco-mestizos* (white mixed-race people), indígenas, and Afro-Ecuadorians. Africans, forced into slavery to labor in gold mines and later plantations, were most populous in the Guayas, Manabi, Esmeraldas, and the Chota valley, and remained at the bottom of the social ladder even after the new nation abolished slavery in 1822. Writing in the 1930s, the Guayaquileño journalist and poet Rodrigo Chávez (1908–81) considered "los negros" inferior to indígenas.[22] No wonder, then, that some Afro-Ecuadorians identified themselves as "blancos."

Meanwhile, through organizing, protesting, and negotiating for their rights, indígenas enjoyed some social mobility and political influence,[23] and by 1929, literate women had won the right to vote. Ecuadorian racism was mitigated by elites' confidence that they would not cede control to indígenas, who comprised a minority of the population.[24] But the combination of literacy requirements and the structural racism working against equal access to education prevented most indígenas in Ecuador from being able to vote until 1979.[25] For their part, blanco-mestizos identified with both their European and indigenous ancestors, while coastal Montuvios who embraced their indigenous, African, and European heritage sometimes were identified as "indios"—a term that was a racial slur in Guatemala, but associated with little denigration in Ecuador.[26] Overall, Ecuadorian racial diversity was complex, sometimes contested, and not entirely fixed. For example, the father of social medicine in Ecuador, Eugenio Espejo (1747–95), has been portrayed as both one of the nation's greatest indígenas and the most "celebrated Afro-Ecuadorian."[27] His father was indigenous, while his mother was of mixed African and European heritage—known, in the terminology of the time, as a mulatta.

In Guatemala, *Criollos* (Creoles, self-proclaimed pure-blooded Spanish descendants) stood atop the social ladder followed by mestizos (of mixed indigenous and Spanish heritage), ladinos (Europeanized, nonindigenous people), and Afro-Guatemalans. A few entrepreneurial indigenous elites notwithstanding, indígenas and Afro-Guatemalans, including Garífunas (an African-Arawak population), were on the bottom rungs. Though hostility arose between indígenas, Africans, and mulattos, intermarriage between them was not uncommon: *mestizaje*, or racial mixing, happened both biologically and culturally. For example, indigenous women were said to have been attracted to African slaves because their physical and social mobility was not as restricted as that of indigenous men.[28]

Yet beginning in the late nineteenth century and in contrast to the more fluid set of identities available in Ecuador, Guatemalan Liberals sought to establish a racial binary with censuses that separated the population into being either indígenas or ladinos. Mestizos populated the nation, but not the censuses. During the first part of the twentieth century, the offspring of German immigrants and Q'eqchi' Maya women were referred to as *la raza mejorada* (the improved race).[29] And while *indígenas* comprised the majority of the population[30]—some 65 percent in 1921[31]—they had little access to wealth and authority. Those who shed their indigenous markers, like language and clothing, could adopt a ladino identity and hope for the spoils that came with it. But many indígenas remained steadfast in their claims of ethnicity and citizenship.[32] Writing to the ruthless dictator Manuel Estrada Cabrera (1898–1920) in 1918, a rural indígena identified himself both as a member of the "indigenous race and citizen of the nation."[33] As in Ecuador, however, the full rights of citizenship were restricted to those who could pass literacy tests, which remained in effect until 1945 for indigenous men and 1965 for indigenous women.[34]

Tainted by such racist disempowerment, public health campaigns often failed to engage, let alone serve, indígenas. Three-quarters of the population of Guatemala was rural (and nearly 70 percent worked in agriculture), but medical professionals were concentrated in cities.[35] Ecuador similarly struggled to provide public health and health care services in rural indigenous areas. Physicians generally cared for a more cosmopolitan elite section of the population, who purchased medications at *farmacias* instead of informal *botiquines* where poor and working class people were attended.[36] When elites fell ill, private doctors shielded them from the deprivations and indignities of hospital care and public health campaigns.[37] By the 1910s, Central American elites enjoyed medical attention and sanitation measures such as screens and piped water that reduced their likelihood of contracting diseases.[38] The concatenations of poverty, racism, and geography that undermined health and convalescence meant that poor, rural indígenas had some of the worst public health indicators in both countries.

THE SHIFTING TERRAIN OF SCIENCE, HEALING, RACE, AND PLACE

Medical science never has been settled terrain. In the early twentieth century, the curative powers of orthodox medicine were often limited, and university-trained doctors struggled to prove they were more competent than Mesoamerican and Andean healers.[39] Antibacterial medicines and antibiotics only began to appear in the late 1930s and mid-1940s, respectively. Most vaccines were developed in the second half of the twentieth century, and thereafter, scientific medicine saved millions of lives. In the early part of the twentieth century, however, scientific medicine was often ineffective and some practices—particularly when applied aggressively—harmed the ill. In those instances, indigenous medicine was preferable. In particularly egregious cases, as when US and Guatemalan doctors injected Guatemalan subjects with syphilis and gonorrhea, scientific medicine actively sought to harm patients.[40] Considered against such brutality, indigenous healers were less of a threat to individual and collective health than medical professionals. Whether considering curanderos, *comadronas* (midwives), physicians, or other providers, my aim is to understand what the meaning, value, and effi-cacy of their practices reveal about race, class, gender, and politics.

Early-twentieth-century public health campaigns demonstrated the effi-cacy of laboratory-based medicine and the ability of state-sponsored scientific medicine to contain epidemics and cure debilitating diseases.[41] Those efforts undoubtedly improved public health, but their agendas foreshortened heal-ing alternatives. What's more, these campaigns were shaped by, and helped perpetuate, racism. For example, as an understanding of miasma (that foul-smelling vapors from the air, water, or ground caused epidemics) gave way to germ theory, with its emphasis on vectors and infectious agents,[42] doctors of medical science framed indígenas themselves, rather than the environment, as contagious threats.

Guatemalan and Ecuadorian authorities, intellectuals, and medical pro-fessionals also mobilized racist thought to promote their priorities by por-traying indigenous healing practices as retrograde and dangerous.[43] Officials argued that elevating scientific medicine and suppressing indigenous and other unlicensed healing were crucial to modernization.[44] They denigrated, and even outlawed, unlicensed healers. They attributed these decisions to the need to maintain public health concerns and continue modernization, but were less forthcoming about another goal: to defend the economic interests of doctors who had graduated with degrees in scientific medicine and whose competition included partially-trained nurses, midwives, pharmacists, and medical students as well as indigenous curers and empíricos.[45] Yet campaigns to persecute unlicensed practitioners stalled in rural areas: medical profes-sionals tended to prefer the cosmopolitanism and higher salaries cities offered, so authorities had to rely on the very empíricos they derided, and indeed criminalized in cities, to treat rural residents.[46] Guatemalan and Ecuadorian officials who rejected indigenous customs as contagious threats often depended on indigenous interlocutors (some of whom were curand-eros) to convince their communities that public health initiatives worked, and to encourage indigenous participation.

Public health campaigns may have advanced humanitarian goals, but they were also articulated in the interests of economic and political elites. In Guatemala and Ecuador, doctors, scientists, and authorities maintained a symbiotic relationship as scientific medicine and state rule emboldened each other. At a 1905 Guatemalan Medical School conference, the conveners noted, "The School of Medicine and Pharmacy owes its existence, progress, and development to the public powers."[47] Legislatures passed health codes and governments constructed hospitals and clinics. Latin American nations established police forces to enforce public hygiene, sanitation, and health standards and to persecute unlicensed practitioners. Increasing surveillance and regulation that characterized public health empowered technocrats to monitor women, the poor, and particular ethnic groups (especially indígenas).[48]

The poor and marginalized populations who were subject to such campaigns tacked between embracing and rejecting them. While national officials used disease as a rhetorical tool to validate domestic interventions, and local authorities unleashed it to stave off labor and other demands from their superiors, local denizens deployed it to attract government resources. The same epidemics that afforded authorities opportunities to intervene in local affairs sometimes emboldened locals who feigned illness to avoid compulsory labor. In May 1928, the Santiago Zamora mayor was unable to fulfill the Sacatepéquez governor's request for three female tortilla makers because the town's "population has been decimated . . . [by] malaria."[49] Malaria provided an opportunity for him to reassert his political power vis-à-vis the Guatemalan state.

Depending on how it affected discrete regions, the same disease meant different things to different people and thus was put to many uses. Whereas Guatemalan officials were more likely than their Ecuadorian counterparts to associate typhus and typhoid with indigeneity, RF representatives generally thought of typhus as a disease of war, poverty, and poor hygiene—the last two of which they associated with Guatemalan indígenas, who predominantly populated the highlands. In both countries, authorities sometimes conflated indigeneity, geography, and disease.

Perceptions of race and place influenced the fate of public health initiatives and responses to crises. By pointing to endemic typhus in the highlands and malaria epidemics in the lowlands, public health reports emphasized the geography of disease. In 1911, the Guatemalan Government and Justice Secretary reported typhus epidemics in the predominantly indigenous towns of Comalapa and Patzicía (2137 and 2135 meters above sea level respectively) and a malaria outbreak in San Jerónimo Baja Verapaz, a town that sits 940 meters above sea level.[50] The highlands, drier and cooler, generally enjoyed better health than the lowlands in the early twentieth century. Two decades later geographical distributions of diseases continued to catch officials' eyes. The 1933 Guatemalan Public Health annual report noted "typhus outbreaks in the [highland] departments of San Marcos, Quetzaltenango, and Chimaltenango and malaria epidemics in many towns on the northern and southern coasts."[51] In a less dichotomous perspective three years later, Guatemalan doctor Romeo de León emphasized the ecology of place: "climates offering... exceptional conditions for human life also [provide] life for their enemies in the struggle for existence."[52]

Concepts about place became intertwined with race and disease in regions populated by indígenas. Medical racialization infused highland but not lowland geography in Guatemala. When Guatemalan officials emphasized lowland and coastal health challenges, they seldom associated them with race or ethnicity.[53] In 1910, the Guatemalan government's official daily *Diario de Centroamérica* reported, "Everywhere there are swamps or stagnant waters, fever germs permanently exist. In warm climates or hot summers, those bad germs multiply with double intensity."[54] Since few indígenas populated the lowlands, journalists and authorities turned to environmental—swamps, stagnant waters, warm climates—rather than ethnic explanations for coastal pestilence.

Where indígenas comprised a majority of the population, officials readily advanced medical racialization. A January 1, 1919, editorial explained the influenza pandemic was ravaging the Kaqchikel towns of "Tecpán, Patzún, Comalapa, Poaquil, Patzicía.... Because of their lack of personal hygiene and their natural ignorance it is in the indigenous race where more havoc was caused due to the reigning plague.... In these places we lack doctors who come to combat the epidemic and stay in the towns to fight for the cure.... The indigenous for their ignorance do a thousand stupidities for which they almost always pay with their lives."[55] Although a dearth of doctors in the rural highlands undermined efforts to combat influenza, the editorialists ultimately attributed indigenous fatalities to indigenous "ignorance," "stupidities," and "lack of hygiene."

Conflating the highlands and indígenas as diseased places and populations was not uncommon. A month later, the *Diario de Centroamérica* proclaimed:

> The poor Indians are defenseless victims of the scourge.... These unhappy people die oblivious of any assistance and lead a miserable life to which they have been accustomed since time immemorial and that is the initial cause among this unfortunate race of certain grave and endemic diseases, as has happened recently with typhus that has seated its realities in the mountains and that does not leave traces of abandoning its position. That is how it will be with all the epidemics that appear in these places because the lack of hygiene aggravates the situation.[56]

Again, even as the author suggested the government failed to provide medical care or public health services, they attributed *indígenas'* "miserable life ... since time immemorial" and "lack of hygiene" to their and to the region's interrelated predilection for disease.

While officials in Guatemala and other countries—including Peru, where legislators blamed Chinese immigrants for spreading bubonic plague in 1903—were quick to racialize disease, Ecuadorians had a less discriminatory approach.[57] Public health officials expressed concern that rural indigenous migrants spread disease in Quito,[58] but they also praised highland health benefits. In 1912, Ecuador's director general of *Servicio de Sanidad* (Health Service) observed, "In the interior of the republic one lives under the healthy influence of a climate of perpetual springtime; the coast suffers instead the rude heat of the tropical environment."[59] Along with meager budgets, the highlands' healthy reputation helps explain why officials seldom sustained rural public health campaigns. Guayaquil's regular epidemics encouraged binary views of lowland pestilence and highland health. With its international reputation as the "pesthole of the Pacific," Guayaquil bore the brunt of official and popular preoccupations with disease.[60]

Associations of geography, race, and disease permeated Latin America. A 1937 map of tropical diseases from Guatemalan public health experts is typical of the overall view, noting region, race, and risk (figure 1). Unlike "blancos," who had virtually no association with disease, "negros" and *"mulatos"* had apparent predilections for *fiebres aguas negras* (blackwater fever, derived from malaria) and the tropical skin infection *pian*. The mapmakers associated *indios americanos* with *Onchocerca volvulus* (river blindness). No matter that, after discovering and treating *Onchocerca volvulus* in 1915, Guatemalan doctor Rodolfo Robles Valverde and his colleagues "firmly dismissed 'race' as a factor." By the 1930s, Guatemalan scientists, journalists, and intellectuals increasingly dubbed it an "indigenous disease."[61] As Guatemala advanced racial eugenics, medical racism and medical racialization (linking illness and race) abounded.[62] Many Latin American scientists, medical professionals, and officials deployed eugenics and race science discourse even after those ideas lost legitimacy in most other parts of the world in the 1930s.[63]

Similar to how early-twentieth-century Argentinian officials established scientific programs to address who they considered a sick race—primarily the Buenos Aires poor—Guatemalan and (to a lesser extent) Ecuadorian officials approached public health crises in rural highlands based on preconceived

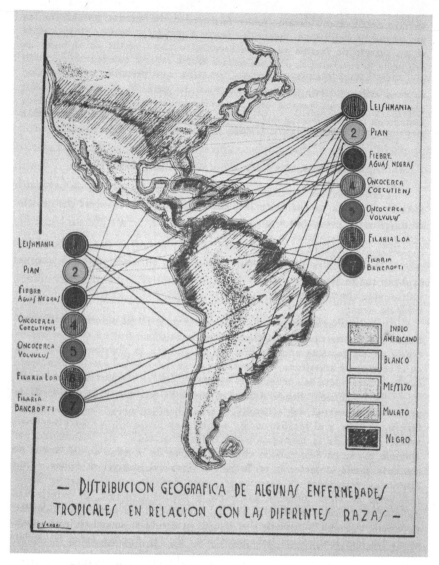

FIGURE 1. "Geographical distribution of some tropical diseases in relation to different races," 1937. *Boletín Sanitario de Guatemala* 46 (1938), 53. Courtesy of Academia de Geografía e Historia de Guatemala.

notions about indígenas propagating diseases.[64] Obsessed with demonstrating that indigeneity undermined public health, Guatemalan health officials and authorities disparaged indigenous medicine and portrayed indigenous customs and practices as vectors of disease rather than bulwarks of mental and physical health. Neither government was working alone—their efforts were supported and shaped, to varying degrees, by the Rockefeller Foundation.

Founded in 1913 with money from the Standard Oil Company, the RF worked in Latin America (and other regions) to "sanitize" the tropics for US business and military interests by curbing tropical diseases. Informed by Cuban researchers' finding that mosquitos were disease vectors, the RF financed and guided yellow fever and malaria control projects in Mexico, Guatemala, Ecuador, and Brazil by the late 1910s.[65] By 1920, success in those nations encouraged them to declare Veracruz, Guayaquil, and other ports "clean" of yellow fever.

The apparent altruism and efficacy of its public health campaigns (particularly against malaria) augured well for the RF's potential impact in rural Latin America, where many states largely neglected public health because their reach was incomplete.[66] Struggling with economic and political crises, Guatemala welcomed RF aid to extend public health infrastructure to rural areas.[67] Providing fellowships to Latin Americans to study abroad, sending technical experts to Latin American countries, and establishing vaccination, sanitation, and other campaigns, the RF shaped how the region approached public health and health care.[68]

Although the RF was the first organization to proselytize scientific medicine globally,[69] its singular focus on particular diseases like hookworm, yellow fever, and malaria diverted resources from urgent local needs. The first RF director in Guatemala, Dr. Walter Rowan, noticed the "destructive effects of 'nigua' or tropical 'jigger,' which is particularly prevalent in Guatemala, where practically all of the Indians in certain sections have their feet deformed as a result of this troublesome insect burrowing into the deep layers of the skin, usually surrounding the nail, to deposit her eggs. Tetanus often results from infections of the wounds which they make."[70] Although Rowan informed his superiors of this "particularly prevalent" public health problem in 1915, the RF made little effort to address nigua. In its focus on diseases for which there was a relatively easy fix, the foundation understandably stayed away from rare diseases such as Madura foot (caused by a vegetable fungus).[71] But its neglect of common diseases among the indigenous peoples who comprised the majority of Guatemalans betrayed a fixation on diseases that affected US soldiers, workers, and other citizens traveling in tropical climates.[72]

Guatemala and Ecuador both solicited assistance from foreign entities to address epidemics and buttress their health systems, but Ecuador was less dependent on largesse than Guatemala.[73] The RF's steady presence in

Guatemala contrasted its intermittent interventions in Ecuador. To ingratiate the foundation upon arrival, Rowan sought to establish close relations with highly respected Guatemalan doctors. His initial overtures to hated dictator Estrada Cabrera only furthered elite suspicions that the RF was an arm of US imperialism and not to be trusted. In turn, Estrada Cabrera mistrusted *Criollo* elites. Rowan had to tread carefully.

Amidst protests against US public health professionals and researchers,[74] Ecuadorian officials sometimes discouraged RF yellow fever commission president William Gorgas from visiting lest his presence incite demonstrations or demands for US aid.[75] Such tensions notwithstanding, Ecuador collaborated with the RF to build water and sewage systems and enforce anti-mosquito campaigns and thus had all but eradicated yellow fever by 1919. That success did little to warm relations, however. "The American nation is [not] in any way popular with the Ecuadorians, who are beset with constant dread that the United States . . . may intervene and treat this country as she has done with . . . unfortunate Central American states that have come within the sphere of her Monroe doctrine," noted the British consul in Quito in 1923.[76]

The RF reacted quite differently to each country's indigenous population. Resonating with Guatemalan elite discourse about impoverished, sick indígenas, Rowan's 1915 photographs from a *finca* (large-landed estate) where indigenous workers earned a pittance for their agricultural labor highlight indigenous poverty, malnourishment, and disease (figures 2, 4, and 6). Barely clad, Rowan's subjects are worlds apart from indígenas recorded in other photographs who proudly wore their traditional clothing (figure 3 and cover top photograph). RF constructions of race and public health were not necessarily negative, however. Rowan endorsed indigenous hygiene by highlighting sweatbaths at a time when Guatemalan authorities considered them disease propagators. Perceptions of how indígenas engaged with (or rejected) public health practices were just as important as any particular science or epidemiology in shaping public health initiatives.

National officials in both countries sought to engage indígenas in public health campaigns in ways that ranged from sincerity to cynicism. Speeches in Kichwa and radio broadcasts aimed at indígenas demonstrate Ecuadorian efforts to integrate indígenas through public health campaigns. More paternalistically and sometime punitively, Guatemalan administrations sought to convey "a very special effort in favor of the health of the *raza indígena*," according to dictator Jorge Ubico's administration (1931–44).[77]

FIGURE 2. "Indian boy, age 14 years, weight 33 lbs." Photograph by Walter Rowan, 1915. Rockefeller Foundation Photographs. Courtesy of Rockefeller Archive Center.

FIGURE 3. Couple from San Juan Comalapa, ca. 1910. Photograph by José Domingo Noriega, ca. 1900–1950. Copyright Colección Fototeca Guatemala, Centro de Investigaciones Regionales de Mesoamérica (CIRMA).

METHODOLOGICAL AND HISTORIOGRAPHICAL INTERVENTIONS

I build on a rich historiography of medicine that advocates transnational analysis.[78] To avoid comparative history's tendency to reify racial and national ideologies and mythologies, I pursue a transnational analysis that destabilizes states and corporate entities as interpretive lenses in favor of analyzing power dynamics through body experiences and indígenas' encounters with illness and healing.[79] Ideas about indigenous humanity and bodies were central to public health practices in Guatemala and Ecuador.[80] Exploring the movement of RF personnel and ideas about medicine, race, and modernization between the United States, Ecuador, and Guatemala, this book traces the transnational circulation and non-circulation of theories of race and racial difference within Latin America.[81] Ecuadorian, Guatemalan, and RF players were part of a vibrant international network connecting Latin American medical professionals, capitalists, and government officials with US scientists, physicians, and philanthropists. Comparing how racism and public health projects shaped each other in Guatemala and Ecuador reveals that explanations of disease in indigenous communities ranged from racial degeneration (in Guatemala) to poverty (in Ecuador). In addition to facilitating analysis of popular actors in ways that change how we write histories of health, integrating transnational and comparative approaches decenters states and multinational organizations without losing sight of nation-state formation or imperialism.

Informed by indigenous scholars who challenge researchers to pursue indigenous desires rather than focus on damage inflicted upon indigenous people, I examine how indígenas like Cuzal and Chalí claimed their rights by seeking multiple forms of health care at a time when government officials, public intellectuals, and medical professionals discriminated against them.[82] By encouraging scholars to highlight "native survivance"—a combination of survival and resistance—Anishinaabe literary critic-author Gerald Vizenor renounces "the unbearable sentiments of tragedy, the legacy of victimry"[83] in favor of narratives that capture "a native sense of presence . . . sovereignty and the skill to resist dominance."[84]

Attempting to focus on indigenous voices and agency sheds light on archival silences and omissions. To bring such marginalized voices to the fore, I am inspired by scholars like Maria Fuentes who, as she describes it, discerns the experiences and perspectives of Africans who were enslaved by "stretch[ing] archival fragments."[85] Often filtered through state actors' and philanthropic visitors' views, evidence of indigenous perspectives, material cultures, and experiences reveal indigenous healers' and patients' motivations and preferences, albeit in incomplete and uneven detail. Historians have explored how doctors have medicalized black, immigrant, female, and other bodies through ideas about typhus, typhoid, smallpox, vaginal fistulas, hysteria, premenstrual syndrome, and other conditions.[86] Yet few scholars have analyzed how indigeneity was medicalized.

Africanist historiography of health similarly offers methodological strategies to capture and comprehend marginalized voices by demonstrating how historical asymmetries of power influenced health systems and the colonial archives that document them. To center Africans' perspectives in histories informed by documents penned by Europeans, scholars searched for multivocal narratives in colonial archives and deployed oral history.[87] Otherwise obscured perspectives and experiences emerge as historians track how distinctions between scientific and traditional medicine were created, contested, and imposed.[88]

Burgeoning in Latin America (and more fully developed in the United States and Europe), history of medicine literature tends to take a top-down approach. National histories of medicine in Latin America often frame medical research as a contact zone where urban (national and foreign) medical professionals studied health and illness among indigenous, impoverished, Afro-Latin American, and other marginalized populations while crafting notions about them that circulated among global health networks.[89] Avoiding the binary between top-down and bottom-up approaches, this book embraces a multidimensional method that includes perspectives from all levels of society and draws upon Latin America's rich tradition of social medicine and ethnographic insights. Intermediaries like curanderos and comadronas informed narratives about ethnicity, class, gender and public health. Informed by a deep grounding in the historical and cultural contexts of Guatemala, Ecuador, Mayas, Kichwas, and the RF, I explore how local— often ethnically charged—dynamics influence public health campaigns and health care delivery. Examining history through multiple lenses affords a more comprehensive understanding of the past.

Since the late 1990s, scholars have explored how the articulation and mobilization of racial categories have influenced the theory and practice of science and medicine.[90] The intersections of public health and racism have enjoyed sophisticated analysis.[91] Some have demonstrated how government and public health officials deployed disease prevention campaigns to pathologize and marginalize particular social groups.[92] More recently, historians of medicine have emphasized marginalized peoples' perspectives in histories of medicine.[93] A few historians and many anthropologists have studied how indigenous people shaped and were shaped by medicine and science,[94] and how nonprofessional actors have shaped medicine in Latin America.[95]

Yet fine-grained analysis of the complicated ways racial thought and public health interventions developed in local, ethnically charged settings eludes us. This book, in response, draws upon popular moments of health, healing, and disease to craft a narrative about race and medicine.[96] Offering a critical history of how marginalized individuals rather than institutions shaped health and society, this book contributes to indigenous histories of Latin

America. Although the historiography of Latin American indígenas is expansive, few scholars move beyond national borders to offer comparative or transnational analysis of indigenous histories.[97] As Guatemala's rich historiography of indigenous people continues to grow, Ecuador's more nascent field boasts excellent studies.[98] Yet few historians examine indígenas in the context of public health or medicine in either country. This book addresses that topic, asking how racial categories intersected with identities of class, nation, and gender to influence rural public health initiatives and the people who were employed and served by them.

No other English-language book explores the history of medicine in post-colonial Guatemala, let alone popular healers' roles in that process.[99] Informed as much by anthropologists as historians, studies of medicine in Ecuador enjoy a rich tradition that tends toward institutional histories rather than close analysis of how epidemics, illness, and public health initiatives influenced the lives of those on the margins of society.[100]

Since the 1950s, three waves of scholarship on the RF have provided rich descriptions and a shifting framing and analysis of its role in the world and Latin America.[101] Over time the predominant themes in that literature have evolved from largely uncritical descriptions of the foundation as an altruistic entity to postcolonial critiques of an imperial organization. Although historians critical of the RF have tended to portray rural working people as ignorant and technical staff as inattentive to local culture, neither stereotype is accurate. Offering more nuanced analysis than their predecessors, historians recently have explored the complex relationships between the RF, imperialism, and tropical diseases.[102] In his study of RF hookworm campaigns in the Caribbean and Central America, historian Steven Palmer found that "local historical dynamics," more than RF public health science, shaped those missions.[103] Rather than centering the RF, I use it as a lens to understand how local and ethnic actors shaped public health initiatives and to analyze distinct relationships between international interlopers, national officials, and indígenas.

BOOK STRUCTURE

While the first half of the twentieth century frames this book, it is organized thematically rather than chronologically. Building on research that reveals how diseases are both biological and social events,[104] *Health in the Highlands* demonstrates how race, place, gender, and politics influence public health projects and their efficacy. Public health is always political, but the politics are not always clear. The first chapter explores the major political, economic, and social phenomena that shaped the histories of Ecuador and Guatemala, and of the transnational RF, with an eye toward how each entity distinctly engaged with and portrayed indígenas. Although they employed people with no medical training in public health endeavors, some RF representatives disparaged indigenous healers as fraudulent practitioners incapable of delivering basic medicine. By exploring Maya and Kichwa health practices and epistemologies, chapter 1 also lays a groundwork for understanding how different cultures approach health and disease.

The second chapter underscores how perceptions shaped the delivery and regulation of health care. Ill-at-ease with their indigenous compatriots, Guatemalan authorities persecuted indigenous healers far more than did their Ecuadorian counterparts, who praised indigenous efforts to stave off epidemics. Race and class, more than science, determined perceptions of health care providers.

As chapter 3 demonstrates, gender too shaped wellness, disease, and healthcare. Whereas Hispanic doctors were predominantly male, many indigenous healers were female. Efforts to reduce infant mortality and improve reproductive health care were as charged with race and class as they were with gender. Notwithstanding a few male midwives and physicians in rural Guatemala and Ecuador, female midwives overwhelmingly engaged with new and expectant mothers. They deepened their relationships with patients through regular wellness visits and house calls. From most any angle, reproductive health was female-centered.

Critically examining portrayals of indígenas as unhygienic and unsanitary vectors of disease, chapter 4 shows that public health projects were shaped not just by medical science, but also by racist perceptions that medical professionals and government officials helped perpetuate in the workings of public health projects. By juxtaposing Guatemalan, Ecuadorian, and RF public health officials who respected indígenas as valuable contributors to the nation's well-being with those who disparaged their culture as a threat to public health, this chapter also highlights the tremendous diversity of interactions between indígenas and medical professionals and authorities. More so in Guatemala than Ecuador, officials associated indígenas with disease to scapegoat them for the nation's ills.

Chapters 5 and 6 examine the framing and treatment of particular diseases in terms of race and place. Typhus and typhoid, the subject of chapter 5, became racially charged in both countries, associated with indigenous populations in the highlands. Malaria, the subject of chapter 6, was framed more broadly as a tropical disease, perhaps because foreign soldiers, workers, and travelers were as likely to contract it as indigenous migrants in coastal regions. Yet it was also prevalent in the highlands, and authorities pointed to its existence there in ways that helped them obscure underlying socioeconomic disparities such as poverty and the absence of potable water and sewerage systems.

By examining how intransigent public health challenges and diseases influenced and were influenced by race relations, racial thought, and indigenous experiences, this study illuminates the ways disease, epidemics, public health responses to them, and ethnicity distinctly shaped two nations with large indigenous populations.

ONE

Hookworm, Histories, and Health

INDIGENOUS HEALING, STATE BUILDING, AND ROCKEFELLER REPRESENTATIVES

WHEN THE FIRST RF DIRECTOR in Guatemala, Dr. Walter Rowan, embarked on an anti-hookworm campaign in 1915, he did so with a keen sense of the challenges undermining indígenas' health, social and economic marginalization chief among them. His description of one young patient with hookworm (figure 4) betrays the connection between poverty and poor health: "This boy is of the type that is usually referred to as '*abandonado*' (abandoned) by the natives, themselves. His mother works in the coffee fields or in the '*beneficio*' (coffee sorting department), all day, and must grind the tortillas for the heavy meal of the day after the work in the fields is over. Of necessity, she has little time to look after her large family of children, and these are left to shift for themselves."[1]

Although hookworm was not at the top of the Guatemalan government's list of concerns, the RF identified it as a problem its agents could solve.[2] RF was one of several international organizations shaping public health in Guatemala and Ecuador, particularly beyond the urban centers, where national public health institutions had limited reach. In addition to RF, the Pan American Sanitary Bureau (PASB), the League of Nations, the United Fruit Company (UFCO), and the United States Public Health Service (USPHS) all influenced the health of Guatemalans and Ecuadorians. These international influences mattered, but national and local actors in both countries largely dictated the relationship between the state and indígenas according to longstanding beliefs about race and nation that were now increasingly intertwined with ideas about healthcare and modernity.

Closely associated with culture, racial typing of indígenas in Ecuador and Guatemala relied more on ethnic markers, such as clothing, than on biological traits or phenology. In turn, Mayas in Guatemala and Kichwas in Ecuador

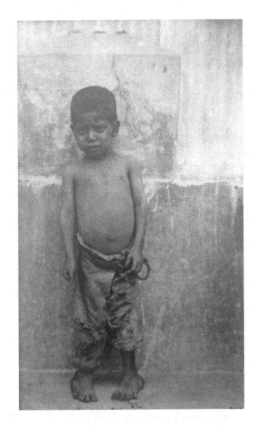

FIGURE 4. "Typical hookworm subject on El Pacayal." Photograph by Walter Rowan, 1915. Rockefeller Foundation Photographs. Courtesy of Rockefeller Archive Center.

rooted their ethnic belonging to shared local cultural understandings. Prior to Spanish contact, both groups had rich healing knowledge and practices informed by their cosmologies and worldviews. Even as they adapted to Spanish influences including medicine, Mayas and Kichwas maintained crucial components of their healing traditions.

In Ecuador and Guatemala, paternalistic elites assumed adopting Hispanic customs around both healthcare and other aspects of culture would improve indígenas' stock, but the underlying motives differed in each country. Both nations exploited and abused indígenas, but whereas Ecuadorian elites framed indígenas' well-being as essential to national development, Guatemalan elites generally disparaged them as ignorant drunks whose health was only important insofar as it did not impede their ability to perform manual labor. Most Guatemalan elites pushed an assimilationist agenda, whereas many Ecuadorian authorities accepted indigeneity, albeit as inferior when contrasted with blanco-mestizo attributes. These divergent attitudes shaped public health initiatives and health care experiences even as both governments deployed scientific medicine and public health campaigns to undergird assimilationist (Guatemala) and integrationist (Ecuador) projects.

Although race relations in Ecuador were seldom conciliatory, they were more productive than those in Guatemala. Ecuador's more pliable, less coercive approaches to incorporating indígenas into public health systems afforded them greater freedom in determining their healthcare. Coastal entrepreneurs developed pro-indigenous discourse to counter highland *hacendados* (hacienda owners) who dispossessed indígenas from their land, harvests, and homes. In contrast, repressive Guatemalan regimes that sought to strip indigenous agency at every turn fostered indígenas who had to fight for every right and opportunity.

Highland healthcare in twentieth-century Guatemala and Ecuador was complex, dynamic, and heterogeneous. Indigenous, Afro-descendant, ladino, creole, and blanco-mestizo patients generally embraced the diverse therapeutic landscapes available to them.[3] What mattered most to the infirm was effectiveness, which was as likely to come from local knowledge and experience as scientific medicine in early-twentieth-century highland Guatemala and Ecuador. Improving individual and institutional health often involved accessing indigenous and scientific medicine in ways that eschewed the racial and social hierarchies scientific medicine and state discourse advanced.

Instead of assessing indigenous or vernacular knowledge as peripheral to or problematic for professional medicine, I approach indigenous and scientific medicines as valid for analyzing ethnic and medical relations.[4] Neither state had the power nor resources to eradicate curanderos or significantly improve indigenous health in rural areas. In the context of two largely indigenous nations that embraced scientific medicine as part of broader modernization projects aimed at cementing their positions in the world order, the politics of indigeneity—particularly the level to which indígenas were included or exploited—was as consequential for public health as advancements in medical science.

INDIGENOUS HEALING AND HEALERS

Andean and Kichwa Healing

Ancient Andeans conceptualized illness as arising from punishments from their ancestors, and as imbalances between the four bodily fluids and between individuals, society, nature, and supernatural entities.[5] Independent of contemporary Europeans, Andeans understood illness as binary (often expressed between hot and cold) and health as humoral.[6] More specific than European humoral notions that bodily fluids influenced health and illness, the Andean cycle theory purported that fluids must continuously move through the body unobstructed to maintain well-being. Since illness occurred as a result of the loss or obstruction of bodily fluids, healers restored health by re-establishing the cycle of bodily fluids.[7] Employed more as preventative than curative measures, purgatives facilitated the flow of humoral fluids.[8] In turn, bloodletting restored imbalances.[9] Ecuadorian indígenas also recognized the role diet played in health and illness.[10] By moderating diet and behavior, Andeans could live long and happy lives that reached upwards of 150 to 200 years, according to Felipe Guáman Poma (1534–1615), the Quechua nobleman who chronicled Andean life and denounced Spaniards' abuse of indígenas.[11]

Andeans had a keen sense of public health and anticipated seasonal spikes in certain diseases. February *aguaceros* (downpours) precipitated diarrhea and other fatal stomach ailments brought on by food scarcity and the consumption of unripe fruits.[12] Any disruption of individual health, particularly if brought on by imbalances, could jeopardize communal health and social welfare.[13] Andeans attributed illnesses to "sin, soul loss, sorcery, rupture of norms."[14] In turn, good health could be maintained through communal efforts. In September, the Inka calendar celebrated *citua* to purify communities and remove illnesses from them. Residents washed and cleaned streets, fasted, abstained from sex, and families bathed together and rubbed their bodies with white corn to absorb and extirpate ailments.[15]

Although they tended to specialize in particular techniques, Andean healers had knowledge of physiology, botany, and cosmology, and spirituality and prayer figured prominently in Andean healing practices.[16] Andean practitioners provided *limpias* (cleansings) and other traditional therapies, deploying amulets, talismans, animals, and medicinal plants and herbs. Often derived from wild plants that grew in surrounding hills and forests, indigenous medicine was eminently local.[17] Curanderos also invoked the ambivalent power of places to heal.[18] For their services, shamans received gifts, including clothing.[19] To downplay Inka (1470–1532) and later Spanish (1532–1820s) rule, Andean healers conjured ancient Moche peoples (200–900).[20] Regularly adapting to changing circumstances and conditions, indigenous healing epistemologies and practices nevertheless enjoyed significant continuity over time.

Ancient Maya worldviews were informed by three interrelated concepts: balance, holism, and spirituality. Balance and harmony between the body, soul, nature, and universe maintained good health; sickness arose when imbalance or disharmony marked those interrelationships. Since individual health was contingent upon good collective health, diagnoses were both individual and communal. Mesoamerican indígenas understood illnesses as originating from both external conditions, whether social or natural (as in the case of evil winds), and from internal, physical conditions.[21] Because harmonious social relations were key to well-being, confessions could reveal the cause of ailments and set the afflicted on the road to well-being.[22]

Religion figured prominently in ancient Maya notions of health and healing. Indígenas prayed to the healing deities of Itzamana, Ixchel, and Cotbolontun for everything from improving their health to easing childbirth or facilitating pregnancy.[23] In turn, the underworld—Xibalba—was populated by demons who represented disease and death.[24] Healers and shamans could both cure and cause illnesses.[25] Trained in divination, confession, prayers, and remedies, some Maya priests specialized in healing.[26]

Male and female healers—from bonesetters and bloodletters to massagists and midwives—drew upon the medicinal characteristics of plants (seeds, roots, leaves), herbs, minerals, and animals to concoct cures that included potions, poultices, salves, and comestibles. Mesoamerican indígenas understood herbs and foods to have temperature qualities that ranged from hot to cold.[27] Indigenous healers used bloodletting, enemas, baths, douches, and masticating and spitting in their practices and fermented corn and fruit beverages and tortillas in cures.[28] A variety of animal fat and parts from fowl, snakes, and dogs also figured prominently in healing.[29] From *zacate ronrón* for malaria to *zopilote* and *junipliego* for fevers, specific cures were created for particular conditions.[30] Cures for typhus and other fever-inducing diseases included *cocolmeca* bark, Savino tree, and pine nuts.[31] Much indigenous healing knowledge and practice was passed from one generation to the next.[32] For many indigenous practitioners, healing was as much a calling as a profession.[33]

The sixteenth-century introduction of European pathogens and religion compelled Mesoamericans and Andeans to reconsider their ideas about disease and wellness. Yet even as those changes were underway, most healers continued to deliver indigenous cures informed by their healing knowledge and epistemology, and plant- and animal-derived medicines.[34]

Indigenous, Hispanic, folk, *casera* (home), Afro-Latin American, and learned or scientific medicine coexisted in an uneasy relationship that was marked by collaboration and conflict.[35] From the sixteenth century forward, learned medicine advocates with the colonial state and Catholic church portrayed indigenous healers as purveyors of superstition and malice. Despite clashes, practitioners often cooperated and adopted healing epistemologies and procedures other than their own. Indigenous curanderos commonly worked alongside doctors and cultivated small gardens of medicinal plants in colonial hospitals.[36] Some Spanish doctors used indigenous medicine to treat indígenas. Surgeons taught vaccination techniques to indigenous healers, who circulated the smallpox vaccine in the early nineteenth century.[37] With shared notions of healing and illness, indígenas and Europeans found common ground in approaches to health care and epidemics.[38] European humoral theory overlapped nicely with indigenous notions of keeping the body in balance, hot and cold foods and liquids, and the importance of moderation. Common concepts did not necessarily produce shared perceptions about disease transmission, however. Some distinct disease etiologies and approaches to healing remained impenetrable.[39] For example, although miasma theory resonated with lowland Maya ideas about *mal aire* (bad air) causing illnesses, indígenas asserted the threat emanated from harmful (*maléfico*) or malevolent wind, not—as Europeans believed—from odors or gases.[40]

As Spaniards sought to extend their control over indígenas, they classified and conflated various healers as curanderos, failing—or perhaps refusing—to recognize their nuanced approaches to healing.[41] When Spaniards perceived superstition as the core component, they framed those practices as *brujería* (witchcraft). The Office of the Inquisition punished such practices and condemned the use of certain herbal remedies.[42]

With poor hygiene and little sanitation, colonial cities like Quito and Antigua were unhealthy places plagued by epidemics.[43] Neither Ecuador nor Guatemala had a *protomedicato*, an institution that regulated medicine and medical practice, until the late colonial period.[44] After Guatemala's protomedicato was formally established in 1793, though, it—in tandem with the region's leading medical school—advanced public health measures to such an extent that, by the time the Spanish Balmis smallpox vaccination expedition (1803–6) arrived in Guatemala, local efforts had already inoculated people.[45]

Ecuador too claimed medical expertise dating to the colonial period, particularly in social medicine. Eighteenth-century Quito doctor Eugenio Espejo posited that poverty, malnutrition, and poor hygiene contributed to disease in his *Reflexiones* (1798).[46]

Outnumbered and often outperformed by unlicensed healers, doctors enlisted authorities to criminalize curanderos and other traditional providers.[47] Since the San Carlos Medical School in Guatemala City refused to admit indigenous, black, or mestizo men, let alone grant them licenses to practice medicine, they had little choice but to practice illegally.[48] Despite persecution, many indigenous healers enjoyed considerable power, as evident in their ability to mobilize people in late-colonial Ecuador—a period during which at least ten revolts occurred in the highlands.[49]

As the rift between medical professionals and traditional healers widened in the mid-nineteenth century, university-trained physicians throughout Latin America deployed the rhetoric of science to validate their practices and denigrate popular notions of health and illness.[50] Evident at the Universidad Central in Quito by 1837, postcolonial Ecuador and Guatemala increasingly embraced scientific medicine and developed robust pharmacopeia by the late nineteenth century.[51] Although indígenas' perceptions of illness, medicine, and public health sometimes challenged scientific medical notions, their knowledge (especially of medicinal plants) and practices were appropriated and adopted by pharmacists and physicians.[52] Aware of attacks on their livelihood and authority, some *curanderos* and other partially-trained or untrained practitioners sowed discord to undermine public health initiatives that competed with their practices by distributing free medicines and providing free health care.[53]

Ancient indigenous medicines and contemporary scientific medicine continued to meld.[54] Both prescribed vermifuges for intestinal worms. Sixteenth-century Mesoamerican indigenous healers deployed the roots of *epazotl* that contained the same chenopodium that twentieth-century RF agents dispensed against hookworm.[55] Curanderas prescribed the fat of snakes and lizards, *floripondio* (angel's trumpet blossom), raw eggs, and red wine for infirmities ranging from infertility to fevers. They also cured children of *susto* or *mal de espanto* (fright) by blowing on their backs.[56] Kaqchikel speakers drew upon curanderos for certain ailments and consulted doctors and admitted themselves into hospitals for others.[57] Remote Ch'orti's concurrently consulted pharmacists and "sorcerers."[58] The turn-of-the-twentieth-century hospital in Babahoyo, the provincial capital of Los Rios located on the

Ecuadorian coast, had a permanent position for a *curandero de establecimiento* (healer of the establishment).[59] In archives in Guatemala, Ecuador, and New York, documentary evidence of medical pluralism paints a story of breaks and ruptures in intertwined lives, politics, and economics, rather than an ascensionist tale building to scientific medical dominance.

Historians have struggled to understand the vast majority of health care that took place beyond the remit of physicians, surgeons, and pharmacists. Outside the clinic, indigenous and unlicensed healers advanced ideas and practices about health that people—particularly poor and working-class patients of color—acted upon.[60] Understanding those exchanges and the epistemologies, worldviews, and lifeways that inform them is crucial to conceptualizing how marginalized people experienced scientific medicine, public health initiatives, and the range of therapeutic options available to them.[61]

INDIGENOUS-STATE RELATIONS

In Guatemala and Ecuador, the state historically has sought to control and curtail indigenous life. Prior to Spanish invasions in the early sixteenth century, indigenous agriculturalists survived and at times thrived in the highlands of Guatemala and Ecuador. But during the colonial period, Spanish and mestizo authorities established economic, political, social, and cultural institutions to inhibit indígenas' autonomy and agency. Such structural racism went hand in hand with racist thought across Latin America, where social hierarchies privileged lighter-skinned people and marginalized darker-skinned subjects. Colonizers forced indígenas to cultivate Spanish colonists' farms, weave textiles, and construct Catholic churches, public buildings, and roads.

In the wake of early nineteenth-century independence movements, economic and labor relations distinctly shaped indígenas' place in their respective nations in ways that influenced public health and health care. From the 1870s to 1930s, Latin America experienced its most intense period of labor coercion and land colonization since the sixteenth century. As the agricultural export economies displaced people and spurred economic development, capitalists transformed the region's undeveloped ecologies. Guatemala stands out as an extreme example of forced labor mechanisms that drew upon a combination of debt peonage, vagrancy laws, and land concentration to compel highland indígenas to migrate to work on Pacific piedmont coffee and cotton plantations.

Areas previously isolated from the centralized state were increasingly drawn into national and international commercial capitalism.[62]

By 1940, Ecuador and Guatemala each had populations of about three million people. Although 39 percent of Ecuadorians and 45 percent of Guatemalans were identified as indigenous that year, both estimates were likely undercounts.[63]

Ecuador

Tacking between advances and setbacks, indígenas navigated Ecuador's nineteenth-century political and economic machinations. Notwithstanding several nineteenth-century highland uprisings, including in the province of Chimborazo where rebellious indígenas aided Fernando Daquilema's 1871 insurrection against church and state taxes, few violent conflicts between indígenas and the state developed in postcolonial Ecuador.[64] A few years after the 1857 abolishment of Indian tribute (taxation), Conservative president Gabriel García Moreno (1860–75) sought to unite the country. His administration both disparaged and liberated indígenas. By suggesting normally timid, cowardly indígenas became violent savages with alcohol, his administration associated indigeneity with inebriation and portrayed indígenas as wards rather than citizens of the state.[65] Yet at a time when highland hacendados, who focused on supplying national markets, controlled even the most personal aspects of indígenas' lives, García Moreno undercut their control over indigenous labor. Nineteenth-century Ecuadorian historian Pedro Fermín Cevallos lauded indígenas' ability to carry heavy loads long distances but otherwise considered them "weak and lazy" and an "absolutely negative" factor "in the civilization of the country."[66] Such perspectives were typical of most nineteenth-century Ecuadorian elites, who framed indígenas as problematic and encouraged their migration to disrupt their cultural, economic, and social systems. With larger estates and more fertile soils, hacendados in the north-central highlands enjoyed more resources than their counterparts in the southern highlands. The 1895 Liberal Revolution marginalized both groups, as coastal entrepreneurs modernized the economy behind the strength of the cacao trade. Creating stability without hegemony, a fragmented oligarchy thereafter facilitated indígenas' autonomy and mobility.[67] As commercial coastal elites shaped the government in the last part of the nineteenth century, Ecuadorian indígenas improved their standing.

Ecuadorian leaders understood that preventing and containing infectious and epidemic disease were among the state's primary responsibilities.[68] Referencing the *Ley de Sanidad* in 1908, Ecuadorian President Eloy Alfaro (1895–1901, 1906–11) insisted, "the most important attribute of government is to protect the lives of its citizens. The propagation of . . . terrible diseases not only decimates our cities and retards their progress, but causes . . . the isolation of the nation . . . and consequently, the ruin of its commerce and industries; it causes immense financial loss to the better classes and suffering and destitution among the poor."[69]

To fortify public health and expand health care services, many turn-of-the-century Latin American nations formed cabinet-level health positions. In 1908, Ecuador established the Servicio de Sanidad (Health Service), which expanded from Guayaquil to Quito in 1914.[70] The former received more attention than the latter partly due to substantial agro-export interests on the coast, though the two offices readily shared information.[71] Articulating the relationship between public health, medical science, and progress, Ecuador's Minister of the Interior, José María Ayora, insisted in 1912 that "no civilized people exists that does not consider its progress to depend, in large part, on perfecting its public health service . . . [through] scientific advance. . . . Good health is the *sine qua non* foundation of all intellectual, moral and material progress."[72]

Fueling that material progress, Guayaquil was the fulcrum of Ecuador's international trade. Considered "the best harbor on the Pacific south of Panama," according to turn-of-the-century US diplomat Thomas Dawson, Guayaquil controlled 75 percent of the thriving cacao trade from the 1870s to the 1920s.[73] More than 20 percent of the world's processed cacao during the late nineteenth century came from Ecuador.[74] Guayaquil's vibrant commerce provided most national revenue. Consequently, Guayaquil enjoyed electricity and other manifestations of modernization before Quito, with which communication was poor. As the highlands became increasingly impoverished and populated by the turn of the century, more than half of Guayaquil's migrants (who comprised one-third of the population) came from the sierras. Even when highland hacendados allied with national politicians and portrayed their economic interests as national interests, the coastal-elite-controlled state resisted such self-serving overtures.[75]

Ecuadorian liberals who controlled cacao (and later sugar) exports on the coast lacked immediate access to highland indigenous communities. Instead of dispossessing indígenas of their lands, liberals passed legislation to advance the free movement of wage labor (facilitated by the contemporaneous construction of the Quito-Guayaquil Railway) to help highland indígenas escape hacendados' paltry pay. Amidst the post-World War I cacao crisis, the 1918 Reforma de la Ley de Jornaleros (Day Laborers' Reform Law) restricted *concertaje* (debt peonage) and coincided with the growth of the coastal sugar economy.[76] After two crop diseases—monilia and witches' broom—devastated cacao production in the 1920s, cacao planters' political and economic power waned and unemployed cacao laborers flooded Guayaquil and other Ecuadorian cities, compounding urban poverty.[77]

That elite power shift did not derail indigenous advances. In contrast to the *indio concertado* (debt peon), argued *indigenista* Pío Jaramillo Alvarado in 1922, "the free *comunero* is . . . well fed . . . knows how to defend his rights before the usurpation of neighboring hacendados, recovers abandoned zones of cultivation, utilizes irrigation, constitutes the nucleus of the demand for agrarian rights of the Indians."[78] Some efforts to defend their rights cost indígenas their lives. On September 13, 1923, a local jefe político ordered seventy soldiers to fire upon indigenous workers who were requesting land rights at Leito hacienda in Tungurahua. Thirty-seven indígenas—women and children included—were killed in that massacre. Such state violence was not uncommon, but it did not deter indigenous protest altogether.[79]

Instead, by the 1920s, indígenas organized and collaborated with other rural laborers in organizations such as El Inca en Pesillo to demand their rights and to improve rural working and living conditions.[80] Even as indígenas increasingly positioned themselves at the center of national discourse and identity, Ecuadorian scholar Diego Iturralde notes, officials considered them "marginal to political participation, [economic] development and social promotion, [and] decontextualized their culture."[81] Officials advocated obligatory military service as an avenue for Spanish acquisition and "indigenous development and progress."[82] In turn, rural indigenous organizations "reframed the content of the problem and demanded new politics" to be valued as "interlocutors and political figures."[83]

By advocating for free indigenous communities, indigenistas and liberal entrepreneurs undercut the economic and political power of highland hacendados. That process continued after a military coup led to the 1925 Revolución Juliana (Julian Revolution) that promised more humane governing and leadership roles for medical (and other) professionals. Although it restricted citizenship to literate men and women (thereby largely excluding indígenas even as it became the first Latin America constitution to grant female suffrage), the 1929 Constitution created a senate seat to represent, guide, and defend indígenas. As the cacao crisis undermined coastal liberals' political and economic power in the 1920s, conservative Catholic hacendados enjoyed renewed and expanded influence. Arguing hacendados had "an intimate union of affection" with indigenous laborers, Ecuadorian historian Pablo Ospina Peralta insists indigenous rebellions were not destructive, partly because indígenas directed their resistance more toward the state than toward hacendados.[84] Contrary to this pollyannaish characterization, archival traces of indigenous laborers' and activists' protests suggest the "intimate union" between indígenas and hacendados was marked as much by contention as affection.

After he came to power with the Revolución Juliana, President Isidro Ramon Antonio Ayora Cueva (1926–31) reorganized and transferred the Servicio de Sanidad national headquarters from Guayaquil to Quito, appointed Dr. Pablo Arturo Suárez general director, and established provincial public health delegates to extend Sanidad offerings to rural areas. Ayora Cueva, previously a doctor and the first Ecuadorian physician to train in obstetrics, prioritized public health. His administration emphasized the state's role in sanitation, hygiene, and curative measures.[85] The following year (1930), two PASB members—traveling representative Dr. John Long and epidemiologist Dr. C. R. Eskey—assisted an intensive campaign against and epidemiological study of bubonic plague in Ecuador. Such targeted responses reduced the need for quarantines that devastated international commerce.[86]

In a region where university-educated doctors enjoyed prestige, politics and health were intimately intertwined.[87] A physician's son who ruled with authoritarian zeal, Ayora Cueva enjoyed the support of congress and the military. But before he assumed the presidency, he hosted a meeting with physicians to explore national medical and social issues. At the height of his power, he insisted he was a doctor first. He attended his clinic daily during respites from his presidential responsibilities.[88] Early twentieth-century Ecuadorian physicians who held or were associated with government positions strove to demonstrate how their efforts benefited the nation. Established in 1928, the Sindicato Médico de Quito, which became the Asociación Médica de Quito in 1933, operated at the intersections of politics and medicine.[89]

After Ayora Cueva's presidency, and with the onset of the economic downturn of the 1930s, the nation plunged into political instability that included fifteen different administrations and many squashed conservative victories.

Absent a clear established power, indígenas could assert theirs more easily, which facilitated indígenas' integration into Ecuador's economy and politics on their own terms in ways that muted opposition to indigenous healing practices.[90] In November 1935, the first Conferencia de Cabecillas Indígenas (Indigenous Leaders Conference) was held in Quito, and the Comité Central de Defensa Indígena (Indigenous Defense Committee) was founded the following year. In turn, the 1937 Ley de Comunas (Community Law) helped indígenas establish their freedom from haciendas and position themselves more centrally in Ecuador's nation-formation process.[91] As the economic crisis lasted into the 1940s, indigenous and other popular groups enjoyed increasing influence.[92]

Financial restraints were a constant challenge for public health offices throughout Latin America, and Ecuador was no exception. From 1900–43, the Ecuadorian government allocated between 1.6 and 6.2 percent of the budget to welfare (which included Sanidad), excepting a spike to 9.5 percent in 1917. The median distribution was 3.1 percent.[93] With limited budgets and state reach, Ecuador's social services were, as a practical matter, available to only 15 percent of the population.[94] Public health resource allocation generally fell along racial (nonindigenous over indigenous) and geographic (urban rather than rural) lines.

Established in 1944, the Federación Ecuatoriana de Indios (FEI) advanced indigenous rights and advocated less derogatory discourse about indígenas. Those were challenging tasks since indigenous autonomy remained "unthinkable" for some blanco-mestizos.[95] Even those who allegedly sought to improve indigenous realities remained rooted in a halcyon past of ethnic relations that disadvantaged indígenas. Indigenista A. M. Paredes insisted national development should "obtain the kind of Indian that suits us."[96] After the May 1944 Glorious Revolution swept Ecuador, populist caudillo José María Velasco Ibarra was elected president with support of the FEI and various center-left groups. Indigenous polities were crucial to his campaign promise of a more humane and just future. Although his proclamations for the poor garnered their votes, Velasco Ibarra, once in office, clearly favored elites. Such sudden shifts in allegiances and goals frequently foreshortened his presidencies: this was the second of his five terms, which were intermittent from 1934–72 and mostly truncated by military coups.[97] Although Velasco Ibarra negotiated with the military and conservative party to instill the social order and peace that facilitated Ecuador's modernization in the 1940s,[98] his reign emulated twentieth-century Ecuador's larger pattern of populist leaders reneging on promises of social reform to preserve oligarchic privileges. In August 1947, the military deposed him.

Ecuadorian indígenas expanded their labor and land rights by continuing to exploit power struggles between Liberal coastal elites and Conservative highland hacendados. The Central Assembly of Public Assistance (Junta Central de Asistencia Pública), which oversaw relations between hacienda owners, overseers, and indigenous workers, regularly defended the latter's interests and rights.[99] Under a new model of exploitation on haciendas, laborers worked four to seven days per week in exchange for a plot of land or *huasipungo* to farm. Hacendados and administrators routinely abused indigenous laborers and families. "*Patrones*', employees', and caciques' [*gamonales*] many abuses, mistreatments, and cruelties are what caused our—*las indígenas* men and women—reaction and rebellion," explained the indigenous leader Neptalí Ulcuango Alba.[100] To evict one cruel overseer, indigenous women disrobed him and gave him a nettle bath in a ditch![101] Indígenas like Dolores Cacuango, who organized *huasipungueros* (huasipungo holders) to advocate for their rights, earned the ire of hacendados and foremen.[102] Labeling Cacuango a "pernicious woman," Anibal Maldonado petitioned the Junta to "change her residence to another region" in 1946, so she could not organize Hacienda Muyurco indigenous laborers.[103] Cacuango's activism thereafter suggests the Junta denied Maldonado's request.

Records suggest that indigenous leaders like Cacuango had ample opportunities to defend indigenous huasipungueros from exploitative administrators. The Junta's archives are filled with petitions like that from the indigenous huasipunguero Felipe Campues, who had worked at the Hacienda Pesillo for ten years "with efficacy, integrity, and punctuality" but, he said, was "harmed" by "interested individuals' intrigue."[104] He wrote that in May 1948, the administrator Jaime Holgun Terran broke his contract and sought to kick Campues off the land and out of the "only home he and his big family had," an act that "was neither just nor humane."[105] A year later, the indigenous huasipunguero Andres Chiguano de José María complained that the Hacienda Zumbagua administrator had taken his harvest, which Chiguano had expanded to "satisfy the subsistence needs of his family."[106] Eighty-five-year-old Joaquin Catucuamba had worked at Hacienda Muyorco for some seventy years when he was threatened with eviction from his huasipungo in August 1949. Insisting his position as the *molinero* (miller) was irreplaceable, Catucuamba assumed he was marginalized by "lies and unjust reasons" because "I had grown old" and "I am a poor father of a family."[107] He asked to be "left peacefully in the huasipungo until I die, and I will continue working and serving as long as I can."[108]

Administrators sent the Junta their own petitions, defending their actions and protesting rulings that favored huasipungueros. But Junta members often supported indigenous claims and reinstated their access to their land, homes, and harvests. As they held landowners, political lieutenants, and priests accountable for actions detrimental to public health, Junta officials enriched their understanding of indígenas' realities, concerns, and challenges. Conciliatory relations between authorities and indígenas established a foundation for efficacious public health campaigns in rural communities.[109]

Those conditions allowed Ecuadorian indígenas to develop considerable autonomy and political power.[110] As Ecuador portrayed itself as a nation that civilized indígenas, some indigenous communities used their genealogies and histories to impress an indelibly indigenous mark on Quito and shape the city's politics and resource allocation.[111] Attention to highland peons' rights facilitated their gradual integration into Ecuador's economy and politics. More than their Guatemalan counterparts, Ecuadorian officials recognized public health campaigns had to account for indígenas.[112]

Engaging with social medicine scholars and practitioners in postcolonial Latin America, Europe, and the United States as part of larger processes of "circulation" of "health and scientific ideologies, policies, and practices," Ecuadorian physicians and public health officials understood that inadequate housing, sanitation, and potable water undermined individual health and fostered epidemics.[113] Social medicine and its integrative focus on economic, political, and social causes of disease generally contended against reductionist scientific medicine,[114] but those tensions waned against the backdrop of indigenous and other traditional medicines in Ecuador that challenged scientific medicine's hegemony.

More distant than Guatemala from the United States and developing a vibrant (if underfunded) public health sector in Guayaquil and later Quito, Ecuador was largely spared international interventions. Few large US-owned companies operated in Ecuador. Founded in 1899, the United Fruit Company (UFCO) identified Ecuador as a source of arable land and inexpensive labor in the late 1920s, but did not purchase its first large landholding there until 1934. Its sanitation campaigns notwithstanding, UFCO had limited influence in Ecuador, where rural workers who protested poor wages and living conditions circumscribed the company's power by the second half of the twentieth century.[115]

Disease has long shaped Guatemalan history. Recognizing that Spaniards introduced illnesses, Kaqchikel Maya chronicles observed in 1558, "After the arrival of the lord President in Pan Q'än [Antigua], the sickness began here. . . . [I]t was frightening how many deaths befell us because of the great lord."[116] Spanish invasions unleashed germs against which indígenas had no immunity. Subsequent Maya mass deaths facilitated Spanish colonization. After independence in 1821, disease continued to shape the nation's and indígenas' political fates. When Guatemalan Governor Maríano Gálvez (1831–38) initiated public health reforms to address a cholera epidemic in 1837, Catholic priests convinced their indigenous congregants that the government was trying to poison them. Angry with the Liberal Gálvez administration for this and other reasons, indígenas joined a successful 1838 revolt led by Rafael Carrera. The Conservative leader, in power from 1844–48 and again from 1851–65, established an era of both authoritarian rule and relative stability.[117]

Conservatives like Carrera largely facilitated indigenous autonomy, but by the 1860s, the Conservative government and Liberal regime that overthrew it in 1871 expropriated indigenous landholdings to access the best agricultural lands and to force indígenas into the labor market. The government redistributed those properties to nonindigenous people who migrated into the western highlands in search of land and livelihoods. Comprised primarily of Creoles and ladinos, political and economic elites deployed racist structures and forced labor mechanisms to compel indígenas from the Western highlands to migrate to coastal coffee plantations. Like Ecuador, Guatemala sent agricultural products, particularly coffee, to the international market.[118]

In the late nineteenth and early twentieth centuries, Guatemala City officials turned their attention to public health. As the government planned to construct potable water infrastructure in the capital in 1890, they turned to the international market for "iron pipes and other materials."[119] To complement such modernizing efforts, Guatemalan officials looked abroad for models of good health and hygiene. In a report to the Guatemala City mayor in 1899, a group of doctors referenced the work of the "prominent Finnish medical hygienist Dr. Alberto Palmberg" to underscore "that the health of the *pueblos* is the supreme law" and to demonstrate that people "should not fear filtering" because "the modern process of purifying water is proven" by "scientific data."[120] Workers repaired aqueducts and relocated the cemetery with an eye toward improving public health. Concurrently, Guatemala beautified its capital: by the turn of the twentieth century, Guatemala City boasted streetcars, electric lights, photoshops, bicycles, cinemas, and the Parque la Reforma, an urban space modeled after New York City's Central Park. A modernized police force and newly outfitted national army perambulated the capital.[121]

Guatemala's Public Health Office maintained centralized control over public health in Guatemala City, and dictator Estrada Cabrera waxed eloquently about the importance of public health. But his regime's actions and allocations seldom reflected such rhetoric: the Office never met regularly in the early twentieth century,[122] and the state's fragmented systems left rural regions devoid of health services. In other words, the state neglected rural indigenous communities, allowing untrained healers whom the state considered incompetent and even dangerous to practice in remote areas.

The nation's skeletal public health infrastructure—comprised of a fledgling Public Health Council, a few urban hospitals, random rural health clinics, and intermittent vaccination campaigns—provided ample room for the RF and UFCO to shape Guatemala's development in the early twentieth century. UFCO's far-reaching influence in Guatemala included developing and controlling railroads that ran from agricultural plantation zones to Puerto Barrios on the Caribbean coast.

UFCO was oriented toward the United States and what Palmer calls "transnational corporate medicine"; in other words, it had little regard for Guatemalan public health priorities.[123] Even though they had to contribute part of their paycheck to UFCO's health care system, Guatemalan workers struggled to gain admittance to its Quirigua hospital. With only occasional access there, UFCO encouraged them to use the Puerto Barrios public hospital at a time when medical professionals there referred malaria patients to Guatemala City. As a result, they had to travel long distances to address that and other ailments. Further betraying its class and racial biases, UFCO provided screens and nets only to plantation managers, claiming that manual laborers were too ignorant to use such technologies.[124] Protesting UFCO's discrimination, myopia, and exclusionary care, Guatemalan workers struck in 1923.[125]

A few pockets of indigenous entrepreneurs notwithstanding, Guatemalan indígenas gained little autonomy during a period marked by authoritarian rule.[126] Guatemalan governments facilitated southern coastal coffee planters' access to highland indígenas. General José María Orellana (1922–26) ignored *finqueros'* (large-landed estate owners) abuse of indigenous laborers as he stabilized the presidential office.[127] His successor Lázaro Chacón's more democratic administration (1926–1930) collaborated with some indigenous communities, but ultimately surrendered the country to another dictator: Ubico.[128] In 1934, Ubico concurrently abolished debt peonage and promulgated a vagrancy law that ensured finqueros and authorities would have sufficient (primarily indigenous) workers for agro-export production and public works.[129]

A dictator who fancied himself a doctor, Ubico was a complicated figure in Guatemala's history of medicine. The extent to which Ubico embraced public health as a cornerstone of his rule is evident in his regime's revisionist history. According to a 1942 government retrospective report, Ubico, as the governor of Alta Verapaz and Chief of Health in the Pacific Zone in the late 1910s, had studied yellow fever "to discover its origins and put in place . . . the drastic measures needed to completely eradicate the disease."[130] Although yellow fever luminary Dr. Joseph White lauded Ubico's management of inspection, fumigation, and quarantine during a 1918 yellow fever outbreak, RF Guatemalan director Alvin Struse was less sanguine about Ubico's public health qualifications. When, as governor in 1918, Ubico diagnosed cases and released patients from quarantine who had been deemed contagious by medical professionals, Struse convinced Estrada Cabrera to remove Ubico's medical authority.[131] His public health (if not medical) prowess resurged thereafter when Ubico was selected to lead the anti-yellow fever campaigns in Los Amates and "other places within the United Fruit Company zone" in 1920. He later visited the United States "to study the sanitary organizations of that advanced country."[132] The 1942 report insisted "The young colonel Ubico . . . exercised a very special effort in favor of the health of the inhabitants of those fertile regions, giving preference to the improvement of the indigenous race. . . . Ubico had the opportunity to demonstrate, with evident proof, his humanitarian efforts for the health of those he governed."[133]

Ubico realized public health campaigns could advance political careers, and as dictator, he championed public health programs. "Prior to the Ubico government . . . people of all ages [were] showing poor blood manifested in weak bones and muscles and even poor spirit stemming from poor health . . . now that vision has completely changed," his administration attested in the same 1942 report.[134] "The Guatemalans who ambulate in our streets and roads no longer look sick, even though they cannot yet flaunt the robust expression that we all yearn for."[135] With a track record of tackling yellow fever and improving sanitation, Ubico targeted malaria and intestinal parasites as the next frontier of the nation's modernization.[136] The report underscored the significance of these efforts and to whom success should be attributed: "The meritorious work . . . in favor of health . . . since Ubico took power is in all Guatemalans' conscience."[137] More than simply biological, disease and public health were political.

Such strong government claims to public health campaigns left little room for other institutions to contribute. While Ecuadorian Catholic priests regularly engaged in public health campaigns, Liberal attacks on the Guatemalan Catholic church weakened its hold among highland indígenas, which left few opportunities for priests to bolster rural health.

In a desperate effort to maintain authoritarian power after Ubico stepped down in 1944, his handpicked successor, General Federico Ponce Vaides, appealed to indígenas for support with a promise to expand their rights and access to resources. On Independence Day (September 15), indígenas demonstrated their allegiance to Ponce's administration by protesting in the capital, Chimaltenango, Chichicastenango, and El Quiche.[138] Those demonstrations had little effect on the growing coalition of students, military reformers, teachers, professionals, urban workers, and an emerging middle class who chafed at fascist rule. On October 20, 1944, they toppled the regime. Two days later, in Patzicía, about twenty-five Kaqchikel men armed with machetes, stones, and axes gathered to support Ponce and protest ladino domination of local resources, particularly land.[139] Local ladinos responded with guns. When the civic guard and national army arrived a few days later to restore order, as many as nine hundred Kaqchikels had been killed.[140] The massacre and its reverberations cast a dark hue over the democratic government of Juan José Arévalo Bermejo (1945–50), who had won free and fair elections shortly after the October Revolution.

The democratic government continued to privilege ladinos, but offered some new benefits to indígenas and Afro-Guatemalans.[141] The 1946 Social Security Law established the Guatemalan Institute of Social Security, which provided workers' compensation, maternity benefits, and childcare, among other provisions, to all citizens.[142] Arévalo also extended suffrage to all men and literate women. Therefore, only 4.8 percent of adult indigenous females could vote by the end of Arévalo's rule.[143]

During Arevalo's administration, the Instituto Indigenista Nacional de Guatemala (National Indigenist Institute of Guatemala, IING) shifted attribution of the "Indian problem" from tired tropes of indigenous ignorance, indolence, and alcoholism to the state's failure to provide for its citizens. Anthropologists and indigenous ethnographers conducted studies that underscored the importance of socioeconomic development and establishing equitable (rather than exploitative) relationships between marginalized people and elites who controlled the state. IING employees asserted that indigenous health would improve if the state provided resources—education, clean water, sewer systems, land—that would combat poverty and ill health.[144] More broadly, IING director Antonio Goubaud insisted ladinos and indígenas come together to cement a Guatemalan identity based on a shared allegiance to the nation rather than acculturation.[145] Guatemalan indigenistas forged a more coherent and efficacious path toward improving indigenous rights and realities than their Ecuadorian counterparts who suffered from disorganization and indifference. And, to the extent that resources afforded interventions in Guatemala, IING officials recognized rural public health was crucial to economic development. They sought to extend public health initiatives to rural areas, oftentimes with the aid of the RF in agro-export regions.

Although Arévalo ushered in a decade of democratic rule, with an administration that sought to increase workers' economic and political power, expand education, modernize health care around a social security model, and extend other social services, the new government regularly undermined the well-being of marginalized populations.[146] Forced labor mechanisms persisted. And from 1946 to 1948, the Ministry of Health collaborated with USPHS to infect Guatemalan prisoners, mental hospital inmates, orphans, and indigenous military recruits with syphilis, gonorrhea, and chancroid.[147] As abhorrent as those experiments were, abuse and inequality in the health care and public health systems were not aberrations.[148] Rather, a long history of disregard for the health of marginalized individuals continued to shape scientific medicine and public health endeavors as the twentieth century progressed.

TRANSNATIONAL THREADS

In Ecuador and Guatemala, international interventions in public health campaigns regularly determined perceptions of both infectious-contagious diseases and the people most susceptible to them. Although the RF is the strongest transnational thread that weaves these histories together, PASB, UFCO, and USPHS all influenced how international, national, and local officials rolled out public health campaigns in nations with large indigenous populations.

During the first half of the twentieth century, Guatemalan and Ecuadorian authorities and researchers engaged the international community of medical professionals and companies from positions of strength. Some stressed their contributions, talents, intelligence, and findings as they collaborated in medical communities beyond their borders. Ecuadorian doctors and public health officials corresponded with and hosted such international health luminaries as William Crawford Gorgas and John Long. In turn, invitations to Guatemalan medical professionals came from the United States, Colombia, Cuba, and El Salvador.[149]

In February 1924, the American College of Surgeons Director visited Guatemala to invite physicians to become fellows "to promote a closer affiliation between the professions of the Americas."[150] In addition to asking for a list of their top surgeons, he solicited their ideas about bringing fellows throughout the region closer together. His use of the term "Americas" to denote the region suggested his attempt to mitigate US-centrism. Such overtures were aimed at cultivating cultural diplomacy through medical expertise as well as spreading US (scientific) medicine in Latin America.[151] While medical professionals in the Americas regularly worked together, collaborating with US doctors and scientists could be perilous.[152] The American College of Surgeons Director enjoyed more resources and power than most Latin American surgeons. Broader trends in Latin American relations with the US government and the American Public Health Association tended to be tainted with imperialism.[153] Yet regional professional organizations in Latin America provide evidence that transnational exchanges of ideas, people, and materials were not contingent on the United States. Fruitful interactions regularly evolved absent its participation.[154]

PASB—founded as the International Sanitary Bureau in 1902 before becoming PASB in 1923 and the Pan American Health Organization (PAHO) in 1949—sought to improve health in the Americas by advancing medical science internationally and adapting it to local conditions. Headquartered in Washington, DC, and comprised of members from different republics in the Americas, PASB ensured that Latin American nations were aware of international interventions throughout the region.

Although the United States had an outsized role in PASB, some of its early leaders understood the interconnected nature of public health in the region. "The growing importance of the relations of the peoples of each

American Republic with those of every other makes it incumbent upon all Americans, North, Central and South, to become fully informed of these relations and to be informed particularly with regard to questions of an international character," noted Dr. Bolivar J. Lloyd, the assistant to the Director of PASB and the Medical Director of the USPHS in the 1930s.[155] By recognizing people of all twenty-one nations as Americans, Dr. Lloyd too moved away from US-centrism toward hemispheric understandings of public health.

HOOKWORM AND THE ROCKEFELLER FOUNDATION

The RF often was in lockstep with US foreign policy and UFCO goals of "sanitizing" the tropics to make the region safe for US investors, workers, and soldiers, but sought to distinguish itself from US imperialism and capital even when its mediations were linked to them.[156] In their shared goals of eradicating yellow fever and malaria, the RF, UFCO, and USPHS occasionally collaborated, but also operated independently.[157]

To legitimize their initial interventions in Latin America, RF representatives defined hookworm as a problematic disease. Although many local populations had learned to live with it as part of their subsistence lifestyles, some governments established anti-hookworm programs in the early 1900s: Guatemala, El Salvador, and Costa Rica in 1910, and Brazil in 1911. To their credit, RF representatives consulted those national experts and used Costa Rica's program as a model.[158] Throughout Central America and the Caribbean, RF representatives embraced bilateral approaches grounded in collaboration with local experts and officials, who at times were paternalistic and condescending.[159] Costa Rican public health official Solón Núñez portrayed his charges as "simple people of the village."[160] As national personnel educated rural residents about the importance of clean water and cleanliness, RF aid helped improve rural hygiene.[161]

RF agents intended to develop local professional elites who would direct changes in medicine and health with scientific decisions, but often worked with less educated populations to staff their programs.[162] With little medical schooling, the microscopists, inspectors, and teachers who advanced the 1914 anti-hookworm program in Costa Rica enjoyed the unusual opportunity of RF training and endorsements. Afforded that affirmation, most sold their services as curanderos thereafter.[163] The RF imprimatur was not omnipotent, however. Accustomed to their own healers, indígenas disputed and resisted early twentieth-century RF hookworm campaigns in Nicaragua.[164] And validating the medical legitimacy of lightly-trained empíricos in Costa Rica did not compel RF representatives to recognize popular healers' legitimacy in Guatemala.

In a manifestation of diverse transnational effects, Guatemalan and Ecuadorian racial thinking distinctly influenced RF representatives. Working primarily with public health officials in Guayaquil, RF representatives in Ecuador seldom interacted with or disparaged indígenas. In Guatemala, however, RF representatives conducted hookworm experiments on *fincas* (large, landed estates) where they observed indígenas, who comprised the majority of laborers.

Hookworm provided the RF an early entrée into Guatemala. When a very young girl was admitted to the Guatemala City General Hospital with intense anemia, abdominal pain, fatigue, "profuse and very foul-smelling diarrhea . . . and extreme depression" in 1909, doctors ordered an examination that revealed teeming hookworm, roundworm, and whipworm eggs.[165] "If the child does not succumb and resists the infection for some time, she will grow up weak, anemic, and of melancholy character," noted the doctor.[166]

To eliminate such deficits by curtailing hookworm, a half decade later Dr. Rowan enlisted Guatemalan medical professionals. Although much of Central America had integrated into what Palmer calls a "Caribbean network oriented by and toward the United States,"[167] RF representatives treaded lightly in a nation ruled by a capricious, cruel dictator who had alienated the oligarchic class from which most medical professionals hailed. Generally coming from families whose conservative outlooks denigrated indígenas, Guatemala's medical elite foreclosed the possibility of working with indigenous communities. During its first three years in Guatemala, the RF did not work in a single indigenous town. Since elite families owned fincas, Rowan established hookworm projects on them that treated laborers—the majority of whom, as mentioned, were indigenous—as patients and research subjects. In sharp contrast, hookworm campaign employees were almost all monolingual Spanish-speaking Criollo medical students and physicians who were largely ignorant of indigenous languages and cultures. As Palmer notes, the Guatemalan staff imposed "their prejudices and preferences on the direction and rhythm of the campaign."[168] Primarily working with such medical professionals and finqueros, RF representatives in Guatemala often disparaged indígenas.[169] Efforts to cultivate multiethnic, multilingual staffs in Trinidad and British Guiana never materialized in

Guatemala.[170] Although RF agents were aware of Guatemalan indígenas' linguistic and cultural richness, they avoided addressing it or racism in civic settings by confining their engagement to indigenous migrant laborers.[171]

Yet Rowan was genuinely curious about indígenas and aware of their diversity. He tacked between lauding them and struggling to convince them of scientific medicine's efficacy. Rowan observed,

> Difficulties encountered: the greatest of all is the type of people with whom we are working. So far our work has been solely among Indians, representing many different tribes, each having its own peculiar language, customs, dress, and worst of all its own systems of medicine. The way they have maintained in the face of Spanish civilization is wonderful. All these Indians are suspicious of any and everything medical. To employ . . . men who know these traits and languages is absolutely out of the question; even the Indian from one tribe does not understand the language of another tribe.[172]

Even as he maligned indigenous medicine, he praised indigenous persistence. He marveled at indigenous languages while his Creole collaborators considered them illegitimate.

Of course, Rowan arrived with his own prejudices, and they dovetailed nicely with those of Guatemalan elites. In his description of forty outhouses built to accommodate a thousand people on Finca Las Mercedes in September 1915, Rowan observed, "No seat is provided because these Indians would not use it" (figure 5).[173] Such assumptions undoubtedly were informed by his colleagues and experiences in the United States. Dr. Andrew Warren, who later directed RF's first hookworm campaign in Mexico, designed an inclined platform for squatting rather than sitting in outhouses because North Carolina farmers "could not defecate when sitting . . . upon the seat of a water closet."[174] Rowan's perceptions and goals were part of what historian Warwick Anderson calls "excremental colonialism," whereby US medical managers in the Philippines and other developing nations assumed dark-skinned inhabitants defecated promiscuously.[175] To improve public health in those places, Rowan and his counterparts in the RF, USPHS, and the US military trained local populations in hygiene and designed and developed sanitary infrastructure. Rowan's successor in Guatemala, Struse, complained that many indígenas refused "to use them [latrines] under any circumstances" because they claimed changing from a squatting to sitting position made them constipated.[176]

Taken for RF clinical, media, and officials' uses, photographs such as those of a fourteen-year-old indigenous boy who weighed thirty-three pounds

Type of "excusado" being built on finca Las Mercedes.
Underneath each is a pit 10 feet deep. No seat is
provided because these Indians would not use it.
Forty of these properly placed will accomodate
about 1000 people.

Another view of the above "excusado."

FIGURE 5. "Type of 'excusado' being built on finca Las Mercedes."
Photograph by Walter Rowan, 1915. Rockefeller Foundation
Photographs. Courtesy of Rockefeller Archive Center.

(figure 2), a twenty-six-year-old indígena who weighed seventy-five pounds, and a hookworm-infected indigenous family of ten (figure 6) conveyed how poverty sapped indigenous vitality and health.[177] Moving beyond portrayals of sick individuals, the photograph of the infected family suggests a systemic problem. When reporting endemic jigger among indígenas, Rowan underlined how a lack of footwear (related to poverty) jeopardized indigenous health. For many Guatemalans, however, being barefoot denoted indigeneity.

A family of ten Indians – all are infected

FIGURE 6. "A family of ten Indians—all are infected." Photograph by Walter Rowan, 1915. Rockefeller Foundation Photographs. Courtesy of Rockefeller Archive Center.

The inextricable intersections of race, class, and disease confounded public health professionals and government officials, and prevented efficacious public health responses. Rowan's descriptions and images resonated with Guatemalan elite discourse about weak, rickety indios. Yet he also noticed their potential.

With a mix of compassion, disgust, and awe, Dr. Rowan understood the capacity of healthy indígenas and the tragedy of their reality. "As a rule 50% of the children die before they have completed one year of such a precarious existence. Another 20% probably never complete 5 years—a terrific human waste that must be checked if Central American countries are ever to make any great progress, since the strongest and best of their people are to be found in the remnants of the aboriginal tribes which remain," he noted in 1915.[178] His successors similarly recognized indígenas' unique contributions such as their native dress, languages, artisanship, and history.[179] Although Rowan's reference to remnants of aboriginal tribes evoked a halcyon past, he also portended a fruitful future should indígenas be afforded conditions in which to thrive. In a nation that framed racial differences along cultural rather than biological lines, Rowan underscored the biological integrity of an otherwise discounted population by calling indígenas "the strongest and best of their people." His problematic biological essentialism notwithstanding, Rowan broke with denigrating discourse about "indios," insisting they were the region's best hope to modernize.

Rowan's replacement was less interested in or hopeful about indigenous people or culture. Serving as the RF Guatemalan director from 1916 until his death in 1918, Struse considered the "class" of indígenas an obstacle to his mission because they resisted hookworm treatments.[180] Struse's thought, informed by US anti-black and anti-brown racism, resonated with Guatemalan government discourse. Guatemalan officials and RF agents transferred their ideas about race and racisms between countries.[181] In contrast to indígenas who resisted RF overtures, Struse claimed, "The Ladino—the inhabitant of the town, represents a much higher scale of civilization. He easily comprehends literature, and is usually willing to cooperate with the work."[182] Struse's prejudice against indígenas surely endeared him to Estrada Cabrera and other Guatemalan officials, medical professionals, and intellectuals.

Rowan's and Struse's portrayals of indígenas as uncivilized and averse to modernization resonated with Guatemalan elite discourse. Nobel Prize Laureate Miguel Angel Asturias argued that "The Indian is the prototype of the anti-hygienic person; proof of this is the facility with which diseases spread among family members."[183] Convinced their "racial background . . . is insufficient," he insisted that education and hygiene could not transform indígenas; rather, he advocated miscegenation with Western European (ideally German) blood.[184] In his 1938 study of Aryan superiority in Alta Verapaz, German military surgeon Gerhard Enno Buß warned about the dangers of interracial mixing, but found that Q'eqchi'-Germans were more psychologically mature than either ladinos or indígenas.[185] Asturias and other Guatemalan intellectuals portrayed indígenas as dirty and diseased to distance them from non-indigenous Guatemalans.[186] RF officers also equated disease with dirtiness.[187] Yet Rowan's positive portrayals of indigenous hygiene and association of disease with poverty suggest he may not have agreed with Asturias and his counterparts that indígenas were anti-hygienic vectors of disease. Beholden to their superiors in New York and national officials in their host countries, RF representatives delicately danced between those power brokers as intermittently influential interlocutors.

Just as Struse was shifting RF's focus from plantations to indigenous and ladino communities, a December 24, 1917 earthquake leveled Guatemala City, opening sewers and cemetery vaults and destroying the system of electricity—all of which compromised public health. When the US Red Cross arrived, Struse organized such an immediate and efficacious response that Estrada Cabrera appointed him head of the emergency medical relief team. The RF-supported hookworm office quickly became an emergency hospital as well as the nerve center of typhoid and other vaccination campaigns.[188] Such goodwill, generosity, and expertise further endeared Struse and the RF to Estrada Cabrera.

On the heels of that disaster, yellow fever struck again, demanding Struse's attention. In 1918, Estrada Cabrera appointed Struse president of the Guatemalan Consejo de Salubridad (Public Health Council). The announcement shocked and dismayed RF leadership, who subsequently prohibited the practice of working directly for governments. After Struse died of influenza in the pandemic later that year, his successor delicately declined the same offer from Estrada Cabrera. Although the paltry $900 US that Estrada Cabrera's dictatorship earmarked for RF initiatives during his reign defied RF requests that national governments assume responsibility for RF-sponsored projects,[189] that Estrada Cabrera selected a US citizen to serve as Guatemala's highest public health official demonstrates how closely connected RF representatives were with him.

The influenza epidemic of 1918 likely originated from US military camps in Guatemala that the RF sought to shield from yellow fever.[190] Influenza's staggering loss of life—the official tally was fifty thousand dead, 3 percent of the population, but a more accurate figure was easily twice that—catalyzed a reckoning. Journalists and doctors blamed indigenous victims for their "miserable hygiene," but such scapegoating failed to conceal government corruption, ineptitude, and exploitation.[191] In 1920, Guatemalans ousted Estrada Cabrera.[192] Even as the Guatemalan medical establishment continued to flourish in ways that built upon Estrada Cabrera's cozy relationship with the RF,[193] the latter never regained Struse's influence or vision, and subsequently made few contributions to indigenous communities.[194]

After Struse's death, RF agents doubted the efficacy of their mission. Concerned that Central American countries were unable "to comply with their end of the financial obligation," RF director Heiser wrote in 1919 that "[u]nless our representative was on the ground to direct the work, it is doubtful whether the planters or other private agencies would continue to support rural health programs in permanent ways," though he expressed enthusiasm for the hookworm campaign in Ecuador.[195] Such doubts haunted RF representatives like RF Director of Medical Sciences Alan Gregg (1930–51) who observed, "We select the kind of work to be done (or they sagaciously anticipate our wishes).

We choose the personnel and we pay the bill. But we don't accept the responsibility for personnel or for the future. . . . The work itself is fragmentary and inconclusive, the employees are timid and restless."[196]

Many Latin Americans considered the RF a cog of US empire—with good reason, since the foundation informally advanced US foreign policy—and thus resisted its personnel and programs.[197] Throughout Central America and the Caribbean, medical professionals mistrusted and thus distanced themselves from the RF and its association with "the new imperial power's preeminent robber baron."[198] Partly to assuage such concerns, the RF provided fellowships, including to five Guatemalan physicians who studied in the United States during the 1920s.[199] Many locals remained unconvinced. On November 15, 1922, the Alotenango mayor thwarted RF interventions when he refused to provide a room or lavatory, not to mention "moral support" for an RF assistant, explained then-RF Director John Elmendorff to the Sacatepéquez governor.[200] Whether the Guatemalan mayor's resistance was informed by RF's ineffective anti-hookworm campaign, a commitment to locally informed solutions, or other factors is unclear, but he demonstrated that even a small-town official could disrupt the intentions of a powerful US organization.[201] Such local actors and conditions have shaped the course of international relations, scientific research, and public health priorities and programs.[202] The 1922 letter hints at competing notions of public health and subaltern strategies for circumscribing foreign interventions.

ROCKEFELLER FOUNDATION AND EMPIRICAL MEDICINE

Although the RF aided Latin American government's and medical elites' commitment to scientific medicine, some RF representatives flouted guidelines and laws regulating medical practice. For example, Struse's successor, Dr. William T. Burres, derided curanderos, but advocated training employees with no medical background to detect and treat hookworm. By the 1930s, a new cohort of RF representatives disavowed such incongruity.

After a few years of limited exposure to popular healing in Guatemala, Burres was unimpressed. "Poorer people . . . seldom see a physician but are attended by old women and other classes of curanderos, and as a rule their word is taken in matter of diagnosis," he explained on October 27, 1919,[203] later adding, "We know that many unlicensed persons prescribe right and left and that these countries are full of 'curanderos' and fakirs of all kinds."[204] Lumping together local curanderos with Middle Eastern "fakirs," Burres discounted indigenous and traditional healing knowledge and practices of all sorts.[205] Unlike Guatemalan authorities, Burres did not associate healers with unrest and disorder, but he doubted they could be redeemed. "A person ... of the ignorant class ... while very useful, is not capable of learning to make exams or administer treatments," he concluded.[206] Informed by his experience on fincas where ladino administrators oversaw indigenous workers, his use of "class" had ethnic undertones. Guatemalan portrayals of inept, ignorant, inebriated indígenas and US anti-black and anti-brown racism influenced Burres, Struse, and their colleagues who perceived ladinos as more capable and of a higher "class" than indígenas.

Throughout Latin America, racism marked RF projects. In a 1920 trip to Brazil, RF International Health Board Director Wycliffe Rose dubbed blacks shiftless and Portuguese people parasitic, in contrast to São Paolo whites who were self-reliant.[207] RF officers working on a contemporary anti-hookworm campaign in Mexico considered indígenas unhygienic, ignorant, and immoral.[208] Their Guatemalan counterparts shared similar sentiments. "Work here is very difficult owing to the fact that the inhabitants are pure Indians, many even not understanding Spanish and in many instances they are opposed to all treatments not given by their native medicine men," reported Elmendorff in 1929.[209] Coinciding with the extent of RF's engagement in each country, RF representatives' racist thought had more traction in Guatemala than Ecuador.

Eschewing collaboration with healers, Burres proposed training technical assistants who could test for and treat hookworm on rural fincas. Unwilling to fund that proposal, his superior in New York, Dr. Victor Heiser, suggested he train a helper from each finca who would remain there, "thus adding to the sum total of education in Guatemala."[210] Burres agreed to pursue that approach under the condition that the trainee was not a *mozo* (manual, often indigenous, laborer), who "is usually unreliable,"[211] but rather "some such person as administrator, book keeper, or other person of that class who would be capable of giving treatments after we leave."[212] Again, Burres's use of the term "class" captures both economic and ethnic status in a nation where both were fraught with multiple meanings, including assumptions of an individual's ability to contribute to the nation's development and well-being. Public discourse portrayed upper- to middle-class ladinos as crucial to national progress and depicted poor and working-class indígenas as backwards. Early-twentieth-century Guatemalan intellectual J. Fernando Juárez Muñoz argued, "this [indigenous] race is the heavy burden that weighs down the nation, threatening to drown it and impeding its full development."[213] Even Guatemalan-German coffee planters who respected some aspects of indigenous culture often insisted indígenas lacked entrepreneurial spirit and thus could neither advance nor benefit from capitalist modernization.[214]

Informed by such biases (and his own), Burres denigrated indigenous healers and promoted educated finca employees whom he insisted "will be of a higher grade material ... [and] better class of man [than mozos]" and could become "microscopists." Aware the Guatemalan Faculty of Medicine "prohibits unauthorized persons from prescribing," Burres knew RF could not sanction such trainees. Still, since the state had a limited presence in rural areas, Burres reasoned, the law "need not prevent a reliable person prescribing a known treatment for one special disease like uncinariasis [hookworm] on an out of the way finca."[215] Maintaining plausible deniability, Burres and his colleagues endorsed the very unlicensed administration of health care they derided among curanderos. Burres's suggestion to ignore Medical Faculty guidelines is all the more remarkable in light of how hard his predecessors, particularly Rowan, worked to placate medical establishment members, many of whom distrusted the RF.[216] Dismissing mozos' capacity to learn rudimentary aspects of scientific medicine and denigrating indigenous healing, Burres carved out moral space within which RF could train educated Guatemalans to practice medicine outside the confines of Guatemalan law.

Convinced that finqueros' interest in a healthy work force would supersede any reluctance to cross authorities or medical faculty, Burres asserted, "When they learn of the advantage of curing their infected workmen, [finqueros] will go ahead on their own responsibility and treat them."[217] Wittingly or not, Burres was tapping into a long Latin American tradition of finqueros deploying empirical medicine to keep their employees healthy.[218] Yet at times, finqueros—particularly, after the United States joined the allies in World War I, those who were German—refused to collaborate with the RF.[219] Despite the "custom in this country to employ by preference medical students," Burres recommended otherwise since "they leave us in the lurch now and then" by returning to finish their medical degree, "which is praiseworthy," but inconvenient.[220] Struse similarly struggled to retain medical students as staff.[221] To achieve its goals "without estranging the Medical Faculty," Burres encouraged finqueros to take the lead.

His superiors must have been impressed with his prescience. Less than a month later on November 25, Mr. J. Antonio Lanuza of "El Siglo" Coffee

Plantation in Tumbador visited RF's New York office. "Two years ago a hookworm campaign reached his plantation and his laborers were treated. He was greatly impressed with the results. He realizes your workers could not be expected to come to his plantation again, he is quite prepared to go on with the work on his own initiative," they reported.[222] After purchasing charts from RF and "other equipment in New York suitable for the work," Lanuza returned to his finca to commence the campaign, apparently approbating Burres's plan.

Yet medical subterfuge rankled some Latin American professionals. The Superintendent of Colón (Panama) Hospital, Dr. Claude Pierce, berated RF representative Lewis Hackett for suggesting his team collaborate in the hookworm campaign, declaring, as Hackett summed it up, that Hackett "had no regard for ethics of the standing of the medical profession . . . that I had no right to send young men without medical degrees out among people to treat them of disease—it was criminal" and "unfair to make doctors out of ignorant young fools and hand them a lot of medicine and let them run loose in the community."[223]

By 1930, the RF was less cavalier with unlicensed practitioners. When a former employee of the RF Department of Uncinariasis established a practice in Chiquimula and marketed himself as a microscopy and intestinal parasite specialist, RF representative Dr. Daniel Molloy kept his distance. In response to the ex-employee's request to purchase a hookworm film from the RF, Molloy informed his superiors, "I doubt it would be advisable for him to use our film since it would give him the sanction of IHD [the International Health Division of the RF] and he would make use of it for advertising purposes. Legally, of course, he is practicing medicine without the necessary authorization and we certainly do not wish to lend ourselves to sanctioning the illicit practice of medicine in this or any other country."[224] Although the state's reach remained limited—Molloy noted the Ministry of Public Health only controlled medical practice in the country "to a certain extent"—Molloy refused to cross the line of supporting unauthorized practitioners even in a remote city some 174 kilometers east of the capital. The shift in RF practice was timely in a nation that was about to expand its campaign against *empirismo* (empiricism).

In Ecuador, as in Guatemala, RF representatives approached medical elites rather than indigenous leaders or communities to facilitate projects. As a result, RF representatives mostly interacted with cosmopolitan and ethnically homogenous blanco-mestizos. Yellow fever and malaria projects occurred primarily in Guayaquil, which attracted few indígenas. When they migrated from the highlands to coastal areas, they tended to work on agro-export plantations for short stints. Neither Ecuadorian officials nor RF representatives reference RF work in rural villages. In the late 1930s, the RF withdrew from programmatic public health campaigns and increasingly focused on laboratory and scientific medical research.[225] Ecuadorian relations with the RF culminated in their 1940s collaboration to develop a nursing school in Quito, the potential students for which were not indígenas.[226]

Betraying their limited interactions with Ecuadorian indígenas, RF agents often portrayed them stereotypically. During the nursing school project, RF employees saw indígenas as laborers. As Dorothy Foley reported to her superior in New York: "the new roof is being put on the recreation room and the house is in usual turmoil: dirt, Indians, and tin roof all over the place."[227] Foley was as likely informed by her own biases about Native Americans as those of Ecuadorian elites. Assumptions of indigeneity could undermine employment opportunities. When Nurse Brackett interviewed a Ms. Villagomez for a teaching position in the nursing school, she noted a number of deficiencies including that she "probably has a good deal of Indian in her."[228] For related reasons, the candidate conceded that her background might be a challenge for her: "She kept talking about coming from a poor family and for this reason might not be accepted in Ecuador," Brackett observed. Pedigree mattered in Ecuadorian medical circles.

CONCLUSION

In Ecuador, RF work yielded few opportunities to observe, let alone engage with, indígenas, but RF agents in Guatemala interacted with indígenas, as well as national and international medical professionals, in ways that made for significant mutual influence. Though the RF was committed to promoting and following medical science, its representatives took a pragmatic approach in rural areas, helping semiliterate farmhands establish laboratories. However, compared to RF laboratories run by scientists in Guatemala City and Guayaquil, let alone the United States, these rural outposts were resource-starved. What's more, foundation representatives labeled curanderos and other popular healers "fakirs" who undermined public health, suggesting a Janus-faced approach to healthcare practitioners.

Among advocates of scientific medicine, a tacit understanding of hybrid health care was well-known. RF representatives tried to produce what they considered the right kind of unlicensed practitioner, though they were not consistent on what that meant or how it should be implemented. Repulsed by one type of empírico, the RF advocated creating another. Although the foundation curtailed its advocacy of empiricism by the 1930s, in the first part of the twentieth century it derided indigenous (and female) healers even as it advocated training finca employees to administer hookworm examinations and treatments. As they advanced racist thought to dismiss experienced indigenous curanderos but disagreed on their utility, a dialectical tension developed between RF representatives and Guatemalan officials. Whereas Guatemalan officials recognized the need for curanderos where doctors were absent, RF representatives preferred to train ladinos with no health care experience.

United to exploit indígenas and neglect rural poor and indigenous populations' marginalized living and health conditions, Guatemalan oligarchs presided over some of the most unequal land distribution in Latin America. To quell indigenous (and other) unrest, they deployed the military, which set the stage for violent clashes. In contrast, Ecuadorian Liberal elites facilitated indigenous autonomy to undercut Conservative hacendados' economic and political power.[229] Of course, even as their power waned, highland authorities and hacendados continued to abuse indígenas. The coastal Liberals and highland hacendados who controlled their own regions but seldom imposed their will on one another, combined with the military's autonomy, resulted in an equilibrium that helped forge a tradition of negotiation and guided Ecuador's relative pacifism by the 1930s and 1940s.[230] Those distinct relations with indígenas meant that public health pursuits and programs tended more toward coopting—rather than controlling or criminalizing—indígenas. They also influenced how officials in each country approached and understood indigenous and other healers who operated outside the bounds of medical science.

Ranging from collaborative to contested, relationships between medical professionals and unlicensed healers reveal myriad ways social relations and imperfect perceptions affected public health campaigns. Shifting our gaze to exchanges between international entities, national governments, medical professionals, and local healers at the intersections of scientific and indigenous medicine offers a nuanced understanding of the contributions of many actors, including curanderos and empíricos, to each locally-inflected version of medicine and healing.

TWO

Curses and Cures

EMPÍRICOS, INDIGENEITY, AND SCIENTIFIC MEDICINE

JORGE UBICO, THE GUATEMALAN DICTATOR, dedicated state resources to criminalizing unlicensed healthcare, ordering the police to arrest uncertified practitioners and working to ensure that urban elites took command of national health. But when Ubico injured his foot, he summoned renowned indigenous bonesetter Ventura Quiacaín. Quiacaín's skill so impressed Ubico that he widely praised Quiacaín's talents.[1] Ubico's actions are part of a broader pattern in which political and economic elites supported the hegemony of scientific medicine but did not necessarily want to close off indigenous healing options altogether. The Guatemalan police gazette, for example, ran stories about its successful arrests of empíricos, but also published articles promoting natural therapies such as "vegetarian medicines" that induced sweating, purified blood, and attacked rheumatism.[2]

From the most powerful denizens of Ecuador and Guatemala to the most marginalized, the embrace of modernity was complicated. Patients tended to pursue the most efficacious healthcare available to them. Ethnicity did not determine healing perspectives. Indígenas did not restrict themselves to curanderos. Nor did ladinos and blanco-mestizos solely consult doctors. According to an ethnographer in the 1940s, ladinos were as keen about "magical illnesses" as "indios."[3] State-run hospitals employed curanderos and comadronas who seldom adhered to a dichotomy of traditional and modern. Instead their approaches, like those of their patients, were pragmatic. Doctors who persecuted untrained healers for their patients' deaths reveal the dangers of unlicensed healthcare. But indigenous healers who saved patients' lives and improved their health suggest their efficacy—most notable in patient testimonies about recovering their health. Exchanges between medical professionals, authorities, unlicensed practitioners, and indigenous people and healers reveal how traditional healing thrived even as the state imposed scientific medicine. In 1939, for example, Ubico's administration requested medicinal plant and seed samples from municipalities to investigate the potential of cultivating them for export.[4]

Indigenous frameworks shaped public health and modern medicine throughout twentieth-century Latin America. In Guatemala and Ecuador, people from all walks of life sought the services of healers, who helped their clients to understand their health in particular (often nonscientific) ways. But by the 1920s and 1930s, authorities in both countries were decrying indigenous healing. More so in Guatemala than Ecuador, elites deemed indígenas incapable of participating in civic life; their healing practices tended to be relegated to the margins of society, and practitioners were oftentimes persecuted.[5]

The officials who targeted indigenous healers portrayed indigenous healthcare as antithetical to state-sanctioned scientific medicine. They were less forthcoming about another motivation: defending the economic interests of medical professionals whose competition ranged from partially-trained nurses, midwives, pharmacists, and medical students to indigenous curanderos and empiricos. These practitioners existed within larger complex ecologies of healthcare in Ecuador and Guatemala.[6] The valorization of social medicine (and relative ambivalence toward traditional medicine) in Ecuador and scant medical professionals beyond urban areas in Guatemala meant popular healers continued to thrive even when authorities sought to curtail their practices.[7]

Popular healers, who operated outside the bounds of state-sanctioned scientific medicine even as they incorporated aspects of it, are difficult to assimilate into histories of public health. But for rural residents, curanderos clearly remained easier to access and less costly than doctors. In Ecuador and Guatemala, empiricos enjoyed popular support that buttressed their practices against legal and medical efforts to undermine them. Persistent indigenous healing practices challenged the hegemony of medical science, contested social hierarchies undergirded by racist thought, and suggested a broader resistance to public health interventions that failed to take their particular circumstances, cultures, and livelihoods into account.

Guatemala and Ecuador had relatively fragile healthcare systems; their archives, and those of the RF, are filled with correspondence and reports documenting various failures and decrying medical fraud. Authorities in both countries sought to advance medical professionalization and modernization by persecuting unlicensed practitioners. Guatemalan officials betrayed a decidedly racial motivation in their attacks, with authorities portraying indigenous healers as inherently inferior to Hispanic medical professionals. In contrast, Ecuadorian public health officials barely mentioned ethnicity as they policed healthcare provision. They, too, took aim at indigenous healing, but in a way that allowed for more continuity, and a more open embrace of syncretism.

SUSTO, SCIENCE, AND SYNCRETISM

With significant funding from the RF, the League of Nations created its Health Organization (LNHO) in 1920 to track and investigate epidemics and pandemics. Over the next few years, it sought to improve public health systems in members states that requested such assistance. While many countries in Latin America generally supported LNHO's coordination and dissemination of epidemiological information, some Latin Americans, who associated the RF with US imperialism, were suspicious of the LNHO in turn.[8] Their wariness extended to LNHO collaborators, such as the PASB; even Latin Americans who regularly attended PASB conferences distrusted US calls for Pan-American health, which they saw as potential precursors to intervention in the region.

The PASB, operating on a shoestring budget, passed the 1924 American Sanitary Code to facilitate member states' ability to organize public health agencies and programs aimed at stemming infectious disease.[9] The document made no mention of indigenous approaches to disease: the assumption was that, as a matter of course, scientific approaches alone had merit. Such coordinated international promotion of scientific medicine in the first part of the twentieth century had profound effects in nations with large indigenous populations. And they often put the PASB, LNHO and its member states, and their collaborators on a collision course with both local traditional medicine and with those who, though they supported scientific medicine, were wary of US imperialism.

Even as divisions between different types of healthcare were constructed, contested, and policed,[10] indigenous and scientific medicine were as complementary as they were competitive. No system had the capacity to eliminate another from the range of therapeutic possibilities. Intending to subordinate *curanderismo* (traditional healing) to scientific medicine, the Guatemalan

National Police Director David H. Ordóñez unwittingly pointed to their similar processes: "The gift of curing is not spontaneously born in an individual, but rather it is a product of collective mentality," he wrote.[11] Like scientific medicine, indigenous healing built on prior collective knowledge. What's more, both deployed trial and error to develop cures and therapies.

Medical professionals, healers, and patients experienced multiple healthcare options, each of which enjoyed some legitimacy in cultural economies of health and wellness. Competing epistemologies informed how people navigated between diverse healing practices to improve or maintain their well-being.[12] More so than any particular indigenous, scientific, or folk medicine, medical pluralism was hegemonic in early-twentieth-century Ecuador and Guatemala.[13] Beyond the purview of medical professionals, unlicensed practitioners advanced health practices that poor patients of color embraced.

Instead of rejecting learned medicine wholesale, indígenas embraced medical pluralism, pursuing a combination of healthcare options depending on their own ailments, social status, economic means, and worldview. Maya ceremonies such as *saneamiento* (cleaning) and practices such as *achi'lib'al* (companionship) whereby sickness was coauthored in ways that contributed to self-healing, helped the infirm to recover.[14] Indigenous midwives asserted lunar eclipses could complicate births, an Ecuadorian public health official prescribed protections against mal de ojo, and ladinos and indígenas alike insisted *susto*, a condition with physical and emotional bodily expressions caused by fright or spirit attack, could be fatal.[15]

On August 20, 1947, a Kaqchikel woman became gravely ill with a bile colic because her husband insulted her with "insolent words." After administering "a special purgative to empty the foul contents in her stomach," the empírico who attended confirmed that the illness "attacked her as a result of her husband's harshness."[16] Like contemporary judges who acknowledged susto, the Patzicía magistrates's guilty verdict against the husband demonstrates that some officials recognized indigenous and popular conceptions of the interconnectedness of psychological and physical well-being.[17]

Susto and mal de ojo are distinct folk illnesses with different causalities. Since pre-Hispanic indigenous records in Latin America are sparse, beliefs and folk illnesses found throughout Latin America often are perceived as Spanish-derived. Most evidence suggests Spaniards had developed the notion of mal de ojo—a curse conveyed by a malevolent glare that many indigenous and Hispanic cultures believed could cause illness—by the sixteenth century, when colonizers introduced it to Latin America. Indígenas then adapted it to their own concepts of disease and healing cultures.[18] Some medical authorities did too. In 1935, the Ecuadorian Director of Public Health encouraged pregnant women and new mothers to put a few drops of lemon in infants' eyes to avoid "mal de ojos."[19] Regardless of whether medical professionals believed in such practices or simply wanted to facilitate popular outreach, their endorsements of maladies like mal de ojo buttressed medical pluralism.

In contrast to mal de ojo, the origins of susto are more firmly grounded in the Americas than Spain.[20] In Maya cultures such as Kaqchikel, men and women have three souls, one of which—the *k'uxaj*—is detachable, wanders when dreaming, and can be "lost." The k'uxaj can remain at a spot where an individual suffers a strong emotion such as fright or other unsettling experience such as near drowning, falling from a mountain ledge, murder of a close relation—or a philandering spouse. When that happens, an *ajq'ij* (daykeeper) or curandero must "call" the soul back to the body through ritual ceremonies. Although both indigenous and non-indigenous people recognize that susto can harm their health, only indígenas attribute soul loss to malevolent sentient beings and underscore the importance of event locations and their spirit guardians. The beings and guardians must be mollified to release the captured soul.[21] Susto is also common in Andean etiologies and Kichwa and Aymara medicines, where healers use live guinea pigs for therapeutic rubbing to coax the soul back to the body. Mayas use hen eggs for the same purpose and branches to "sweep" the body.[22] In both the Andes and Mesoamerica, symptoms of susto include lethargy, anemia, loss of appetite and strength, diarrhea, fever, restless sleep, disinterest in dress and personal hygiene, depression and introversion, and even death.[23] One recorded Andean woman claimed susto caused her miscarriage.[24]

The plurality of medicine in Latin America compelled medical professionals and popular healers to adapt their practices and account for notions of healing and illness distinct from their own. While legislation betrayed preferences for medical professionals over curanderos and empíricos,[25] some Latin American doctors worked with healers. And while early-twentieth-century Guatemalan officials, for example, cautioned against using medicine "without a prescription,"[26] thereby excluding the vast pharmacopeia of medicinal plants administered by traditional healers, some pharmacists nevertheless filled popular healers' prescriptions.[27] Neither hegemonic nor toothless, scientific medicine promoted by medical schools, public health agencies, and nation-states and traditional medicine advanced by indigenous, Asian, African, mestizo, and other popular healers coexisted to varying degrees in such state-sanctioned institutions as courtrooms, clinics, and hospitals.[28] During the failed French attempt to construct the Panama Canal (1881–89), officials invited Bolivian Kallawaya healers to treat malaria that was devastating workers.[29] Like medical professionals whose responses to indigenous healing practices varied, indigenous healers similarly approached medical science in ways that ranged from collaboration and acquiescence to resistance and rejection.

Political instability sometimes animated tensions between providers. Reflecting Ecuador's 1930s political volatility, a "division between radical liberals and radical socialist liberals" in Ibarra catalyzed tensions between professional and empirical providers. In 1933, Ibarra governor Dr. Joaquín Sandoval fined a curandero one hundred sucres for practicing without a license. The curandero's brother was a radical socialist liberal pharmacist and "enemy of Dr. Sandoval." To defend his brother the curandero and to "demonstrate his hatred of Dr. Sandoval," the pharmacist had sowed discord.[30] Although both Dr. Sandoval and the pharmacist were medical professionals, they had dramatically different views about the legitimacy of empíricos. Shared training in scientific medicine did not engender united approaches to curanderismo. Nor did filial ties produce universal approaches to healthcare, as the pharmacist and curandero who were brothers attest.

The three men's relationship reminds us that healthcare providers—whether physicians, surgeons, pharmacists, or popular healers—worked in complex and often competitive environments.[31] This was true in both Guatemala and Ecuador. Though the interactions between indigenous, scientific, and hybrid healthcare played out differently in both nations, neither authoritarian nor democratic governments could establish a medical monopoly.

HEALERS AND DOCTORS IN GUATEMALA

Both Ecuador and Guatemala faced a shortage of trained medical practitioners—particularly in rural areas. Medical schools in Guayaquil, Quito, and Guatemala City graduated medical students slowly, and most of them preferred to practice in cities, where salaries were higher. In 1920, for example, Guatemala had a population of 2.5 million people, but only 132 doctors, 74 of whom worked in Guatemala City.[32] Absent other options, Guatemalan officials felt obliged to recognize empíricos' capacity. While doctors and military surgeons ran municipal offices that distributed free vaccines in department capitals, the Superior Council of Public Health authorized empíricos to serve such offices in towns and villages in 1923. Their service proved crucial the following year, when a smallpox outbreak compelled the government to quickly reopen inoculation offices and fine anyone who did not carry proof of vaccination.[33] When health crises erupted, empíricos figured prominently. Some indigenous communities only accepted treatment delivered by their curanderos.[34]

To be recognized by the state, empíricos had to be Guatemalan citizens of notable honor and good conduct as verified by a Health Tribunal investigation into their lives and customs. Indigenous claims to being "citizen[s] of the nation" indicate indígenas considered themselves eligible for such recognition.[35] To facilitate indigenous input into rural healthcare, indígenas served on municipal public health committees, as was true when Sebastian Coché and Marcos Yojcom were nominated to those positions in San Pedro la Laguna in 1933.[36] By 1935, empíricos additionally had to pass an aptitude examination (for which they paid three quetzals), obtain a certificate of good health, and pay a five-quetzal fee to practice medicine as first-class empíricos.[37] With those qualifications, they could be named municipal empíricos. Although such fees were prohibitive for many empíricos, anyone who practiced without completing the process was open to legal consequences.[38] Under the jurisdiction of the regional health inspector, empíricos were held responsible for any ignorance, malice, or negligence that caused their patients harm.[39]

According to some officials, rural indígenas invariably were subjected to such harm. In 1933, the El Quiche governor insisted that the "indigenous race" was "neglected as much by bad customs and invalid medicines, as by the ignorance of those who prescribe them."[40]

Indígenas, however, already understood that curanderos' power emanated from their abilities both to cure and to curse, so they approached the possibility of harm distinctly from their nonindigenous contemporaries. The same healer who made one's ailment vanish could be employed to undermine a rival's health. Ranging from nineteenth-century hermaphrodites and *brujas* (social healers, spiritual guides, witches) to twentieth-century *elefanciacos* (elefantitis patients) and healers, individuals with dramatically distinct physical, mental, and emotional attributes elicited fascination and fear. Those considered unfortunate and disabled in some contexts might be recognized as gifted and venerated in others; being malevolent could have a positive valence.[41] Ch'orti' Mayas, wrote the ethnographer Charles Wisdom, expected curanderos to have a "slight strain of insanity."[42] Individuals who displayed "mental and emotional peculiarities" could be identified as potential sorcerers, who were both respected for their power and dreaded for their evildoing.[43]

Indigenous languages convey more nuanced conceptualizations of medicine and poison than the dichotomy common in US and Western European notions. In Kaqchikel, the word for medicine is the same as the word for poison: *aq'om*. To indicate giving people or animals either medicine or poison, Kaqchikel speakers use the verb *aq'omaj*. For example, someone might say "*Xinwaq'omaj ri nutz'i'. Chanin xk'achoj*" (I medicated my dog. He got well quickly) or, on the other hand, "*Xe'inwaq'omaj ri tz'i' pa b'ey. K'a ri' xekäm*" (I poisoned the street dogs. Then they died.)[44] Indigenous curanderos understood the properties of plant and other medicinal sources to operate along a continuum between medicine and poison. Suggesting how closely intertwined health and illness were in indigenous worldviews, the same substance that could cure you could kill you. In contrast to medical science that generally distinguished between medicines and poisons and portrayed doctors as saviors, that Janus-faced power extended to curanderismo and brujería (which conflated witchcraft and social healing, though the latter was more akin to social work or psychotherapy) whose practitioners could improve or undermine one's health.

Curanderos often operated on a hierarchical spectrum. In many indigenous communities, diviners and curers who possessed spiritual power enjoyed greater prestige than healers who relied on medicinal plants or aspects of scientific medicine.[45] Most bonesetters, for example, learned to treat musculoskeletal disorders empirically, though some of their counterparts were spiritualists.[46] The classification of an illness often determined the type of healer to consult. Mid-century Kaqchikels in Magdalena attributed intestinal worms to physical disturbances so they consulted "practical" rather than spiritual healers.[47] For spiritual healing, patient-healer rapport and each patient's trust in and perceived efficacy of the treatment were crucial.[48] With a reputation for gifted healers, the town of San Pedro la Laguna attracted patients from as far as El Salvador and Mexico.[49] Even when demand for their services was high, most bonesetters had other occupations or specializations—intestinal worms, toothaches, female disorders—to support themselves.[50] Empíricos were a remarkably diverse group.

In 1935, the Ubico administration permitted empíricos to practice where there were no doctors within a ten-kilometer radius.[51] That description captured the majority of the nation. Whereas "The healing system of *brujos* is intimately bound in the life of the Indian," explained a *Liberal Progresista* journalist, "doctors roll around the capital in their snazzy automobiles going from cocktail to cocktail, [and] deliciously earn a little salary from the Nation."[52] This hyperbolic depiction suggests why so few doctors were willing to trade their comfortable cosmopolitan profession to work in what they considered primitive indigenous villages.

That reporter's critique notwithstanding, Guatemalan journalists generally were more concerned about advancing medical professionals and persecuting healers than improving rural health. Describing provinces characterized by "expensive medicine, a lack of young doctors, and a shortage of medications in pharmacies," the *Liberal Progresista* reporter encouraged the police to undertake a "campaign against wild *brujos* and curanderos."[53] In a seven-point plan that sought "to maintain the State's privilege in favor of the Doctor," he encouraged young physicians to serve at least two years in rural areas because they "have an obligation to go where their services are needed and not stay in the capital to pursue a salary and good life." Yet he conceded that in many villages, "professionals could not live . . . because the people were extremely poor and cannot afford the services of a physician." In one such community, "three *empíricos de medicina* live in difficult economic circumstances" because of residents' poverty and "competition of brujos and curanderos . . . who practice freely, despite being prohibited to." Charging the National Police with pursuing "curanderos, empíricos, brujos, *parteras de ocasión* [opportunistic midwives], etc.," the journalist concluded, "What is urgent . . . is to kick out those scum and then, to see if it is possible to establish a certified doctor." According to his plan, eradicating popular healers was more important than ensuring rural residents had access to healthcare.

Medical professionals perceived power struggles with indigenous healers too. In 1935, Dr. Hernán Martínez Sobral described indigenous curanderos as hybrid healer-witches: "CHUCH-KAJAU [w]as a good witch [who] combined healer and fortune-teller functions. . . . He bewitched people, cursed the enemy of those who paid him. . . . He could make an individual feel as if they had a toad in their belly."[54] Even as he warned that indigenous curanderos were "most dangerous when [t]he[y] prepared concoctions with herbs that only [t]he[y] know," Dr. Martínez Sobral conveyed astonishment: "This witch healer knows a vast number of medicinal plants and resorts to the strangest treatments for healing: he passes a toad over the skin of erisypelas victims; he puts ground sloth spines with fly oil in the eardrum for ear pain;

he makes ointments with lard, incense, and salt, that according to him, have great curative virtues; he prepares poultices by splitting a live black chicken and placing its palpitating innards on the sick region; he considers dog urine with chile and carbonated water a magnificent remedy to cure tonsillitis."[55] What most concerned Dr. Martínez Sobral and his colleagues was the tremendous social power indigenous curanderos enjoyed: "His word is infallible: it is enough for him to declare the infirm terminally ill and their relatives will no longer feed them and actually let them die. He is paid in advance, in part with moonshine and hens and the rest in cash and corn, and he is so well known that they look for him from as far away as twenty leagues. For that reason, finqueros, to avoid problems, keep him on retainer on their fincas." (At the time, officials obligated fincas to establish health clinics for workers, and curanderos were popular and efficacious enough that they were often hired in lieu of medical doctors.)

Another doctor, Dr. José Pacheco Molina, reported in 1935 that "Quetzaltenango [province] has magnificent medicinal waters, discovered by chance, though probably the *indios* already used them for therapeutic ends."[56] He was not the first outsider to note the popularity of such waters. Around 1910, US engineers working on the Los Altos railroad, tired and dusty, were searching for water when they came upon "*un indígena*" who directed them to a pond and river from which originated "a watershed of hot crystal clear water." They noticed that the water was "astringent and acrid and for that reason a woman named it '*Aguas Amargas*.'" Thereafter, people documented its healing powers. *Aguas amargas* cured a ladino and a woman with a facial skin infection that "rebelled against the usual medicines." Sent to investigate, a government commission discovered the water had "radioactive power."[57] Even as science confirmed its unique characteristics, Dr. Pacheco Molina warned about the tendency to portray the water as a "panacea and . . . some clown saying 'it cures poverty' and naturally all those patients who resort to it with their illnesses and maladies . . . will suffer disillusionment."

When curers, empíricos, and medicinal waters failed, some indigenous patients consulted doctors.[58] Indigenous cities such as Quetzaltenango and Tecpán (located along the Pan-American Highway) had resident doctors who regularly referred indigenous patients to hospitals, as Dr. Miguel Antonio Giron did when the indígena Inés Tzurez's dog bite became infected in November 1940.[59] At times, though, medical professionals in indigenous towns failed to diagnose, let alone treat, illnesses.[60] Although they generally entered hospitals as a last resort, the frequency with which Guatemalan indígenas consulted doctors suggests they perceived themselves as medical citizens with rights to healthcare.[61] Yet these doctors remained in short supply: even after the completion of the Pan-American Highway afforded medical professionals access to communities along it, few serviced rural areas.[62]

In their stead, officially-sanctioned empíricos treated indigenous and ladino patients. When San Martín Jilotepeque's *empírico en medicina* diagnosed Jerónimo Tun Bernadino with sciatica in 1942, an *intendente municipal* (municipal official) referred the indigenous patient to Guatemala City because he "lacked the funds to attend to his cure."[63] The next day an empírico in Nueva Santa Rosa referred another patient who was "injured in a sensitive area."[64] Local and national authorities alike had confidence in those empíricos' practices. The following year the local *"Empírico en Cirugía"* (Empiricist in Surgery)—the capital letters suggest it was a formal title—treated a young girl's burns in Barberena.[65] When experts in scientific medicine were lacking, other healthcare providers, with a range of expertise, stepped in. All in all, this meant that care in the highlands was syncretic, with patients consulting curanderos *and* empíricos as well as the occasional expert in medical science.

PURSUING EMPÍRICOS IN GUATEMALA

By the early twentieth century, nations across Latin America increasingly built infrastructure and deployed personnel to advance medical science's hegemony. Latin American professionals demanded, and politicians passed, penal codes that outlawed practicing medicine without a license. To enforce that accreditation process, officials established regulatory and police bodies.[66] Guatemala was no exception.

Despite his facilitation of indigenous culture in the military and other public venues, as well as his personal, heterodox approach to healing, Ubico persecuted healers and other empíricos during his administration. His first Director of National Police, Brigadier C. Rodrico Anzueto, explained in 1933 that his officers would pursue anyone practicing "physician and midwife professions without a degree and in a very special way curanderismo and 'brujería' that are so harmful to public health and at times order."[67] A year later, Anzueto proclaimed that, thanks to a constant campaign, "There are almost no departments where we have not apprehended a curandero and *hechicero* [witch doctor, sorcerer], ignorant subjects, unaware of the most basic hygiene and specialist principles" and "all kinds of diseases and ill-nesses." He asserted that "their harmful participation has caused much dam-age, because they do not only exploit by deceiving the public, but indifferent to their responsibility, they administer nasty drinks and remedies that on more than one occasion have caused a patient's death."[68]

Although fatalities at the hands of curanderos were rare, journalists took up the cause of authorities who were criminalizing healers and portraying them as threats to public health. Newspapers publicized curanderos' failures widely. In 1935, at least three Guatemalan newspapers carried the story of the empírico José Luis Godoy who "without medical expertise . . . applied certain potions" that caused the painful death of his patient.[69] Contextualizing such reports, Anzueto insisted that wherever police perambulated, curanderos would flee and that in "no time a true dike will be placed . . . against those unscrupulous and ignorant subjects."[70] Anzueto's declarations reflected the larger goals of the authoritarian state—one whose dictator had already appointed loyalists to replace local mayors and other municipal leaders as *intendentes* (military leaders assigned to act as local governors) throughout the countryside. But Anzueto overestimated the National Police's capacity and underestimated curanderos' resilience. The criminal record provides evidence of curanderos being apprehended, but oral histories suggest many evaded arrest and thus the written record.[71]

The National Police crafted narratives that attributed curanderos' ram-pant practice to the previous regime and referenced—but did not actually cite—statistics purportedly demonstrating curanderos' decline during Ubico's reign. "Brujos' and *embaucadores'* [swindlers'] incursion commenced in previous years," read one annual report, but 1935 police "statistics show that it is succeeding in ending this fatal plague."[72] Even without hard evi-dence of the police state's efficacy, however, such discourse had power, align-ing with—and likely contributing to—perceptions that unlicensed healers were dangerous.

Police pursuit of "false curanderas" suggests that officers distinguished between rogue and credible healers.[73] Regularly studying "legal medicine [and] urgent surgery,"[74] police officers differentiated those who practiced medicine without a license from "people who recommended certain curing methods, but did not [pretend to] practice professional medicine."[75] Police lenience with some empíricos thus seems to have resulted not from bribery or corruption, but from an understanding that some healers did improve health.

Even as officers differentiated curers, they conflated healers they considered fraudulent with brujas. This suggested a belief that healers are good, and witches are evil—a dichotomy at odds with indigenous understanding of brujería as encompassing a wide range of powers that could be harnessed to heal or harm. Accused of brujería, María Teresa Rodríguez was arrested in February 1933. The police confiscated Rodríguez's "trances, love potions, hot dolls, magic dolls in vinegar, vodu doll (with remedy sewn inside), love salves ... all to the detriment of her fellow man's honor, health, and self-interest."[76] The item "magic dolls in vinegar," or *"Diabillos a la vinagreta,"* refers to a practice in witchcraft of making dolls or "poppets" out of a piece of clothing of someone you are targeting for harm and placing the poppet in a jar of vinegar. In some cases, practitioners crafted dolls to look like specific individuals.[77] Dolls or other effigies could be used to cause pain or death. Putting someone's name or effigy in a bottle could cause drunkenness. Putting them under a bed could promote licentiousness.

Curanderos' healing objects could defy, counterbalance, or mitigate other forces at play in people's lives.[78] For indigenous healers, such forces ranged from racism and discrimination to domestic violence and disease. In the same way that knives could cure or kill people, and that leaves and powders could be both medicines and poisons, Guatemalan curanderos and brujos used dolls, moonshine (taken orally or applied through baths or poultices), beans, herbs, candles, and locks of hair to help people recuperate or to hasten their demise. "Beans" were probably the *tz'ite'* that were commonly deployed in divination, though curanderos could also employ black beans or corn kernels. With colors indicating to whom they were offered and for what, candles were traditional offerings. Cebo candles were offered to and for one's ancestors. Purple candles warded against evil influences. Black candles invoked or countered negative energy. That the precise uses of healers' accoutrements remained a mystery to most authorities added to those objects' allure and authority. Their cultural nearsightedness, evident in *La Gaceta* (the police gazette), enhanced curanderos' enigmatic power.[79]

Authorities cracked down on wily curanderos with an enthusiasm that matched their desire to punish moonshiners.[80] According to *La Gaceta*, both groups were comprised of "swindlers, men and women, who exploit people's naïveté and ignorance."[81] Some individuals, like Juana Lucas of Quezaltenango, were said to traffic in both *"hechicería ... and bootlegging."* When officers arrested her in 1935, they confiscated "an arsenal of very strange objects," including two bags of beans, two flags, two metal chains, nine metal

FIGURE 7. "Galería de brujos, adivinos, zahories y curanderos de ambos sexos" (Gallery of witches, diviners, dowsers, and healers of both sexes), *La Gaceta*, May 5, 1935. José López Guinac is at top with his wares. Guadelupe Acuña Velasquez is in the bottom center. Note the bottle of poison at lower left. Courtesy of Hemeroteca Nacional de Guatemala.

and wood crosses, and ten bottles with traces of moonshine. Although few of those items were extraordinary—the crosses demonstrate the integration of Christian symbols and spirits to be invoked—in the possession of an alleged bruja, they became evidence of her "evil arts." Police regularly presented "witching equipment" as evidence against unlicensed healers.

Police officials underscored the difficulty of their task by claiming that clients and local authorities who feared brujas and curanderas refrained from denouncing them.[82] In 1935, a Guatemala City police station chief reported that his team only apprehended the *brujas y curanderas* Cecilia Pirir Chamalé (age sixty-two) and Isabel Pirir Mansilla de Morales (age twenty-six) because they had not yet intimidated their new neighbors.[83] Though the neighbors may have been daunted by what the chief called "the smell of witches," they were still ready to talk. Although class is difficult to discern in the police record, persecuted practitioners were diverse in ethnicity, gender, and generation: young, old, indigenous, ladino, married and single men and women.[84]

When Quetzaltenango police captured the "witch, healer and even midwife" José López Guinac in 1935, they explained that he operated with "boundless audacity . . . in the heart of the highland metropolis."[85] The fifty-four-year-old merchant, who was the legitimate son of a ladino father and indigenous mother, had earned widespread "popularity" with numerous clients from "distinct social categories soliciting" his services. He served as midwife to at least two women. In addition to the many wares of his trade on full display in the photograph that graced the cover of the May 5, 1935, *La Gaceta* (figure 7), López Guinac had "a collection of medicinal herbs, candles; locks of hair ('from different sites from women of various ages')," photographs of people who lived in different parts of the country, and "a list of those who should die." Faced with prosecution, "the outrageous criminal" attempted to bribe a police officer. That same year, police arrested Reyes Ordóñez Izet, aka Santo Viejo, who also "acquired fame" as a "brujo, *partero* [midwife] and curandero." Among other accoutrements, officers confiscated his photographs of well-known locals and his "Great Magical Fish . . . [an] enormous dried hake" to which his "devotees" prayed (figure 8). Like López Guinac, Ordóñez Izet was the legitimate son of a ladino father and indigenous mother, who enjoyed a wide following "first in indigenous circles and then among ladinos, exploiting them all. . . . He counted on the discretion of his clientele; none of whom denounced him because of fear or other motives."

Although the criminal record suggests more men than women were healers (or that *curanderas* better concealed their practices), and that some of these male healers also practiced midwifery, midwifery itself was a field dominated by females. Yet authorities seldom feminized the male midwives they apprehended. Nor, for that matter, did they feminize the healing methods and practices associated with curanderismo. Perhaps curanderas instilled enough fear in authorities to neutralize notions of female curers as the weaker

FIGURE 8. "Galería de brujos, adivinos, zahories y curanderos de ambos sexos," *La Gaceta,* May 5, 1935. Reyes Ordóñez Izet, aka Santo Viejo, is shown in the top left alongside his magical fish. Albertina Garcia Revolorio is shown on the top right along with "some implements of" witchcraft. Courtesy of Hemeroteca Nacional de Guatemala.

sex. At any rate, incarceration did not necessarily dampen curanderas' entrepreneurial spirit. According to *La Gaceta,* Albertina García Revolorio (figure 8) made the most of her time in jail by seeking "to profit from fear, illnesses, or the desire to harm others, from the prisoners who trust in such *curanderas-brujas* . . . with blind faith."[86]

In 1937, National Police Director Anzueto's successor David H. Ordóñez declared that "The campaign against folk medicine and witchcraft continues with intensity."[87] To demonstrate "the fight was gradually obtaining the desired result," he cited (but like Anzueto did not divulge) "pertinent statistical data" of cases diminishing in 1937. Even as he distinguished between folk medicine and witchcraft, Ordóñez saw the two as intertwined: "Alongside those who perform witchcraft, exist people who do the opposite, they undo it; and here we arrive at the origins of folk medicine, that date . . . to the earliest eras of history." Ultimately he condemned both curanderismo and brujería. They were, he said, informed by the "extremely widespread phenomenon" of superstition that "principally occurs in the least civilized regions, even . . . in cultured nations like ours."

Under Ordóñez's leadership, the police highlighted their critical role in preserving public health. On September 16, 1938, agents caught Francisco Samayoa Monroy, Rosa Penagos y Monroy, and Victoria Castro Méndez in their home performing "curses and cures by means of concoctions that they provided to the sick woman Isidra Castro v. de Limatuj, who in a grave state . . . was transported by the police officers to the hospital and the criminals to jail."[88] While authorities believed such potions were lethal, poor and working class indígenas readily consumed them.[89] Snatching a deathly-ill woman from the jaws of empirismo and delivering her to a doctor, the police saved the day, according to their official mouthpiece.

Tipped off two months later, officers caught two women and a man who "practiced strange sorcery rites, cures, and all kinds of spells."[90] Shortly thereafter, on December 16, the police captured a couple administering "concoctions to Mrs. Dolores Velásquez Alonso, who suffers from paralysis . . . exacerbated by those cunning crooks with the application of substances."[91] Given such efficaciousness, authorities asserted that there were "very few cases" of practicing medicine illegally by 1939.[92] Kaqchikel oral histories suggest otherwise.

The government's own records suggest police pursuit of empíricos was not a singular attack on indigenous curanderos. Officers sometimes protected indígenas. Carlos Vásquez was arrested for defrauding an indigenous couple in Sololá of nine and a half quetzals "by making them believe he could cure their mother-in-law Rosa Piscul through his magic art" in 1941.[93] Meanwhile, Afro-descended healers also attracted police. Samuel Richard, whom *La Gaceta* described as "from the black race, although some of his compatriots can pass as 'light' [*claro*]," migrated from Belize to practice medicine on the Guatemalan coast, where police arrested him for being a "false doctor."[94] As a "healer, midwife, and very occult half witch," Richard "filled his pockets" by providing medicines and surgery supplies.[95] He also maintained a *tienda* in Jutiapa where he prepared, prescribed, and sold medicines he "invented." Dubbed "The Grave Man," Richard allegedly could induce "human mutations" and insanity (figure 9).[96]

TAMBIEN EN EL ORIENTE DEL PAIS HA VENIDO ACTUANDO UN IMPOSTOR, ORIUNDO DE LA COLONIA BRITANICA

JUTIAPA

1935

(Fotografía tomada con exclusividad para LA GACETA de la Policía.—Propiedad registrada)

EL DOCTOR RICHARD, O SEA «EL HOMBRE TUMBA»

FIGURE 9. "The Doctor Richard, or rather 'The Grave Man.'" *La Gaceta*, May 5, 1935, 1075. Courtesy of Hemeroteca Nacional de Guatemala.

Unorthodox foreign healers like Richard were not uncommon. On October 16, 1941, Cobán (Alta Verapaz) authorities arrested Holger Holm for practicing medicine "without any authorization," sentenced him to fifty days in jail commutable by a fifty quetzal fine, and insisted he be put to work in prison with "no exonerations for any distinctions"—presumably based on his German nationality.[97] Just a month before, Ubico had ended Guatemalan neutrality, declaring support for the Allied campaign. When Guatemala formally declared war on Germany that December, there were public celebrations.[98] Ladinos called on the government to deport Germans, nationalize their properties, or force them to become Guatemalan citizens— all suggesting that nationalism informed authorities' persecution of Holm.[99] Cobán police portrayed him as a "scheming and concealing type who abuses the ignorance of the indigenous class, to cause trouble for the authorities, and he is smart enough not to leave any traces, to apply the law; furthermore his medical practice is even dangerous, he prescribed calomel [mercury chloride] to a woman who had recently given birth and the baby died from it."[100]

Germans in Alta Verapaz generally considered themselves superior to Q'eqchi' indígenas. While most German coffee planters exploited (and often abused) indigenous laborers, a few, such as Erwin Paul Dieseldorff (1868–1940), espoused Q'eqchi' ethics of reciprocity and instructed foremen to facilitate the efflorescence of indigenous religions.[101] Intent on making Guatemala their new home even as their loyalties remained to their families overseas, many Germans started families with Q'eqchi' women. Early twentieth-century Guatemalan intellectuals like Asturias promoted miscegenation between European immigrants and indígenas to improve the stock of the latter. Asturias's celebration of "robust and well-endowed" Q'eqchi'-German children notwithstanding, by the 1940s, anti-German sentiments grew in Alta Verapaz, where Cobáneros insisted Germans be limited to fifteen *caballerías* of cultivated land.[102] Depending on their location and socioeconomic positions, Germans were both privileged and persecuted in Guatemala.

Authorities' pursuit of curanderos was part of a larger project to eradicate primitivism and atavism, but Germans generally were portrayed as the opposite of those traits. Holm hailed from a nation associated with excellence in laboratory medicine, science, and drug development—the German pharmaceutical company Bayer operated in Guatemala—yet Cobán police arrested him for prescribing dangerous chemicals.[103] Perhaps homeopathy, which we know was practiced by early nineteenth-century European immigrants to Guatemala, was part of Holm's trade. Although Mexico, Colombia, and Brazil endorsed and regulated homeopathic practices by the turn of the century, most medical professionals derided them.[104] Just as authorities understood that not all indigenous healers were a threat to public health, they knew some European practitioners were. Instead of broadly grouping practitioners (such as illicit indigenous healers or accomplished European practitioners) officers approached empíricos as individuals who might or might not be competent practitioners. Those distinctions likely lent legitimacy to their pursuit of curanderismo and brujería.

Although determining the extent to which Holm employed indigenous healing practices is difficult, the value some of his compatriots placed on indigenous medicinal plants must have buoyed Q'eqchi' healers in Cobán. Dieseldorff wrote a book about medicinal plants in the region, conducted ethnographic studies of indigenous medicine, and treated plantation workers with

cures from such curanderos as Félix Cucul.[105] Some German planters exoti-
cized indigenous healing by associating it with "wizards... and fortune-tellers,"
which dovetailed nicely with police conflations of indigenous curanderismo
and brujería.[106] Ladinos too studied and documented indigenous medicine. *El
Norte* editor Emilio Rosales Ponce included medicinal cures in his study of
Q'eqchi' culture. By pairing medicine with "superstitions," Ponce stopped
short of legitimizing indigenous "customs" and practices.[107] Nonetheless,
German and ladino interest in indigenous medicine lent legitimacy to curanderos. Not all Q'eqchi' embraced this attention, however. Domingo Caal
accused Dieseldorff of appropriating and commodifying indigenous knowledge and customs.[108] Often productive, intersections and collaborations
between indigenous and scientific medicines remained contested.

The prevalence of medical pluralism notwithstanding, authorities and
journalists celebrated medical professionals such as the Guatemalan sibling-
doctors Juan and Salvador Ortega.[109] In a 1941 story entitled "Sages Who
Visit Us," *La Gaceta* lauded an European ophthalmologist who extracted a
cataract "in the modern operating environment of our Military Hospital. ...
The Spanish physician's lessons left in our midst positive confirmation of his
prestige" (figure 10).[110] Evoking modernity, the physicians clad in white, the
operating table, and a suction device (for removing cataracts) starkly con-
trasts with the same paper's collages of curanderos and brujos portrayed as
primitive, infantilized simpletons (figures 7 and 8).

Some curanderos associated themselves with state-sanctioned scientific
medicine, thereby indicating the extent to which that discourse had prolifer-
ated in Guatemala. When the National Police arrested indigenous curandero
Paulino Salohuí Cuc in July 1942, they also confiscated the tools of his trade,
which included red beans, idols, hollowed-out stones, and a wooden crucifix.
Most troubling to them was the *oficio* (official notice) from the Sololá Health
Authorities to the Director of the Guatemala City General Hospital stating
that Salohuí Cuc had been admitted to that hospital—"a document that
helped further him in his punishable deeds by making it appear that he was
authorized to practice such illicit maneuvers."[111] Apparently authorities recognized the *oficio* as a totemic document with the power to imbue the appearance of legality, accusing the curandero of using his admission as a patient to
give credence to his work. The *oficio* suggests one of the self-conscious ways
Salohuí Cuc and his counterparts marketed themselves and their services.[112]
The illusion of modern medicine's sanction, made possible by his clientele's
illiteracy, likely did legitimize his practice among some patients.

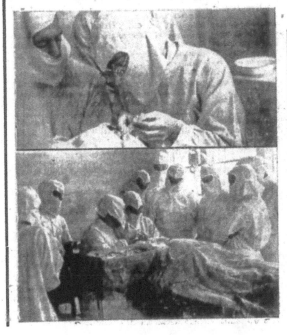

Sabios que nos visitan

El eminente oftalmólogo español Doctor José Gómez Márquez, que en los ambientes de la medicina europea se ha hecho notar al lado del no menos ilustre cirujano Médico Doctor Barraquer, fué motivo de cálidos homenajes de parte del cuerpo médico guatemalteco en su estancia en el País. Las gráficas exhiben el instante en que el sabio oftalmólogo practica una extracción de catarata en el moderno ambiente operatorio de nuestro Hospital Militar. La técnica del Doctor Gómez Márquez empleó de preferencia en sus labores, el aparato denominado erisífago que se debe a la invención del Doctor Barraquer y el cual permite extirpar la catarata por succión. Las lecciones del galeno español, dejaron en nuestro medio, positivas ratificaciones de prestigio.

FIGURE 10. "Wise men who visit us." *La Gaceta*, January 12, 1941. Courtesy of Hemeroteca Nacional de Guatemala.

Police also persecuted ladinos for unlicensed medical practices *or* witchcraft, but seldom for both. When police in San Marcos arrested the father-son duo of Tranquilino Velasquez Joachin and Domingo Velasquez Fuentes—the "soul of . . ridiculous witchcraft"—in May 1943, they charged them with "sorcery," but not illicit curing (figure 11).[113] Their "fraudulent practices damaged civilization," according to the police. Racial thought influenced who officers believed could meld witchcraft and healing and who could merely practice one or the other. Combining the two was a talent only indígenas possessed, according to authorities.

Determining police officers' decision-making process is difficult because few agents explained their rationale for arresting or sanctioning empíricos. Officers most fervently persecuted indigenous curanderos associated with brujería and afforded leeway to partially-trained practitioners who did not perform procedures beyond their expertise.[114] Geography often determined arrests. Whereas the National Police persistently persecuted empíricos in the

El fraude a la sombra de ridículas brujerías en el departamento de San Marcos

En la aldea Piedra Grande del municipio de La Unión del predicho departamento, son capturados TRANQUILINO VELASQUEZ JOACHIN y DOMINGO VELASQUEZ FUENTES, quienes en compañía de otras personas más se dedicaban a actividades de hechicería, contrarias a toda civilización y cultura, estafando mediante las mismas a los incautos

A los detenidos se les incautan los elementos que utilizaban en sus prácticas misteriosas

A la izquierda TRANQUILINO VELASQUEZ JOACHIN; a la derecha DOMINGO VELASQUEZ FUENTES. Se exhibe la remesa de objetos que se les incautó

FIGURE 11. "Fraud in the Shadow of Ridiculous Witches.... On the left Tranquilino Velasquez Joachin; on the right Domingo Velasquez Fuentes. They exhibit the remittance of objects that were seized." *La Gaceta*, May 9, 1943. Courtesy of Hemeroteca Nacional de Guatemala.

capital where doctors abounded, rural healers who avoided fatal mistakes in lightly-patrolled regions without doctors enjoyed considerable autonomy. Those policing patterns reflected the Guatemalan state's prioritization of urban over rural healthcare.

Even in the broader context of authorities persecuting and Germans exoticizing curanderos, Guatemalan officials and foreigners created spaces within which empíricos contributed to officials' and planters' goals of maintaining a healthy workforce. Unlike RF representatives, who advanced empiricism when they could train providers, some Guatemalan authorities and German planters recognized curanderos' crucial roles in the broader pantheon of healthcare even though their epistemologies, knowledge, and practices operated beyond the bounds of scientific medicine.

ECUADORIAN HEALING ECOLOGIES

Whereas national authorities in Guatemala persecuted healers, their Ecuadorian counterparts were more concerned about the absence of healthcare, particularly in rural areas, than about the dangers of its unlicensed practice. Beginning in the colonial period, Ecuadorian authorities sought to apprehend untrained and unlicensed practitioners, but tolerated indigenous healers and endorsed medical students where physicians were absent.[115] That pattern continued into the twentieth century.

Ecuadorian public health officials were also less concerned than their Guatemalan counterparts about practitioners' ethnicity. Highland indígenas were as likely to encounter racist medical professionals and authorities as enlightened public health officials who celebrated indigenous ingenuity and industriousness. With its pursuit of national eugenics—rather than, as in Guatemala, racial eugenics—Ecuador made space for medical professionals and officials to endorse indígenas' healing and prophylactic practices. In turn, a 1913 decree mandating that Ecuadorian municipalities provide free healthcare facilitated indigenous access to healthcare.[116]

Though Ecuadorians pursued syncretic approaches to healing and healthcare, some officials disparaged distinct healing traditions they associated with insufficient training, or even no training at all. In 1914, Subdirección de Sanidad officials in Quito warned that empíricos constituted a "social plague" because they lacked "scientific knowledge."[117] Then again, knowledge alone was not a free pass. Medical students who treated patients but did not report infectious-contagious diseases to the Sanidad irked officials too.[118]

Authorities prosecuted itinerant practitioners who allegedly peddled quack remedies. In urban and semi-urban highland Ecuador, shamanism was obscure, at least to blanco-mestizo authorities and scribes, but other figures were still targets: the 1920 Ley Boticas (Pharmacy Law) prohibited unlicensed physicians, pharmacists, and other practitioners from prescribing drug therapies unless no licensed providers served the area. Yet that was often the case in the remote highlands.[119] So while the Sanidad was tasked with punishing unlicensed practitioners, it simultaneously authorized some of them to practice.[120] Andean healers regularly served clientele who could not afford professional assistance.[121]

An exception that proved the rule, mid-twentieth-century doctor Manuel Núñez Butrón served Puno, a predominantly indigenous region in the Peruvian highlands. Many of his colleagues resigned their provincial physician positions when forced into rural practices.[122] Frustrated by paltry resources, Núñez Butrón asked, "[W]hat can a man do, no matter how much a scientist he may be, if his mission is to cover thousands of residents distributed over hundreds of kilometers? What does a young doctor do . . . if he has but a thermometer and prescription pad? A thermometer that doesn't last long and a pad to prescribe remedies that arrive . . . days after the death of a patient?"[123]

Without medical professionals or public health resources, indígenas adapted learned medicine and public health strategies to maintain their communities' wellbeing. Some authorities marveled at this ingenuity. Working in the indigenous town of Sigchos in Latacunga in April 1930, a public health inspector learned of the "the practice of smallpox inoculation as a traditional custom among the *campesinos*."[124] When "a case of smallpox presents itself, they wait until the pustule matures, from that they use the pus to inoculate children," he explained.[125] Latin American doctors and indigenous curanderos had been using the human production of live vaccine to inoculate populations against smallpox since the colonial period,[126] when variolation (immunizing people by infecting them with the substance from pustules of patients with a mild form of smallpox) was understood as a municipal obligation. But by the 1930s, variolation was unusual in most places, having declined in the early twentieth century when Latin American laboratories deployed bacteriology to develop smallpox vaccine from a bovine lymph that could be preserved in calves.[127] The Sigchos inoculation campaigns and other such

FIGURE 12. Vaccination campaign in Ambato, Ecuador, 1926. Courtesy of Museo de Medicina, Quito.

archival evidence counter anthropological studies that "have tended to fetishize popular medical phenomena and systems as forms of 'otherness' with a kind of prepolitical authenticity," as historians Cueto and Palmer note.[128] Remote from state power and public health amenities, Sigchos campesinos were exemplars of modernity.[129]

Compliance was best developed within indigenous communities. Sigchos's smallpox vaccination tradition offers an example of indígenas co-opting learned medicine into their larger panoply of pluralistic healing. It also lends credence to Palmer's assertion that "coexistence, complementarity, and dialogue more than outright rivalry and ideological warfare," marked public health in Latin America.[130]

While Sigchos indígenas embraced inoculation, not all Ecuadorian indígenas did. In Riobamba, a public health official noted that resistance to vaccination campaigns was especially strong among "indios."[131] As a result, any large scale campaign was nearly impossible: "a sole employee without support cannot obligate them," he insisted.[132] Efforts to bring vaccination campaigns to rural populations often only made it as far as train stations. In 1926, the Tungurahua public health delegate Dr. Luis Joaquín Martínez orchestrated a vaccination post at a rail station in Ambato (figure 12). For rural indígenas, even just arriving at a railroad station when a vaccination campaign arrived was often prohibitive.

Of the nine vaccination methods Latin American doctors had identified by 1938, they considered the one employed by Sigchos indígenas "painful and bloody."[133] It also risked contaminating the liquid with diseases such as malaria that were carried in blood.[134] In light of how slow the Ecuadorian government was to respond to rural epidemics, however, the benefits of such practices likely outweighed the risks. Sigchos indígenas buffered their public health when the government could not.

ECUADORIAN EMPÍRICOS

Whereas local and regional authorities generally agreed that untrained practitioners endangered public health and warranted punishment, Ecuadorian national officials were less concerned about the threats empíricos posed. Consider, for example, the case of Delia María Robayo, who opened an office in Tacabundo's central plaza. After her practice had fatal consequences, local leaders realized she had no formal training in medicine, let alone obstetrics. Of the six births she had attended by October 25, 1946, at least one had gone poorly. One pregnant woman became "incapacitated" after Robayo injected her with Ergotina.[135] Although Robayo also advertised herself as a pharmacist, "her medication consisted of the juice of whatever vegetable she found at hand," according to municipal doctor Carlos Fabara.[136] Some were made from "Marijuana and other narcotics."[137] For that care, "she charged very high prices."[138]

Characterizing her as "an abnormal woman, with criminal instincts," Fabara insisted her "cures were eminently dangerous."[139] When the "quite robust" Miguel Cahuanas, who had "a magnificent constitution," developed gastritis after drinking some beer, Robayo's "disastrous treatment" killed him within twenty-four hours.[140] By December, a number of her clients had died who "could well have been saved if treated by a doctor," lamented the Head of Pharmacy and Medical Profession Inspection Dr. Abel Alvear.[141] In that capacity, he supervised regular inspections of pharmacies and healthcare practices and responded to complaints about them. (Although inspectors tended to operate independently, police assisted when needed.) Dr. Alvear suspended Robayo's practice for a year.[142]

Concerned about the dearth of rural healthcare, national officials regularly endorsed untrained practitioners, and just one month into Robayo's suspension, the national Public Health Service compelled Dr. Alvear to reduce her suspension to two months.[143] Upset with the weakened sanction, Dr. Alvear insisted Robayo be suspended for the full year, "as a warning to the many nurses, who we know perform medical and obstetric works without a license or training."[144] Robayo, according to Alvear and his colleagues, was part of a pervasive problem.

When inspector César Augusto Salvador "confirmed the existence of another nurse of the same nature, in Malchinguí," Dr. Fabara warned, "I can deduce that this fleet of charlatans are almost entirely spread out through the Republic, and represent a real threat; one that should be eradicated and punished to the full harshness of the law; otherwise we will have denounced and acquired terrible enemies like the current one."[145] Perhaps because two nurses hardly constituted a "fleet of charlatans," the Public Health Service prioritized pragmatism—namely access to unlicensed healthcare for residents who had few options—over professionalization.[146]

The clashes between local officials and national authorities' approaches to empíricos reflected broader tensions between municipalities and national organizations. Elected by residents, municipal councils were rooted in place among townspeople, whereas jefes políticos and tenientes políticos were appointed by the president to serve at the local level.[147] National officials and municipal doctors like Fabara shared concerns about the health of local residents, but while doctors believed their practices (and livelihoods) to be sufficient, national officials considered municipal doctors too sparse to serve rural regions. Those tensions were informed by municipal officials (including doctors) seeking to expand their autonomy from an increasingly regulatory state. Ironically, the state's diminished capacity and presence in rural areas fueled the need for alternative medicinal methods and practitioners.

Events the following year suggest that Dr. Alvear may have been complicit with the pattern he railed against, as he was learning to toe the national line. In September 1947, explained the hospital director E. Herdoíza, "The empírico Olmedo Solís, former nurse of this hospital, killed a young child of one year of age by having given him 2 grams of quinine causing an instant death by collapse." (Dr. Herdoíza had examined the corpse.)[148] After being imprisoned in Quito for a week, Solís had resumed his practice and control of the pharmacy. "Since having received permission from Dr. Abel Alvear to install a pharmacy, he [Solís] has dedicated himself to illegally practicing medicine and furthermore he pretends to be a doctor tricking and harming those who fall into his hands. . . . Because they haven't tried him today he has returned with more hate," explained Herdoíza. In response to Dr. Herdoíza's critiques, Solís accused him of selling medications the state provided for free. Dr. Herdoíza complained that such slander threatened his honor and professional standing. "The ex-laundress, ex-gardener and a circle of illiterate people are in charge of signing these accusations and others of all categories making common causes with the charlatan Solís," Dr. Herdoíza wrote. The empírico's association with the working class seems to have been raised to discredit him further. Before asking his superior to "judge the facts," Herdoíza wanted him "to feel the struggles and the sorrow that is felt when fighting against unscrupulous, ignorant, and rude people."

The Technical Health Inspector of the Central Zone, Dr. José Gómez de la Torre, sent a copy of Dr. Herdoíza's report to Dr. Alvear, asking him "about the validity behind the operating permit for a pharmacy given to Mr. Olmedo Solís."[149] If Dr. Alvear responded, no evidence of it surfaced in the archives. The documents preserved today shed little light on why Dr. Alvear severely punished Robayo but failed to punish and instead endorsed Solís. Both were unlicensed blanco-mestizo practitioners. The most glaring distinction between them was gender; if sexism did shape Dr. Alvear's actions, he would certainly be in crowded company. But it may also be the case that, just a few years after sanctioning Robayo, Dr. Alvear was shifting his priorities to keeping businesses open, per the federal government's goals.

By punishing some empíricos while authorizing others, Dr. Alvear embodied ambivalent and contradictory public health responses to partially-trained and untrained practitioners operating in towns and hospitals. National officials seldom expressed alarm, perhaps because so few medical professionals were available in the countryside. Even as he railed against uncertified nurses and his colleague warned about a "fleet of charlatans," Dr. Alvear apparently recognized that empíricos could improve as well as undermine highland health. With such comprehension common among regional and national authorities, Ecuadorian highland healthcare enjoyed an easier syncretism than that in Guatemala. Cooperation and co-optation, rather than conflict, characterized relations between empíricos and officials in Ecuador.

CONCLUSION

The relationships between indigenous and scientific medicine and unlicensed practitioners and authorities tell us not just about healthcare, but also about social relations. If the arrest record of empíricos, curanderos, and brujas is any indication, authorities in both Guatemala and Ecuador tended to have a fairly nuanced sense of healing, medicine, and the need for uncertified practitioners in rural areas. While the Ecuadorian archival record portrays the state's balanced approach to critiquing some traditional practices and practitioners while extolling others, the case for Guatemala more clearly skews against indigenous curanderos and healing practices. Police pursuit of foreign and non-indigenous empíricos complicate that unambiguous assessment, however. Racist thought shaped but did not overdetermine Guatemalan efforts to advance medical professionals and persecute untrained practitioners.

Even though scientific medicine was an integral part of modernization and nationalism, states have seldom consistently suppressed indigenous and traditional medicine. Although curanderos and empíricos had more leeway in Ecuador than Guatemala, both nations facilitated spaces for them to practice medicine. Indigenous and other healing traditions were simply too popular for scientific medicine to curtail, and neither medical professionals nor government officials could fully sway all the Guatemalans and Ecuadorians they hoped to serve.[150] With bureaucrats promoting pragmaticism and indigenous healers borrowing methods and resources from state medicine, the relationship between traditional and modern medicine was fluid and syncretic.

So seamless had different health practices become that during trainings aimed at bringing empíricos into the fold of scientific medicine, advocates of the latter mined the minds of the former for their expertise. An elderly Kaqchikel woman from highland Guatemala recounts an incident with the renowned indigenous midwife Germana Catu (1879 [1889?]–1966) that further complicates our understanding of indigenous influences on medical professionals: "One time many doctors came and held a meeting to show midwives the techniques of their work, but then they asked Germana what she would do in certain circumstances. For example, when the baby was not coming out right. She never lost a mother to a bad birth and the doctors admired her for that."[151] Doctors who learned from indigenous midwives offer one example of ways medical professionals legitimized the work of traditional healers.[152] Just as indigenous epistemologies and practices that differed from learned medicine shaped it, gender influenced healthcare delivery and public health initiatives.

THREE

Engendering Infant Mortality and Public Health

MIDWIFERY, OBSTETRICS, AND ETHNICITY

REPORTING FROM THE ECUADORIAN CENTRAL highlands in 1947, the Technical Health Inspector of the Central Zone, Dr. José Gómez de la Torre, praised the "modern orientation and great enthusiasm" of public health employees "who ignored the low salaries and inherent hardships of their duties" to improve Ecuadorians' health.[1] Such advances notwithstanding, high rates of infant mortality persisted, in part because a lack of potable water and latrines continued to undermine rural health. "The reality in the villages is bitter; according to statistical studies by this office, the villages have one of the highest infant mortality rates," he lamented. Among other measures, he proposed "creating sanitary units … like those seen in countries more advanced than ours," raising salaries, and improving transportation because carrying patients on men's and mules' backs was "unhygienic and inhumane." Like his contemporaries and predecessors who warned of depopulated cities and unhealthy labor forces, Gómez de la Torre analyzed infant mortality through a social medicine lens.[2] In a nation that avoided the 1918 influenza pandemic, eradicated yellow fever from its main port by 1920, and established maternal-infant care clinics in 1935, infant mortality continued to defy mitigation at mid-century.

Throughout the Americas and Europe, high infant mortality rates in the late nineteenth and early twentieth centuries compelled countries to improve maternal and infant health. Such concerns began surfacing as early as the 1850s in the United States.[3] While Europe approached the problem from an economic perspective (to ensure a productive industrial labor force and, in nineteenth-century France, to buttress the nation's military defense), most Latin American nations considered infant mortality a moral crisis and advocates wanted governments to assume responsibility for maternal and infant health.[4] At a time when the Pan American Sanitary Bureau had little interest in maternal or child health, Latin American nations petitioned the organization to tackle infant mortality.[5] By 1923, a Pan American Health Association study of infant mortality was circulating in Guatemala.[6] In 1927, Montevideo founded the first American International Institute for the Protection of Childhood. Shortly thereafter, Costa Rica joined Uruguay in pioneering child and infant care legislation and reform.[7] Many Latin American nations followed suit, designating a day or week of the child and holding Child Congresses.[8]

Despite scientific medicine's expanded influence and geographic reach during the first half of the twentieth century, babies continued dying at an alarming rate. As governments and healthcare professionals in the Americas and Europe dedicated more resources to the problem, officials like Dr. Gómez de la Torre realized the solution lay not in scientific medicine but in improving the environmental and social conditions into which babies were born. Since confronting those issues demanded clear communication with rural impoverished communities, traditional healers—particularly *comadronas empíricas* (untrained midwives)—were uniquely poised to counteract the crisis. Dwarfed by those who considered uncertified midwives dangerous, some Guatemalan physicians and authorities lauded them.[9] Those contrasting perceptions fueled both conflict and collaboration, which in turn shaped hybrid healthcare.

Since neither scientific nor indigenous medicine had the capacity to singlehandedly cure all ailments or solve entrenched public health challenges, hybrid healthcare was often the most efficacious approach to highland health. By legitimizing indigenous and other vernacular knowledge about health, some medical professionals gained insight into local realities, particularly obstacles to individual wellness such as poverty and a lack of potable water. Only as nations began addressing those issues did infant mortality rates begin to drop. Akin to indigenous healing practices, holistic approaches to public health crises generally enjoyed success. Yet many medical professionals were singularly wedded to scientific medicine. In 1938, Central American doctors noted, "Infant mortality is one of the greatest problems that science must resolve, as much in the old world as in the new world."[10]

Efforts to improve outcomes for women and children took place amidst a growing professionalization of medicine that involved usurping female and indigenous power. Even when indigenous and hybrid healthcare thrived in some areas, seldom did officials or medical professionals universally endorse it. Institutionalizing medical professionalization through nursing and midwifery schools further demarcated medical professionals from indigenous midwives at a time when more than 90 percent of births in indigenous communities were attended in homes by midwives,[11] most of whom practiced independently of the state.[12] Guatemalan police who considered indigenous and unlicensed midwives "detrimental to public health and at times order" eagerly persecuted them.[13] In a reality that cemented associations between untrained midwives, indigeneity, and criminality, indigenous midwives' poverty and isolation largely precluded their capacity to attain, let alone, maintain a license. Contested perspectives on the legitimacy of different types of reproductive healthcare undermined efforts to reduce infant mortality.

Beginning in the seventeenth century, the push to professionalize medicine in Latin America involved arrogating gynecological and natal care from indigenous and other traditional midwives, transferring the authority to diagnose and cure illness to licensed male doctors. Enlightened medicine was the intended norm, and male physicians the intended experts.[14] As part of this process, in 1750 the *Real Tribunal del Protomedicato* established requirements for practice (including literacy) and issued examinations to circumscribe midwives' medical roles. Yet throughout the colonial period, traditional and learned approaches to healthcare often coexisted without much conflict.[15]

That changed during the late nineteenth and early twentieth century as authorities and physicians proclaimed the advances of obstetrics and gynecology, subverting traditional midwives' knowledge and legitimacy, such that male doctors could take control of female bodies, particularly in the birthing process.[16] Decrying their ideological battle against doctors in his award winning *Infante hygiene* (1900), the Cuban physician Benjamín Céspedes claimed, "women empirics ... bring sterility and death to all homes."[17]

In 1916, the Ecuadorian director of the Maternidad (maternity hospital) in Quito, Dr. Isidro Ayora, sounded a similar warning: since "empirical" obstetrics could be "fatal," he said, physicians and medical students should handle patients in the maternity hospital "where [midwives] can come from time to time to forget the negligence and routine to which their professional exercise tends."[18] While medical professionals were concerned by high infant mortality rates in the country, their dismissals of midwives' knowledge also reflected the desire, among a growing number of medical school graduates, for lucrative employment.[19] Dr. Ayora advocated training women to assist, not compete with, physicians.[20]

Midwives' experiential learning and alternative epistemologies were the antithesis of what postcolonial Latin American states advanced. Assumptions about midwives' ignorance or incapacity undoubtedly informed plans to establish obstetric studies in both countries. Like other early-twentieth-century Latin American governments that partnered with hospitals and medical professionals to train midwives, Guatemala's and Ecuador's leaders recognized that midwifery was critical to addressing infant mortality and thus set about training and licensing midwives (partly to subordinate them to medical authority).[21] The twentieth century saw new courses in midwifery and nursing in Ecuador and Guatemala and new regulations around birth and maternal-infant care. Throughout the 1920s, 1930s, and 1940s, records of teachers, students, and graduates from the Guatemala City Nursing School show ladino, rather than indigenous surnames, partly because powerful Creoles and ladinos wielded their influence.[22] Among RF representatives and Ecuadorian doctors, a preference for non-indigenous educated women similarly characterized recruitment to Quito's nursing school.[23] RF representatives generally endorsed their host government's focus on training for both midwives and nurses. Though they decried appalling maternal and infant care, Foundation agents tended not to highlight the state's responsibility for abysmal living conditions.[24] Latin American health officials favored a push for education over reforms that might undermine elite assets.[25]

In 1936, Guatemalan Dr. Manuel Hernández Jurado advocated "a tireless war against *parteras empíricas* [untrained midwives] where they have been irresponsibly certified and exercise their trade, constituting one of the principal causes of our infant mortality."[26] Yet he knew that midwives—predominantly indigenous, and lacking formal training—attended the majority of births in rural areas, so that, even as he railed against these "shameful cases," he knew regions lacking certified midwives would have to "regulate empirismo" by providing parteras with "indispensable elementary instruction."[27] A decade later, the Escuintla Hospital Director proposed that "hospitals register cases of post-partum complications with the names of empíricas who assisted and report them to public health court, cancelling the license when punishable negligence or noteworthy incompetence is proven."[28] Midwives policed each other too.[29] The daughter of the Guatemalan midwife Germana Catu recalled, "She was called to attend a woman who was suffering ... because she had a bad comadrona. My mother threatened to send her to jail because she did such a bad job."[30]

In 1946, Guatemala launched an "Enlightenment campaign for comadronas empíricas . . . to gradually reduce until extinguishing the danger represented by untrained care to women in prenatal, natal, and postnatal periods."[31] Proposing to replace midwives who dominated rural natal care with obstetricians and "medical advancement," the government promised that "in addition to scientific training and teaching," trained midwives would receive tools of their trade.[32]

The persecution of midwives notwithstanding, some midwifery practices that contravened contemporary scientific medical procedures have been proven particularly effective. Taking advantage of gravity, indigenous midwives advised mothers to assume squatting or kneeling positions or to hang from a rope looped around a rafter during delivery. Professional obstetricians working in hospitals almost invariably positioned women lying on their backs to give birth, which made labor more difficult (but kept the obstetrician in a position of power).

As cultural brokers, indigenous midwives determined the extent to which they were agents of change, control, and continuity. In contrast to other traditional indigenous healers such as *oyonela'* (soul therapists), whose practices were so far outside the realm of scientific medicine that they were never officially authorized, midwives had the opportunity to be recognized by the state.[33] Indigenous midwives tacked between thwarting the state's goals and educating medical professionals.[34] Indigenous and other unlicensed midwives who incorporated aspects of medical science, and doctors who adopted indigenous practices, indicate that attempts to delegitimize traditional healing were countered by popular demand for both its helpfulness and its affordability.

In the complex tapestry of reproductive healthcare providers, medical professionals, Ecuadorian *obstetrices científicas* (scientific midwives who received university training), Guatemalan *comadrona tituladas* (trained and certified midwives), and indigenous and uncertified midwives complemented, collaborated with, and competed against each other. Female professionals struggled to distinguish themselves from untrained practitioners.[35] With few female doctors in early twentieth-century Latin America, nurses and midwives represented the vast majority of female reproductive healthcare providers.[36] Various groups of medical professionals, healers, and authorities had cultural stakes in reproductive healthcare.[37] Yet it was female providers—from indigenous midwives to visiting nurses—rather than male doctors who attracted new and expectant mothers to the milieu of hybrid healthcare.

By the turn of the century, the medicalization of birth was gaining strength in Ecuador.[38] In 1899, a new maternity hospital opened in Quito to serve poor expectant mothers and offer classes to midwives.[39] Four years later, Guayaquil established a maternity ward. Yet even into the 1920s, Guayaquil hospital directors complained the ward was "utterly inadequate," and some provincial hospitals lacked maternity services entirely. Infant mortality rates remained high.[40] To gauge the nation's needs, the Ecuadorian government asked obstetric doctors to register with the state in 1929.[41]

The Universidad Central Faculty of Medicine in Quito offered a midwifery program for women. Set against male doctors and authorities who attempted to control human reproduction, training female professionals to lead interventions in reproductive health was remarkable.[42] The school had a stringent secondary education requirement for admission, but it was only loosely enforced, perhaps because so few schools offered a high school diploma for girls. For sixty of the sixty-one students who enrolled from 1890–1911—many of whom were poor illegitimate daughters, orphans, or widows—the requirement was waived. Ultimately, character and morality seem to have mattered more than educational background. A Supreme Court official wrote the school a letter endorsing the "honorable" and "distinguished" character of an "extremely poor" student who ended up being admitted and graduating in 1898.[43] With minimal prior education, some students struggled academically. From 1890 to the 1930s, forty-four women who studied midwifery at the Universidad Central did not graduate. Some pursued empirismo.[44] And while the Ecuadorian Faculty of Medicine matriculated many marginalized women—a half-century before the university admitted women in other areas of study—no indigenous women enrolled in the program.[45]

Those midwives who had received specialized training generally enjoyed more prestige and respect than hospital or visiting nurses: their elevated backgrounds, levels of education, social profiles, professional statuses, and comparatively comfortable working conditions set them apart.[46] But they still fought for space in a complex ecology of practitioners that included physicians, who often invaded midwives' spheres, as well as unlicensed midwives—including indigenous parteras who employed Andean medicine, mestizo matronas who had some scientific medical training but also used home remedies, and empíricas who learned their craft through informal personal experience with births and home remedies—who had loyal clienteles.[47] Although they provided similar services, those uncertified reproductive healthcare providers did not have the university education midwives did. While Ecuador's Sanidad endorsed Delia Robayo even though she lacked formal training,[48] Ecuadorian women who enrolled in full-time university training often were fierce critics of untrained midwives. Consuelo Rueda Sáenz, one of these women, proposed an infant and maternal care outreach program in Quito. She insisted that replacing partially- or un-trained midwives with scientifically-educated midwives would reduce infant mortality. Her 1929 proposal languished until 1935 when the Ecuadorian government launched a maternal-infant care program that greatly resembled Rueda Sáenz's vision and rationale.[49]

Far from uniform, maternal and infant care in highland Ecuador was as dependent on the regulatory bodies and individuals enforcing the dictates of medical science as on the decisions, knowledge, and practices of trained and untrained midwives and nurses. Without a license or degree, empíricas were susceptible to criminalization. Completing four years of midwifery studies before being expelled in 1920, Carmela Granja established an obstetric clinic in Quito that thrived into the 1930s. Suspecting her of performing abortions, which were illegal, Quito authorities incarcerated her at least twice for practicing without a license. When police raided her business in 1929, they discovered boiling water, electric heating elements, and sterilized obstetrical instruments that suggested she adhered to modern mechanization and science. By threatening to make public the (many elite) women who had consulted her for an abortion, Granja avoided incarceration for that aspect of her practice. Midwives who prescribed (and pharmacists who dispensed) "rue, savin, mugwort, saffron, rye ergot and other similar substances known as abortifacients" also alarmed Sanidad officials.[50]

Such scrutiny notwithstanding, tacit approval for unlicensed work continued into the mid-twentieth century. Ecuadorian officials permitted untrained practitioners where no licensed professionals existed. Even the fiercest critics could be quieted when they considered the large swaths of the population that lacked formal healthcare. When medical professionals opened offices, they could petition the Public Health Service to prohibit unlicensed midwives and healers from practicing (though national authorities did not always enforce sanctions, as the 1946 case of Robayo, discussed in chapter 2, demonstrates).[51] Even after it employed university-trained midwives throughout the country, the Public Health Service tended more toward

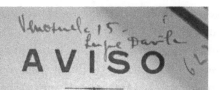

AVISO

Se pone en conocimiento del público que la Dirección General de Sanidad, a fin de completar la obra de la protección infantil, ha creado en esta ciudad los cargos de Partera y Enfermera, para la atención gratuita de partos a domicilio a mujeres menesterosas que, por circunstancias especiales, no pudieran recurrir a la asistencia en la Maternidad.

Para merecer este servicio, las interesadas deberán hacerse inscribir, con oportunidad, en la Oficina de Sanidad, situada en la Carrera Veloz, Casa Municipal.

Riobamba, junio 12 de 1935.

A. Villagómez R.
Delegado de Sanidad del Chimborazo.

FIGURE 13. Public notice announcing infant protection program for poor women, Riobamba, Ecuador, June 12, 1935. Courtesy of Museo de Medicina, Quito.

leniency than censure with unlicensed midwives in places that lacked professional midwives.

In 1935, Ecuador launched a natal outreach program that employed university-trained midwives (who provided prenatal care and attended births) and visiting nurses (who oversaw infants' health) to provide free care to poor populations in Andean provincial cities and county seats.[52] Ecuador's maternal-infant healthcare program could be selective,[53] and officials seem not to have prioritized foreign expertise. For example, a Chicago School of Nursing graduate who had worked in Panama, Esther García, assured her prospective employer her references could attest to her "aptitude ... as a trained midwife in difficult cases."[54] Six months after her initial inquiry on May 22, 1935, she still was asking "authorities to employ me in something."[55]

Public notices informed women: "The Health Service has created the positions of midwife and nurse for free consults for home births of needy women, who because of special circumstances, cannot go to a maternity ward" (figure 13).[56] The Health Service adeptly deployed discourse of infant mortality to validate its domestic interventions, but their outreach efforts seldom reached rural villages, and thus had little capacity to advance programming in indigenous communities.

For the young mothers and families who received care from female providers within the program, the midwives' and nurses' skills, solidarity, and empathy were impressive. One husband contacted the Ministry of Health to thank midwife Emma Franco and nurse Rosalía Vaca for their "professional services" and for attending to his wife "with caring resolve and true philanthropy."[57] Another husband praised: "American Medicine ... [and] the competent, charitable, and selfless professional, Ms. Leticia Rosas de Navarrete, whose virtues are a gift to all who know her and whose integrity and honor have earned her the trust of those she has served."[58] According to Consuelo Rueda Sáenz, who became the state midwife for Ambato (1936–41) and Machachi (1942), local gratitude extended to the Ministry of Health: "The people are grateful for the humanitarian labor displayed by the General Director who ... comprehends the needs and hardship of the indigent."[59] Rueda Sáenz deserved thanks too: she could boast of never having lost a life or causing puerperal infection during a time when her caseload was often twice what was expected.[60]

Beneficiaries who wrote to express their gratitude generally underscored their poverty. Too poor to pay the doctor who attended her, María Hermilida insisted God would. After a "very violent birth," she had "symptoms that she had not felt in other births." When the female attendant's care did not suffice, they called the doctor "at the last minute."[61] For saving her life, she offered him "affection and gratitude."[62]

Many midwives empathized with their poor patients' plights. Even as Rueda Sáenz characterized them as "poor, unhappy, without aid ... [and] in imminent danger of their and their children's lives," she felt "fraternity with her neighbors."[63] Such sentiments inspired women to surmount rather than submit to the program's deficiencies. Insisting committed workers could overcome the state's financial constraints, the university-trained midwife Dolores A. de Lippke noted: "Economic hardship is great in Ecuador, but the good will of midwives should reach all homes, preferentially the proletarian class to leave in them instructions for mothers and future mothers."[64] Indicating she perceived differences between her middle- and lower-class patients' intellect, Lippke "advised women about healthcare in general and childcare according to the social class to which they belonged." Aware few clients could afford healthcare, Lippke considered it a "crime to charge fees." Complaints about her counterparts doing so suggest that other midwives were less sympathetic to their clients' challenges.

Healthcare officials praised midwives like Esperanza Calderon for their "selfless and disciplined" work, but authorities struggled to assess midwives' performance, especially since most were unaccompanied when they made house calls.[65] Authorities relied on patients for feedback, and the police fined professional midwives for failing to attend patients who requested their services.[66] After hearing several complaints from expectant and new mothers that one nurse—if she even arrived, which was seldom—only took their pulse and temperature, Dr. Alvear Pérez was convinced she only visited patients when she was being observed. When a patient's umbilical cord was bleeding, the nurse did not offer any "obstetric attention to the mother or care to the baby."[67] Such reports of incompetency or indifference were exceptional, however, and most of the complaints around the maternal-infant care program came from people who simply wanted access to more personnel.[68]

That lack came, in part, because of Ecuador's failure—whether through inability or unwillingness—to adequately fund the infant protection program. In 1934, the government had dedicated a mere 4.7 percent of the national budget to welfare, which included public health. The military and education consumed nearly 20 percent each. Public works consumed 12.7 percent, while much of the remaining budget (42.9 percent) went to "other expenditures." By 1937, the next year for which figures are available, the welfare budget increased to 6.8 percent, though natal care was not prioritized among public health needs.[69] In 1935, midwives in the program wrote to the Director of Health, Dr. Alfonso Mosquera Narváez, soliciting "the necessary medicines and objects that they lacked."[70] Dr. E. R. Rickard concurrently informed Mosquera Narváez that he could not exhaust his 50,000 sucre budget to study yellow fever.[71] No matter that the nation proudly claimed to have eradicated yellow fever in Guayaquil by 1920: a tropical disease the nation had controlled received a more generous allocation than female medical professionals on the front lines of reducing infant mortality—a legitimate national scourge.

Among the vital components that budgetary constraints precluded were vaccines. In 1935 Ecuadorian physician and tuberculosis expert Rafael Quevedo Coronel insisted, "There is no country in the civilized world that does not have a laboratory for preparing and distributing the Calmette vaccine."[72] Administered to infants shortly after their birth, the Calmette (known today as the Bacillus Calmette–Guérin or BCG) vaccine is effective against tuberculosis. Referencing data from the Pasteur Institute in Paris that indicated the vaccine reduced infant mortality from 40 to 5.75 percent,

Quevedo Coronel wrote that his nation's failure to procure it condemned babies to death.

Other basic supplies were lacking as well. In November 1935, midwives and doctors wrote to the Minister of Health asking for medicines and sterilized supplies that they needed when attending to births, including thermometers, pelvimetros, scales, soap, talcum powder, alcohol, gasoline, and oxygenated water. Their lists were punctuated with notes like "this order is URGENT."[73] Transferred to Ambato after her stint as a health inspector in Machachi, Lucila Valencia insisted a visit from the Minister of Public Health was necessary because of the "many complaints and needs that are not possible to explain by mail."[74] In Latacunga, Dr. Pilliariz reported in November 1935 that an adequate shipment was "indispensable . . . as quickly as possible."[75] A few days later, he followed up: "There is no medicine or supplies and the Nurse and Midwife can only offer their personal attention."[76] Another clinic (in Ibarra) faced eviction for unpaid rent.[77] The financial woes persisted for at least half a decade. By April 1940, the Director of Sanidad promised to procure office supplies and, "if it is possible, other materials needed" for the obstetric program in Ambato.[78]

Supply shortages were not the only difficulties midwives faced. Educated and largely enjoying a middle-class lifestyle, professional midwives tended to be single; many had been orphans. Without husbands or fathers in a society where male protectors defended women's honor, midwives had to forge their own paths of good standing, sometimes working against the association of their career with abortion. Their peripatetic lives required regularly reestablishing reputations.[79] Considering expectations that university-trained midwives' behavior be irreproachable, their senior male supervisors' accusations of sex work or alcoholism were particularly damaging.[80] In response to an "unjust and false" complaint that she never showed up to work, Leopoldina Padilla Cos explained that the doctor did not see her because *he* seldom came to the clinic and when he did, she was often out on a call. While the office assistant insisted they wait for the doctor to commence work, Padilla Cos explained, "I came not to *pasearme* but to work," and visited Ambato and its surrounding communities.[81] Since doctors' professional status trumped that of midwives, midwives like Padilla Cos may have enjoyed the autonomy afforded them during house visits where they could diagnose and treat patients freely in a doctor's absence. Writing with "truth and frankness," Padilla Cos was not alone in feeling distant from doctors.[82] Though they shared a commitment to scientific medicine, educated midwives and doctors seem to have seldom formed affinities, let alone alliances. Rueda Sáenz,

Padilla Cos, Lippke, and their colleagues often clashed with doctors. In 1946, a doctor fined Lippke for "insubordination and a lack of discipline."[83] Some midwives operated practices parallel to doctors.[84]

Midwifery was laborious. The program expected midwives to attend at least ten births a month, though some assisted in as many as thirty.[85] To reach a woman suffering from infection after a stillbirth, Rueda Sáenz endured "the hardship of a bad road, distance and bad weather, but with a desire to fulfill my obligations."[86] The following month she attended four births and six miscarriages in addition to the "innumerable daily consultations wherein she did not simply prescribe but personally cured them."[87] Reaching pregnant women could be daunting. Rueda Sáenz regularly traversed "indescribable roads," mountains, and ravines often putting herself in danger to "fulfill her professional obligations."[88] So did Padilla Cos. On November 15, 1935, she accompanied the comadrona empírica on a trip of "two kilometers in strong sunshine (insolación) which gave me a brutal headache."[89]

Given the time-consuming work of serving people "at any hour and in every place," Rueda Sáenz did not want to "spend much time and paper" noting everyone's name and illness.[90] One month, instead of a full report, Rueda Sáenz offered her supervisor a synthesis "so as not to exhaust your attention." In the next correspondence she emphasized the importance and limited nature of her own, rather than her superior's, time—suggesting she felt increasingly emboldened as her experience expanded.[91] She was not alone in her bureaucratic neglect. The head of the Chimborazo (Riobamba) public health delegation, for example, conceded that his reports had been "very laconic and scarce," explaining that because of a "lack of order and discipline in procedures, many issues" required his time.[92] Yet the broader archival record offers evidence of their peers' voluminous labor, indicating that both he and Rueda Sáenz may not have been simply shirking paperwork, but charting a strategy for increased autonomy.

Nascent maternal and infant care clinics afforded professional midwives the autonomy and authority to buttress their confidence and expertise. Aware of their crucial contributions to pregnant women and babies on the margins of state-sanctioned healthcare, midwives became brokers between compromised citizens and the nation's public health systems. The government paid professional midwives a modest salary to serve indigent patients, but some midwives became entrepreneurial, establishing private practices with wealthier clients.[93] In September 1935, Severa Urresta provided healthcare to a hatmaker, servant, cook, weaver, and seamstress.[94]

Further legitimizing university-educated midwifery, the government persecuted untrained practitioners with rhetoric that portrayed them as a threat. Officials sought to extirpate dubious healthcare that jeopardized infants' and expectant mothers' well-being. Some flyers warned against the dangers of empíricas' care. Others threatened to punish "very severely" mothers whose children died because they consulted empíricas—though the archives betray nary a document suggesting authorities in fact punished anyone.[95] Rueda Sáenz lamented "the terrible consequences" suffered by "the majority of women ... who have been victims of ignorant empiricism."[96] According to her, a combination of geographic isolation and spurious healthcare put them at risk. The rail pass that facilitated her transportation "to the neighboring communities where her visits were urgent" enabled her to "save a child [from] empirical hands without knowledge" in July 1935.[97]

The marginalization of untrained midwives among medical professionals and popular clients contributed to their relative invisibility in the archives. Practicing in rural communities, indigenous midwives and other parteras were not eligible to register as obstetrices científicas. An enduring urban bias—evident in the limited reach of Ecuador's Health Service beyond municipalities—means indigenous midwives largely are absent in Ecuadorian archives. Yet it is clear that some locals insisted parteras, matronas, and empíricas served them well. Other families understood untrained midwives as associated with risk, but could not access professional providers.[98] Too poor to give birth in a maternity ward, for example, a Riobamba woman felt compelled "to turn to empiricism, with the grave danger for her life and that of the fruit of their love," her husband explained.[99]

Professional midwives were concerned that indigenous and local culture jeopardized wellness. Working in the Andean mestizo town of Alausí and its surrounding indigenous villages where "the entire population complains of absolute poverty ... [and thus] wants free midwives and medicine," Rueda Sáenz was shocked by some traditions.[100] Since Andean traditional midwives generally did not charge fees because it would have "cheapened the value of their work," expecting free midwifery was common.[101] "There is much to do to educate these people and be able to if not eliminate then at least attenuate certain customs," Rueda Sáenz insisted.[102] She alarmingly observed "*el lavado a vano del quinto*," whereby a variety of herbs were mixed in an enormous pail so the "*puepura*" could be submerged up to the throat for a few minutes. Much to her "horror," when she tried to stop the practice, they explained it is "custom ... we cannot stop doing it because in that way the mother is seasoned."[103] That custom, which could be translated as "bath of the fifth space/ doorway," reflected Andean cures for susto that included a mixture of flower petals, leaves, and wheat or corn that healers blessed and distributed over the patient's body.[104] Such purification or cleansing rituals intended to expel illnesses date to the pre-colonial period.[105] Those healing rituals differed dramatically from the medical science and midwifery taught at the university.

For poor women, hosting middle-class professionals may have been fraught with peril. One such pregnant woman "shouted insults and dirty words" at two midwives who visited her home.[106] Although their supervisor insisted the outburst was unwarranted, baring poverty that compromised hygiene and sanitation to medical professionals must have been stressful to poor women. Historical anthropologist Kim Clark argues that midwives perpetuated "state projects of moral regulation of poor mothers."[107] Such moralizing likely inflamed tensions between women of different socioeconomic statuses, ethnicity, class, and linguistic backgrounds.

Few midwives and nurses seem to have considered their charges equals. Lippke, for example, insisted that "jokes, messes, chatting are typical of unoccupied people, without culture, and typical of cooks and lower classes."[108] That view extended to the untrained midwives who often cared for indigenous and poor populations—people whom, she maintained, should not be hired by clinics. Writing to Dr. Alvear, she advised "From the beginning, select scientific, patient, and conscientious people who are talented professionals, that is, people [who are] cultured, adult, and normal and [do] not employ a person without any professional responsibility," a description that, to her mind, excluded poor and indigenous would-be workers.

Even as she warned about the dangers of "empirical hands," however, Rueda Sáenz recognized empíricas' contributions. She advocated a measured approach, endorsing unlicensed midwives as families slowly became accustomed to professionals, eventually rejecting empirical for professional care. Evidence supported her hypothesis. By September 1938, professionals attended more than half the births in Ambato, compared to 1930 when empirics attended twice as many births as professionals. Although discerning Rueda Sáenz's influence is difficult, the absence of evidence indicating authorities punished mothers who consulted comadronas empíricas suggests her method won the day. In Ecuador, conciliation often characterized intersections of scientific and traditional medicine.[109]

Some officials who critiqued untrained healers still advanced traditional practices. In a 1935 memo to pregnant women and new mothers, the Director of Public Health advocated hybrid approaches to infant healthcare. After he warned them not to allow "ignorant people to perform internal exams because of the danger of infection," he advised them on how to prevent mal de ojo. Referencing another popular notion about health, he instructed them not to "eat heavy foods, that is baked, fried … *aji* [chile], [or] alcohol . . . because it could make the baby sick."[110] Although the International Office of Public Health similarly advised pregnant women to avoid fatty foods,[111] medical professionals championing traditional beliefs and practices reveals that approaches to healthcare were syncretic even at the highest levels of Ecuadorian authority. Rather than reject certain approaches outright, everyone from professionals to poor patients tended toward pragmatism predicated on the multiplicity of medicines that permeated their societies.

GUATEMALA

Guatemala shared Ecuador's preoccupation with high infant mortality rates. Without Ecuador's robust midwifery school or government-sponsored natal care program, however, Guatemala depended on indigenous and other uncertified midwives even as officials disparaged them. Despite limited resources and reach, the Guatemalan government sought to train midwives.

As early as 1879, the Guatemala Ministry of Public Education established an obstetrics class for midwives. Constanya Marino taught it at the San José Hospital in Guatemala City with supervision from a male physician. According to the presidential decree that authorized the course, "experience has demonstrated the very grave problems caused by midwives who lack knowledge of the art."[112]

Four years later, the Guatemalan government founded a midwifery school in the General Hospital directed by faculty at the School of Medicine and Pharmacy "to educate . . . if not true midwives then at least lesser midwives who understand something."[113] To supplement the curriculum, the hospital delivery room created two positions for midwifery interns who earned eight pesos a month and room and board at the hospital. Interested students had to be between twenty and forty years old with a vaccination certificate, to have graduated from a "complementary [presumably secondary] school," register verbally with the Dean of Faculty, be of "notably good conduct [*notaria buena conducta*] . . . and present a statement from a distinguished person who could confirm the integrity [*honradez*] of the postulate." Indigenous midwives generally began to practice later in life. Coupled with the term *honradez*, the phrase "buena conducta" referred to female honor. The need for a certificate from a distinguished individual (read: a Creole or ladino male) pointed to other forms of virtue and to cross-class and cross-gender patronage relations that would not have been available for most indigenous women. Because of their ethnicity, few rural indígenas would have been recognized by a faculty dean as honorable, let alone appropriate for evaluating candidates' conduct. Moreover, interviews were conducted in Spanish, which precluded participation for most indigenous women, who were likely to be monolingual and illiterate. Few rural indigenous women completed elementary school, if they attended at all. In short, the midwifery school cast a narrow net aimed at educated ladinas.

Deploying medicinal plants to treat snake bites, intestinal problems, and other issues beyond their expertise in natal care, Guatemalan comadronas empíricas included naturalists and spiritualists. The latter divined through prayers and ritual calendars.[114] Many combined herbal medicines with magical rituals.[115] Some incorporated aspects of gynecology.[116] While medical training encouraged midwives to critique "old beliefs," many maintained traditional practices such as burning the placenta to shape the infant's future.[117] With their different paths to healing, indigenous and other traditional midwives who incorporated aspects of their state-sanctioned training into their practices demonstrate the multiple layers and complex continuum of indigenous healthcare.[118]

By preserving local traditions even as they incorporated aspects of medical science, Maya midwives and healers provided historical and cultural continuity without rejecting modernization. Often responding to a calling that many initially resisted, indigenous midwives learned through spirituality, healing hands, experience, and their predecessors. Midwives who called upon such ancient practices as massages, spiritual counseling, and sweat and herb baths drew on deep knowledge acquired and shared over generations.[119]

Neither obstetrics nor midwifery were hegemonic. Just as indigenous midwives walked a fine line between resisting and accommodating regulations that disrupted age-old practices, authorities weighed their desire to enforce regulations against the realities of rural healthcare. Targeted by officials as ignorant, irresponsible, and dangerous, Guatemalan comadronas empíricas struggled to advance their expertise when authorities expected them to register with the state and adhere to its notions of healthcare. Yet the state's intermittent presence beyond urban areas curtailed professional obstetrics' march toward hegemony.

In rural areas, authorities' preference for university-trained practitioners was difficult to institute. Of the thirty-eight Guatemalan midwives who registered in Antigua in 1931, only two were comadronas tituladas.[120] The following year a survey of Sacatepéquez province turned up only two comadronas tituladas and eighty-seven comadronas empíricas.[121] The vast majority of midwives who were listed without an address reveals Guatemalan authorities' inability to locate, let alone control, them. Evident in oral histories and inferred from archival omissions, midwives' ability to continue practicing without a license was facilitated more by their elusiveness than open resistance.[122]

On the frontlines of natal care, midwives worked tirelessly to improve infant and maternal health. One such midwife, María Castro de Morales, proposed opening a free obstetric clinic in Guatemala City in 1911 to reduce infant mortality. With 400 pesos a month for rent and salary, she pledged to attend her clinic in the afternoons and do outreach in the mornings. She mapped out different parts of the city where she would make home visits to poor and working-class women Monday through Saturday.[123] The archival silence thereafter suggests municipal officials never approved her proposal. A midwife-centered institution may not have resonated with early-twentieth-century authorities' notions of modernization.

The following year, however, Estrada Cabrera's administration established the Joaquina Maternity Ward. Confident "Guatemala has the elements to initiate reform . . . tending to the revitalization of humanity," officials highlighted scientific medicine's role in Estrada Cabrera's quest for modernity.[124] Named after the dictator's mother Doña Joaquina Cabrera, the ward was "equipped with the most modern elements that exist in America and Europe." The majority of patients were "poor people who probably would have lost the fruit of their wombs because they lacked resources." For bringing Joaquina's vision of an "elegant, comfortable, and hygienic building" into reality, his Minister of Government and Justice dubbed Estrada Cabrera "the protector of children." Of the 336 births at the Joaquina Maternity Ward in 1915, only 38 infants (13 of whom were premature) died—11.3 percent, much lower than mortality rates in the nation (and region).[125]

In 1923, the Guatemalan Red Cross opened a Nursing School and School for parteras that, like the midwifery school at the General Hospital, largely excluded indígenas.[126] Students at the nursing school had to be between eighteen and twenty-five years old. A midwifery diploma required three years of daily classes. To become a first-class midwife, students had to extend their studies a fourth year and earn a degree in Arts and Sciences. Hinting at socio-economically and culturally biased admissions, they had to demonstrate "good behavior as verified ... by three people of recognized honor and selected by the Dean [of the School of Medicine]." To underscore the importance of formal studies, the Guatemalan Red Cross proposal explained that anyone who practiced midwifery without a degree or beyond their sanctioned capacity would be "persecuted and punished." Betraying an urban bias in midwifery education and access, each department capital was tasked with selecting and financially supporting a midwifery student, who in turn would serve their sending community after graduation.[127]

Across Guatemala, midwifery training and formal positions were largely reserved for non-indigenous people. The prevalence of ladino, foreign, and foreign-educated midwives and nurses in the records punctuates the absence of indigenous surnames.[128] The expertise and status of comadronas tituladas trumped that of comadronas empíricas. In Guatemala, the latter were overwhelmingly indigenous and poor whereas the former were nonindigenous. Comadronas tituladas' ability to pay for their training betrayed their resources. As one example of the preference for educated elite women, Estrada Cabrera earmarked 4,495 pesos to hire two British midwives to manage the Asilo Joaquina Maternidad in 1913,[129] and "to teach those [midwives] from the country the methods that they use."[130] Installing two European women educated in obstetric science was a manifestation of Guatemala's attempt to position itself as a modern nation among its peers in the Atlantic world. When it celebrated "prominent nurses," the Guatemalan Red Cross similarly looked to foreign nations such as the United States and Japan.[131]

With scholarships to Mexico's Infant Hospital, some Guatemalan nurses expanded their expertise. The Guatemala City Hospital General Director Dr. Victor Giordani conceded that permission to Alma Marina Chavez in 1945.[132] But when she won a scholarship to study in Panama the following year, he threatened to take her to court if she did not finish her requisite three years of service to the hospital first.[133] Apparently studying infant care afforded privileges that other nursing specialties did not.

Early-twentieth-century trained midwives and nurses enjoyed similar statuses, but by the 1940s, their specializations made them increasingly distinguishable. Insisting that nurses were essential to infant, family, and national health, the Red Cross director explained they also needed obstetric training.[134] When the National School of Nursing opened in Guatemala City in 1926, midwives attended.[135] A shared curriculum and goals may have helped to bridge nurses and midwives. In 1930, obstetric students requested that a "weekly practice class in the maternity ward" be added to their curriculum.[136] Wittingly or not, they recognized the importance of midwives' experience.

The Ubico administration, for their part, approached midwives and nurses as equals.[137] In 1935, the Ubico administration laid out requirements to receive a title in midwifery and nursing. Midwives could assist in the birth and "normal postpartum activities," but not surgery unless there was an "absolute lack" of medical professionals in the area. They could prescribe medicine, but if they facilitated abortions, they faced a year-long suspension. Anyone who practiced midwifery without the corresponding license would be punished. Since the cost of acquiring a license and supplies—among other accoutrements of their trade trained midwives needed a thermometer, stethoscope, and catheter—was prohibitive for many women, they had little choice but to practice illegally.[138] The stipulation that midwives wear white blouses and caps would have compelled indigenous women to abandon ethnic markers that their hand-crafted clothing denoted. But few indigenous women had the training to get a license anyway, given the educational barriers.

Despite their contributions, midwives struggled to secure positions in Guatemalan hospitals. The Nursing School *directora* and other female officials had to petition the hospital director to license midwives who worked there.[139] When two obstetric nurses resigned their posts at the General Hospital in 1943, the directora suggested replacing them with midwives.[140] She also petitioned for more hospital space and pay raises for midwives, and separate housing for nurses and midwives.[141] The Guatemalan superintendent of nurses, meanwhile, advocated for a raise for midwives who had worked at the hospital for more than three years.[142] If the archival silences in response to these petitions are any indication, the requests may have been turned down. When midwives were foreigners, though, the Nursing School directora enjoyed more influence. In 1943, she informed the hospital director that Kate Hyden, a midwife sent through the Pan American Sanitation Office in Washington, would be working at the hospital.[143]

In 1944, the Guatemalan Revolution set the government on a democratic course, but many midwives ended up losing rights. The new government decreed that midwives could only practice after completing training and passing an examination. Like the 1923 midwifery school proposal, the 1945 decrees mandated training that was inaccessible for poor and working-class indígenas. Few rural comadronas empíricas could afford the time or money required to take two courses a month in Guatemala City.[144] Midwifery training programs commenced in the highlands in the mid-1940s.[145] Located close to the capital, Chimaltenango had 201 comadronas empíricas registered with the state in 1944, only a few of whom had attended midwifery conferences.[146] The following year, 132 comadronas empíricas there registered and received monthly training from a doctor "to best perform their mission."[147] Further west and north, however, fewer indigenous midwives sought the state's approval. Only five comadronas empíricas registered in Sololá.[148] Similarly, in Quetzaltenango, only five women applied for the "certificate of authorization for parteras empíricas.... Three possessed the knowledge and skill necessary to exercise that profession.... The other two did not answer or demonstrate satisfactorily and moreover lacked the indispensable tools for that purpose."[149]

Although few indigenous midwives had licenses, they remained vital to natal care, particularly deliveries. Comadronas empíricas dominated rural Guatemala. Even though the licensing program expanded its influence and reach thereafter,[150] Guatemalan indigenous women generally thwarted the medicalization of childbirth that characterized other parts of Latin America.[151]

Government efforts to control midwifery were part of a broader attempt to staunch infant mortality. Guatemala's history, like Ecuador's, reflects global concerns to keep babies alive and well; in both countries, as in Latin America more broadly, infant death was considered a moral crisis. When the Guatemalan government established a newborn clinic, disinfection office, and *Gota de Leche* (Drop of Milk) program (which was informed by public hygiene and dietary science) in 1908, it underscored that such efforts enjoyed "notable success ... in countries at the vanguard of civilization, like France, Belgium, and Switzerland."[152] To ensure a "good constitution for their growth," Guatemalan newborns attended health clinics where they received "good quality sterilized milk," if their mothers could not breastfeed.[153] Since the majority of infant deaths could be attributed to enteritis or gastroenteritis— gastro-intestinal ailments caused predominantly by bacteria-laden milk, water, and food entering still-developing immune and digestive systems—sterilized milk was critical for young bodies.[154]

Throughout the 1920s, 1930s, and 1940s scientists researched infant mortality in Central America.[155] Beginning in 1929, Guatemalan Dr. Luis Gaitán studied infant mortality, which demanded "the help of the entire medical class in the country to find resolutions through experiential observation."[156] Gaitán insisted that "infant mortality was of vital importance."[157] The head of Public Health similarly argued, "The fight against infant mortality will be another of our activities that requires significant expenditures."[158] Gaitán's study with Johns Hopkins University malaria expert Julio Roberto Herrera found that malaria figured prominently in infant deaths, which ranged from 19,486 (1923) to 32,537 (1925) and outnumbered adult deaths from 1922 to 1928.[159] Another Central American study demonstrated that infant mortality (from gastro-intestinal diseases) increased during coffee harvests.[160] UFCO Scottish doctor Neil MacPhail concluded that malaria and gastrointestinal diseases were the leading causes of infant mortality in northern Guatemala.[161]

When the Amatitlán Hospital inaugurated its maternity ward on November 6, 1928, Guatemalan officials noted, "much is needed in this department to partially prevent infant mortality and diseases that mothers contract in birth because of a lack of medical assistance and midwives' care."[162] Even as officials highlighted the hospital's modernity (via the maternity ward) and distinguished between medical science and midwifery, they suggested both were crucial to reducing infant and maternal death and illness.

Eugenics often informed reproductive health initiatives. "Protecting infancy is the tutelary action exercised by the State and Society . . . to obtain generations of capable and healthy citizens," argued Alvaro Idigoras in 1935.[163] He warned that rampant infant mortality invited "the degeneration of children and criminality of minors," and encouraged Guatemala to emulate Uruguay's pioneering Infant Protection Code. Noting that the number of children who died before their first year was "alarming," Idigoras recognized the causes were diverse. He articulated a litany of threats including working mothers' inability to rest or maintain a good diet during pregnancy; syphilis, mental illness, alcoholism, malaria, and other diseases; and climate and poverty that undermined poor families' ability to feed, shelter, and care for themselves. He also cited "the seduction and abandonment of the woman" as a moral failing that undermined mothers' ability "to raise and support children." By framing seduction and abandonment as threats to motherhood, Idigoras tapped into Latin American notions of women's honor that were grounded in virginity and fidelity. Even as mothers forfeited the former, they had to maintain the latter to uphold their own and their family's reputations.[164] Rather than race, Idigoras invoked gender to analyze infant mortality.

Emerging from French strands of eugenics, puericulture—scientific child-rearing based on biological and social factors—found fertile ground in Guatemala and other Latin American countries. Neo-Lamarckian ideas of inheriting acquired characteristics fueled puericulture's spread throughout Latin America. Intended to enhance the quality of the population with medical approaches to protect pregnant women and infants, puericulture in Latin America had eugenic undertones. Since puericulture did not separate social and biological factors in dysgenics (the inheritance of undesirable characteristics), it mapped nicely onto Guatemalan eugenics, which leaned on culture rather than phenotype to identify race. Convinced of puericulture's analysis and efficacy, the Ubico dictatorship distributed pamphlets outlining puericulture and responsible mothering at annual state fairs. One manifestation of puericulture advocates' efforts to arrest maternal and child malnutrition and its hereditary defects was the healthy baby contest. As judges evaluated and ranked participants, the contests organized by municipal officials generally encouraged well-fed (and light-skinned) rotund babies. Those activities betrayed how eugenics shaped efforts to medicalize infant health, maternity, and childbirth in Guatemala (and elsewhere in Latin America).[165]

Mothers figured prominently in Latin American efforts to reduce infant mortality.[166] The Salvadoran delegate to the 1937 Central American Health Conference in Guatemala City, Dr. David Escalantes, advocated for mothers: "The future of a nation lays in the MOTHER's womb. Savage are the countries that do not protect women even during pregnancy. If you want to form a true nation, educate and prepare the woman to be a healthy and conscientious mother, good wet nurse, and perfect ... teacher of body, soul, heart and mind."[167] To his mind, reducing infant and mother mortality was "indispensable ... for the progress of these countries."[168] Lacking in knowledge, mothers had to be educated, nurtured and protected to aid infants and the nation, according to Escalantes.

The 1937 Central American Health Congress charged Costa Rican delegates with drafting a Child Code "to protect infancy."[169] Guatemalan delegates insisted race figure prominently in the discussion. Secretary General Dr. Gaitán explained that protecting infancy "favor[ed] population growth and the racial quality of the Central American isthmus."[170] The previous year Dr. Hernández insisted, "In the presence of eugenics and protecting infancy, I want us to consider nothing else ... as important among the multiple public health activities carried out in Central America. The century of the child has arrived and Central America must also launch its redeeming crusade."[171]

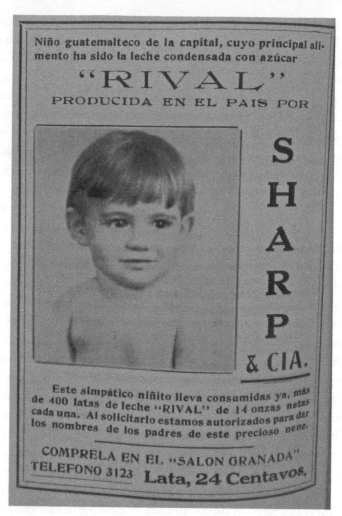

Niño guatemalteco de la capital, cuyo principal alimento ha sido la leche condensada con azúcar

"RIVAL"

PRODUCIDA EN EL PAIS POR

S
H
A
R
P
& CIA.

Este simpático niñito lleva consumidas ya, más de 400 latas de leche "RIVAL" de 14 onzas netas cada una. Al solicitarlo estamos autorizados para dar los nombres de los padres de este precioso nene.

COMPRELA EN EL "SALON GRANADA" TELEFONO 3123 Lata, 24 Centavos.

FIGURE 14. "Pleasant little boy." *Revista de la Cruz Roja Guatemalteca* 14, October 1936. Courtesy of Hemeroteca Nacional de Guatemala.

Deploying nationalism—"BE A PATRIOT PROTECT INFANCY"— Hernández detailed a plan that began with prenuptial clinics and culminated in a "MAGNA CARTA OF CHILDHOOD" because "YOU ONLY REAP WHAT YOU SOW."[172] Lest there be any doubt about the phenotype and race of children eugenicists preferred, Guatemalan newspapers provided ample images of white babies and children in a nation that had far more brown ones (figures 14 and 15).

Aware of high infant mortality rates and regional challenges with natal care in the predominantly indigenous department of Alta Verapaz where he lived, wealthy German coffee planter Guillermo "Willi" Dieseldorff (Erwin Paul Dieseldorff's son and heir) sought to buoy his national position during World War II by addressing infant mortality.[173] In addition to fulfilling requests from the Sociedad Protectora del Niño (Child Protection Society) for such medical implements as forceps, knives, and Davis' mouth gags, Dieseldorff organized and funded raffles to raise money for the Sociedad.[174] Dieseldorff funded the construction of a "Maternity ward for the hospital equipped with all the elements of modern science" in 1942.[175] A hospital administrator emoted that the donation allowed the maternity ward to "operate indefinitely under superb conditions."[176] Dieseldorff also purchased a dozen cribs and beds.[177] Convinced modernization would improve the lives of those (including indígenas) who embraced it,[178] Dieseldorff endorsed "all the enthusiasm of persons who loved cultural progress . . . [that] undoubtedly will yield optimal results."[179]

Media coverage overtly addressed the project's class consequences. *Nuestro Diario* considered the maternity ward a crucial contribution to public health and "even more valuable for . . . its sentiment of cooperation between social aid and the state."[180] In an assertion that aided (perhaps unwittingly) authorities' efforts to undermine indigenous midwifery, a journalist insisted the ward would "fill a great void among poor mothers in the region."[181] A *Norte* reporter insisted the hospital was extremely important for marginalized Cobaneros: "Our national House of Care is improving humanitarian conditions that respond to necessities of pauperism . . . and that will be a great comfort for many poor mothers who in the supreme hour, will have a secure roof to shelter and a caressing crib for those who come to receive the kiss of life."[182] The article concluded, "Works like this that have been sponsored by a generous soul, endure in the heart of those who receive its positive benefits."[183] Since government funding failed to fully finance natal care, Dieseldorff's generosity was welcome.[184]

Not everyone approached science and modernity as panaceas, however. In 1930, the director of Antigua's Pedro de Bethancourt Hospital suggested that Guatemalans' obsession with the trappings of modernization, including science, could be detrimental. He wanted to "restrain our customs, shifting them away from vices and the misery of nature that our unbridled zeal to reach an illogical and violent progress has driven us."[185] Critiquing modernity for exacting high costs distinguished him from other Guatemalan elites. Though they had little success countervailing modernization's march, other Latin Americans similarly warned against development's excesses.[186] In turn, some medical professionals recognized science's limits. In 1941, Guatemalan public health official Dr. Epaminondas Quintana concluded chemical analysis of breastmilk was "useless." Since it could not be improved upon, he encouraged "increasing the weight (or amount) of the nourishment." Breastmilk was universally good, he noted, but many infants did not drink enough.[187] In a critique that spoke to "an illogical and violent progress," Quintana attributed high infant mortality rates in Central America to governments dedicating more money to militaries than public health.[188]

Others blamed female caregivers. Sometime lauded, women were more frequently criticized and even criminalized for their role in infant health. In 1930, the director of Antigua's Pedro de Bethancourt Hospital studied Guatemala's high infant mortality rate at the Sacatepéquez governor's request. He conducted a survey of Guatemalan doctors about their experiences with and observations of natal care. Among a litany of causes that ranged from a lack of sanitation and hygiene (particularly contaminated water) and expensive medicine to climate (coastal lowlands), alcoholism, and poor families' "excessive birth rate," the respondents singled out "mothers who do not know [anything] . . . about childcare" and midwives who "are completely ignorant of the physiology" of birth "and propagate absurd harm."[189] Vilifying the women most intimately involved in childcare, Sacatepéquez physicians seem to have been seeking to legitimize their own interventions in pre- and postnatal care.

While scapegoating untrained midwives adhered to a broader pattern, Sacatepéquez doctors' reluctance to blame indígenas for infant mortality is noteworthy in a nation where medical professionals regularly associated indigeneity with disease. Sacatepéquez doctors concluded that infant mortality rates were "almost equal" for indígenas and ladinos, only slightly favoring ladinos who sought medical care quickly whereas indígenas generally only did so after it was too late.[190]

Yet the hospital director who authored the 1930 study disagreed with his colleagues. In his response to the report, he insisted, "the true determinant of INFANT MORTALITY in all its manifestations is: *THE DEGENERATION OF THE RACE*."[191] Exploring the causes of what he considered their intellectual, moral, and material degeneration, he lamented that indígenas "sacrifice their well-being" and that "their children are propitious victims of any disease" who depend on "scientific means to save them." The director's medical racialization was as ill-informed as his colleagues' denigration of mothers and midwives. Without addressing the "*problema del indio*," the director argued, no scientific advances could save the nation, let alone infants. He wanted "to regenerate our impoverished race."[192]

Other authorities disregarded such racist discourse, even in indigenous regions devastated by infant mortality. When infant mortality and illness increased in Chimaltenango in June 1933, the military surgeon who coordinated the province's public health ordered water be boiled for children's consumption, prohibited consumption of unripe fruits, and "published instructions for mothers in respect to the care that must be observed in preparing children's food to prevent digestive disruption."[193] Since most infants and children were suffering from "infant cholera, acute enteritis, and wormy fevers . . . the undersigned noted for the hundredth time the pressing need in the provincial capital to provide the population good potable water since what is presently supplied could not be any worse, especially during the rainy season."[194] Instead of emphasizing ethnicity in that predominantly indigenous province, the surgeon underscored that contaminated water introduced parasites and intestinal worms that caused numerous deaths.

The Sacatepéquez physicians who disparaged midwives, however, had many allies. Guatemalan police arrested practitioners who combined brujería with midwifery, including both women and men who were brujas, curanderas, and parteras. In 1935, police arrested two women who had earned "fame on the margins of the city" as "diviners," midwives, and healers. In addition to their "home remedies . . . [and] poorly dried animal's foot," the women provided "intimate massages" and performed a witchcraft ceremony involving an ox heart.[195] Officers arrested Albertina García Revolorio, who practiced witchcraft, healing, and midwifery (figure 8) in Guatemala City in 1935. When they searched her possessions, they found a painting of a devil, cigarettes with people's names written on them, herbs and liquids of various colors, a catalog of hygienic condoms, "a notebook with instructions for married women who wanted to be butches," and abortifacients. Authorities called her "audacious and quite intelligent, though without any intellectual cultivation," suggesting at least some respect for empíricas' epistemology even while stifling its practice. Confiscated accoutrements from other midwives like a "Magical Fish" and "forceps of . . . wood for vaginal explorations" revealed supernatural and scientific syncretism in reproductive care (see figure 8).[196]

Discounting social medicine, Dr. Gaitán rejected the idea that "economic indigence caused many ills, principally infant mortality."[197] In regions without doctors, he wanted to "fight ignorance first . . . the woman who knows how to apply even the most rudimentary knowledge of hygiene with few economic

Ignorante del peligro que lo acecha.   ¿A quienes culpar?

(Véase artículo en la pág. 1.)

FIGURE 15. *"Who is at fault?"* *Revista de la Cruz Roja Guatemalteca*
15, November 1936. Courtesy of Hemeroteca Nacional de Guatemala.

resources at her disposal, it will be easy for her to take advantage of them in
defense of their health."[198] Images in Guatemalan newspapers similarly suggested women contributed to infant mortality. "Ignorant of the danger that
stalks her. Who is to blame?," asked a 1936 *Guatemalan Red Cross Magazine*
caption below an image of a cherubic white toddler descended upon by a fly
the size of her head (figure 15). With its attention to domestic hygiene, the
accompanying article indicated that mothers and other female care givers
largely determined—for better or worse—infant and child health.[199]

Despite misogyny and the vilification of midwives, they continued to be
crucial protectors of infant health. Indigenous and other unlicensed midwives maintained reputations as highly-skilled experts.[200] A few exceptions
notwithstanding—such as the 1900 conviction of an illiterate widow who

was sentenced to ten years in prison for decapitating a newborn while assisting a birth—the Guatemalan judicial record buttresses that view.[201] Called to testify about a discarded fetus in 1914, one fifty-year-old illiterate midwife insisted all the babies and mothers she had assisted were in "perfect shape."[202] Though such self-reporting is prone to hyperbole, other litigants lauded midwives. Rosa Álvarez proclaimed that Petronila de León saved her newborn grandson who was born with a bruised back and lame leg in 1915.[203]

Demonstrating the persistence of traditional knowledge in highland women's reproductive health epistemologies, the midwife de León attributed the infant's ailments to a lunar eclipse during the birth.[204] That de León expressed that view in a legal system bent on modernizing the nation suggests her confidence in her position in the pantheon of healing and the nation. When they testified in court, rural midwives often advanced traditional knowledge even when it contradicted medical science.

Judicial officials sometimes solicited unlicensed practitioners' opinions. After de León's testimony, the Chimaltenango judge requested that another comadrona empírica give an opinion. Like de León, she attributed the bruises to the lunar eclipse.[205] By requesting their expertise, justices validated untrained midwives' professions, epistemologies, and knowledge. Set against the broader criminal record in which judicial officials overwhelmingly consulted physicians, the 1914 and 1915 cases are exceptions that prove the rule: Latin American courts generally deferred to medical science and its male providers to inform judicial rulings regarding physical and mental well-being.[206] Yet traditional midwives also influenced the courts.

When they emerged in courtrooms, traditional notions of health and illness countered medical hegemony. Convinced traumatic or violent events triggered susto, Guatemalan municipal magistrates forwarded such claims to provincial judges.[207] Such was the case when Álvarez and her daughter Juana Tobar attributed her newborn's death to susto from the father threatening Tobar and the infant with a machete. "From ... susto her daughter Juana carried in her very delicate condition, the infant became ill and died," declared Álvarez.[208] Even though he ultimately found no grounds for conviction, the judge entertained that explanation of the baby's death.

Elites too consulted comadronas empíricas. A few years after Estrada Cabrera contracted those British midwives, Doña Amelia Lanuza de Samasoya requested a license for "the midwife Doña Adela de Danovan to come to the *Asilo* to verify the recovery" of Doña Magdalena Lanuza.[209] At the modern maternity ward named after the dictator's mother, at least one elite woman (as evidenced by her title) requested the services of a comadrona empírica, whom she also distinguished with title "doña." In urban and rural areas alike, the lines between traditional and scientific healthcare often blurred.[210]

In areas devoid of doctors, trained and untrained practitioners enjoyed wide latitude. "Recently a comadrona titulada has invaded the area; knowing the ingenuity of the people and the tolerance of the authorities, she has dedicated herself to curing the sick," explained a Guatemalan reporter in 1935.[211] Recognizing "the Republic did not have a sufficient number of comadronas tituladas," the government allowed comadronas empíricas to practice where there were no comadronas tituladas within a five-kilometer radius.[212] Even with that concession, however, the Guatemalan government considered comadronas empíricas to be operating illegally if they did not apply for the right to practice, pass a "theoretical exam" administered by a health technician, and register each birth.[213] Like most indigenous midwives, comadrona empírica Francisca Tacen was illiterate, so she could not read the license that conferred her state-sanctioned status. Before renewing it in 1943, the official read the formulaic warning that reminded her of the "grave responsibilities inherent in her occupation ... [and] the obligation to inform authorities in severe cases so the sick woman could be transported to a hospital or a physician's care."[214] Officials who endorsed comadronas empíricas did not concede scientific medicine's preferential status.

Even as the new democratic government increased regulation in the wake of the 1944 revolution, rural care continued largely as before because of the state's limited reach. The democratic government offered little reprieve for comadronas empíricas. The Amatitlán Hospital Director insisted they were overpaid. "The midwife salary of 40 quetzals is too much, because those we have had and have are empíricas and we are the ones who attend to patients," he argued in 1945.[215] The following year, his contemporary at the Escuintla Hospital portrayed comadronas empíricas as harmful and asked that their licenses be revoked.[216] He wanted the Dirección General de Asistencia Social to prepare "regulations for the vigilance and improvement of the techniques of comadronas empíricas."[217]

Midwives and mothers remained crucial components of infant mortality analysis and solutions. During the transition from dictatorship to democracy, Totonicapán public health official Constantino Alvarez reported, "Gastroenteritis [inflammation of the stomach] causes infant mortality, as a result of poorly regulated diet after the suppression of maternal lactation."[218]

Without explicitly scapegoating mothers, Alvarez suggested their poor diets and insufficient breastfeeding exacerbated infant mortality. He noted infants comprised most of the 433 cases and 190 deaths from gastroenteritis in the provincial capital. "The majority of deaths were not treated because no one solicited medical assistance and from that arises the high number of deaths in comparison to the cured, which were those who were attended to," he observed.[219] Alvarez insisted medical science could reduce infant mortality. To that end, Totonicapán public health officials instituted a program in 1945 "to prevent infant mortality, obligating comadronas empíricas to come to the hospital maternity ward to practice the best way to learn births, since the . . . municipality's infant mortality rate is alarming." By the end of the year, 525 infants and children had died in Totonicapán—more than three times the number of adults (170).[220] Solving the enigma of infant mortality remained elusive during democratic rule, as well.

To address the problem, Arévalo's administration established four dispensaries in Guatemala City to provide prenatal care and infant hygiene. In 1945, the dispensaries treated 75,000 mothers and infants and sent visiting nurses throughout the capital with the same goal.[221] The following year, the United Nations International Emergency Children Fund (UNICEF) established one of its first field offices in Guatemala City to help reduce infant mortality.[222]

Attention to infant mortality was bearing fruit by the late 1940s. Amatitlán enjoyed a "marked decrease" in infant mortality rates in 1949.[223] Yet some programs buckled under their own success. From December 1950 to November 1951, the Public Health Department's Maternal Hygiene Section had a physician's assistant in each dispensary and a doctor who saw patients each morning. Babies born in the nursery were sent to Healthy Child Clinics. Thereafter they hit a bottleneck at Infant Hygiene Clinics. "Each day turnout is greater and our budget does not permit us to increase personnel. . . . A good number of children are unattended because of a lack of personnel," the annual report lamented.[224] Publicity, education, and outreach had attracted more clients than dispensaries could accommodate. Archival records offer no evidence of officials articulating if or how that affected infant mortality.

As the official commitment to providing natal care expanded into rural Guatemala, trained midwives increasingly enjoyed formal positions. In 1950, the Department of Public Health and municipalities collaborated to provide "special attention" to mothers and pregnant women.[225] With a structure and goals similar to Ecuador's maternal and infant care program, municipalities paid nurses' and midwives' salaries. Whereas midwives made house calls, nurses operated dispensaries.[226] By mandating that municipalities hire midwives, the Guatemalan (and Ecuadorian) Public Health Department validated multiple forms of natal care.[227]

CONCLUSION

Absent reliable historical data on infant mortality in Guatemala and Ecuador, assessing the efficacy of government responses is difficult.[228] Even as scientific medicine's advances were undeniable, reducing infant mortality was dependent on addressing socioeconomic issues of poverty, potable water, sanitation, and hygiene. Few healthcare providers had a better perspective on those realities than midwives who routinely made house calls.

Trained midwives were the norm in each nation's capital. Through at least May 4, 1943, when President Ubico appointed América Amaya the maternity ward's head comadrona titulada, Guatemala City's general hospital had a midwife trained in obstetrics.[229] Such recognition of the legitimacy of midwifery was akin to university-educated midwives' central role in Ecuador's infant and maternal care clinics.

In the complex negotiations surrounding healthcare and public health, some authorities and medical professionals acknowledged the expertise of indigenous and other untrained midwives, many of whom adopted aspects of medical science. Guatemalan and Ecuadorian national officials knew unlicensed midwives were essential to highland communities. A growing demand for healthcare as populations increased and a scarcity of medical professionals in rural areas facilitated the persistence of indigenous and other uncertified healers in these modernizing nations. Individuals who contravened modernization—a doctor critiquing modernity, an urban doña who insisted her unlicensed midwife practice in the maternity ward, the Director of Public Health warning of mal de ojo, university-educated midwives, physicians, and public health officials endorsing empirical midwives—also facilitated empíricos' ongoing abilities to provide care. Healthcare offered a site where modernity could be contested.[230] Characterized by historical processes that shaped indigenous, Hispanic, hybrid, traditional, and scientific medicines in Guatemala and Ecuador, modernity engendered a cacophony of critiques.[231]

As evidenced by indigenous midwives who sanctioned peers for malpractice and poor patients who criticized empiricism's "grave danger," rural reproductive healthcare was policed informally. Yet women who consulted indigenous and other unlicensed midwives sharply contrasted medical professionals who attributed infant mortality to midwives' ignorance. Regardless of one's training, title, and epistemology, the ability to practice was dependent on efficacy and reputation.

More evident in natal care than other fields of medicine in Guatemala and Ecuador, hybrid healthcare permeated obstetrics. A gendered tension emerged in how male doctors, authorities, and journalists referred to obstetrics and midwifery as arts that incorporated some science, whereas male-dominated medical fields fell squarely in science's domain. In 1928, a Guatemala City government official distinguished between "medicine and other branches of the art of curing."[232] Infant and maternal care blurred those lines. Rodolfo Castello advocated practicing obstetrics "in the most scientific manner in that art" in 1942.[233] Although evidence from Ecuadorian archives is less clear, Guatemalan oral histories and archival records suggest that indigenous and other midwives welcomed rather than thwarted opportunities to cross ethnic and healthcare lines.

As natal care outreach clinics in Ecuador demonstrate, interactions between medical professionals and target populations in local contexts largely determined the efficacy of public health projects. For the Health Service, infant mortality offered a pretense for entering poor and working-class families' homes. Primarily urban middle-class women, university-trained midwives articulated problems posed by house calls, customs, and traditional healing without disrespecting the people they served, whose lives were so different from their own. Acutely aware of infant mortality and the delicate nature of giving birth, most poor (and often illiterate) women welcomed those outsiders into their lives. Tensions arose in some exchanges, but for the most part the marriage of obstetric specialists and poor mothers was conciliatory and productive. Bridging class and ethnic differences was crucial to medical efficacy and each nation's social fabric. Those fabrics were woven more strongly in Ecuador than Guatemala.

FOUR

"Malnourished, Scrawny, Emaciated Indios"

PERCEPTIONS OF INDIGENEITY, ILLNESS, AND HEALING

ALTHOUGH PUBLIC HEALTH INITIATIVES were based on science, they also reflected state politics around race, and often reinforced established tropes of indigenous inferiority. Frustrated by a December 1939 typhoid outbreak in Tocachi where the "population . . . is almost completely indigenous," the Ecuadorian health inspector Dr. Rogelio Yañez wrote: "They live reprehensibly: completely ignorant of hygiene in their houses [and] with their bodies. To this, add the bad quality of water, which is insufficient for public service, [and] a minimal economic situation. The life of the inhabitants unfolds primitively. . . . At each step one finds idiots, morons and the majority with mental deficiency that forces one to despair. This complexity will be very difficult to improve."[1] Further jeopardizing public health, he noted, the school and jail were in the same building.

Yañez was writing at the end of a tumultuous decade that saw fifteen different administrations assume power in Ecuador, all of which neglected to provide clean water, alleviate indígenas' poverty, or separate incubators of disease (schools and jails). His recognition that such conditions undermined health made his analysis more nuanced than that of many of his contemporaries, but he did not go so far as to implicate the government for facilitating, or at least failing to ameliorate, these conditions. Instead, he seemed to blame indígenas themselves. He was by no means alone. Three years earlier, another Ecuadorian official insisted the challenge of convincing "indigenous *parcialidades* [factions] to subject themselves to medical treatments: [was due to] prejudices and superstitions."[2] In fact, all across Latin America, medical professionals and authorities often attributed ill health among the poor and working classes to their alleged lack of hygiene or resistance to modernization,[3] while others recognized that poverty and other conditions beyond their control overdetermined individual health.

In impoverished Latin American nations with large indigenous populations, intersections of race and medicine were complex. RF and US public health representatives deployed medical science in Latin American nations similar to how national governments used it in indigenous communities. RF, Guatemalan, and (to a lesser extent) Ecuadorian medical professionals and officials turned to medicine to homogenize each nation.[4] The RF sought to make Guatemala safer for US investment and intervention, but congruous RF efforts in Ecuador were less pervasive.[5] Both Ecuadorian and Guatemalan politicians and economic elites argued that indigenous health was essential for economic development and national progress: capitalists depended on healthy indígenas to produce agricultural goods for export and domestic markets. Some authorities portrayed indígenas as vectors of disease, and worried about epidemics that would stunt economic development and "Human Capital," according to an Ecuadorian inspector.[6]

Conceptions of health were bound up with conceptions of the nation. For Guatemalans who encouraged indigenous assimilation, indios would never be healthy until they acculturated to ladino norms and embraced scientific medicine and hygiene. In contrast, Ecuadorians' interest in indigenous health was not contingent upon eradicating indigeneity. Even as they critiqued cultural contributors to disease such as raising guinea pigs in homes, some Ecuadorian public health agents recognized indigenous ingenuity regarding health and hygiene. In turn, RF representatives ranged from lauding indígenas and highlighting some of their hygienic customs like the sweat bath to denigrating their intelligence and healing systems. Even though US, RF, Ecuadorian, and Guatemalan officials put public health campaigns to different uses, they all used narratives of scientific medicine to modernize what they perceived to be backward, lazy subjects.[7]

Diverse approaches to healing among Guatemalan and Ecuadorian patients, practitioners, and public health officials hint at the complexity of health care provision in Latin America. While many indigenous patients embraced hybrid health care, some only turned to doctors, clinics, and hospitals as a last resort. Others avoided scientific medical care even on their deathbeds. In turn, doctors' and nurses' perceptions ranged from seeing indígenas as ignorant vectors of disease who precipitated their own demise to understanding their patients as marginalized members of society who possessed knowledge crucial to their own well-being. As was true elsewhere in Latin America, Guatemalan and Ecuadorian medical professionals had a keen awareness of ethnic differences between themselves and their patients.[8] Informed partly by national elites, officials, and medical professionals with whom they worked and socialized, RF representatives developed stronger opinions about indígenas and public health in Guatemala than in Ecuador. As such, RF officials' perceptions of indigenous salubriousness had a greater impact on Guatemalan than Ecuadorian public health initiatives.

Analyzing relations between indígenas and the state through the lens of public health campaigns reveals a complex dialectic between indigenous practices and healthcare interventions. Among indigenous populations that maintained longstanding healing traditions, the imposition of scientific medicine as normative was far from a foregone conclusion. Indigenous responses to epidemics and public health outreach varied across time and place. In both nations, indígenas resisted state-sponsored (and often imposed) public health interventions in ways that ranged from violent uprisings to flight. Their most intense responses could topple governments. Yet when public health officials approached indigenous communities and healing practices with respect, residents often acquiesced and sometimes embraced their programs. At times, indígenas invited interventions. Those varied responses shaped how contemporary medical professionals perceived indígenas. The extent to which healthcare and public health initiatives in Ecuador and Guatemala advanced, retreated, changed, and came to resemble something uniquely local was attributable to the influence of indígenas—both healthy and sick—since they far outnumbered healthcare providers and public health officials. In different ways in each nation, indígenas were crucial contributors to how public health evolved, particularly in rural areas.

RACE RELATIONS, RACISMS, AND PUBLIC HEALTH IN ECUADOR AND GUATEMALA

Traces of discourse correlating indígenas and their customs with disease date to the colonial era. As early as 1764, Ecuadorian doctor, lawyer, and writer Eugenio Espejo called pestilent fevers "*peste de los indios*" (Indians' plague). Accompanied by spots, such fevers were likely caused by smallpox or measles—diseases introduced by Europeans.[9] Colonialism's public health effects were dramatic. "Since first contact with European invaders, indigenous people on the whole have been sicker and died younger than non-indigenous inhabitants of the same colony or state," observes historian Warwick Anderson.[10] Ignoring the effects of colonial exploitation and deprivation, settler colonialists framed indígenas as perpetrators of their own ill health.

Common colonial pasts deviated as Guatemala and Ecuador charted divergent approaches to indígenas after independence. Most Guatemalan and Ecuadorian intellectuals adhered to neo-Lamarckian eugenic assertions that altering behaviors could transform society.[11] While Guatemalan and Ecuadorian intellectual elites both framed mestizaje, or racial mixing, in terms of social behaviors and culture rather than biological mixing or genetics, perceptions about how indigeneity affected mestizaje differed along national lines. Ecuadorian blanco-mestizos embraced integrating European and indigenous influences whereas Guatemalan ladinos celebrated European associations but denigrated indigeneity.[12] While blanco-mestizos generally respected indígenas, ladinos vilified them in ways that distinctly shaped public health initiatives. Whereas Guatemalan authorities and medical professionals persecuted indigenous healers, many Ecuadorian officials recognized indígenas' capability to maintain their well-being.

Interactions between authorities, medical professionals, and indigenous healers and patients differed markedly within and across Ecuador and Guatemala. If archival records are any indication, Ecuador experienced more frequent but less momentous revolts partly because some officials managed race relations in ways that encouraged indígenas to believe the public health system could facilitate their best interests even in a broader context where many authorities and blanco-mestizos exploited and abused them. Even as some Ecuadorian public health officials communicated in Kichwa, they seldom understood the panoply of indigenous worldviews, let alone their perceptions of healing and disease. Guatemalan authorities, meanwhile, tended toward more repressive and violent race relations. Many Guatemalans denigrated indígenas who engaged with public health initiatives, although a few Guatemalan doctors consulted indigenous midwives.[13]

Indigenismo—movements that advocated for indígenas but often demanded their assimilation—similarly differed along national lines, especially during the 1930s when Guatemala's steady authoritarianism contrasted Ecuador's political instability. Ecuadorian indigenistas advocated fomenting social change and appropriating state resources to improve indígenas' plight, thereby mitigating racial tensions.[14] Recognizing indígenas' socioeconomic challenges, Latin American indigenistas met in Patzcuaro, Mexico in 1940, to expand indígenas' rights, resources, and participation in their nations. Specifically, the Patzcuaro congress advocated creating national indigenous institutes to study, promote, and protect indigenous social, cultural, economic, and physical well-being, including researching indigenous medicine and nutrition.[15] Delegates stressed that economic underdevelopment, not racial inferiority, doomed indigenous health. Ecuador was one of the first nations to endorse Patzcuaro and establish an indigenous institute. By 1943, Ecuador had established the "Day of the Indian" and translated official statements into Kichwa. Indicating Ecuadorian indigenismo was more radical than Guatemala's, Ecuadorian school director Reynaldo Murgueytio suggested, "it is necessary to Indianize mestizos and whites."[16]

Although Ubico did not send official delegates to Patzcuaro, the few Guatemalans who attended returned to advocate engaging indígenas in the nation-formation process and addressing their poverty to improve their health. By 1940, some Guatemalan officials and intellectuals recognized that a lack of resources (rather than culture) undermined health. Armed with knowledge about Mayas of Quetzaltenango, Guatemalan minister José Gregorio Díaz attended the second "Day of the Indian" event on April 20, 1944. Still in the minority in the mid- to late 1940s, IING ethnographers challenged Guatemalan government discourse about biological inferiority by depicting indígenas as engaged citizens who needed resources to improve their lot.[17]

GUATEMALA: PUBLIC HEALTH CRISES AND POLITICAL CHANGE

When Guatemalan indígenas considered government healthcare interventions ineffective or counterproductive, they revolted. Indigenous outrage at the government's response to the 1837 cholera epidemic precipitated the downfall of Governor Mariano Gálvez (1831–38). As cholera devastated Mexico in 1833, the Gálvez administration quickly established sanitary quarters, opened new water supplies and sewage facilities, and prohibited burials inside churches.[18] Despite those efforts, cholera was still ravaging Guatemala by April 1837, so the government quarantined areas, tightened sanitary cordons, and expanded water treatment efforts. While those initiatives followed the logic of contemporary scientific medicine (which did not identify the causes of cholera until the 1840s), religious forces undermined them. Chafing at Liberal attacks on their institution, Catholic priests convinced their congregations that water treatments were poison. In light of the Gálvez government's encroachment on their communal land and curtailment of their political autonomy, perceptions of poisoning encouraged many indígenas to join Rafael Carrera's revolt. By 1838, Carrera had ousted Gálvez and established Conservative rule that would govern the new nation for the next forty years.[19]

Indicating how memories and oral traditions are shaped over time, looking back on the 1837 cholera outbreak through the lens of a thirty-six-year civil war (1960–96) and the genocide of the early 1980s, many Kaqchikel elders interviewed in the late 1990s framed the government's intervention in 1837 as pernicious at best. One man asserted, "With cholera, the people thought the government poisoned the water in an attempt to terminate our people. Many people died."[20] Oral traditions also underscore ethnic tensions. "Ladinos poisoned the water because they do not like us.... They do not value us. Many died from cholera, almost all the people were wiped out. The people dug a huge hole in the hills to bury the dead but no one was left to bury them," explained a Kaqchikel woman who learned history from her elders.[21] More than 150 years later, the terror of the 1837 epidemic and suspicion of state malice remained palpable in Kaqchikel oral traditions.

Some eighty years after the cholera epidemic, the influenza pandemic catalyzed another coup in Guatemala. After a severe earthquake in 1917 compromised public health, some rural indigenous communities lost 50 to 90 percent of the population to influenza the following year. Set against the backdrop of brutal authoritarian rule, influenza's decimation compelled indigenous and other Guatemalans to overthrow Estrada Cabrera's dictatorship in 1920.[22]

As the 1918–19 influenza pandemic devastated indigenous communities, Guatemalan officials, doctors, and journalists attributed the spread of disease to indigenous housing. Mariano López claimed that the "Indians' vicious customs," such as their tendency to sleep huddled together on the floor surrounded by their "secretions... have been valid factors for the rapid propagation of the disease and greatly diminishes the success that the humanitarian efforts of the government should have."[23] The *Diario de Centroamérica* concurred: "An efficacious prophylactic is absolutely necessary in the Indian housing. These dwellings are the most unhygienic that one can imagine.... What admirable land for the propagation of the bacillus that kills us!"[24] A manifestation of socioeconomic status, housing signaled inhabitants'

An Indian vapor bath

FIGURE 16. "An Indian vapor bath." Photograph by Walter Rowan, 1915. Rockefeller Foundation Photographs. Courtesy of Rockefeller Archive Center.

salubriousness for many public health officials.[25] Informed by racist assumptions that indígenas lived in filth, finqueros failed to provide humane (or any) housing,[26] which undermined indigenous migrants' health.[27]

In 1915, the aforementioned RF Guatemalan director Dr. Rowan portrayed indigenous housing—ranchitos and huts—in a less critical light and richly described aspects of their personal care.[28] Rowan noted the "Indian vapor bath" was a "very old custom among them, antedating the Spanish conquest" (figure 16).[29] Andean and Mexican indígenas similarly used sweat baths that predated European contact.[30] Rowan observed that "the dome-shaped mud bathhouse [was] used almost universally by the Indians."[31] Although he detailed how the vapor bath functioned, he betrayed no hint of his perception of its effects, offering only that "they sometimes remain in these hot baths until completely exhausted."[32] His RF contemporaries, such as W. M. Martin who insisted, "A home without a bath ... is menace to the community," regularly emphasized the importance of personal hygiene.[33] Perhaps Guatemalan elite discourse about dirty "indios" influenced Rowan's reluctance to articulate steam baths' hygienic benefits. He pointed to indígenas' healthy habits without endorsing them. Countering historians' portrayals of RF technical staff as insensitive to local culture, Rowan was a keen observer of indigenous practices.[34]

Unfortunately, Rowan's balanced assessment of indigenous life failed to sway Guatemalan authorities, who spuriously decried indigenous customs during the 1918–19 influenza epidemic. Without offering contemporary scientific evidence to support their claim, Guatemalan authorities cited the *temascal* (sweat bath, *tuj* in Kaqchikel) as a propagator of disease and outlawed its use.[35] Whether officials were unaware of the science (germ theory and bacteriology were still nascent fields) or simply allowed their prejudices to cloud their reason is difficult to discern, but banning the *tuj*, which killed syphilitic spirochetes and other microbes, contributed to the spread of disease.[36] Condemnations couched in racist tones persisted across time even as scientific advances such as bacteriology offered opportunities for Guatemalan authorities to move past their prejudices.

Revealing the persistence of long-standing hygienic and healing practices, highland indígenas consistently reestablished the *tuj* after epidemics subsided. Like Rowan and other RF representatives, indígenas recognized the vital role bathing played in maintaining good hygiene. But when influenza "dangerously returned" in El Quiche in 1933, authorities again attributed the outbreak to "the disastrous customs of the indigenous class . . . [particularly the] temascal."[37] To ensure those "very harmful customs would disappear,"[38] authorities prohibited and ordered "the destruction of . . . sweat baths."[39] Without a hint of irony, the Quiche jefe político attributed contemporaneous "epidemics that threaten collective health" to "the little attention that the indigenous race pays to hygiene."[40] Yet destroying indígenas' baths undermined indígenas' hygiene. It also eliminated the very structures where midwives and bonesetters conducted much of their healing, particularly medicinal massages.

Blaming indígenas for their ill health despite evidence to the contrary remained a cornerstone of public health discourse in Guatemala throughout the first half of the twentieth century. Contrasting the department capital's good health with rural epidemics in 1926, Sololá police impugned the region's indígenas. When the predominantly K'iche' Maya community of Nahuala lost 959 people to smallpox, the police insisted "epidemics . . . found their development in the indigenous class that is accustomed to living without any foresight."[41] To their minds, indígenas catalyzed disease. Seven years later authorities in Santa Cruz el Quiche reported, "The sanitary regulations are slowly being put into effect, which is difficult because . . . this population of a majority indigenous elements [is] devoted to their customs."[42] In his effort to "improve the orientation of residents' customs with conferences for them," the Huehuetenango jefe político concluded, "the majority are indígenas [who are] opposed to all advancements."[43]

Even early-twentieth century advocates for indigenous rights disparaged indigenous hygiene and health. Indigenista J. Fernando Juárez Muñoz decried: "The Indian is filthy."[44] Other indigenistas, like newspaper editor David Vela, attributed indigenous illnesses to their "absurd" beliefs and "lack of civilization" and hygiene.[45] Government and health officials who blamed indigenous cultural beliefs and practices for the outbreak "transformed individual bodies into natural bearers of disease."[46]

When medical and public health officials' assumptions about indigenous filth and susceptibility to disease morphed into portrayals of indigenous customs as unhealthy, Guatemalan public health mandates discounted indigenous healthcare practices and knowledge. Contravening indigenous culture and practices, Guatemalan government prohibitions of sweat baths in 1918 and 1933 undermined national efforts to improve personal hygiene. Sanitation campaigns that outlawed spitting had little knowledge of (or concern for) Guatemalan curanderos who healed and protected sick patients by cleaning them with *escupitajos* (gobs of spit) and incense.[47] Indígenas who considered blood sacred and finite resisted blood draws.[48] Guatemalan public health officials who attributed epidemics and disease outbreaks to indígenas' alleged lack of hygiene and general depravity made collaboration between indigenous communities and authorities less likely.

Yet scientific medicine had a powerful allure for many indígenas. In the 1930s, Ch'orti' Mayas attributed special powers to capsules and pills. They also believed medicines that came in bottles with labels and pictures on them had additional powers. Illiterate indígenas considered medicine that came with instructions they could not read to be particularly potent. Even though many medications were prepared with the same plant material curanderos prescribed to treat illnesses, some indígenas preferred the packaged industrialized remedy.[49]

Not all indígenas were impressed with scientific medicine, however. Mam speakers from Santiago Chimaltenango were skeptical of modern medicine and remedies they associated with ladinos.[50] Kaqchikel contemporaries from Magdalena Milpas Altas, who consumed Mejoral to treat influenza and other ailments, were critical and discontinued use of medicines they found ineffective. Informed by healing knowledge that made use of distinct herbs (with discrete physical characteristics) for specific ailments, they struggled to distinguish between different treatments for different diseases with pills that each looked alike. They encountered the same problem with injections.[51]

Constructions of Race and Indigenismo

First established by Liberal politicians in the 1880 census, Guatemalan binary notions of race pitted indios against ladinos.[52] Eschewing the term mestizo to further isolate indios, the 1893 census insisted, "The Ladinos and indios are two distinct classes; the former march ahead with hope and energy through the paths that have been laid out by progress; the latter, immovable, do not take any part in the political and intellectual life, adhering tenaciously to their old habits and customs. The indios do not participate actively in the progress of civilization."[53] Not all leaders accepted that national narrative. By abolishing forced labor and establishing the Indigenous Agricultural Institute in 1894, President José María Reyna Barrios (1892–98) hoped to "civilize indígenas ... [and] redeem the once great" Mayas.[54] Some elites too rejected that racial dichotomy. In their interlocutory role, early-twentieth-century indigenous accommodationist elites in Quetzaltenango, Tecpán, San Juan Comalapa, and elsewhere helped non-indigenous elites and medical professionals understand that indígenas—particularly those who had acculturated to some extent—were not monolithic.[55] Nonetheless, when praising indígenas, Guatemalan officials emphasized their labor and halcyon past rather than their contemporary entrepreneurial or intellectual contributions.

Guatemalan census takers distinguished between ladinos and indígenas by such cultural traits as whether individuals wore Western or hand-woven clothing, wore footwear or walked barefoot, and ate with silverware or tortillas. Ignoring genetic mixing, Guatemala encouraged assimilation through cultural changes. With the exception of Asturias' celebration of blue-eyed, brown-skinned offspring (raza mejorada) from Q'eqchi' women and German men in Alta Verapaz, most Guatemalans denied mestizaje's biological function.[56] At the same time, some elites maintained it could provide a solution: one contemporary advocated impregnating "our Indian women with Saxon semen!"[57]

At the interface of medical science and race relations, 1920s Latin American scientists and intellectuals reinterpreted deterministic ideas about social degeneration.[58] Led by Mexican and Peruvian intellectuals, Latin American nations with large indigenous populations developed different strands of indigenismo.[59] In the late 1920s, Latin American indigenistas shifted from portraying indígenas as backward to critiquing their socioeconomic challenges, such as poverty and exploitation.[60] Reflecting that shift, a few Guatemalan intellectuals (including Asturias and Vela) advocated integrating rather than acculturating indígenas.[61] Yet most Guatemalan indigenistas harkened back to a halcyon past of indigenous glory, but saw little purpose in advancing contemporary indigenous culture and healing. They lamented the misery in which indígenas lived but thought them incapable of improving their lot. Whether through miscegenation or education, they reasoned, the improvement of indigenous lives was contingent upon their acculturation.

Their perceived ownership over indígenas—"*our* Indian women"— combined with a preference for European immigrants informed the sense of superiority felt by Asturias and other intellectuals of the *Generación del 20*.[62] By the 1930s, such self-aggrandizement harbored concerns about unleashing indígenas' independent thinking and actions. Juárez Muñoz likened indigenous activism to a "disease [that] spreads through the towns and decides destinies by way of tumultuous crowds."[63] Ubico similarly portrayed certain indigenous practices—curanderismo, brujería, moonshine production—as threatening the nation even as he endorsed some indigenous traditions and customs.[64] Such circumscribed indigenismo deepened racial tensions between ladinos and indígenas when set against portrayals of the latter as drunks, criminals, and vagrants.[65] Guatemalan officials advanced what historian Nancy Stepan calls "preventive eugenics" through public health initiatives that framed indígenas as fundamentally inferior.[66]

After a broad coalition of reform-minded junior military officers, students, middle-class activists, and urban workers overthrew Ubico's dictatorship in October 1944, democracy reigned in Guatemala. Yet President Arévalo's (1945–51) promise of more egalitarian relations failed to significantly improve indígenas' lives. Indígenas' rights, access to education and healthcare, and mobility expanded little during democracy's short reign (1944–54).[67] Contentious debates surrounding Guatemala's 1945 constitution reflected racial tensions that restricted indigenous rights.[68] Despite those failings, some indígenas believed democracy improved public health. As much as officials portrayed indígenas as dirty and diseased, they cared deeply about individual and public health. When asked about Arévalo in a 1997 oral history interview, a Kaqchikel Maya raconteur recalled, "Arévalo established health and education agencies. He gave more to the people."[69]

During the 1930s and 1940s, Ubico both exploited and accommodated indígenas. To attract tourists, he invited indígenas to create model villages at national fairs in the capital where they performed traditional labor. While he celebrated their ethnicity, which included indígenas wearing their traditional dress in military parades,[70] Ubico did not want them "to consciously poison themselves with politics"[71] and insisted indígenas only understood "the law of the whip."[72] Journalists similarly dismissed indigenous intellect. In 1933, one insisted, "the indio . . . did not understand scientific reasoning."[73]

Faced with recurrent epidemics in highland communities, authorities focused on indigeneity rather than poverty or other structural causes of disease. When measles threatened Sololá in 1939, the governor blamed the outbreak on "the indigenous race due to their complete lack of cleanliness in their homes, despite the sanitary exposure that the sanitation inspector explained in all his visits to municipalities . . . among the said race . . . so they could slowly learn and put into practice the most basic rules of hygiene."[74]

Amidst elite and government discourses of dirty, diseased indígenas, other understandings of etiology emerged. Some officials who considered "natives' opposition systematic" nevertheless conceded that indigenous customs alone did not undermine health.[75] As typhus incidences increased in the early 1940s, the Ministry of Health's chief of epidemiology insisted, "In spite of all the difficulties that stall the campaign [against typhus], it intrepidly continues, the most notorious is the opposition of the indigenous race who is precisely the most attacked, for their customs, dirtiness, and the cold regions of the country where they generally live." While seeing indígenas as victims of their customs and (alleged) filth, he also recognized that geography, climate, and environment contributed to typhus outbreaks.

Often associated with ethnicity, geography and topography had public health implications. In 1933, the Huehuetenango jefe político explained the challenges of maintaining public health in his jurisdiction: "The department is vast, its means of communication are bad and the towns are distant from each other, inhabited by indígenas; the topographical conditions, inhabitants' customs, and economic situation do not allow for as active a public health campaign as one would want."[76] Further denigrating indígenas, the Huehuetenango military surgeon repeated the jefe político's report verbatim, except for substituting the derogatory term "indios" for "indígenas."[77] Even as officials broadened their explanations to include economic and environmental factors, indigeneity remained a primary cause of ill health in their discourse.

If poverty made healing hard, many authorities believed indigeneity compounded the problem. Guatemalan officials explicitly connected ethnicity and poverty. According to the Chichicastenango intendente, José Mejía and María Quino had been suffering from venereal disease for many months by January 1938 because, "as the ignorance of the indigenous class is extreme and complete, their solemn poverty has resulted in the disease taking grave characteristics."[78] He further explained how their marginalization undermined their health, "If said indigenous people were given shelter, their extreme poverty would not allow for their procuring even the most inexpensive medicine."[79] Of course, such portrayals ignored the indigenous healers and traditional medicines that indígenas could access.

As was true in Costa Rica, over the first half of the twentieth century national belonging in Guatemala was contingent upon bathing daily, using a toilet, vigilance against disease vectors and pathogens, and maintaining good health.[80] To encourage such practices, Guatemalan municipalities held contests for the oldest indio, the healthiest baby, and *indias bonitas* (pretty Indians)—all of which suggested indígenas often appeared healthy (and attractive) despite portrayals of them as filthy vectors of disease.[81] Yet even leaders who celebrated indigeneity and afforded indígenas autonomy did not envision them as modern, but rather as foils for the nation's progress. Intellectuals, authorities, and Catholic priests regularly portrayed indígenas as superstitious and ignorant.[82] In 1935, Guatemalan public health inspector Dr. Hernán Martínez Sobral depicted indígenas as "extremely superstitious" because they believed "some jade stones" could protect them from harm.[83]

So ingrained were Guatemalan perceptions of dirty, diseased indios that observations to the contrary shocked public health officials. In "San Andres Xecul—a distinctly indigenous town in the department of Totonicapán . . . I was surprised to find that the owner of the only butcher shop in town had spontaneously fulfilled [Public Health] Regulation's requirements, it was in very good hygienic condition even though no one demanded that it be . . . the town had never been inspected," noted the regional public health inspector in 1933.[84] He was not always so forthcoming, however. When he lauded Chichicastenango as a town that "satisfactorily completed [Public Health] Regulation's requirements," he omitted that it too was predominantly indigenous.[85] Populated primarily by K'iche' speakers, Almolonga similarly enjoyed good health because of the "superb quality of its waters and excellent topographical situation." The inspector failed to mention that he was describing an indigenous population among whom "longevity was not unusual."[86] Apparently water and topography trumped ethnicity when emphasizing positive outcomes.

Some public health officials endorsed educating indígenas. Dr. Martínez Sobral advocated a three-pronged approach to eradicating typhus, which had mortality rates exceeding 20 percent in 1933.[87] He envisioned an educational campaign aimed at "the indigenous masses by using cinematography and posters in a rural Maya Quiche style" (which he did not define further).[88] He also considered prophylactic and scientific campaigns crucial to his plan. To overcome "prevailing sanitation illiteracy," the Ubico administration similarly was convinced that "it was necessary to teach about a hygienic dwelling, personal hygiene, coupled with a widespread policy of using soap, nutritious … food, [and] specialized reproduction in accordance with eugenic principles."[89]

Like other Latin American eugenicists, Ubico contrasted clean, healthy, light-skinned citizens with filthy, diseased people of color.[90] In targeting indígenas, the Ubico administration adopted a eugenic lexicon that framed national inclusion in proper hygiene and good health and national exclusion in foulness and pestilence.[91] "One had to convince parents that malnourished, scrawny, emaciated indios, due to the poor hygiene in which they live, including misguided defective diets, could become strong boys and girls, archetypes of life and health, thanks to the principal elements indicated in scientific hygiene," asserted the administration in 1942.[92] The phrase "malnourished, scrawny, emaciated indios" evoked Rowan's portraits of indigenous families and children on Guatemalan fincas (figures 2, 4, 6, and 18). Yet Ubico was confident they could become excellent workers and models of good health and high energy via the knowledge and practices of scientific hygiene and medicine. His encouragement of indigenous clothing in military parades and references to eugenics and the "improved race" of Q'eqchi'-Germans conveyed mixed messages about whether the transformation of indígenas was contingent upon acculturation.[93]

Ignoring that poverty undermined indigenous hygiene and sanitation, Ubico-era officials believed information could buoy indigenous lifestyles. Sending public health officials to indigenous communities was far less expensive than investing in those communities' infrastructure, schools, marketplaces, and other facilities. After Ubico's overthrow, some officials considered education efforts fruitless. "Unfortunately, among us we should take into account the almost primordial ignorance of the majority of inhabitants, that leads them to truly oppose the observance of any prophylactic, hygienic, or treatment measure," opined a public health official in 1945.[94]

Guatemalan discourse about indigenous filth, ignorance, and resistance that framed indígenas and their customs as vectors of disease was not unique. Even among Latin American governments such as Bolivia's Movimiento Nacionalista Revolucionario that were intent on avoiding racial terms to define rural populations, medical professionals and officials claimed indígenas' "loathsome practices" spread highland diseases.[95] Racist thought blinded many Guatemalan public health officials and authorities to the beneficial aspects of indigenous hygiene practices such as the temascal. Those perceptions' persistence across dictatorial and democratic rule suggests the power of such racist discourse.

Indígenas and Scientific Medicine

Scientific advances regularly resonated with indigenous concepts. With its emphasis on eradicating microscopic pathogens in bodily fluids, bacteriology echoed indigenous and humoral notions that bodily fluids influenced health and illness.[96] Late-nineteenth and early-twentieth-century discoveries that diseases were spread by vectors—particularly mosquitos and flies—affirmed indigenous understandings of insects as carriers of disease. Among lowland Mayas, brujos sent illnesses via insects. In indigenous communities where victims protected themselves by killing insects before they could inflict harm,[97] public health campaigns to control mosquitos and flies found welcome audiences. RF teams regularly translated scientific terms to other sociocultural contexts using parables, folk tales, songs, and other genres. At times such translations contradicted scientific disease etiology.[98] After learning about germ theory in the 1930s, many Ch'orti' Mayas called germs *animalitos* (little animals).[99] Working in the Guatemalan highlands in the 1940s and 1950s, a doctor explained bacterial infections as *animalitos* to his indigenous patients to bridge scientific and indigenous notions of disease.[100]

Commonalities did not cement confidence, however. Pre-Hispanic, colonial, and republican-era Mesoamerican indígenas used the common plant *Chenopodium* (*apazotl* in Nahuatl, later Hispanicized as *apazote*) as a vermifuge to treat roundworms. When the RF adopted it for hookworm treatments in 1915, *Chenopodium* was hardly innovative for rural indígenas.[101] Because the vermifuge followed by purges of castor oil or salts so closely mirrored indigenous deworming methods, RF hookworm campaigns lost any mysteriousness scientific medicine may have evoked. Because "familiarity breeds contempt," according to RF representative in Nicaragua Daniel Molloy (1915–22), some people associated RF public health campaigns with "'quack medicine' ('*medicina de curandero*')."[102] While some Mam speakers in Santiago Chimaltenango purchased pills from Huehuetenango pharmacies, most residents "had very little faith in ladino remedies" even into the 1930s.[103]

Even as indigenous patients regularly used aspirin and other drugs,[104] scientific medicine did not eclipse indigenous understandings of illness. Many Mam speakers were convinced spirits (guardians) sent smallpox and typhus, whereas chronic diseases were punishments from God.[105] As one Ch'orti' man explained, his headache went away when he took aspirin, but unless God forgave his sins, his headache would return.[106] When medicines such as Mejoral were effective, indígenas readily consumed them, but they were quick to dismiss ineffective medications.[107] If a patient did not improve after medical treatment in Chichicastenango, family members publicly confessed their transgressions and asked for forgiveness of wrongdoings because they attributed illnesses to sins.[108] A Kaqchikel teacher recounted how her great-great-uncle struck a stone repeatedly and had his children do so before burying it, as a means of attacking her great-grandmother, who subsequently developed rheumatism in her knee and had to have bees sting her joint to combat swelling and pain.[109] Malevolence too caused illnesses.

When Guatemalan officials realized that indigenous cooperation facilitated public health campaigns, they enjoyed success. In 1945, Arévalo's government "selected personnel for a more successful [public health] campaign including a training course for indigenous interpreters known as '*principales*' to facilitate the work with indigenous masses, without causing trouble or fear among indígenas, who previously evaded sanitary efforts."[110] Arévalo sought to expand indígenas' access to medical care.[111] In addition to collaborating with indigenous leaders, public health officials discontinued measures indígenas abhorred and deployed the "new system" of applying DDT to homes, clothes, bodies, and heads "with good results."[112] The head of the epidemiology section of the Ministry of Health explained, "This insecticide has among its multiple advantages, that it can easily be applied to the indigenous race, since their principal opposition lies in their not tolerating having their hair cut or their clothing boiled."[113]

Even as the Ministry of Health recognized the importance of indigenous personnel, culture, and languages, racism persisted. To facilitate rural public health campaigns, "various natives from Huehuetenango, Totonicapán, El Quiche, and Chimaltenango, who understand and speak their dialect and the Spanish language perfectly as well as knowing how to read and write were brought" to the capital to learn about "the advantages of DDT" with Dr. Enrique Padilla.[114] Contrasting "the Spanish language" with indigenous "dialects" instead of recognizing them as languages was a manifestation of racist structures that discounted indigenous intelligence. After applying their new skills and knowledge in Sumpango and the Guatemala City Insane Asylum, "natives" were sent to their home towns to serve public health campaigns as interpreters. "With that process one can say indigenous opposition to the campaign will vanish," the chief of epidemiology predicted. Officials adhered to indigenous priorities (such as preserving the integrity of long hair and hand-woven clothes) and practices (communicating in indigenous languages) to facilitate smoother public health campaigns. Even embedded in broader contexts of racism, cultural sensitivity could advance technology, science, and medicine.

ECUADOR: ETHNICITY AND BUBONIC PLAGUE

Late nineteenth- and early-twentieth-century Ecuadorian government discourse around indígenas tacked between portraying them as backwards, inebriated, and passive and insisting their labor and economies contributed to ill health.[115] To move indígenas out of the capital, Quito's municipal council restricted cattle sales and *chicherías* (corn-beer establishments that catered to indígenas).[116] Some nineteenth-century elites considered drunkenness "innate" in indígenas.[117] To discourage intoxication, the council passed a chichería tax in 1909.[118]

Scapegoating indígenas as public health threats was part of a larger turn-of-the-century effort to shed Ecuador's reputation for poor hygiene and sanitation. To accommodate spitting—a common contemporary habit—most *salones* (meeting halls) and houses had spittoons. At the time, few homes in either Quito or Guayaquil had indoor toilets. Consequently, much waste was destined for street gullies, which during the rainy season washed out to canyons, but during the dry season created infection focal points and typhoid epidemics. In 1900, Quito established the Cuerpo de Salubridad to police public health. With mule-drawn carts, sweepers perambulated the capital to clean up trash and canals. Hygiene manuals encouraged bathing and changing underwear weekly. The latter was considered a luxury while the former was more likely along the coast than in the sierras. *Juntas de Sanidad* (Sanitation Committees) were organized in each province's capital.[119] Those efforts did little to curb associations of indígenas with filth and disease, however.

Writing to the Minister of the Interior in February 1916, one public health agent who worked in the indigenous community of Tixan explained that the bubonic plague had returned, "particularly among the indigenous class and has caused many victims . . . gravely threatening public health."[120] At a time when Ecuadorian authorities generally associated the plague with urban coastal areas (and railway cars and rats), the Tixan report preceded a shift in perceived bubonic plague demographics. In the mid- to late 1920s, Ecuadorian officials increasingly attributed bubonic plague to rural indigenous regions. During a plague outbreak in 1926, the Chimborazo health delegate insisted that "all the plague cases have occurred among indigenous people."[121]

Located in the highlands above Alausí, Tixan was one of the first highland towns where the railroad introduced infected rats that took refuge in empty crates sent back to the dairy production area of Guaytacama near Latacunga. When bubonic plague broke out in Alausí, indigenous laborers were conscripted into municipal public works to disinfect the railway station and houses. Some contracted the plague and subsequently infected their highland villages. Conscription, not culture, spread the disease.[122] "Since the time you noticed the mortality of indios . . . the number of deaths has risen rapidly," Dr. Alfonso Mosquera informed his superiors in 1929. "Danger currently exists in Latacunga," he warned.[123] Without blaming indígenas for bubonic plague, Mosquera suggested they were a threat to public health. To contain the plague the following year, the Imbabura Public Health Delegate collected fleas from "indígenas' houses."[124] Most Ecuadorian social medicine practitioners, who understood that destitution undermined health, attributed high incidences of disease among indígenas to structural determinants of poverty rather than their culture.[125]

Eschewing facile associations of indígenas with disease, Ecuadorian officials criticized local authorities who undermined public health. The mestizo Andean town of Alausí similarly struggled with regular outbreaks of the bubonic plague into the 1920s. "Almost every year the Bubonic plague appears. There is a need for perfect vigilance. [Yet] in this parish there is perfect neglect on the part of local authorities and they never concern themselves with hygiene ... they ignore political lieutenants' orders and instructions," explained regional public health officials.[126]

By the 1930s, Ecuadorian thinkers and officials downplayed racial identities.[127] Reflecting the rise of communist and socialist parties and workers' organizations in 1920s Ecuador, efforts to improve rural lives focused on class, not ethnicity.[128] Dr. Pablo Arturo Suárez, director of the Public Health Service in the late 1920s, later conducted studies of workers' living conditions, insisting, "we do not take into account ethnic issues."[129] Dr. Suárez advocated improving the customs, hygiene, nutrition, and living conditions of "campesinos" (not just indígenas), and reducing alcoholism to better the national stock.[130] In a nation that heralded mestizaje to promote national unity, indigeneity persisted mainly in the periphery.[131] Whereas Guatemalan government discourse focused on civilizing *la raza indígena*, Ecuadorian state discourse advanced a national ideology of mestizaje that emphasized improving the "*raza ecuatoriana*."[132]

Those most in need of aid were rural residents. A 1942 report about Santo Domingo de los Colorados—located 133 kilometers west of Quito in the Andes foothills—bemoaned that residents "live and die like dogs: without any help, without any attention, without any solace, in short without anything. It is truly shameful to travel the mountain and find all kinds of diseases that have victimized people. ... They don't have anything with which to defend themselves against the diseases that consume their lives."[133] In response, the Ecuadorian Director of Health lamented, "the absolute lack of resources ... makes it impossible for me to attend to them."[134]

Rural poverty notwithstanding, politics sometimes favored indígenas. Ecuadorian indigenistas' dysfunction and weakness created openings for indigenous communities to foster collaborative relations with each other, political parties, and urban workers that blunted derisive comments about indígenas and advanced economic and social justice—the effects of which were evident in the 1945 Constitution that expanded indigenous rights.[135] A pact the following year cemented the military's autonomy and guaranteed it would not be used by the state to advance oligarchic interests.[136] With its 1944 founding, the Federación Ecuatoriana de Indios consolidated various indigenous polities and thus wielded considerable power and influence as the nation embraced modernization in the 1940s. Thereafter indigenous healing, languages, and cultures became increasingly integral to Ecuador's march toward progress.

Indigenous Responses to Public Health Tensions

In contrast to public health-inspired political turmoil in Guatemala, some Ecuadorian officials strategized how to preempt and diffuse unrest. When smallpox appeared in Eastern Ecuador in 1911, public health and government officials sprang into action. Aware that news of smallpox would alarm indígenas, authorities stressed the immediate need for vaccination and a plan for treating the ill. Jefe político Rafael Aguila pleaded, "Immediately send vaccine to attend to the indígenas who are extremely alarmed with news of the smallpox invasion in this area, if it is true, . . . it would be calamitous in the East . . . given the terror that the indios have of the plague for its horrific ravages among them."[137] He explained, "I am taking measures to avert an *aborigenes* uprising . . . with promises to attend to their illness if they are attacked by it."[138] With a keen sense of local indígenas, Aguila addressed their concerns. He was quick to convey the particular parameters of smallpox among indígenas to his superiors and implore a swift response from them. That neither a revolt nor smallpox epidemic were reported thereafter suggests his strategy worked.

While a systematic public health approach to epidemics among indígenas is difficult to discern in Ecuador's archival record, Aguila's sensitivity to indigenous concerns was mirrored by other public health professionals who knew effective communication was crucial. When he traveled to Alausí in July 1928, Inspector Michelan visited people's homes "with the indio *gobernador de* Ninze, first because he is very respected among the rest of the indios and then as an interpreter."[139] If Michelan's report is any indication, employing a revered indigenous leader as an interpreter facilitated the inspector's interactions with indígenas, many of whom were otherwise "enraged" at the state of affairs and panicked about the spread of the bubonic plague.[140] Suggesting they were amenable to state-sponsored public health initiatives, some indígenas followed public health protocols for the bubonic plague.

As plague spread in Azuay province in March 1928, indigenous uprisings compelled the President of the Red Cross and other public health officials in the area to offer their services as government troops clashed with rebellious indigenous masses. "We went to the sinister place and dedicated ourselves to treating an injured man, and immediately we were brutally and savagely attacked by a great quantity of indígenas, who without giving any importance to the mission we were completing, cruelly abused us in a special manner. . . . Inspector Urbano Darque . . . putting his own life in danger, stayed by my side, running the same risk and enormous danger of being murdered by the indígenas [who were] thirsty for blood and revenge," explained one official.[141] Violent indigenous uprisings in Ecuador were rare, but officials' fear of them was palpable. If this account is any indication, some medical professionals portrayed themselves as heroic deliverers of healthcare in the face of such threats.

The constant threat of bubonic plague made *caza-ratas* (rat hunters) crucial. Because they focused on neutralizing environments and conditions that bred rats, their work often put them in conflict with residents and entrepreneurs. In his 1928 annual public health report regarding Chimborazo (in Riobamba province), the regional public health delegation director underlined "the problem of uprisings of the indios," particularly when "inspectors strictly fulfilled their duties."[142] Those working in indigenous communities had to delicately balance public health guidelines with indigenous needs, customs, and perceptions. Not everyone did.

The career of Juan Pedro Aimacana offers a window into the world of caza-ratas and their interactions with indígenas. Aimacana upset enough indígenas to suggest he veered more toward following the letter of the law than prioritizing indigenous concerns. Although his role in a 1926 indigenous uprising against health services employees is unclear, he was among the victims.[143] Seven years later Juan José Toapanta complained about Aimacana and his partner Manuel María Guamani. Their surnames suggest all three were indigenous. Since Toapanta's pig died after cutting its neck on a wire that caused "an injury that was terribly infected to the extreme, . . . the meat was dangerous to the health of anyone who eats it."[144] When Aimacana and Guamani confiscated the meat in his Guaytacama home, Toapanta was furious and wanted to recover his losses or exact "revenge."[145]

Intruding into the intimacy of indigenous homes and assessing fines vacated any good will Aimacana and Guamani may have enjoyed from their shared ethnicity with Guaytacama residents. By the time Toapanta launched another complaint a month later, it was clear he was not the only indigenous resident who despised Aimacana and Guamani. On February 8, 1933, the governor explained, "There exists rancor on the part of some Guaytacama *pobladores* [settlers] towards the public health employees, who in fulfilling their duties, monitor the cleanliness of indígenas' houses . . . and impose fines. From that the *pobladores* became enemies of the employees, that enmity reached the point whereby Aimacana and Guamani have been mistreated and faced death threats; not too long ago Aimacana was stabbed and almost killed, the trial for that crime is proceeding. Unable to kill the employees, [residents] have resorted to false accusations."[146]

His account reveals that indígenas' strategies ranged from verbal and physical abuse to turning the legal system to their own ends. Although few authorities questioned the right to violate indigenous privacy to inspect their homes, the governor's description suggests Aimacana's and Guamani's strict adherence to their duties afforded little accommodation for indigenous cultures, lifestyles, or subsistence. Evidence of authorities exploiting indígenas by charging them unwarranted fines and other improprieties abound in the archival record.[147] Already suspicious of state agents, many indígenas perceived public health officials who entered their homes as threats to their livelihoods and lives. That tension frequently fomented resistance. As such, the governor recommended that Aimacana be transferred to another region just as he had been nine years earlier when he was at the center of another indigenous uprising.[148] When relations between individual public health officials and indígenas soured, authorities relocated the former.[149] That pattern demonstrates an institutional awareness of indigenous communities' realities and reservations. On the other hand, with regular complaints about the same agent from different communities, such rotations seemed more akin to moving rather than remedying problematic employees.

Unlike in Guatemala, revolts in response to public health concerns seldom became widespread or serious enough to threaten Ecuadorian governments. That may be attributable to public health officials' ability to manage infectious-contagious disease spikes, which thus generated better Indian-state relations. Recognizing the importance of gaining their trust, some Ecuadorian medical professionals, like Dr. Pedro Zambrano, empathized with indígenas and recognized the legitimacy of their resistance to some campaigns, particularly those that cost their counterparts their lives.[150] Ecuadorian public health professionals' recognition of indigenous intelligence and rationality facilitated fruitful exchanges during public health campaigns.

In light of indígenas' constrained voices in public health archives, determining the extent to which indígenas felt threatened or valued in public health initiatives is difficult.[151] As public health inspectors, Aimacana and Guamani almost surely felt empowered by the very efforts Guaytacama indígenas like Toapanta perceived as threats. Power (and likely class) differentials trumped any empathy or understanding that may have emanated from the inspectors' and pobladores' shared ethnicity. Even public health campaigns that help people can catalyze beneficiaries' suspicions.[152] Efforts to establish the truth amidst such ambiguity reveal as much about the scholars who analyze those campaigns as the indígenas who responded to them.

Evolving Customs and Adaptable Indígenas

Early twentieth-century Ecuadorian authorities and politicians recognized the capacity of indígenas to be productive members of society without assimilation. When officials approached indígenas regarding public health issues, they generally sought changes in personal decisions or collective lifestyles to facilitate improved health, not the reformation of indigenous culture. Many Ecuadorian leaders considered indigeneity and modernization symbiotic, even if a few indigenous customs allegedly threatened public health.[153]

Indigenous and Catholic funerary traditions troubled public health officials. In 1918, Dr. Alberto Jo, the public health delegate from Cotacachi (a Kichwa town five miles northwest of Otavalo) felt one such custom was "undoubtedly damning public health: in the entrance of churches [there are] cadavers, mainly of indígenas, who many times are in a state of putrefaction without a moratorium bed, barely wrapped in a sheet."[154] He asked that such customs be "decisively prohibited" by enforcing the sanitary code.[155] Although the response to Dr. Jo's request is lost, other regions outlawed wakes in indigenous communities.

Into the 1930s, indigenous funerary practices continued to concern authorities.[156] PASB doctor John Long attributed the 1930 spread of bubonic plague to indigenous wakes during which "participants drink large quantities of *chicha* [corn beer], become intoxicated, and fall asleep on the floor of the *choza*. As this harbors infected fleas, the Indians are infected or carry back to their dwellings infected fleas, leading to a new outbreak of the disease."[157] Indígenas often handled, washed, and even caressed cadavers. Rather than burning the deceased's clothing, as Long and other public health experts advised, indígenas often redistributed it.[158] Long warned that such practices spread disease, particularly when indígenas returned to their communities after attending the funeral of an infectious indígena in another community.

Complementing efforts to reform customs, focusing on indigenous hygiene was part of a broader change in the 1920s as Ecuadorian public health officials downplayed the importance of public works projects to improve sanitation and emphasized eliminating "bad habits" to prevent contagion.[159] The state's priority shifted "from an effort to change the environment in which people lived to a concern with changing how people lived in that environment," explains Clark.[160] In a thinly veiled accusation that indigenous women were vectors of disease, the 1926 "Special Regulation Regarding the Provision and Sale of Milk" stipulated that "to obtain corresponding permission, every female vendor should abandon . . . clothing of *centro y mantas de bayeta* [cloth blankets]."[161] Another regulation outlawed "*follon* [a gathered skirt] *o mantas de bayeta y bayetilla*."[162] Assimilationist in nature, both mandates prohibited clothing traditionally worn by indigenous women. Similar provisions were passed for the sale of meat, groceries, and other foodstuffs.[163] Portrayals of insalubrious indígenas persisted in highland Ecuadorian markets where indigenous vendors were regularly accused of undermining public health. Because they prepared food and worked in public markets, indigenous women often were under more scrutiny than their male counterparts.

Campaigns to exclude indigenous female vendors from public markets were accompanied by attempts to curtail indigenous domesticity. Public health officials (including Dr. Suárez) targeted *cuyes* (guinea pigs)—a significant source of indígenas' protein and component of indigenous healing and other cultural practices—as disease vectors because they carried fleas. Their subsistence threatened, indígenas resisted cuy eradication campaigns, which dated to the early twentieth century.[164] Public health officials and authorities who simultaneously sought to reform the home and marginalize women who left it to work reveal how public health practices were bound up in ideas about decency, honor, gender, and race.

Ecuadorian officials also emphasized the role housing played in public health. In 1927, housing was a focal point of Dr. Suárez's instructions for curbing bubonic plague. He sought to prevent indígenas from sleeping on floors where they were susceptible to flea and rat bites and to remove cuy corrals from "sleeping quarters . . . so that there is less promiscuity between man and these rodents, who . . . serve as a means of contagion."[165] To entice residents, he offered one- or two-sucre stipends to build raised sleeping platforms.[166] Suárez also provided architectural specifications for huts which were cost-prohibitive for most rural Ecuadorians. When Sanidad destroyed plague victims' dwellings, it sometimes financed their reconstruction.[167]

In addition to housing, diets captured Ecuadorian public health officials' attention. Reporting from Sigchos, Latacunga in 1933, Dr. Terán noted, "The straw shelters [are] anti-hygienic and small, with characteristics of indigenous shelters. . . . The food is insufficient and [has] little variety, cereals, barley, corn and zest, they drink little milk and consume almost no meat."[168] Some eight years later, conditions had improved little, according to indigenista

Victor Gabriel Garcés.[169] While a lack of hygiene and poor diets made indígenas susceptible to disease, Terán also considered their culture and knowledge problematic. "My labor has been . . . arduous, I have had to fight many prejudices," he explained, referring to indigenous worldviews and healthcare practices.[170]

Whereas Guatemalan officials generally perceived indigenous hygiene as static, Ecuadorian officials recognized that indigenous habits evolved. By the late 1920s, some authorities marveled at indígenas' ability to adapt to the state's public health guidelines. With thirty to forty deaths having already occurred before the public health official arrived in Alausí on July 22, 1928, the plague set off a "true panic among poor people."[171] Eager to share how people responded, Inspector Oc. Michelan confessed, "It is not possible to remain silent when my impressions are so strong. . . . One indígena burned his hut together with the cadaver of his son and daughter-in-law and once they were consumed in the fire and bright sparks, he looked for the ashes of the remains of them both. He found the bones and then he fit them very deeply in the same land and buried them and finished saying: 'That is for the best.'"[172] Informed by broader public health campaigns that advocated destroying structures deemed public health threats, the indígena prioritized protecting himself and neighbors from contagion. Sacrificing his home for the greater good speaks volumes about his public health commitment. Given indígenas' funerary rituals, cremating his loved ones was also a significant sacrifice with equally altruistic motives. Far from foils to medical modernity, indígenas were perfectly capable of embracing public health practices distinct from their own.

When communities and individuals altered their customs in favor of public health concerns, authorities delighted. In his 1934 report to the Otavalo municipal council, regional health inspector Dr. J. M. Espinosa explained that Ecuadorian inspectors were working hard to improve urban, domestic, and food hygiene and "fight against infectious-contagious diseases."[173] It was not simply inspectors' vigilance that increased the reporting incidence of such diseases, however. "I dare say, residents' habits and customs have changed, as they form and develop a sanitary conscience," he boasted. Espinosa was particularly proud that "the health labor was reaching even indigenous sections where one no longer looks upon health work with mistrust but rather to their liking." Suggesting a broader trend of changing customs in Imbabura's towns, Espinosa submitted an almost identical report to the Cotacachi municipal council. Ecuadorian indígenas particularly understood how individual and collective health shaped community and social welfare.[174]

Some indígenas traveled great distances to access scientific medicine. In 1942, the sublieutenant of Military Health Services in northwest Ecuador, Gonzalo Fabara, observed that "Sometimes people come from very far away knowing that there is someone who can treat their illnesses. They are very poor, they do not have [resources] to acquire medicines."[175] Fabara continued, "It is necessary to medically attend to the *colonos* [tenant farmers] of this region.... Due to the climate and conditions of the environment, they are almost all frequently ill ... indígenas."

In turn, Ecuadorian healthcare professionals recognized indígenas were crucial to national development and well-being. In an August 27, 1945, radio address about health, nurse Luila López de Paz called attention to indígenas' health and encouraged their integration into the nation's healthcare system. "The health of the indio is the soul of the nation, we must help one another for the general well-being," she said.[176] She implored indígenas "to come to the office, it is yours, the government is giving you the tools your community needs ... they are your rights that you will demand."[177] Even before Kichwas and other Ecuadorian indígenas received national citizenship, López de Paz used the language of rights to summon what scholars such as Alex Nading have referred to as "health citizenship" that "entails the enumeration of health needs to which governments must respond."[178] Far from expecting assimilation, López de Paz enticed indígenas to use government resources as their own. She affirmed their rights as health citizens and encouraged them to use Ministry of Health clinics. Assimilationist aspects of health clinics whereby the state advanced scientific medicine and other manifestations of its brand of modernization notwithstanding, López de Paz primarily wanted indígenas to be healthy, not to become blanco-mestizos.

Even as she recognized Ecuador's shortcomings, López de Paz's goals were lofty. "We don't have even one remedy of the Health offices in more civilized countries, [but] we do not lack the yearning or desire of health from living hygienically and sharing healthful hands.... In that way we can repeat what Hippocrates said: 'healthy mind in a healthy body.'"[179] By moving forward from healthcare origins that traced back to Hippocrates, López de Paz conveyed a shared cumulative experience of healthcare and healing. Whether her indigenous listeners would have been enticed or alienated by such references is difficult to discern.

Despite outreach to encourage indígenas' engagement with state-sanctioned medicine, portrayals of insalubrious indígenas persisted. Concerns about vendors' products often had racist overtones. "We have

FIGURE 17. Ecuadorian milk vendor at Latacunga train station, November 1945. Courtesy of Museo de Medicina.

observed that indígenas from the east of Pasto sell *Guayusa* (traditional Amazonian tea) leaves, rosewood, *sima-yuca*, and other vegetable and animal products of questionable origin," asserted Dr. Alvear in 1945.[180] He claimed indigenous vendors were selling products that "introduced . . . sanitary problems and no benefit." Dr. Alvear, and his counterparts in Quito who prohibited the sale of such goods, worried their unhygienic condition could compound consumers' already compromised health (figure 17). Instead of inspecting each indigenous vendor's products, some officials targeted them as a group based on assumptions of indigenous insalubriousness. Such medical and marketplace racialization impinged upon vendors' livelihoods and healers' practices.

CONCLUSION

Ethnicity, poverty, and rurality all shape people's access to healthcare. That is as true today as it was in early-twentieth-century Guatemala and Ecuador. "Indigenous communities continue to have worse health outcomes than those of other ethnicities in Ecuador and across Latin America. These differences seem to be deeply rooted in socio-historical contingencies such as isolation, gender, racism and poverty," noted Ecuadorian public health expert Estefanía Bautista-Valarezo and her colleagues in a 2020 study of indigenous Ecuadorians' concepts about health and illness.[181] This and previous chapters have demonstrated as much for the first half of the twentieth century. Poverty undermined people's capacity to maintain good health, particularly where potable water, sewers, waste treatment, and other sanitary measures were absent. Overcrowded in deteriorating homes made from cane or straw, indígenas struggled to keep their bodies healthy.

Public health and medical professionals in Ecuador and Guatemala sought to stamp indigenous bodies and culture with scientific medicine as part of larger projects of integration and assimilation, and in the process, they often advanced ugly stereotypes about indigenous biology and culture.[182] Racism seemed to blind officials to beneficial aspects of indigenous hygiene practices and obfuscated their path toward improved public health. In Guatemala, officials and authorities pathologized indígenas as vectors of disease and claimed their customs undermined public health. In contrast, some Ecuadorian medical professionals, like López de Paz, advanced public health without scapegoating indígenas or their customs. Even Ecuadorian public health officials who alleged indigenous funerary rituals spread disease did not demand assimilation, but rather the cessation of just those rituals. That response facilitated a more collective approach to maintaining the nation's and its residents' well-being than in Guatemala, where health officials and authorities seemed intent upon demonstrating that indigeneity itself undermined public health.

Since the RF had a greater and more sustained role in Guatemala than Ecuador, foundation representatives' disparaging attitudes towards indígenas had more power in the former than the latter. With his extended stay in Guatemala and observance of indigenous people, Dr. Rowan recognized their potential (and heralded their halcyon past) even while documenting the crushing poverty, malnutrition, and disease that marked their plight. In descriptions of deprivation that hint at social medicine analysis, he raised points that contradicted Guatemalan professionals' insistence that ethnicity undermined indigenous salubriousness. On the eve of the 1918–19 influenza epidemic, when Guatemalan officials blamed indigenous sweat baths for the spread of disease, Rowan described those hygienic structures but refrained from praising them the way he did other aspects of indigenous realities. His frank assessment of some aspects of indígenas' lives and reluctance to opine about others suggests a dialectical tension between US-based RF representatives and Guatemalan medical professionals and elites.

Efforts to advance modern scientific medicine in nations with large indigenous populations were fraught with contradictions. Allocation of limited public health resources in both nations prioritized nonindigenous urban residents. As such, the combination of indigeneity and rurality all but guaranteed that states left indígenas to their own devices—some of which authorities accused of spreading disease to mask larger socioeconomic conditions that undermined rural indigenous health. As Palmer asserts, "To be pathologized can also imply inclusion."[183] The extent to which authorities and public health officials disparaged and abandoned indigenous and rural health speaks to the marginalization of indígenas. With its recognition of mestizaje and history of negotiating with indígenas, Ecuador encouraged indigenous participation in public health campaigns. In contrast, Guatemalan binary notions of race that pitted indios against ladinos bled into public health campaigns that portrayed indigenous customs and practices as vectors of disease rather than bulwarks of mental and physical health. Ecuadorian officials facilitated a more welcoming environment for indígenas but a less welcoming one for RF representatives than their Guatemalan counterparts. Yet as Ecuadorian inspector Aimacana's experiences intimate, respecting indigeneity did not necessarily mitigate tensions between public health inspectors and indígenas. Neither Guatemalan nor Ecuadorian indígenas doubted their right to healthcare or public health initiatives, but they faced different challenges in convincing others of their worth and medical citizenship.

FIVE

Infectious Indígenas

THE ETHNICITY OF HIGHLAND DISEASES

"THE ILLNESS OF THE INDÍGENAS in this zone is typhoid," explained Ecuadorian Dr. J. M. Espinosa on June 8, 1936.[1] So many people had succumbed to it that he planned to rent a truck to transport them to the Hospital in Ibarra and vaccinate "the indígenas against typhoid."[2] His portrayal of typhoid as an indigenous disease resonates with the broader archival record in both Guatemala and Ecuador.[3] Public health officials regularly related typhoid and typhus to indigenous living conditions and customs. Few of his compatriots or Guatemalan counterparts were as proactive as Dr. Espinosa, but most agreed with his assessment that typhoid was a serious public health threat among indígenas.

A few years later Guatemalan doctor Carlos Catalán Prem published a history of typhus in Chimaltenango province that similarly associated that disease with indígenas. Between 1912 and 1940, Tecpán, Comalapa, Patzicía and other Kaqchikel towns were among the most adversely affected by typhus. "Almost all of the province has paid tribute to [typhus], more than anything the indigenous class; the Ladinos of a different cultural level understand much better what hygiene means," he noted.[4] Like his predecessors and contemporaries, Dr. Catalán Prem portrayed indígenas as unhygienic contributors to epidemics. His Ecuadorian counterpart Dr. E. Salazar Pazmino also associated typhus with indigeneity when he classified a 1945 outbreak at Hacienda Zumbahua as "typhus of the indigenous race."[5] Framing typhus as indigenous perpetuated notions that indígenas were vectors of disease, which marginalized their positions, mobility, and autonomy. Public health officials like Salazar Pazmino and Catalán Prem considered indígenas incapable of maintaining their health. Deployed by blanco-mestizos and ladinos to distinguish themselves from their indigenous counterparts, such associations were part of larger popular discourses disparaging indígenas, as the previous chapter demonstrates.

Betraying racist thought, many Guatemalan and Ecuadorian medical professionals and officials attributed high incidences of typhus and typhoid among indígenas to culture rather than to structural determinants of abject poverty. Once they reified associations of indigeneity with typhus and typhoid, causal relationships between race and disease were difficult to extirpate. As much as medical science, race shaped how physicians and public health officials approached infectious-contagious diseases and indígenas who contracted them. Even officials who noted indígenas' impoverished and unsanitary living conditions called for cultural rather than structural change. By emphasizing indígenas' alleged unhygienic practices as catalysts of disease, officials deflected attention from the massive land ownership inequalities in the Guatemalan and Ecuadorian highlands that circumscribed indígenas' access to wealth and the sanitation infrastructure, such as piped water and sewer systems, so crucial to good health.

Such medical racialization undermined public health initiatives by foreclosing indigenous participation in them. In contrast, when public health officials communicated in indigenous languages, acknowledged indigenous healing knowledge and practices, or simply conveyed respect rather than denigration, public health campaigns often enjoyed efficacy. By the 1940s, public health officials and departments in both nations recognized that multilingual materials mattered. Building on the rich historiography that uses race to complicate and enrich histories of medicine and public health, this chapter demonstrates how racial categories intersected with identities of class and nation to influence healthcare systems and the people who were employed and served by them.

Although medical racialization had strong roots, a few officials deployed class rather than race to frame public health analysis. When in 1917 the Guatemalan Minister of Health attributed various infectious diseases, such as malaria, typhus, typhoid, and influenza, to heavy rains, he quickly sent "extraordinary doctors and sufficient medicine to attack those ills and prevent their propagation principally among the proletarian class, which is the one that suffers most in these cases."[6] Although unaware that heavy rains would not have contributed to typhoid, typhus, or influenza, the Minister resisted pathologizing indigeneity, unlike many of his contemporaries and successors.

Even as understandings of disease etiology sharpened over time, racial scapegoating persisted. In truth, neither trend was linear. Well after the

Ecuadorian government began vaccinating people against smallpox, Sigchos indígenas practiced arm to arm smallpox inoculation in their remote community.[7] Similarly, by the 1920s medical professionals understood that lice propagated typhus, yet in 1933 the Guatemalan Minister of Health was still attributing it to high altitudes and indigeneity.[8] Knowledge frequently was imperfect. Some contemporary Guatemalan medical professionals incorrectly claimed flies could spread typhoid at least a decade after most of their counterparts had identified contaminated water as the culprit. Guatemalan officials who recognized potable water could reduce typhoid mitigated racist scapegoating. Yet well into the 1940s, knowledge about the connection between lice and typhus often precipitated pathologizing indígenas for their alleged lack of hygiene. Disparaging indígenas persisted throughout early-twentieth-century medical science's fits, starts, setbacks, and advances.

Often confused during the colonial and early national periods, typhoid and typhus are distinct diseases caused by different types of bacteria. Similar in symptoms and causes, both diseases were classified as typhus or *tabardillo* until the 1830s. Into the twentieth century, Latin American medical professionals continued to confuse typhus and typhoid. Both diseases can be prevented through good hygiene, sanitation, and potable water.[9]

Typhoid is caused by ingesting drink (most often water) or food contaminated with human feces and the bacterium *Salmonella typhi*. Severe sewerage system shortcomings and little access to potable water led to epidemics. The disease was slow to develop; symptoms included coughing, headaches, digestive disturbances, and physical weakness. In 1880, German scientists Carl Eberth and Edwin Klebs identified the typhoid bacillus. Some sixteen years later in 1896, Fernand Widal discovered that most people developed O and H antibodies to *Salmonella typhi*, which informed his diagnostic test for the disease. Contemporaneously, British scientist Almroth Wright developed a typhoid vaccine. By 1916, the US army deployed the typhoid vaccine because it afforded temporary immunity. The vaccine doubled as treatment prior to 1948, when doctors and scientists discovered that the antibiotic chloramphenicol dramatically reduced mortality.[10] Injected once or twice a day until the fever subsided, the vaccine initially increased the patient's body temperature and often caused a painful local reaction. Those side effects compelled some patients to request treatment cessation. Although many Andean indígenas initially evaded vaccination, after realizing its benefits, some early twentieth-century highland parents requested their children be inoculated.[11]

Like typhoid, typhus is enabled by poverty and poor sanitation. Spread by the *Pediculus humanus* louse that lives and lays eggs in clothing and hair that maintain body warmth, typhus occurs in cold, dry climates where bathing is infrequent. Typhus generally broke out during seasonal droughts that created conditions favorable to louse populations. Another casual factor was overcrowded dwellings with multiple people sleeping together, of the type Guatemalan and Ecuadorian officials associated with indigenous housing. Feasting on human blood, louse nymphs take two weeks to become adult lice and excrete the *Rickettsia prowazekii* micro-organism, halfway between a virus and bacteria, that irritated the skin, which induced itching that allowed the micro-organism to enter the body. Some five to fifteen days after infection, the skin rashes which inspired typhus's classification as *tifus exantemático* appeared on patients who also experienced headaches, body aches, prostration, fever, and chills. Victims who contracted meningoencephalitis from typhus could be incapacitated or die. In crowded marketplaces and religious ceremonies (such as wakes and funerals), lice (and thus typhus) could spread quickly among people.[12]

Focusing on typhus and typhoid reveals fault lines between race, public health, and national development. In both countries, associating indígenas with typhoid or typhus stigmatized them as disease carriers, thereby diverting attention from each government's inability to improve rural health.[13] Although racism permeated relations from the highest levels of government and society to the most marginalized populations in each country, Ecuador's strands of discrimination were less virulent than Guatemala's blatant bigotry. Whereas race relations in Ecuador allowed for cracks in the public health system through which indígenas could slip to advance their own interests on their own terms, most privileged Guatemalans refused to recognize indígenas as anything beyond ignorant, inebriated laborers, which made for some chilling interactions with medical professionals.

Archival evidence of the perceived ethnicity and geography of typhus and typhoid demonstrates how disease was racialized. Triggered by unsanitary living conditions, in Guatemala and Ecuador both diseases often were associated with mountainous villages where indígenas predominated. Neither disease depended on elevation, but both were common in high altitudes. While public health campaigns against tropical diseases provided ample opportunities for engagement with foreign actors, few were interested in typhus and typhoid. Informed by assumptions about infected indígenas and diseased landscapes, these stigmas influenced the tenor and effectiveness of public health campaigns.

LEVERAGING TYPHOID AND TYPHUS IN ECUADOR

Although the mortality rate was low, Ecuador struggled to combat typhoid in the late nineteenth and early twentieth centuries. In 1913, Dr. Carlos A. Miño fought typhoid with Quito's Servicio de Sanidad Subdirección office. Only 0.03 percent of Quito's approximately 80,000 residents died from typhoid.[14] It was more common and lethal in Guayaquil where it represented one of every twenty deaths.[15] When the White Company excavated parts of Guayaquil to lay potable water infrastructure in 1915, it unearthed "bacillary flora deposited in the layers of soil, where the residents dispose of their feces and all manner of waste."[16] A typhoid outbreak soon followed, demonstrating how efforts to improve public health could backfire.

As tempting as scapegoating indígenas for typhoid was in the early twentieth century, some Ecuadorian officials emphasized socioeconomics. When seven cases of typhoid emerged in Puembo in 1914, Dr. Nicolás Baca, Miño's assistant at Quito's Servicio de Sanidad Subdirección office, observed, "All of the sick belong to the indigent class and for that reason need free assistance from a physician, with the indispensable elements for a reasonable recovery."[17] His recognition that poverty undermined health and healing was part of Ecuador's burgeoning social medicine movement that encouraged nuanced and sympathetic perspectives on indígenas and their culture and healing practices.

Because typhoid spread easily, identifying its origins was crucial to public health responses. Reluctant to associate poor hygiene and sanitation with their communities, some authorities claimed the disease was exogenous. Dr. Baca reported, "the fever has been imported by a person who contracted the fever in Pifo."[18] Four years later, Otavalo suffered from typhoid that local officials insisted arrived via commerce with Quito and its indigenous neighborhood of Cotocollao. They explained that since "the majority of people did not have any custom of cleanliness, it is very just to assume they can bring us new cases."[19] That officials from a town with a significant indigenous presence cast aspersions on an indigenous community in the capital suggests some rural leaders deployed discourses of anti-hygienic indígenas to distinguish some indigenous populations from others. Perhaps aware that public health officials from the capital and elsewhere assumed Otavalo indígenas were dirty and unsanitary, Otavalo officials externalized the origins of a disease associated with poor sanitation, hygiene, and indigeneity.

Portrayals of indígenas undermining public health notwithstanding, state institutions often infringed on indígenas' well-being. "A true focal point of infection," the overcrowded Sangolquí jail (outside of Quito) was one such place.[20] The majority of "unhappy indios" were held in two small rooms without ventilation or windows. "At times they were not allowed to leave to satisfy their needs, turning it into a pigsty," an August 29, 1918 report noted. "We do not look after the hygiene of the population, leaving behind humanitarian sentiments for which we are all responsible," chided the author, who insisted the *chuqueros* (uneducated officials) who ran the jail were a greater threat to public health than indigenous prisoners. Tight sleeping and living quarters made jails incubators of disease; authorities' neglect made them death chambers. After contracting typhoid, one prisoner was sent to a Quito hospital where he died.[21] Instead of blaming indigeneity for typhoid, the author suggested the jail's living conditions had catalyzed the indigenous prisoner's demise. Perhaps incarceration's setting compelled the author to decouple disease from ethnicity. Few other scenarios could so starkly shift the balance of typhoid's etiology from ethnicity to hygiene and sanitation.

Assertions that indigenous customs threatened public health often were as much about self-perception as ethnic differences, as a 1918 complaint about indigenous funeral processions demonstrates. "The custom of the indígenas is to take a break where *aguardiente* is sold, staying there for more than an hour during each break, which makes the current location of the cemetery [on the outskirts of town] extremely dangerous," a few Quito residents warned.[22] At a time when typhoid was ravaging the capital and "we contemplate the daily disappearance of our family members, friends, and acquaintances that fall under the claws of that terrible disease," the petitioners asked that the cemetery be moved "alongside or behind the parish church," to minimize processions and thereby reduce exposure to infectious corpses and inebriated indígenas.[23]

Their request was part of a long historical debate about the location of cemeteries and cadavers. Informed by the miasma paradigm that proposed decomposing corpses and other decaying organic matter poisoned the atmosphere by emitting foul vapors that generated infectious diseases, colonial officials had prohibited burials in churches and mandated that cemeteries be located far from populated areas. As the colonial era and learned medicine progressed, authorities increasingly positioned cemeteries closer to town centers.[24] By the first half of the nineteenth century, churches again hosted cemeteries, as was the desire of these early-twentieth-century Quiteños, who lent urgency to their request by framing it in the broader context of a typhoid epidemic.

In addition to distinguishing their drinking habits from those of indígenas, the blanco-mestizo petitioners pointed to geographical and class distinctions between those living in urban centers and the peripheries. They described themselves as "a handful of citizens who have the same privileges and rights as those who have the good fortune to live in the center of the capital . . . and are carrying out the unbreakable good energy of a patriot."[25] During the first half of the twentieth century, many remote working-class districts felt marginalized from cosmopolitan urban areas.[26] By the 1930s real estate speculation allowed elites to inhabit Quito's most desirable sections (in the center and north of the city).[27] After appealing to notions of justice and nationalism, the petitioners made a personal plea: "Save us, Dr. Miño, and our gratitude will know no limits in the annals of our lives. Save us! And see that our request is not impossible. Save us and we will pronounce your name with religious respect and eternal GRATITUDE."[28] What began as a public health complaint about indigenous customs and the spread of typhoid culminated in a thinly-veiled attempt to gain respect and equal access to resources. Indigenous insalubriousness was a common trope to attract authorities' attention. Absent Dr. Miño's response, assessing that strategy's efficacy is difficult, though petitions such as this likely encouraged city officials to expand drainage to marginalized neighborhoods in 1924 and 1925.[29]

Public Health Campaigns in Highland Ecuador

Sparse finances regularly curtailed state efforts to tackle individual diseases and broader public health concerns related to them. Lotteries helped to raise money for hospitals and public health institutions,[30] but governments often wasted scarce resources.[31]

Without a budget, Dr. Miño observed, Ecuadorian municipalities could not proactively prevent epidemics. If "a scourge appears," Miño warned in February 1914, my office "does not have a single cent in the treasury . . . to combat it."[32] The National Treasury had given the Quito Servicio de Sanidad Subdirección office only six hundred and some odd sucres—an "insignificant sum, that has not been used except to pay day laborers and buy indispensable material for sanitary work." Dr. Miño's office only worked "on a small scale" because they had purchased disinfection materials on credit, but their creditors were demanding payment. Protesting meager funding a few years later, Director of Public Health Dr. León Becerra threatened to resign in 1921 (he unexpectedly died before he could).[33] Public health officials repeatedly complained that they lacked the resources and funding to anticipate and address public health threats.[34]

Miserly budgets disrupted continuity and undermined confidence in the nation's health services, which in turn restricted subordinate institutions' ability to respond to disease outbreaks. Filling the void left by skeletal national health offices, municipalities coordinated and sponsored public health campaigns, inspecting markets, collecting garbage, and installing sewerage and potable water systems. Not until 1926 did the Ecuadorian Public Health Office gain centralized control over municipal public health issues. That did not secure stability, however, as the rapid turnover of Ecuadorian Directors of Health thereafter (three in 1933 alone!) attested.[35] Since few medical professionals ventured beyond municipalities, public health campaigns were intermittent at best in rural areas.[36]

Absent state resources, indígenas engineered their own public health initiatives. Such was the case with Sigchos indígenas who practiced arm to arm "smallpox inoculation as a traditional custom" (as analyzed in chapter 2) as late as 1930.[37] Whereas local officials often panicked, Sigchos indígenas devised ways to maintain their well-being when faced with incompetent or inadequate government responses to epidemics.

In May 1930, typhoid was devastating Sigchos. "I have not received any help to date for the health of this town that finds itself seriously threatened," the local *teniente político* complained on May 10th.[38] Assigned to address the epidemic in Sigchos, the regional public health official Dr. R. Jeráud concluded that typhoid would claim "many victims, taking into account the manner of living, customs, etc. of the people who live in that territory."[39] That he could so quickly dismiss the capabilities of people who coordinated their own public health campaigns suggests his counterpart's report about Sigchos indígenas' smallpox inoculations did little to change the minds of prejudicial colleagues. Indeed, Dr. Jeráud intended to vaccinate Sigchos residents against smallpox while he coordinated the anti-typhoid campaign.[40]

Even as he disparaged indígenas' alleged "manner of living, customs, etc.," Dr. Jeráud's professional integrity was compromised. On May 19, he postponed his trip because he was not feeling well and needed to finish a monthly report that was overdue to Dr. Miño—lest his superior interpret Jeráud's tardiness "as negligence."[41] Three days later Jeráud decided to "suspend the trip to Sigchos until he could arrange a substitute for his post ... and my health improves."[42]

Over the next three months, typhoid wreaked havoc in Sigchos. On August 20, a local leader decried: "There are various cases of typhoid, resulting in calamity in many homes. One cannot combat this plague, leaving so many sick."[43] The ill outnumbered the healthy. On September 6, public health workers finally arrived with two gallons of Kreso to disinfect houses. Quarantining the sick proved more challenging. "Moving the *tíficos* to the Latacunga Lazareto [quarantine station] is very difficult because the distance between the towns is great and the road rough. In this case, it is better to set up a pest house here," explained a public health official.[44] With those interventions, the crisis subsided.

As important as the public health department's belated assistance was, Sigchos residents were instrumental in halting the epidemic. On October 11, Franciso Arrieta reported, "The state of the epidemic in Sigchos is in much better condition, thanks to the aid offered by the Health [department], through the Mobile Inspector and the resolute support of the community's residents."[45] Disproving Dr. Jeráud and other officials who dismissed indigenous public health measures, Sigchos indígenas facilitated their community's recovery. A long history of neglect and intermittent and often delayed assistance compelled Sigchos indígenas to rely on themselves. Their tradition of smallpox inoculation was but one manifestation of that self-determination and preservation. Their mobilization to stem a typhoid epidemic was another.

As health inspectors increasingly fanned out to rural communities to address epidemics and improve sanitation, they developed closer relationships with indígenas, who began to accept care in clinics and hospitals. In 1928, a Tixan health inspector noted indígenas "naturally resist taking those sick with infectious-contagious diseases to the department health clinic."[46] But by the early 1930s, President Ayora Cueva's efforts to extend Servicio de Sanidad offerings to rural areas were bearing fruit. Working in Otavalo and Cotacachi in 1934, Dr. Espinosa observed, "Effortlessly, one can move typhoid patients to the isolation ward in the Ibarra Hospital."[47] Buoying indígenas' confidence, none of those admitted to the hospital died from typhoid. Increased hospital use was part of a larger pattern whereby indígenas gravitated toward rather than avoided scientific medicine, which Dr.

Espinosa attributed to "health deputy inspectors, who do their work in accordance with the police, teachers, and priests ... [for] the towns' health."[48]

When health inspectors enforced mandates that contravened indigenous customs, however, indigenous acquiescence was not always forthcoming. Adhering to their funerary rituals, indígenas defied Imbabura province's prohibition of wakes.[49] In turn, officials like Dr. Espinosa identified indigenous communities as disease propagators. Because typhoid cases increased "sporadically in indigenous villages that were the origins of epidemic outbreaks of that disease," 1933 "was very difficult" in Cotacachi, he explained.[50] A concurrent typhoid epidemic in nearby Otavalo had similarly "alarming characteristics."[51] By pointing to the propensity for typhoid in highland indigenous communities, Espinosa was neither blaming them for that fate nor claiming only indígenas could contract it. Such observations more likely reflected reality than racism.

In response to those epidemics, Dr. Espinosa recommended constructing cemeteries in indigenous neighborhoods so cadavers could be buried a few hours after death. He wanted to achieve two goals: "First, to prevent wakes, origins of typhoid epidemic outbreaks, and second to prevent the danger of infection of city residents when decomposing cadavers, deceased from infectious-contagious diseases, are carried through the streets ... in coffins that are not hermetically sealed."[52]

It is unlikely that wakes contributed significantly to typhoid infection among those attending. Since typhoid largely has a fecal-oral transmission route, the extent to which wakes could spread disease depended on how much people ate and drank at them (and who prepared the food and drinks). Whether or not Espinosa and the aforementioned petitioners scapegoated indigenous wakes for that reason is unclear, but their observations and complaints speak to a longer tradition of blaming transmission on a fetishized differentiation of funerary rites. To marginalize certain groups, officials and neighbors portrayed their rituals as barbaric and attributed their illnesses to spending too much time with corpses.

According to Espinosa, implementing reforms aimed at arresting contagious diseases contributed to healthier communities the following year, when neither Otavalo nor Cotacachi had typhoid outbreaks.[53] When four people contracted and one died from typhoid in June 1936, public health officials again prevented "the customary wake among the indígenas."[54] Improved relations between public health officials and indígenas facilitated negotiations over such traditions, which indígenas sometimes altered or suppressed but seldom extirpated.

Although they fell under the National Funerary Society (Sociedad Funeraria Nacional), which included private tax-paying companies, nonindigenous funerals and wakes did not differ significantly from indigenous practices.[55] Recognizing that grieving families were ill-equipped to adhere to public health regulations around their deceased loves ones, Dr. Miño asked the President of the National Funerary Society to ensure his members and employees maintained public health measures related to cadavers.[56] In rural parishes, funerary regulations had little sway. Dr. Becerra insisted authorities "extirpate the ill-fated and uncivil custom to conserve cadavers for more than 24 hours in homes, as a pretext for immoral and anti-hygienic orgies."[57]

Although Becerra did not conflate offending wakes with indigenous customs, his colleague Dr. Miño sometimes did. "Today I saw a cadaver in an almost open casket, completely nude and carried by two indígenas for a wake in a private home," Dr. Miño exclaimed a few months earlier.[58] Even as the indigenous wake disturbed him, he was "horrified to see the desecration of the cadaver." Apparently, the *anfiteatro* (dissection hall) porter had delivered the cadaver "just as he had found it on the dissection table." In an observation that further revealed his prejudices, Dr. Miño concluded that is how "one sees cadavers in savage *pueblos*."[59]

Whether informed by racist thought or not, Ecuadorian public health officials continued identifying indigenous wakes as typhoid propagators. When the Guaranda Hospital housed twenty typhoid cases in 1939, public health officials warned about an epidemic. Arguing that wakes jeopardized public health, the Guaranda public health inspector explained, "Indígenas are accustomed to holding a wake with cadavers for more than two days and in most cases . . . without knowing the cause of death." He implored his superiors to "urgently order severe prohibitions and employ effective measures to banish those customs."[60] Rather than exclude indígenas, such prohibitions (forcefully) included them.

When authorities enforced lifestyle changes, rural residents sometimes circumvented them. After Ecuadorian Inspector Viteri banned domestic guinea pigs and *chancos* in 1939, he noticed most animals had disappeared. Then he realized, "Some people adopted a defense mechanism . . . whereby they moved the animals outside the city during the day and brought them back during the night—animals damaging to hygiene—many houses keep doing it."[61] In another indication of how indígenas thwarted the state's aspirations, people hid the infirm from authorities. Such was the case in 1939, in Tocachi.[62] By the end of Ecuador's tumultuous political decade, Dr. Espinosa's observation of increased hospital use did not hold throughout the region. Like scientific medicine, indígenas' hospital use was not a linear ascent.

Many public health officials considered attempts to change indigenous lifestyles ephemeral. In 1943, the director of the campaign against bubonic plague Cornelio Sáenz Vera characterized indígenas as "a population completely lacking in the most elemental norms of hygiene, who live in the most complete filth and the most frightening promiscuity with all kinds of animals."[63] He was buoyed by the campaigns' progress but pessimistic about long-term success, noting, "I think that we have improved hygiene considerably, but given the nature of the indigenous population, I doubt very much that these good customs will be conserved when we cannot continue exercising the strict monitoring we have applied during the current year, during which we made 189,048 house visits." Even when indígenas embraced learned medicine, public health officials assumed they perpetuated their own demise.

Typhus and Indígenas in the Andes

Ecuadorian authorities also associated typhus with indígenas. In his 1931 state of health report, General Director of Public Health Dr. Mosquera noted that public health was generally satisfactory "except for frequent outbreaks of typhus in the indigenous population."[64] By contrasting an otherwise healthy nation with regular attacks of typhus among indígenas, Mosquera portrayed them as the source of the nation's ills. Indígenas' aversion to medical care fueled impressions that they exacerbated epidemics. Notified he would be transported to the hospital on October 27, 1931, an "indio" who had contracted typhus hid in "una chichera."[65] Generally portrayed as "dens of corruption and vice where la raza india degenerates"[66] and diseases flourished in malnourished, inebriated bodies, chicherías were considered public health threats. Although health inspectors eventually located him, they noted that "resistance and a tendency to hide sick people" pervaded the indigenous population.[67] Some Ecuadorian indígenas resisted hospital care even when they were deathly ill. Coupled with concerns about indigenous wakes, infectious indígenas who refused medical care were particularly problematic for public health officials.

Into the 1940s, Ecuadorian officials continued to racialize typhus. When it erupted "with very alarming characteristics . . . in Caserio Yuracrucito very close to the city" in 1942, an official lamented, "Not one of those affected survived. In less than a month, fifteen people died, infecting the indígenas from Yuracruz Grands."[68] Desperate for "funds, medicine, and specialized personnel to attend to the sick and avert this terrible scourge that proliferates in Ibarra," he heralded the municipality's previous public health campaigns and emphasized that government aid was crucial for Ibarra, "the residents of which are justifiably alarmed because of the appearance of that lethal pestilence." Officials who assumed indígenas were particularly vulnerable to contagion insisted immediate action was critical "to prevent the propagation of typhus." Unfortunately, no archival evidence of a response surfaced, but the broader archival record suggests deploying images of indígenas on the cusp of contagion was a powerful trope that regularly elicited swift action.

Informed by racialized medicine, public health officials targeted indígenas for typhus education outreach. Even when delivered in indigenous languages, health information was often laden with biases and stereotypes. Recall Dr. Enrique Garcés's speech about typhus in Kichwa when he visited his birthplace Otavalo on June 10, 1945, noted in the introduction to this book: "In your language . . . I come again to teach you how you should live and how you can guard against this illness that is in your land."[69] Assuming indígenas distrusted scientific medicine, Garcés deployed several arguments to change their thinking. Asking them to consider evidence, he insisted, "You have seen how many sick people I have sent to Ibarra where they get well." He also shared a cautionary tale: "Recently I heard that an indígena from this area, having returned healthy from Ibarra, once again [fell ill] because he lived in the same filth, without listening to what I have told you to kill lice and wash clothes; he has died, as you well know." In addition to evidence and anecdotes, Garcés used the legal system to motivate conformity: "The law imposes a strong sanction" against anyone who does not report typhus in their home. As he tacked between coercion and cooptation, he offered them a vaccine "that has worms that attack typhus."[70] By depicting the vaccine as "worms," he encouraged indígenas to associate scientific conceptions of disease with their notions that the natural world was integral to healing.[71]

Beyond conveying information in Kichwa and conjuring images of the natural world—typhus in the land and healing worms—Garcés exhibited little cultural or economic sensitivity. Aware many indígenas raised guinea pigs, he advised their removal from domestic courtyards because they had fleas. Both species carried typhus.[72] He insisted livestock be kept far from courtyards. Such mandates could be difficult to implement in poor households that lacked space to raise animals beyond the family compound. In what must surely have been the most insulting assertion in a speech filled with offensive comments, he implored: "do not eat lice because you will get sick."[73] Although his contemporaries similarly critiqued indígenas' consumption habits and alleged predilection for insects—Sáenz Vera decried indígenas' "repugnant customs of consuming dead animals they encounter and chewing ticks and fleas"[74]—Garcés misunderstood that indigenous practice. Indígenas bit lice to kill, not to consume them. Indigenista art and literature regularly presented indígenas killing lice by biting them.[75] Ever patronizing, Garcés concluded, "Do not forget what I told you, wash well [and] sweep your homes. . . . If you want, I can come back to speak with you again."[76] The lack of an invitation thereafter suggests his message was not well received.

Officials' assumptions about indigenous culture, lifestyles, and behavior shaped public health policies and initiatives. Garcés was both a keen observer of indigenous realities and ignorant of their healthcare practices and knowledge—a counterproductive combination. By couching important information about typhus and the role of medical science and hospitals within patronizing portrayals of ignorant, dirty indígenas, Garcés failed to gain the trust, let alone interest, of Kichwas he hoped to sway by speaking in their language.

As flawed as his speech was, Dr. Garcés demonstrated his and the Ecuadorian public health office's commitment to communication through indigenous languages. One Ecuadorian public health official prided herself on understanding "indigenous psychology."[77] Many Ecuadorian medical authorities recognized the important role indigenous culture, language, and epistemologies could play in public health campaigns.

THE ETHNICITY OF TYPHOID AND TYPHUS IN GUATEMALA

The beginnings of associating typhoid with indigeneity in Guatemala can be discerned in Mirano B. Padilla Matute's 1865 study of typhoid. Although the causes of typhoid were as of yet undetermined, "age, change in climate, and customs have been considered underlying" factors for the disease associated with "the *campo* [countryside], exposure to cold and hot, extreme vicissitudes, strong moral impressions, etc." he argued.[78] Locating the disease in

FIGURE 18. "El tambor—subject with severe case of hookworm, dirt-eater." Photograph by Walter Rowan, 1915. Rockefeller Foundation Photographs. Courtesy of Rockefeller Archive Center.

rural areas—the campo—Padilla Matute introduced the idea that customs and morals played a role without naming indígenas. When fourteen patients at the Guatemala City General Hospital died of typhoid in 1888, hospital officials neglected to note their ethnicity.[79] Apparently Liberal attempts to portray Guatemala as a nation divided between indios and ladinos in the 1881 census had not yet shaped medical observations. By the turn of the century, however, some Guatemalan authorities explicitly identified indigenous customs, lifestyles, and ignorance with the propagation of typhoid.

Informed by Guatemalan elites' prejudices and their own biases, foreign healthcare interlopers similarly disparaged indígenas. Referencing geophagy (a condition most common among rural poor pregnant women and children) whereby individuals eat earth (especially chalk or clay) in response to iron deficiencies, RF representative Rowan dubbed some indigenous subjects "dirt-eaters" (figure 18).[80] RF officers often equated disease with filth.[81] Primed by US Anglo elites' racist perceptions of their southern neighbors,

RF representatives absorbed Guatemalan elite portrayals of indígenas as being diseased and dirty.[82] Conveyed by such high-level authorities as PASB director and USPHS Surgeon General Hugh Cumming (1920–47), a distrust of social medicine among US public health officials resonated with Guatemalan medical professionals.

Facilitated by ladino and Creole denigration of indígenas, corvée labor could catalyze typhoid. Such was the case when Guatemalan authorities drained Lake Quinizilapa in 1927. Conscripted to dig trenches and construct canals, migrant workers contracted typhoid and other diseases.[83] "Indios from neighboring towns and even from the department of Chimaltenango come to consume energy and lose their health in that work," reported a journalist.[84] Yet authorities were suspicious of ill workers. When Gabino Siquinajay got sick while working at the lake, the Chimaltenango governor asked his Sacatepéquez counterpart to investigate the veracity of the claim.[85]

When causation was obscure, Guatemalan authorities blamed indígenas. When thirty-four people died of typhoid fever in Totonicapán in 1933, the jefe político attributed their demise "to the neglect among families for the recovery of the infirm, whether for a lack of resources or because they did not submit to treatment at the appropriate time."[86] Like many of his contemporaries who advanced medical racialization rather than social medicine, he betrayed racist thought by highlighting their poverty, but insisting their neglect and ignorance precipitated fatalities.[87]

When typhoid broke out in nonindigenous regions and towns, however, authorities embraced explanations that avoided ethnicity. In 1929, typhoid epidemics hit Sacatepéquez, Quetzaltenango, Suchitepéquez, Retalhulew, and San Marcos. All were combated with containment measures and the Mulford vaccine. Only in the non-indigenous areas of Retalhulew and Mazatenango did typhoid persist, but those reports largely ignored ethnicity.[88] Officials only rarely maligned ladino or Creole hygiene and health.

By the late 1920s, Guatemalan authorities recognized that vaccination and potable water were crucial to curtailing typhoid. But "where it [vaccination] is not obligatory and sanitary awareness still is not thoroughly developed . . . [those places] require a quick solution to the problem of potable water, which avoids not only the transmission of that type of infection but many other dangerous consequences for individual and collective health."[89] Without extensive vaccination in 1929, potable water became the focal point of anti-typhoid campaigns. In 1930, when typhoid was the fourth most commonly contracted disease, the Minister of Health encouraged authorities to distribute vaccines widely to "obtain the greatest number of immunizations" because "the preventive antityphoid vaccine has indisputable value."[90] By 1933, local authorities distributed typhoid vaccine in such indigenous towns as Santa Apolonia and Tecpán where typhoid was common.[91]

During Ubico's dictatorship, the Guatemalan public health department and rural populace were steadily gaining ground against typhoid. In 1933, the government formalized its campaign against "transmissible diseases" such as typhoid and typhus by passing an agreement that laid out the public health strategy: vaccination, isolating (and quarantining if necessary) the sick, killing insects and rats, purifying water, and distributing certificates of good health.[92] The campaign was successful. Treating a growing population, the incidences of typhoid per 100,000 inhabitants decreased from a high of 23.5 in 1935 (and 23.3 in 1930) to a low of 5.3 in 1939 (and 6.7 in 1940).[93] The average incidence decreased by half from 16.7 from 1930–1935 to 8.1 from 1936–1940.[94] Such successes built on the glowing public health reputation Ubico earned by combating yellow fever as a governor and public health official in the late 1910s and early 1920s. Public health gains were crucial to his rule.

As knowledge of typhoid etiology evolved and responses became more efficacious, racist portrayals of indígenas receded. In the 1930s, Guatemalan medical professionals claimed flies could spread typhoid.[95] By the 1940s, they understood contaminated water was the primary culprit. When typhoid struck Guatemala in 1941, the chief epidemiologist noted that most victims were in the capital even though typhoid also struck the indigenous departments of Sacatepéquez, Totonicapán, and Quetzaltenango.[96] Within a few years, officials attributed increasing typhoid cases in the capital to the "water of public consumption" lacking chlorine.[97] Working with PAHO, officials arranged to have chlorine immediately flown from Washington to Guatemala City to disinfect water supplies. Even though it was "truly flattering the percent by which the disease [typhoid] had diminished in the last three years," Mazatenango Health Department director Dr. Ramón Rivadeneira insisted, "the cause persists . . . the waters today are the same as always."[98] He continued, "The rare cases that present themselves during the rainy season appear with first-time visitors to the area and the reason is they lack vaccination."[99] Without indígenas to scapegoat, contaminated water and excessive rainfall emerged as causes of typhoid. The first cause was accurate; the second was not. While scientific medical advances sometimes reinforced racial thought, progress against typhoid diminished disparaging depictions of indígenas.

Throughout the 1940s, typhoid vaccination programs continued in highland Guatemala.[100] In 1945, Sololá officials vaccinated against typhus and typhoid, isolated the sick, surveilled public water sources to prevent typhoid, and administered *piojocida* (lice poison) to students to reduce typhus.[101] Often identified as disease propagators, highland schools and their students and teachers were monitored by authorities. Vaccination campaigns via schools and other public institutions were effective. Despite rumors to the contrary, "not even a single true outbreak" occurred in 1945, the Minister of Health's chief epidemiologist boasted.[102]

Indicating that medicine became less racialized as diseases diminished, the minister ignored ethnicity and attributed the campaign's shortcomings to medical professionals. It "was not possible to develop a systematized and perfectly organized campaign owing to the doctors who do not report the cases that they know about."[103] In light of such omissions, he proposed requiring doctors to report all cases of transmissible diseases. "Without a perfect notification system, this department finds it impossible to work effectively," he lamented.[104] Medical professionals and technology, not indígenas, were the problem.

Typhus

Typhus figured prominently in postcolonial Guatemala's first efforts to establish a public health office. Founded in 1906, the Primer Consejo Superior de Salubridad Pública (First Supreme Council of Public Health) named a medical commission to address typhus epidemics. Indigenous resistance would not have surprised commission members.[105] According to the 1893 census, "Indios do not advance as rapidly as the whites or Ladinos. . . . The efforts of the government to instill into the indios new customs, showing them new paths to success, have been met with but little reward, due to their systematic ways and unchangeable proclivities and ideas."[106] As stereotypical as that portrayal was, the author recognized nuances within the indigenous population. "This condition of affairs does not exist amongst the entire Indian population. Those who have been thrown in direct contact with active society develop an astonishing amount of energy which is not noted at a superficial examination of the race; this activity and intelligence is more remarkable amongst the women," he continued.[107] His attention to indigenous women's talents notwithstanding, he assumed indígenas would reject scientific medicine, suggesting rural public health campaigns would fail. Yet even when indigenous disease etiology differed from scientific medicine—Mam Mayas in Santiago Chimaltenango, for example, believed *guardians* (spirits) sent typhus—they did not necessarily reject public health campaigns.[108]

Throughout the early 1900s, typhus threatened populations in Europe and the Americas. Western Guatemalan highland residents regularly contracted typhus.[109] When typhus erupted in the Kaqchikel towns of San Andres Itzapa and Patzún in 1915, Drs. Catalán Prem and Federico Azpuru España quickly deployed a control plan that included disinfection. Their efforts staved off an epidemic, but Minister of Health J. M. Reina Andrada emphasized that "superb hygienic conditions in almost all of the country" were crucial to prevent epidemics.[110] The following year typhus erupted across the Atlantic. Three million typhus deaths in Eastern Europe and Russia between 1916 and 1920 spurred the League of Nations to establish its Health Organization.[111]

By the 1920s, Guatemalan public health officials focused on lice as the key to curtailing typhus. In 1923, the government established an Office of Disinfection in Chimaltenango (a predominantly Kaqchikel province) "to eradicate white lice, the transmitting agent of typhus."[112] Although a 1928 public health department publication insisted, "Science has demonstrated ... that TYPHUS (not to be confused with Typhoid fever) IS SOLELY AND EXCLUSIVELY TRANSMITTED BY LICE,"[113] fleas too transmitted it.[114] "Where there are no lice, there is no typhus. A typhus patient without lice is not contagious," public health officials argued.[115] Simply put, "The fight against typhus has been reduced to a fight against lice and against those who have lice." Without explicitly identifying indígenas, this publication suggested their role in contagion by emphasizing the disease was common *"among dirty and abandoned people* in some populations that can constitute the point of departure for major propagations if they disregard sanitation authorities' prophylactic prescriptions." That description reflected derogatory discourse about indígenas.

Calling on "all citizens, even those who consider themselves free from" typhus, the publication insisted the disease was "very easy to prevent by just obeying the most basic hygiene principles and personal cleanliness."[116] The authors asserted typhus "is a disease that should not endure in cultured nations, which is precisely why it should be definitively banished from our country." After subtly scapegoating indígenas, the authors maligned mothers whose children contracted and transmitted lice "to the mother and then because she does not know to destroy the nits, it turns into a family plague."

According to nonindigenous elite men, typhus was a disease of class, gender, and (less explicitly) ethnicity. Public health officials tailored narratives of typhus to reinforce (or obscure) hierarchies of power.

When typhus broke out in the ladino city of Tejutal (San Marcos) in 1933, "Superior Authorities" sent medicines and a police force to "maintain discipline during the three-month epidemic" and used "scientific order" to establish the cause of the epidemic.[117] Dealing with a ladino population, public health officials emphasized "poverty, hardship, and murkiness of homes" instead of ethnicity. Whether those particular public health officials were more inclined to adhere to scientific explanations or simply could not deploy an argument about ethnicity absent an indigenous population is unclear. Yet the same officials showed sensitivity to indigenous culture when typhus broke out in the *aldea* of Chiquilaja (Quetzaltenango). When they discovered students with lice, they ordered their heads shaved, "conceding to the girls a period of three days to delouse" since cutting females' hair would have been experienced as an attack on indigenous culture. Devoid of racist portrayals of indígenas, the two-pronged approach snuffed out typhus shortly thereafter.

Authorities and public health officials noted intersections of ethnicity and geography of typhus. In 1933, the Guatemalan Minister of Health observed that typhus outbreaks occurred primarily in the predominantly indigenous highland departments of San Marcos, Sacatepéquez, Quetzaltenango, and Chimaltenango.[118] "In Chimaltenango, for its highland climates and mountain ranges populated mostly by indios, one saw the threat of sporadic outbreaks of typhus," he asserted.[119] Apparently ignorant of contemporary typhus etiology, the Minister of Health incorrectly attributed typhus to high altitudes and indigeneity rather than lice, which was exacerbated by drought, poverty, and poor sanitation. The Kaqchikel towns of Tecpán, Patzicía, and Santa Apolonia all had typhus cases throughout the year.[120] In Patzicía, victims were immediately isolated in a provisional hospital or interred outside of town, salvageable clothes were boiled while the rest were incinerated, and sulfur was applied in homes.[121] With close economic and social relations, indigenous towns sometimes spread typhus from one to another. In April 1933, two cases in Tecpán "were imported from Patzún."[122] In other indigenous highland departments such as Totonicapán, El Quiche, and Huehuetenango where "populations separated by great distances, made them relatively unharmed by epidemic invasions, there were only a few sporadic cases of typhus," the minister noted.[123] When typhus "seriously threatened" municipal capitals or other densely populated towns, authorities "immediately install[ed] a *lazareto*."[124]

Lazaretos, or isolation facilities, did not necessarily provide better care or succor than families did. When twenty-seven people contracted typhus in Quetzaltenango in 1933, patients were attended to in their homes with "truly appropriate conditions ... good ventilation and hygiene."[125] In contrast, the lazareto was "little more than a locale where the sick are not well cared for." Governor Carlos Enrique insisted, "Without a doubt people can recover in their homes under the watchfulness of the municipal doctor and military surgeon."[126]

Two years later, however, Dr. Francisco Quintana insisted recovery in rural houses in Huehuetenango was impossible. After thirty people died of typhus, Dr. Quintana visited the sick in their homes, "going down and over deep valleys and hills, convincing myself that there was no hygiene, inhabitants' extreme poverty and the distance between the sick made combating the epidemic in patients' homes useless."[127] He quickly opened a lazareto and accepted twelve patients; shortly thereafter it housed thirty-three people and the epidemic subsided. "Before being hospitalized, the sick were subjected to a 'toilet,'" insisted Dr. Quintana, so he ordered clothes boiled and furniture and houses fumigated and washed.[128] Since only two patients perished, the mortality rate (6 percent) was low for typhus. To his mind, lazaretos provided better care and more quickly arrested typhus epidemics than remote poverty-stricken families could. Although the "deep valleys and hills" were populated primarily by indígenas, Dr. Quintana grounded his argument in class and geography rather than ethnicity.

Some lazaretos were focal points of contagion. When the head of the Tecana lazareto Dr. Agusto Gonzales was struck by a "great desire to return quickly to the capital" in 1933, he released thirty-nine typhus patients isolated there.[129] "That act was completely negative because it delayed the elimination of the disease that spreads in those villages," warned the San Marcos governor.[130] Among other effects was a 15 percent mortality rate.[131]

To lower mortality rates, Guatemalan doctors experimented with vaccines. (An effective typhus vaccine remains elusive.) Dr. José Bernard y Sarti developed a serum that reduced the mortality rate in San Pedro Sacatepéquez from 18.95 percent in 1934 to 9.16 percent the following year. Of the 130 people who contracted typhus, only 12 died. Only 13 of the 825 people who were vaccinated contracted the disease. Dr. Bernard y Sarti concluded that the serum "protected individuals against infection and in cases where protection was not absolute, the disease evolved benignly."[132]

Highland officials who racialized typhus were hypervigilant about it.[133] When typhus broke out around Lake Atitlán in the indigenous communities of Santa Lucía Utatlán and San Pablo la Laguna in 1939, Guatemalan public health officials' quick response averted an epidemic. They emphasized, however, that typhus, measles, and other contagious diseases remained a threat because indígenas had poor hygiene habits.[134] "The indigenous race does not observe any cleanliness in their homes, despite the verbal dissemination the inspector provides in his visits ... among the said race and by order of this office, so that slowly they will learn and put in practice the most basic regulations about hygiene," noted the Department's Director of Public Health.[135] Such allegations of indigenous filth contradict contemporary ethnographic studies that portray indigenous homes as clean and indígenas as regular bathers attuned to personal hygiene. State efforts to prohibit and destroy sweat baths similarly suggest authorities' ignorance of (or biases against) indigenous hygiene.

Even when typhus declined in indigenous regions and spiked in nonindigenous areas, associations of indígenas with typhus were difficult to extirpate. Director of field work Dr. Julio Roberto Herrera reported that typhus cases and deaths diminished in 1940, with "possibly a few in Alta Verapaz where since the last epidemic of 1917 a few epidemic outbreaks have been observed."[136] At times typhus attacked lowland fincas. When families from San Juan Sacatepéquez visited workers at finca El Zapote and finca El Naranjo, typhus erupted there.[137] Despite those counterexamples, old tropes died hard. In 1941, the head of the Guatemalan Ministry of Health's Epidemiology department insisted typhus "is a difficult disease to eradicate among us because the indígena maintains unharmed one of the principal factors of transmission (lice) with their dirty habits and opposition to all hygiene measures."[138]

Although it is difficult to discern the reach of his influence, in July 1944 the public health official and author Dr. Epaminondas Quintana criticized the Guatemalan government for blaming indígenas for their health problems. Presented at the University of California, Berkeley, his report on Central American sanitary conditions was later published in Guatemala.[139] Suggesting his sway, by the mid 1940s, medical professionals increasingly highlighted geography and climate rather than indigeneity. When public health officials initially identified a typhus epidemic in the Guatemala City Insane Asylum in April 1944, they attributed the "invasion of typhus in the capital" to "the flood of a great number of people from the departments."[140]

The disease was spreading at an "extraordinarily rapid rate by virtue of disastrous hygienic conditions of the ill, who enter in an indescribable state of filth."[141] Such language resonated with that used to portray indígenas as dirty and diseased, but Dr. Miguel Molina emphasized geography rather than ethnicity in his report in the waning days of the Ubico dictatorship. The shift away from pathologizing indígenas continued into the democratic regimes. "Typhus exantematico has been one of the scourges that causes more mortality in the cold zone of the Republic (Occidental)," explained Public Health Director Dr. Roberto Candana Lacape in 1951.[142] Rather than associating the western highlands with indígenas, he attributed typhus fatalities to the cold climate.

Similarly averting references to ethnicity in the predominantly indigenous province of Huehuetenango, officials recognized the anti-typhus campaign faltered because of the "scarcity of personnel and considerable distance between villages."[143] After dismissing the physician's assistant in charge of the campaign, Dr. Isidro Cabrera went to Huehuetenango to fire other personnel. When Cabrera reorganized the campaign, typhus incidents decreased.[144] In 1945, Huehuetenango had 377 cases of typhus and 78 deaths compared to 110 cases of typhoid and 43 deaths.[145] While nationally typhus cases increased from 2144 to 2834 between 1944 and 1945, the mortality rate decreased from 381 to 323 during that period.[146] Although it is difficult to trace their direct impact, PAHO also developed programs to fight typhus in the 1940s.[147]

Even as some Guatemalan officials skirted associations of ethnicity and typhus, others continued to emphasize indigeneity, suggesting the limited reach of Dr. Quintana's views.[148] In 1944, the Ministry of Health's chief epidemiologist reported, "Rickettsiosis [typhus group] has remained endemic in the Republic in the cold regions of the country, principally in the zones where the indigenous race predominates, for that reason it boldly endures: [they] hide the sick, oppose fumigation of those who have come in contact with them, and in general they make very difficult the arduous struggle undertaken and maintained to eradicate this disease."[149] Even as he recognized cold temperatures as incubators of typhus, the epidemiologist insisted that indígenas undermined anti-typhus campaigns. Although the Public Health department seldom provided statistics that tracked ethnicity, in 1944 they noted that 1015 "indios" and 174 ladinos contracted typhus.[150] Without any context (the department also reported 2144 cases of typhus, with 381 deaths, in 1944, nearly double the 1189 cases that "indios" and ladinos comprised for the year), those numbers confirmed officials' claims that indígenas were more susceptible to typhus than other Guatemalans, even though the demographic preponderance of indígenas may have accounted for the statistical disparity.

When typhus outbreaks occurred among predominantly ladino populations, ethnicity seldom appeared in public health narratives. Shortly after authorities in the Jalapa *aldea* (village) of El Paraiso reported a typhus outbreak in January 1944, special brigades arrived to combat it. As in indigenous communities, Flores (Jalapa) municipal officials created a lazareto for typhus patients and a "disinfection room" to treat the clothes of those suspected of having typhus. Authorities applied lice poison to municipal school students instead of shaving their heads like officials did with indigenous boys.[151] When typhus concurrently broke out in the capital, officials established quarantines. Annexed to the General Hospital, the Insane Asylum had a high-mortality typhus epidemic. Public health officials promptly disinfected and quarantined both institutions. Despite those efforts, 198 patients contracted typhus, 63 of whom died during the forty-day epidemic.[152]

With their long-standing relationship with residents, empíricos had developed a level of trust and familiarity that advanced anti-typhus campaigns and counteracted tendencies to hide the sick. In Totonicapán and other rural Guatemalan departments short on medical professionals, empíricos were crucial to controlling typhus. In 1944, "the system of municipal empíricos" in the department capital, where an empírico worked in each canton, "contributed greatly to locating and treating those sick with typhus."[153]

The following year, the new democratic administration's public health department created a division to fight typhus with an eye toward engaging indígenas in its campaigns. The 1947 decree mandating Cox typhus vaccination in the highlands conveyed the democratic government's commitment to highland health. In truth, brigades sent to fumigate people, homes, and clothes with DDT to kill lice that spread typhus likely had a greater impact than the Cox vaccine. By sending Kaqchikel and other indigenous intermediaries to explain the vaccine, the Arévalo administration convinced many indígenas to comply voluntarily.[154] Collaboration with instead of accusations against indígenas boosted public health campaigns.

Language, Dialects, and Portrayals of Indigenous Intellect

To reach rural monolingual indigenous language speakers, astute public health officials adapted modes and means of communication. On fincas where indigenous laborers spoke distinct languages, RF officers used illustrations to convey hookworm eradication programs.[155] Dr. Juan Funes, a Guatemalan recipient of an USPHS fellowship, advocated using indigenous languages in public health campaigns at a time when the democratic administration of Arévalo (and later Jacobo Arbenz Guzmán [1951–54]) was developing literacy materials in indigenous languages.[156] Kaqchikel oral histories recall that residents appreciated public health officials' efforts to educate them about typhus in Kaqchikel during Arévalo's regime. Some elders' memories so associated anti-typhus campaigns with the democratic government that they claimed Arévalo had visited their homes to talk about typhus.[157] Regardless of the veracity of that claim, Arévalo convincingly communicated through indigenous brokers and languages the need and means to eliminate typhus.

In 1943, Dr. Epaminondas Quintana proposed creating anti-typhus education materials in the four most widely spoken indigenous languages: Kiche', Kaqchikel, Mam, and Q'eqchi'. Insisting posters and records were the "most appropriate means to achieve indigenous comprehension . . . of contagion," he explained, "the efficacy of flyers is nonexistent because the majority are illiterate."[158] Neither radio programs nor movies were effective because rural areas lacked electricity and cinematography was too expensive. He suggested providing short courses and pamphlets to teachers and priests who could advance public health campaigns. Dr. Quintana conceded that "traveling exhibits and education and visiting nurses would be more effective, but we do not have the personnel, material, or sufficient funds to initiate it."[159] Two years later, the Ministry of Public Health held a competition to design an anti-typhus poster. It also distributed some forty thousand brochures about hygiene and typhoid to schools throughout the republic. Among agriculturists, the Ministry circulated articles illustrated with drawings and photographs to convey sanitation ideas.[160]

An indigenista who understood indígenas' aversion to outsiders—particularly authorities—Dr. Quintana chided officials who did not respect indígenas and their contributions to public health.[161] Yet even as he encouraged developing anti-typhus materials in indigenous languages, he belittled them. He suggested producing "Records in the most widespread vernacular tongues [*lenguas vernaculas*], alternating the vocal language [*lenguaje vocal*] with popular music: brief, concise, synthesized advice that can be adapted to the local conditions of the population that determines the norms of the dialect [*dialecto*]."[162] Refusing to recognize indigenous languages as such, he referred to "vernacular tongues," "vocal language," and "dialect" to portray indigenous language speakers as less intelligent. Incapable of developing a language, indígenas spoke a creole that lacked the sophistication and complexity of European languages, according to Dr. Quintana.

Like Dr. Quintana, many Guatemalan officials assumed indígenas were ignorant or ambivalent. According to Quetzaltenango public health representative Rigoberto de León, "Much of the work is lost because of the indifference of the inhabitants where the indigenous element prevails."[163] The shift from dictatorship to democracy did little to change those attitudes. Even at the highest levels of democratic government, indígenas were associated with disease. President Arévalo explained that the anti-typhus campaign focused "on the indigenous race, because of the misery and lamentable hygiene in which they live."[164] In 1945, the anti-typhus campaign director insisted, "The illiteracy of our indigenous race and the high percentage also of ladinos, makes the fight against typhus very difficult. One sees that in all the infected areas and especially in [the primarily indigenous] department of Huehuetenango where the lack of roads also obstructs" progress.[165] Recognizing illiteracy and infrastructure as obstacles to better health, he paternalistically referred to "*our* indigenous race" and situated typhus as particularly virulent in the highlands where indígenas predominated. "As is well known by all doctors and erudite individuals, typhus is an endemic disease not only in Guatemala where the indigenous race predominates, but also in many countries of the world where for life circumstances, unnatural masses of people, poverty, etc. the observance of essential hygiene regulations declines."[166] While he attributed typhus in other nations to poverty and urbanization, in Guatemala he blamed the allegedly less hygienic indigenous race.

As democracy progressed, some officials refrained from scapegoating indígenas. In January 1946, El Quiche governor Rogelio Morales reported "various cases of *Tifus exantemático*, which caused some deaths in the indigenous population that is very dense in these regions."[167] He claimed that "because of the lack of doctors and suitable medicine, it was not possible to combat the epidemic immediately." Morales asserted that insufficient medical professionals, not indigeneity, doomed indígenas. Although a health brigade from Chiché contained the outbreak, remote indigenous communities often suffered through epidemics while authorities mobilized health teams. Indicating that typhus was often the primary health threat in the highlands, public health reportedly was good in the region except for typhus outbreaks.

Portraying indígenas as vectors of typhus, typhoid, and other diseases related to poverty and poor hygiene justified and framed public health interventions. Yet when medical professionals disparaged indígenas, medical science struggled to become relevant in indigenous communities. Ecuadorian officials and blanco-mestizo neighbors who targeted indigenous funeral rituals as catalysts of disease further marginalized indígenas from the broader body politic of healthy citizens. Unlike officials who denigrated indigenous languages and portrayed indígenas as ignorant, those who communicated in indigenous languages and made respectful accommodations often found receptive audiences. Garcés knew communicating in Kichwa could mitigate fears of scientific medicine and legitimize public health practices. If the content of the message was disrespectful of indígenas and their lifestyles, however, such overtures could be counterproductive, as Garcés's speech suggests.

Demonstrating how categories of disease and categories of race were intertwined, even as the allopathic medical community started understanding typhoid and typhus better, they still entangled their explanations with ethnicity and race. Instead of acknowledging the ways indígenas embraced modernity, elites framed the former as averse to the latter, which set the stage for pitting indigenous healing against scientific medicine—as chapter 2 also demonstrates. Resisting efforts to ameliorate poverty by redistributing resources (particularly land), Guatemalan and Ecuadorian oligarchs insisted assimilation or integration, respectively, could modernize indígenas and improve their well-being.

While at first glance anti-typhus and anti-typhoid campaigns appear parallel in Ecuador and Guatemala, a close read of archival material reveals that Ecuadorian public health officials offered more varied and nuanced understandings of the role race played in public health endeavors than their Guatemalan contemporaries. When Ecuadorian public health officials witnessed indigenous ingenuity and diligence firsthand, they generally credited those traits with buttressing public health. Although Sigchos indígenas impressed one Ecuadorian inspector with their smallpox inoculation technique, his counterpart ignored that prophylactic procedure and attributed a typhoid outbreak to their "manner of living, customs." While that official never arrived in the community, his successor did and praised indigenous residents for helping to eradicate the epidemic. The range of Ecuadorian public health professionals' perceptions of indígenas speaks to how some officials lauded them, while others peddled racist stereotypes even as they highlighted socioeconomic conditions that undermined indigenous health. Both groups recognized that race alone did not predetermine well-being.

Despite the frequency with which racism and ignorance shaped public health interventions, indígenas' efforts to maintain and restore individual and public health and local officials' recognition of those actions' efficacy suggests that Ecuador sometimes cultivated fertile ground for collaboration between public health officials and indígenas. Set against government discourse that presented indígenas as degenerate carriers of typhoid and typhus, indigenous interaction with public health outreach ranged from careful accommodation to resistance. Race often shaped officials' assessment of infectious diseases, but indígenas and medical professionals could find common ground in efforts to stem them.

Officials who recognized the importance of indigenous languages were exceptional and intermittent at best in Guatemala, whereas many Ecuadorian public health officials communicated in Kichwa. Those distinctions reflected broader differences between nations that shared racist tenets, whereby Ecuadorian blanco-mestizos were more apt to approach indigenous peoples, languages, and cultures as worthy of respect (if not equality) than their Guatemalan counterparts who generally dismissed indígenas' intellectual acumen and languages. Even Guatemalan indigenistas like Dr. Quintana, who advocated producing public health materials in indigenous languages, discounted indigenous intellect.

Indigenous responses to public health initiatives offer a window onto how the give and take between authorities and local residents played out around public health interventions. Guatemalan Kaqchikel speakers celebrated public health measures that were explained in their language. Even as Ecuadorian indígenas collaborated in anti-typhus and anti-typhoid campaigns, many resisted mandates to banish domestic animals from their courtyards. Regardless of the level of expertise in scientific medicine that informed the state's plans, indígenas and other marginalized rural residents often determined the extent to which authorities' aspirations matched their accomplishments.

Racist thought persisted in Ecuador and dominated popular discourse and social relations in Guatemala. Ecuador's rich social medicine threads only infrequently evoked a broader sentiment of looking beyond indigeneity and indigenous bodies for explanations of highland epidemics. In Guatemala, where elites defined "indios" as problematic, social medicine had little fertile ground upon which to develop. Rather than identify poverty as a catalyst of illness, Guatemalan and, to a lesser extent, Ecuadorian authorities and intellectuals focused on indigeneity. In so doing, they masked the very unequal distribution of resources (particularly land) that often undermined indigenous health. As we will see in the next chapter, public health and government officials similarly spuriously framed malaria as a highland disease to obscure the government's inability to redress vast income and asset inequalities.

excuses...
race.

SIX

"Prisoners of Malaria"

A LOWLAND DISEASE IN THE MOUNTAINS

WHILE ECUADOR AND GUATEMALA had successes fighting yellow fever in the early twentieth century, malaria continued to plague both countries to such an extent that antimalarial campaigns were framed as patriotic.[1] For example, after decrying a "malaria scourge" in 1934, a Guatemalan official insisted, "an active prophylactic and curative campaign would allow [us] to dominate the epidemic, saving thousands of lives useful to the *patria*."[2] Ecuadorian leaders similarly framed malaria as a threat to national development and the labor that fueled it. In regular visits to indigenous communities in 1947, a public health official pressed the urgency "to change the awful unhygienic conditions that are the cause of villages' stagnation and highways' slow progress because workers are prisoners of malaria."[3] Echoing an argument made by public health officials around the world, he underscored that reducing malaria would improve manual laborers' lives and the nation's infrastructure. In another international pattern, public health officials framed malaria as a cause of poverty, when in fact, infection was increasingly due to poverty's effects.

Malaria, which is caused by parasites transmitted through female anopheles mosquito bites, causes fever, chills, bodily pains, malaise, and sweats.[4] Malaria was primarily a lowland disease: mosquitoes had a hard time surviving beyond 2000–2500 meters above sea level. At the turn of the century, it barely registered as a public health threat in Quito, where the malaria mortality rate was 0.01 percent. Yet highland malaria did emerge from time to time.[5] Infected laborers who seasonally migrated to coastal regions to mitigate their poverty regularly introduced malaria to the highlands. By the early twentieth century, much of the most arable land was controlled by elites, leaving poor rural indígenas to eke out a living on small, marginalized plots. As a result, highland indígenas often had to migrate to coastal agro-export (often coffee, banana, and cacao) plantations to make ends meet. When coastal residents and others living in malarial areas survived repeated bouts of the disease, they could develop or inherit resistance (but not immunity).[6] But indigenous migrants who were born in the highlands lacked heritable shields from malaria, or the resources to keep mosquitos at bay, so they often spent their coastal earnings recovering from it. Poverty further compounded malarial highlanders' plight because their family members could ill afford to accompany them to urban hospitals. As a disease that generally originated in the lowlands, malaria exposed the multiple marginalizations of poor, highland indígenas.

Historical evidence from Guatemala suggests droughts that created lakeshore pools and flooding that filled puddles sometimes spawned malaria mosquitos in the highlands. Female anopheles lay their eggs along the edges of lakes, marshes, or flowing streams. Blood provides high-energy food they need to complete the production of eggs. When they bite vertebrata to extract blood, infected anopheles inject parasites into bloodstreams. Only about twenty of the nearly five hundred different varieties of anopheles spread diseases to humans.[7] Of the five malaria parasites that infect humans, *Plasmodium vivax* and *Plasmodium falciparum* are the most common in Latin America.[8] Because it infects nearly 90 percent of red blood cells, *falciparum* is lethal. As many as 25 percent of those infected with *falciparum* die, whereas only about 1 percent of *vivax* victims die. If treated promptly and properly, malaria is curable.[9] Prior to European contact, Andeans discovered that cinchona tree bark, or *quina*, which contains quinine, could combat chills and fevers. A curative and prophylactic, quinine attacks *falciparum* and *vivax* malarial parasites circulating in human bloodstreams (but not in livers).[10]

From the colonial era through the twentieth century, malaria etiology preoccupied public health officials in tropical Latin America, and they deployed a diverse array of strategies to control it—as did affected nations across the globe. European, African, and North American nations tended to focus on attacking mosquitos or parasites. European and US health authorities' approaches included screening, bonification (improving housing conditions and farming practices), adjusting water levels, oiling, deploying chemicals like Paris Green (a highly toxic copper-based insecticide), and introducing larvae-eating fish.[11]

In some respects, antimalarial campaigns in Ecuador and Guatemala depart from histories of malaria control in other parts of Latin America, particularly Mexico and Brazil where the RF and the United States established models for malaria eradication to be implemented elsewhere. Even though US and Mexican officials put antimalaria campaigns to different uses, they both deployed narratives of scientific medicine to modernize what they perceived to be backward subjects (Mexico in the case of the United States; Chiapas and indígenas in the case of Mexico). Neither Ecuador nor Guatemala were central to RF efforts to establish exemplars or expand RF influence, as reflected in sparse resource allocation in those countries.

Resource-poor governments lacked capacity to establish universal antimalarial campaigns like those in Western Europe.[12] Officials understood that malaria campaigns were long-term efforts that demanded at least ten years of persistent work to achieve their goals.[13] But with meager budgets, officials often had to adjust and adapt to local conditions and individual circumstances. Guatemala regularly reinvented its antimalarial campaigns with approaches that tacked between quinine, draining, and insecticide from the 1920s through the 1940s.[14] Ecuador too varied its strategies, which ranged from environmental sanitation (draining, petroleum, and salt) to personal prophylactics (quinine and anti-mosquito housing).

As a lowland disease in two nations where the coasts were largely devoid of indigenous populations, malaria was not indigenized like typhus or typhoid. Other countries framed it differently: international stereotypes that portrayed malaria as a manifestation of peasants' penury, indolence, fatigue, and fatalism sometimes morphed into accusations that indigenous peoples and cultures were vectors of malaria.[15] That was particularly true in places like Panama where sanitary officials "chalked up the persistence of a malarial reservoir among nonwhites to particular racial habits."[16] In Guatemala and Ecuador, however, officials did not decry indígenas as vectors. Instead, they focused on what they framed—incorrectly—as malaria's transmission in the highlands to deflect attention from the structural economic disadvantages that brought it there to begin with. They were not alone in such machinations. From Italy to Brazil, experts (including RF agents) argued that malaria was the single most important obstacle to regional and national development in what Peter Brown calls the "malaria blocks development" model.[17] Public health campaigns were an easier sell, it seems, than redistributing wealth or otherwise addressing poverty head-on.

Ecuadorian healers harvested *quina* in the southern highlands, on the Eastern slopes of the Andes above 1500 meters, near the cities of Cuenca and Loja, which had abundant groves of diverse cinchona trees. (There are ninety varieties.) By the seventeenth century, European merchants and Jesuits had profited from introducing quinine (alkaloids in the form of powdered bark) into European pharmacopoeia and markets.[18] Within the next hundred years, Cuenca and Loja were enjoying cinchona bark booms. In the 1850s, the British government imported cinchona bark from Ecuador, Peru, Bolivia, and Colombia and distributed quinine to protect its soldiers from malaria in Africa and India.[19]

Indigenous knowledge and research were crucial to developing both a cure and prophylactic for malaria. A prominent British quinine manufacturer insisted botanists learned about Calisaya bark from "the experience and practical sagacity of an Indian."[20] The Bolivian indígena Manuel Incra Mamani was renowned for his vast knowledge of cinchona trees: while some tree bark had 2 to 3 percent quinine content, Mamani's samples—which helped shape research across the world—were remarkably potent, with 14 percent quinine content. In the 1860s, Mamani befriended British naturalist, explorer, and merchant Charles Ledger,[21] who wrote "[T]he little I know has been acquired practically and from what I heard from my faithful old servant and friend Manuel and other most intelligent Bolivian Indians."[22] To facilitate his mid-nineteenth-century pursuit of cinchona in Ecuador, English botanist Richard Spruce also hired indigenous guides and experts.[23]

Intending to control and profit from the boom, by the mid-nineteenth century, the Ecuadorian government forbade foreigners from exporting cinchona plants, cuttings, seeds, or bark and required quinine to be produced in country. The government also demanded *cascarilleros* (bark harvesters) plant six trees for every one they felled. Retaining sufficient stores of quinine could still be challenging, given both its escalating price and—during World War I—interruptions to supply chains.[24] After learning that a group of Ecuadorians suffered severely because they lacked quinine in November 1918, Dr. Miño "personally took measures and remedies arrived" within a week.[25] Yet Dr. Miño, like other public health officials, was keenly aware of quinine's limitations: its potency diminished so dramatically over time that some "wretched souls suffered relapses while taking it.[26]

By the late nineteenth century, quinine's attributes were well known in Guatemala too.[27] Guatemalan President Justo Rufino Barrios (1873–85) cultivated quinine trees on his plantation, and, "[a]ttentive to the well-being and health of the nation," dropped customs taxes on the importation of quinine.[28] Some patients had an intolerance for or simply refused to take quinine;[29] UFCO mixed quinine with rum to get laborers to ingest it.[30] Pelletier Pharmaceutical company sold quinine capsules it claimed "resolved the problem of administering quinine without disgust."[31] In 1910, the company insisted "all doctors have adopted [the capsules] because of their efficacy against ... malarial fevers," and other ailments.[32] Ten days later, the *Diario de Centroamérica* highlighted a different "heroic medicine that will cure fever quickly."[33] Taking one or two little cups with each meal, "The cure obtained with Vino de Quinum Labarrague is more radical and more secure than taking quinine alone."[34] The Paris Academy of Medicine allegedly approved Vino de Quinum Labarrague's formula.[35]

In 1904, when malaria and yellow fever were decimating Panama Canal workers, US military Surgeon General William Gorgas and his counterparts used quinine and other drugs to treat malaria, and drained puddles and ponds, cut down grass, cleared brush, and spread oil to destroy breeding sites. After the canal was completed in 1914, authorities discontinued the use of quinine because they considered it unnecessary and were skeptical of mass quininization's effectiveness.[36]

Guatemalan highland healers had little experience with chronic or acute malaria. Climatic and environmental conditions (particularly high altitudes) tempered tropical diseases in the mountains, and indigenous healers lacked access to *quina*. When malaria did present itself, Guatemalan indigenous healers suggested preventative measures but had few remedies. Ch'orti' used natural remedies (aimed at changing body temperature) for mild malaria, which they believed was caused by hot *aigre* (malevolent air or wind) entering the head and cold *aigre* entering the body.[37] Kaqchikel recommended sucking on lemons and drinking *guaro* (rum) instead of water while on the coast to prevent malaria.[38] In some cases, traditional remedies could be counterproductive. A Salvadoran curandero killed two patients with a potion intended to cure malaria in 1935.[39] When the Guatemalan indígena Mariano Cucul died "mysteriously of an unknown ailment" three days after experiencing "strong fever, intense cold ... swelling ... [and] yellow water coming from his pores"—symptoms that suggested he had malaria—Izabal residents were convinced he had been bewitched by an indigenous curandero.[40]

Some communities turned to traveling doctors to diagnose and treat malaria.[41] (Apparently some Guatemalan officials over-diagnosed malaria. Noting that malaria had caused more deaths than other diseases in 1944, Quiche health specialist Dr. Federico Castellanos warned such statistics must be taken in context since rural councilors attributed "any fatal fever" to malaria.[42]) Many highland residents sought relief in Guatemala City hospitals. Even in tropical regions like Puerto San José and Puerto Barrios where RF and Guatemalan officials had established antimalarial campaigns, medical professionals referred malaria patients to the capital.[43] Instead of transferring a malaria patient from Tenedores where it "was not possible to cure him" to the department capital of Puerto Barrios, authorities sent him to Guatemala City in February 1943.[44] At times, transferring patients was remarkably slow. Referred to the General Hospital in Guatemala City on July 5, 1943, one malaria patient from Santa Lucía Cotzumalguapa (Escuintla) did not arrive until July 30—more than three weeks later.[45]

MALARIA IN GUATEMALA

Climate and topography were as likely to catalyze malaria as poverty and standing water.[46] Predisposed to warm humid climates, malaria sometimes was evident in highland valleys where lakes and streams produced conditions where malarial vectors could proliferate. As an 1898 Guatemalan Government Ministry report noted, "The *pueblos* immediately [surrounding] the lake called San Antonio [Aguascalientes, henceforth Aguascalientes] . . . suffered from malaria that naturally develops in . . . stagnant waters."[47] A malaria outbreak the previous year had been particularly devastating.[48] By the turn of the century, Guatemalan doctors were convinced malaria was common among indígenas,[49] whose mountainous regions were "threatened by outbreaks of their own malaria."[50] At 1539 meters above sea level, Aguascalientes could still allow malaria-carrying mosquitos to spread.[51]

Migration—often of highlanders seeking work in plantation agriculture—also introduced malaria to the highlands.[52] When a Presbyterian minister lauded the Kaqchikel community of Santa Catarina Barahona (henceforth Barahona) as "very clean and [with] abundant water" in 1874, he noted that "some residents tend to return from the coast with malaria."[53] Twenty-five years later, the mayor of Aguascalientes insisted, "Fevers only come from other climates where people come and go for their work and *mandamientos*. . . . The climate is . . . healthy" in Aguascalientes.[54] Many highlanders feared traveling to humid tropical areas where malaria flourished.[55]

Some locals deployed malaria to invite government intervention that could advance their interests. In 1910, Guatemala City neighbors petitioned the municipal council to relocate a tannery that "is a true focal point of infection and makes [our lives] unbearable because of the bad odors it emits principally at night."[56] Claiming that the "great voices of public health demand" the tannery be moved out of their neighborhood, residents declared, "our children are malarial and the law is clear to arrange [the move] that way."[57] Miasma concepts like these continued to percolate, but mostly were known to be wrong.[58]

Guatemala City medical inspector Morales reported that the tannery "cannot be the cause of an epidemic" because "tanneries are not considered focal points of infection nor [do] bad odors cause epidemics."[59] Nonetheless, he suggested public health police vigilantly inspect it. Although residents failed in their bid to remove the tannery, they captured the attention of state agents by highlighting malaria—and in children, no less—in a city that was 1,492 meters above sea level.

When malaria broke out in Baja Verapaz (a province elevated at between 940 and 1,540 meters above sea level) in January 1904, the Guatemalan medical commission sent to address it reported: "It was our work to dispel many erroneous ideas about treatment that those simple people followed: some treated it with baths, others with tobacco and white lead [salt] infusions, and those who took quinine believed they had cured themselves after only one or two Pelletier pills; this explains the considerable number of deaths."[60] Even as some aspects of scientific medicine (malaria pills) penetrated remote regions, traditional medicine (baths, tobacco, and salt treatments) persisted. Neither could effectively combat malaria in Baja Verapaz. Attributing malarial mortality to indigenous and other highland populations' ignorance, medical professionals and authorities obfuscated how poverty undermined rural health.

Aware of the relationship between the lived environment and malaria, some Guatemalan officials attributed malaria to UFCO's ecological disruptions. "One observes malaria in almost all the places where the Fruit Company tills for its banana plantations, undoubtedly for the great quantity of anopheles that develop in those sites," noted a government minister in 1909.[61] The relationship between banana farming, mosquitos, and malaria exacted a high human toll. Nearly half the patients UFCO treated in 1914 had contracted malaria.[62] When UFCO began an antimalarial campaign in earnest in 1926, mortality dropped,[63] such that in 1928, 27.6 percent of all UFCO workers were diagnosed with malaria.[64] Between 1914 and 1931, 1,672 UFCO patients died from malaria.[65]

Because it devastated workforces and troops, malaria was regularly in the crosshairs of foreign entities that operated in Guatemala.[66] In its 1915 annual report, the RF asserted, "Malaria is . . . probably the number one obstacle to the welfare and economic efficiency of the human race."[67] More than any other disease, malaria undermined "economic efficiency and . . . mental and physical development." The report concluded, "malaria must be considered the . . . most serious medical and hygienic problem that we have to face."[68]

In 1918, the Guatemalan government warned people not "to resort to quinine,"[69] and throughout the 1920s, it preferred draining stagnant water to administering quinine to local populations.[70] This strategy was right in line with recommendations from the RF. Although quinine was cheaper than environmental sanitation projects, both the government and RF were concerned about poor indigenous and ladino residents' ability to regularly consume medication.

British and RF doctors and scientists similarly discouraged quinine's use. "Breaking the circuit between persons with germs in their blood, the infectious mosquito and the person who doesn't have malaria," was the best approach, according to the RF President in 1926.[71] Six years later, the 1932 RF annual report discounted quinine and social medicine: "In areas where efforts to control malaria have been based on the use of quinine, more nutritional diets, improved housing and improved hospitals, the effect on prevalence of disease has been virtually nil. On the other hand, where efforts have been directed against vector mosquitos, the incidence of malaria has been significantly reduced and its spread has been controlled."[72]

Yet the RF did deploy quinine to protect its field workers. At least two Guatemalan microscopists died of malaria and yellow fever in the late 1910s.[73] Working in Guatemala, RF representative Dr. William T. Burres advanced an economic argument about quinine's value: "Since our men are working almost all of the time in malarial sections, these [quinine] pills were ordered for their use. If two or more men become ill with malarial fever in a year the loss is more than the cost of the pills."[74] His New York supervisors immediately sent a thousand pills "for conserving the health of the field men."[75] Such gradations of quinine deployment hint at diverse responses to malaria control and treatment based on class and nationality. By the late 1920s, however, Guatemala had changed course, promoting quinine to fight malaria. A 1929

Public Health Department publication declared, "QUININE TAKEN IN TIME OVERCOMES DEATH!"[76] In 1933, the Ubico administration distributed and sold quinine to those suffering from malaria.[77]

If the archival record is any indication, malaria in the highlands was quickly worsening. Attributed to the adaptability and mobility of humans, insects, and diseases, highland malaria was "a new phenomenon," according to malariologist Dr. J. Romeo de León and other early twentieth-century Guatemalan officials.[78] By 1936, de León attributed malaria's spread to "vast extensions of water . . . malarial men . . . and *anophelismo* that adapted to different climates [after being] transported by railroads and highways. . . . The new ease offered by transportation . . . [allowed] masses of workers to go to the coasts, . . . contract malaria, returning ill to their place of origin."[79] De León erroneously claimed, "Previously highland towns were unscathed by malaria."[80] In response to Guatemala's high levels of malaria in 1936, the government commissioned a study of malarial mosquitos' geographic distribution (figure 19).[81] When Guatemalan RF representative Benjamin Washburn advocated pursuing "malaria control mainly through permanent drainage" in 1936, the Guatemalan Director of Health requested that a RF expert on drainage "be assigned to his department to reorganize the section on malaria upon the basis of mosquito control."[82] Although scholars and scientists have developed more sophisticated understandings of malaria since the 1930s, contemporary studies provide valuable insight into how early-twentieth-century scientists and authorities framed the disease and its propagation.

In 1939, the Sacatepéquez governor explained, malaria "always causes damage in neighborhoods, principally among the workers who return from agricultural labor on the coast."[83] That same year Rabinal (Baja Verapaz) suffered an outbreak when "a labor broker took 400 *peones* to work in Tiquisate, which resulted in 100 percent of them contracting malaria, returning to their houses to become disseminators of the disease with a high percentage of mortality."[84] Although mosquitos rather than migrants would have been disseminators, at 982 meters above sea level, Rabinal could house them. Given the high death toll, Tiquisate's "great problem with malaria" was probably *falciparum*.[85] Destroying mosquitos there would take significant resources, "but save many lives."[86] Tight finances undermined individuals' health. When Guatemalan police agent Canuto Estrada Díaz contracted acute malaria in 1939, he "lacked the resources to cure it."[87]

Since most highland indígenas who contracted malaria did so through migration, national public health officials seldom associated malaria with

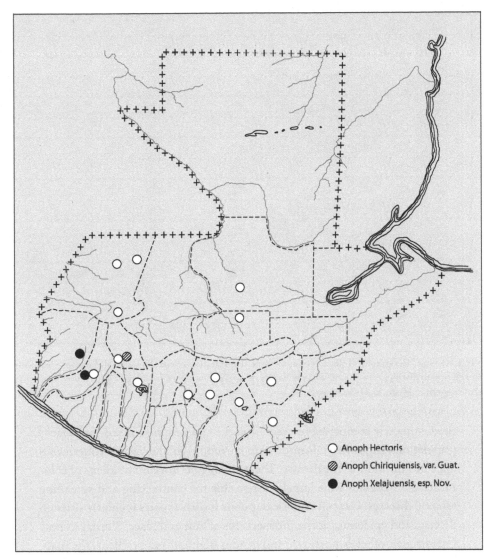

FIGURE 19. "Map of geographical distribution of the mosquitoes A. Hectoris, A. Guatemalnesis, and A. Xelopiensis." *Boletín Sanitaria* 46 (1938), 415. Courtesy of Academia de Geografía e Historia de Guatemala.

indigeneity. At the First Central American Health Congress in 1937, participants were keen to establish relationships between race, place, and disease. Elites often racialized space to marginalize ethic groups.[88] When Central American health delegates mapped *fiebre aguas negras*, a complication related to malaria, they attributed it to lowland populations that were

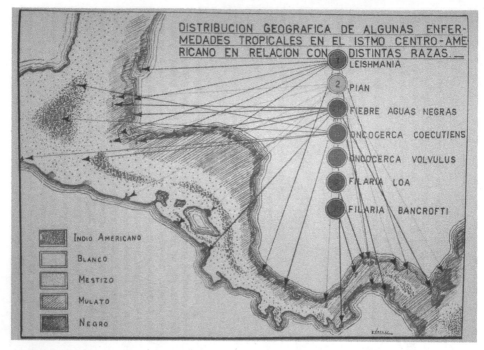

FIGURE 20. "Geographical distribution of some tropical diseases in the Central American isthmus in relation to distinct races," 1937. *Boletín Sanitario de Guatemala* 46 (1938), 55. Courtesy of Academia de Geografía e Historia de Guatemala.

predominantly comprised of *Negro* (black) and *Mulato* (mixed-race black) populations (figure 20). Represented in red, highland *Indios Americanos* appeared immune to the disease. The map suggests lowland residents of color rather than *Blancos* were largely responsible for contracting and spreading tropical diseases. Central American public health experts regularly situated diseases and epidemics at the intersections of race and place. Similar to how Guatemalan officials portrayed indigenous highlands as pestilent, the mapmakers suggested certain regions were more disease-prone because they were racialized as Afro-Central American spaces.

Maintaining a healthy rural workforce for the agricultural economy spurred many public health initiatives. "In the rural zones . . . our day laborers' work is deficient, with a great loss for the national economy, they could not perform the necessary tasks, they could not finish the normal work of any healthy worker because of their poor health that was the result of malaria or intestinal parasites," the Ubico administration lamented.[89] By 1942, the administration lauded "the satisfaction to contemplate those poor workers of the land, alleviated and cured of their habitual ailments, to extract from the bountiful Guatemalan land, the gift of farm work conducted with powerful muscles and invaluable mental energy, that knows how to give . . . one hundred percent."[90]

Draining Lakes, Marshes, and Swamps

Awareness that environmental conditions could jeopardize health dates back thousands of years. Ancient Rome, China, and other agricultural societies learned that stagnant water, irrigation, and (clogged) canals bred swamp fever, later known as malaria. During the Middle Ages, the papacy planned to drain the Pontine marshes to reduce malaria. Devasted by malaria from the seventeenth to the nineteenth centuries, Romans realized neglecting drainage perpetuated the problem.[91] As scientific understandings of tropical diseases evolved in the early twentieth century, public health specialists and authorities throughout the world drained wetlands and lakes to sanitize landscapes, reclaim land, and reduce mosquito populations.[92]

In the late 1920s, Guatemala embarked on environmental drainage projects aimed at eradicating mosquito breeding grounds. Located in a highland valley about 55 kilometers west of Guatemala City and 1530 meters above sea level, the three-square-kilometer Lake Quinizilapa was readily accessible to the capital, which both heightened national officials' concerns about malaria outbreaks there and made the location an ideal site for a major environmental project. In 1924, the Barahona municipal council forbade irrigating from the Quinizilapa because as its water level decreased, swamps developed. To drain stagnant water into a nearby river, council members proposed building a canal. In neighboring Aguascalientes, which bordered the lake, evangelical missionary Paul Townsend, a US citizen who ran a school, hospital, and free health clinic, responded with a call to conserve rather than redirect water from the lake. "We urgently need a sufficient quantity of water," he insisted, warning, "without it, a hygienic and healthy life is not possible."[93] The Aguascalientes municipal council wrote that Townsend's own entities' water consumption altered the physical environment enough to undermine public health. "Every time Mr. Townsend takes the amount of water he requests [he] is drying the lake and as a result . . . a fever is developing that if not stopped," they wrote, will leave *pueblos* "completely abandoned."[94]

Townsend enjoyed a privileged position vis-à-vis indigenous locals, though he highlighted their shared fates. "With respect to the *laguna*'s decreasing water level, we are the first to recognize given that we live in the same place and run the same risk as everyone else in San Antonio [Aguascalientes], because no one is protected in life from death, we are all humans. . . . The use of those waters is a guarantee of hygiene for everyone," claimed Townsend.[95] By highlighting hygiene, Townsend extended considerations about the lake beyond merely addressing malaria to broader issues of public health. He also played on ladino fears of unhygienic indígenas. Finding no "reasonable basis to oppose Mr. Townsend's request," the Sacatepéquez governor allowed Townsend to continue siphoning water for his enterprises.[96]

President Lázaro Chacón (1926–31) ended Townsend's hegemony. His administration facilitated the draining of Lake Quinizilapa.[97] As was true of most public (and private) works in Guatemala, indigenous corvée labor was key to the project's completion in July 1927. Efforts to phase out forced labor in the early 1920s had been short-lived. Chacón's predecessor José María Orellana (1921–26) ignored coffee planters as they reinstated forced labor and directed authorities to violently suppress indigenous-organized land invasions and labor strikes. In contrast, Chacón's lake-draining project stands out for its efforts to protect indigenous residents and to foster domestic agriculture. Those goals were noteworthy in a nation that disparaged indígenas and promoted agro-exports—particularly coffee—sustained by indigenous forced labor.[98] Redistributing three hundred hectares of lakebed land to indígenas allowed Chacón to shore up support for a regime that had clashed with indígenas elsewhere. Moreover, reducing malaria and expanding agricultural land in indigenous communities allowed Chacón to utilize the public health effort to undercut critiques from the nation's unions and newly formed Communist Party.[99] Unlike Estrada Cabrera, whose lackluster response to influenza contributed to his downfall, Chacón addressed public health concerns before diseases became crises, thereby solidifying his political standing.

While Chacón and the lead project engineer Felipe Castillo hatched a plan based on mosquito and parasite etiology, the Sacatepéquez governor attributed malaria to "a foci of miasmas."[100] Against the backdrop of national efforts to privilege medical science over indigenous healthcare practices and philosophies, Guatemalan state representatives were not necessarily in agreement or equally informed about what caused and spread diseases. When Chacón learned that the lakebed was producing a "bad odor" a few weeks after it had been drained and "disinfected" with petroleum, he ordered that more oil be sprayed, suggesting he also adhered (at least partially) to the miasma theory.[101] Even at the highest levels of power, diverse disease etiologies emerged as traditional and scientific knowledge evolved. But since standing water that bred mosquitos was place-based, Guatemalan officials with different understandings of disease etiology could agree on a solution: draining the lake.[102] Their exchanges reveal much about the myriad ways societies, groups, and individuals gave meaning to illnesses and the threats they posed.

Local indígenas responded to the project in different and complex ways. In oral histories, some Kaqchikel elders recount malaria's devastating effects: "The lake ... was a breeding ground for mosquitoes that spread malaria amongst the townspeople.... No doctors or medicine could combat the disease.... In some cases survivors brought the infirm to the cemetery before they were dead." For Guatemalan indígenas, wakes and funeral processions were crucial conduits to the afterworld, but malaria meant that "the custom of a wake had to cease.... The loss of the lake was a devastating blow to our community but our people knew drastic measures were necessary."[103] The public health crisis catalyzed collaboration. Aguascalientes elder Ka'i' Kawoq supported Chacón's order that authorities enter homes as part of the public health campaign and drainage project. For him, state interventions into private lives were justified.[104] Aguascalientes residents seem to have endorsed the project because they benefited from lakebed land distribution thereafter. Barahona residents, however, received no land, and Barahona elder Kab'lajuj Kan was less sanguine about the drainage: "The lake provoked malaria and dengue so they built a trench to drain it. Now Aguascalientes suffers from a lack of water, because their water has disappeared. It's their own fault."[105] Although he recognized public health benefits, he insisted that destruction of an essential natural resource was short-sighted.

The Lake Quinizilapa drainage project suggests that ethnic divides, more than scientific knowledge, influenced the reception of distinct notions about disease etiology. On May 20, 1927, an *El Día* reporter wrote: "According to the *inditos*, the river has a *nahual*. The *nahual* is a young child who lives in a cave along the river. He does not allow the water of the lake to join with the river.... [The *inditos*] said the lake could never be united with the river and that malaria would continue its work of destruction."[106] Capturing indigenous worldviews that emphasized interrelationships between water, malaria, and the supernatural, the article documents Kaqchikel understandings of ecology that coincide with other material in the archives. "Perhaps the lake will not disappear because it has a *nahual*," noted another indígena in a 1927 letter.[107]

The *El Día* journalist's goal was not to understand indigenous epistemologies, however. Conjuring images of indigenous ignorance, the journalist quoted indígenas saying "*misme ingenier*" and "*buene*" as if they spoke less sophisticated, creole Spanish. Deploying the pejorative "*inditos*" was one way journalists and ladinos infantilized and denigrated indígenas. Portraying them as fatalistic was another. Whereas ladino authorities could maintain miasma theory alongside entomological and parasitological understandings of disease without any major trouble, contemporary indigenous notions of a *nahual* protecting water and facilitating malaria provoked disdain and incredulity. Yet malaria's persistence in the region thereafter—the lakebed refilled and malaria returned in 1929 and 1934—lent credence to indigenous assertions that it would take more than draining a lake to control malaria.[108]

A few years after draining Lake Quinizilapa, malaria broke out around another (much larger) highland lake. Sitting 1,563 meters above sea level with a surface area of 130 square kilometers and 20 cubic kilometers of water, Lake Atitlán was surrounded by indigenous villages that had long used the water's resources for their livelihoods. When RF representative Dr. Daniel M. Molloy investigated the outbreak in September 1930, local indígenas explained that drought catalyzed malaria. While wave action generally kept mosquito breeding to a minimum, a drought lowered the water level such that water accumulated along the lake shore precisely when summer temperatures rose sufficiently to support breeding. When indigenous fishermen cleared dense vegetation along the shore to attract and capture small fish, they exposed existing mosquito larvae in the water to fish predators but also inadvertently reduced shade, thereby further raising the water temperature, which facilitated breeding.[109]

Although Molloy had witnessed a severe malaria outbreak at 3000 feet (914.4 meters) in Tegucigalpa in 1927, he surmised that "autochthonous malaria in epidemic form must be rare" above 5000 feet (1524 meters).[110] Yet in 1933, malaria "invaded" Lake Atitlán shoreline towns again.[111] Thanks to RF experts in the field, knowledge of malaria in locales generally understood to be immune from it expanded. According to Molloy's superior, malaria outbreaks occasionally occurred in Puerto Rican mountains below 3000 feet "where ordinarily malaria is practically absent."[112] Imported from the lowlands, those outbreaks generally were "benign malaria, which is usually easily and quickly controlled by quinine medication and the use of Paris Green."[113] As Molloy's successor B. E. Washburn explained in 1936, malaria in Guatemala "exists under a great variety of conditions at altitudes ranging from sea level to high mountains and offers opportunities for studies probably not found elsewhere."[114]

By the 1930s, Guatemalan scientists had identified two malarial mosquitos: *Anopheles hectoris*, which lived in the highlands, and *Anopheles pseudopunctipennis*, which survived from the coast up to 1500 meters above sea level. Those mosquitos were found in Coban (1320m), Guatemala City (1480 meters), Antigua (1525 meters), and Quezaltenango (2440 meters).[115] Malarialogist de León found *A. hectoris* and two others—*A. guatemalensis* and *A. xelopiensis*—at 4500 feet (1372 meters) above sea level. The map of their geographic distribution suggests why contemporary officials and scientists surmised malaria regularly struck the highlands (figure 19).[116] Yet twenty-first-century epidemiologists generally consider only one of these, *Anopheles pseudopunctipennis*, a main malaria vector in Guatemala.[117]

Research aside, Guatemala had a limited budget for antimalarial campaigns, which made for limited results. In the 1930s and 1940s, malaria consistently had the highest morbidity and mortality rate of any disease in Guatemala. In 1933, 59,645 people contracted and 8,946 (roughly 15 percent) died from it.[118] Comprising nearly 20 percent of all disease-related deaths in 1935, 10,627 people died from malaria and other fevers.[119] Despite dramatically decreasing malaria incidences and "epidemic outbreaks,"[120] the department of public health reported 67,371 malaria cases in 1939. As part of an effort to bring scientific medicine to rural areas, the dispensary rail car treated 5,109 of those cases.[121] In some areas, "malaria is the only disease that worries inhabitants," according to one public health official.[122]

Other nations were concerned too. In 1939, Dr. Lieutenant Colonel James Stevens Simmons observed, "Malaria remains a major scourge, exceeding all other diseases in reducing vitality, and in impeding the industrial development and political progress of the inhabitants of many tropical and subtropical countries."[123] His explanation resonated with Guatemalan officials who conflated racialized populations, disease, and backwardness. Dr. Simmons's observation continued to ring true five years later for the US military, which declared malaria "the number one enemy . . . it has been responsible for more death and disability than any other" disease.[124] At the 1937 Central American Health Congress, Dr. Julio Roberto Herrera proposed a "minimum plan that could be implemented with the economic resources" that, he knew, were scarce in the region.[125] Based on an efficacious approach in Dougherty County, Georgia, his strategy had four parts: draining, larvicide, antimalaria drugs, and a public education campaign. "Long considered a specific effective remedy against malaria," quinine figured prominently in Herrera's plan, which coincided with a request to abolish Guatemalan customs duties on it.[126]

Throughout the 1930s and 1940s, Guatemala pursued such multilateral approaches to malaria control. When recurrent rains wracked Sacatepéquez in 1933, authorities distributed a list of sanitation regulations that included spreading oil or lime over stagnant water and immediately incinerating cadavers that flooding "spontaneously exhumed."[127] In 1933, Puerto Champerico had a 50 percent decrease in malaria patients, which a public health official attributed to its use of petroleum, Paris Green, "the Famous Flint (chemicals), larvae-eating fish, burning Eucalyptus leaves and other materials to produce dense smoke that banished anopheles, window and door metal screens." Not everyone could afford screens, but "the majority have mosquito nets."[128]

Even as Ubico cast a wide net, his administration increasingly emphasized environmental management. "Unwavering, General Ubico looked for all the means to achieve the objective [reducing malaria], ordering the cleaning of lake shores and supporting swamp drainage," announced the government's 1933 annual report.[129] Informed by Italian malariologist Dr. Giaquinto Mira and an RF-sponsored Central American tour, Ubico followed a path charted by the RF, which advocated environmental sanitation over social medicine.[130] RF thinking about malaria had evolved from a preoccupation with reducing transmissions in the 1920s and by the mid-1930s was focused on eliminating mosquitos.[131] RF representatives were impressed by Guatemala's commitment. "Malaria is a problem to which Guatemalan Health Department gives the greatest attention and money," Washburn explained in 1936.[132] Despite those efforts, "As always, malaria has been the disease that has decimated the country," Luis Nuñez lamented in 1935.[133]

Aware the battle against malaria was a worldwide endeavor, Ubico's administration engaged with the international community of scientists and researchers. Guatemalan dailies and periodicals regularly translated and republished articles about antimalaria efforts in Europe and the United States.[134] At a time when the United States was successfully draining lowlands, Guatemalans were optimistic.[135] The May 1936 issue of *Revista de la Cruz Roja Guatemalteca* (figure 21) was emblazoned with an image of a mosquito and the question: "Can malaria be destroyed in the world?" The *Revista* journalist praised one researcher's "new way to end malaria efficiently, quickly, and cheaply."[136] Such hyperbole captures the allure of science and the Guatemalan medical community's confidence that malaria could be defeated.

15 DE MAYO DE 1936.   Núm. 9.-Vol. I.

REVISTA DE LA
CRUZ ROJA
GUATEMALTECA

¿Se puede destruir la
Malaria en el mundo?
(Véase artículo en la pág. 4.)

FIGURE 21. "Can malaria be destroyed in the world?" Cover, *Revista de la Cruz Roja Guatemalteca*, 9, May 1936. Courtesy of Hemeroteca Nacional de Guatemala.

Ironically, rather than learning from his nation's Lake Quinizilapa draining project, the Guatemalan Director of Health Dr. Carlos Estevez observed other Central American countries' strategies to "reorganize the Malaria Section."[137] At the behest of the RF, Estevez visited El Salvador, Costa Rica, and Panama in 1936. "Greatly impressed with demonstrations in malaria control by drainage measures," he "expressed desire of having work of this nature *started* in his country."[138] Throughout Central America, the RF emphasized "malaria control mainly through permanent drainage work,"[139] based upon "the plan employed in Panama,"[140] where workers constructed nearly eight million feet of ditches and spread fifty thousand gallons of kerosene to eliminate mosquito breeding sites.[141] Ubico and the Minister of the Interior were interested in introducing the methods Dr. Estevez observed on his "Travel Study tour."[142] Perhaps because the new effort focused on the lowland Escuintla province, populated primarily by ladinos, neither Ubico, Estevez, nor the Minister thought to plumb the antimalarial strategies employed in their nation's indigenous highlands. Instead, they were "anxious to organize work which has been found to be useful in other countries of Tropical America."[143] To offset drainage's high cost, the RF funded equipment to make concrete inverts and tiles for drainage systems and to construct mosquito traps.[144] In another manifestation of RF influence, the Guatemalan engineer who oversaw the drainage work had studied engineering in the United States on a RF fellowship.

Just a few years after Estevez's Central American tour, the policy shift toward drainage was evident throughout Guatemala. In settlements with high incidences of malaria, the government built drains and dried larvae habitats. By opening canals that drained to the Rio de la Plata, workers dried Lake Pereira, located near Santa Rosa de Lima. Three kilometers of canals drained a swamp measuring twenty square kilometers near San Agustín Las Minas in 1939.[145] Throughout the lowlands, authorities built canals to "eliminate marshes."[146] Highlighting "channeling" projects that reduced malaria infection rates, the administration showcased lowland municipalities that enjoyed improved health.[147] According to the administration, drainage projects maintained the health of residents and the "great number of visitors all over the Republic."[148] As was true at Lake Quinizilapa, the main challenge was maintaining clean canals. If canals became clogged with debris, swamps, lakes, and marshes (re)filled and mosquitos propagated.[149]

To buttress its policy shift, the Ubico administration sought the support of finqueros. In 1932, the director of public health suggested, "The battle against malaria and parasitism is to defend the country's human vitality and energy.... Finca owners happily spend on mechanics that check and lubricate the machines of their operations and do not look to [improve] workers' well-being or health, emigrant laborers who transform their muscular force into pure gold and whose machines are surrounded by malaria and unicinarias [hookworm], could be three or four times more productive, with just one small sanitation campaign."[150] A few exceptions notwithstanding, Guatemalan finqueros seldom invested in their permanent, let alone itinerant, work force. Despite employing many workers, Alta Verapaz finqueros were notorious for paying medical personnel low salaries.[151] Even landowners who pledged their concern for public health selectively chose which aspects of it they supported.[152]

If the notoriously corrupt Ubico-era statistics—most egregiously, Ubico fabricated 1940 census data—are at all accurate, draining campaigns were effective. Santa Rosa de Lima's 100 percent infection rate in 1929 dropped to 61 percent by 1938.[153] A year after cleaning canals in San Jeronimo, Baja Verapaz, the infection rate decreased from 87.5 to 34.7 percent. By 1941, the malaria infection rate was 12.5 percent[154]—a remarkable achievement in an area where in some years malaria had "practically decimated the population."[155]

By World War II, malaria control and treatment in Guatemala reduced malaria incidences even as death rates increased. From 1943 to 1945, malaria again topped the charts, infecting 94,945, 75,004, and 64,115 people while causing 1500, 2174, and 2253 deaths respectively.[156] Declining malaria morbidity rates continued into the second half of the twentieth century: 39,809 and 41,821 people contracted, and 1337 and 1633 died from, malaria in 1950 and 1951.[157]

The Class, Ethnicity, and Politics of Malaria

Since living conditions and resources shaped one's ability to pursue prophylactic measures, malaria had a class bias. Turn-of-the-century Kaqchikel oral histories underscore how seasonal migration to coastal plantations put highland families at risk. "The workers suffered. Some brought their families, but the children became sick with malaria or fever. The insects carry diseases. The houses only had tin roofs . . . no walls," explained a Kaqchikel teacher and linguist from Tecpán.[158] Kaqchikel migrants from Santiago Sacatepéquez considered the coast "deadly."[159] A Kaqchikel elder recalled that when she migrated as a young girl, the owners provided no housing so her family made a structure out of banana tree leaves, which left them exposed to malarial mosquitoes.[160] "People slept in the weeds and made their home out of nylon, which they brought with them," added another woman.[161]

Public health officials recognized that these privations jeopardized migrant health. When more than three hundred people died in a 1931 malaria outbreak,[162] Dr. Luis Gaitán reported, "Individuals from the highlands on the coast have been dismantled by the effects [of malaria] without the provision by the landowners of adequate means to protect themselves."[163] Conditions improved little over the next fifteen years. In December 1947, a labor inspector asserted, "Workers have a right to complain, not even pigs could occupy these lodgings. The problem of the rains is that [the roof] is a sieve and the floor, because it is dirt, remains moldy and damp. . . . They are victims of all the inclemency of the weather. As the workers made clear to the *patrón*, they are more secure under the canopies of the trees."[164] A few months earlier workers from Finca Australia informed President Arévalo, "We *campesinos* are [suffering from] bad conditions, poor vision, bad food, and poor sleep and we cannot live happily nor sleep happily. . . . We cannot endure it any longer."[165] Those conditions and concomitant illnesses resonate with historian Eric Carter's observation that malaria "flourished opportunistically in bodies worn down by . . . malnutrition, overwork, and material deprivation."[166]

Guatemalan (and Ecuadorian) archives reveal class biases in malaria care. Whereas medical professionals tended to be middle- or upper class, most malaria victims were poor and working class. When referring patients for treatment, authorities and medical professionals emphasized patients' poverty, notwithstanding exceptions like Doña Mercedes Oliva who had been suffering from acute malaria for "a very long time" by December 1930.[167] Throughout the 1930s and 1940s, the majority of Guatemalan patients suffering from malaria were identified as "poor" or "lacking the funds to *curarse*."[168] Arriving at the Guatemala City General Hospital from Barberena on April 21, 1938, Angel Blanco was a "truly poor person who could not even afford to buy the medicine needed to get better."[169]

A few months later, Herminio Saquil was admitted because he lived in such "extremely poor circumstances that he could not recover."[170] Offering a broader description than simply personal finances, the phrase "extremely poor circumstances" speaks to health problems related to compromised hygiene, poor diet, and lack of potable water and sewage systems. Saquil's surname, which suggests an indigenous heritage, should remind us of the relationship between poverty and ethnicity. Anti-typhus/anti-typhoid campaigns often targeted indigenous subjects, but antimalarial campaigns tended to be less racially marked. In 1945, however, when the Ministry of Public Health and Social Assistance collaborated with PASB to launch a new system to control and combat malaria, they paid particular attention to *indígenas*.[171]

In addition to undermining health, poverty isolated rural patients by precluding family members from accompanying them to Guatemala City hospitals. Shortly after Christmas in Morales (Izabal), Manuel Samayoa wrote to the Guatemala City hospital to inquire about "my *mujer* Julia Gutierrez" who had contracted malaria in 1944. "It pains me immensely that I still do not know if she has been hospitalized. . . . I would appreciate information," he pleaded.[172] Desperate letters from marginalized rural residents inquiring about the status of loved ones offer a window into the isolation felt by family members who sent the infirm to the capital as a last hope of healing. Although the archives reveal only fleeting glimpses into the details of patients' experiences, it is clear that many died alone.[173]

MALARIA IN ECUADOR

In observations that resonated with their Guatemalan counterparts, Ecuadorian officials from Tulcán, the city with the highest elevation in the country, insisted that migrants were the main culprits in the spread of malaria and yellow fever. The town is situated at 2950 meters above sea level, but the floor of nearby Chota Valley, nestled between the highlands in Imbabura and Carchi provinces, is at 1700 meters, and haciendas there employed numerous migrant workers who returned to their villages with malaria. In 1933, 10 percent of Tulcán's population suffered from influenza and malaria, and Tulcán officials were convinced that Chota Valley jobs were to blame.[174] In October 1936, 90 percent of day laborers from haciendas in Chota and Ambi contracted malaria.[175]

When malarial migrants returned to their communities, they seldom transmitted the disease to highland residents, since malarial mosquitos generally did not survive at those altitudes. Although some public health officials directed vector control measures in the highlands, treating those infected with quinine was more appropriate. With an elevation of 2225 meters, Ibarra was not generally susceptible to malaria. Yet local authorities asked hacienda owners to maintain clean water sources for "the development of Ibarra."[176] They also prodded national officials by explaining they could count on the "gratitude of the residents of this unhappy parish battered by malaria and hunger."[177] Highland authorities used a lowland disease to attract national attention and aid.

Even in regions where malarial mosquitos did not survive, Ecuadorian officials deployed malaria to advance their public health and political agendas. Like officials across the globe who used malaria to explain underdevelopment,

Ecuadorian authorities made claims about highland malaria to rationalize inhabitants' poverty and deflect attention from its root causes.[178] "Inhabitants find themselves in a permanent state of misery in this place that makes [life] impossible: there is no good water or food; the land does not produce anything as a result of many plagues and for that reason the inhabitants have to earn their livelihoods working in malarial . . . very unhealthy places," noted Ibarra officials in November 1936, when half the population suffered from malaria.[179] Even as they understood that geography and scarce resources condemned rural residents to migration, authorities who lamented highland villagers' need for lowland migration ignored the massive inequalities in land ownership that necessitated migrant labor. Ibarra officials referenced unproductive land, but not its unequal distribution.

Like other contemporary Latin American leaders, Ecuadorian officials deployed public health to improve national well-being without disrupting the socioeconomic status quo. Aware that diets low in iron and other essential nutrients made people more susceptible to malaria and premature death,[180] many prominent twentieth-century malariologists recognized that "social and economic forces shaped the epidemiology of malaria."[181] Addressing both the social and medical realms of infectious diseases bolstered Ecuador's public health.[182] Yet even as antimalarial campaign delegates in Imbabura province recognized that poverty created these conditions, they suggest a sense of powerlessness to rectify them. In Tumbabiro, "a great number of people are sick with malaria through the special circumstance that its inhabitants earn their living working outside the parish . . . in . . . extremely malarial" regions.[183] Since "it is not possible to improve the situation of Tumbabiro inhabitants' extreme anguish . . . the National Health Service [should] aspire to ERADICATE malaria."[184] Delegates proposed investing in disease control instead of addressing poverty that fueled migrant labor. Dependent on the latter for the agro-export economy, Ecuador was reluctant to restructure rural economies to accommodate poor migrant laborers.

Ecuadorian authorities who emphasized how climate imperiled residents similarly obscured the simultaneous harm of existing socioeconomic structures. "The cause of . . . poverty and prostration is in the deterioration of man. In his indefensible state in front of the climate and inherent affliction of the tropics," noted an official in October 1942.[185] Insisting "it is irrefutable that the first labor the state should develop is the defense of its associates' lives. Protect them against disease . . . [and] hunger," the official cajoled, concluding, "campaigns against malaria . . . should begin immediately."[186] He estimated a budget of four million sucres could cover two doctors in each region earning a salary of one thousand sucres a month.[187] His colleague similarly chided: "Given the climate etc., three million inhabitants lack a qualified doctor, . . . to attend to the malaria plagues that frequently decimate . . . the inhabitants . . . who are victims of a lack of attention."[188]

Remote mountainous topography that inhibited access exacerbated public health crises. When requesting a medical post be created for Intag (Imbabura province) in 1947, Dr. Roberto Nevárez Vásquez suggested the salary should be greater than the 1500 sucres offered for analogous posts in Cotacachi and Otavalo because Intag "is very distant and unhealthy, dominated by parasitic and malarial diseases, and for the same distance, bad roads and other reasons, this zone can only be visited with difficulty . . . [and] needs a doctor so the residents do not live in complete abandon. . . . Make a reality of this wish that will bring benefits to a town that merits attention and lives in complete neglect."[189] With a cloud forest at 1800–2800 meters above sea level and a subtropical rain forest, Intag enjoyed rich biodiversity. Yet the same isolation that afforded indígenas and Afro-Ecuadorians autonomy jeopardized their access to scientific medicine. Since public health officials' responses to malaria seldom addressed its root causes, even when innovative multipronged strategies arrested epidemics, malaria often returned to highland regions where poverty drove lowland labor migration.

Strategies and Politics

When malaria appeared in Pomasqui, a village 2600 meters above sea level and 16 kilometers north of Quito, the local political commissioner notified authorities immediately in May 1914, shortly after Dr. Miño was named the first Subdirector of the Quito Sanidad office. Informed by the public health study of malaria he conducted the previous year in the region, the chief of vaccination Aurelio Vaca R. and the commissioner visited the infected, about sixty of whom were suffering through an "advanced period and entering the chronic phase."[190] Then Vaca "toured a long stretch of the river . . . to study . . . the cause of the malaria epidemic, since science has taught us that the vector of malaria is *Anofeles*, mosquitos who deposit their eggs in stagnant water." Along his route, he found "stagnant water and numerous muddy watersheds from which sprout thousands of mosquitos that bite the inhabitants who go to retrieve water, wash clothes, bathe." His response closely adhered to strategies based on contemporary scientific knowledge regarding mosquitos as malarial vectors and stagnant water as their breeding grounds. Yet malaria was more likely introduced by migrant workers returning from coastal harvest than anopheles that seldom survived in elevations above 2500 meters. Absent malarial mosquitos in Pomasqui, it would have been impossible for malaria to spread from returning migrants to local residents. Operating with imperfect information, Vaca strove to "extirpate ... the reigning illness and at the same time treat the many patients with efficacious scientific therapeutic resources."

Shortly after Vaca submitted his May 19 report, public health officials implemented a plan that reflected his multifaceted recommendations. The first phase was to "cure the sick, killing the parasite in the blood by scientifically administering quinine." The second step was "to abolish mosquitos, addressing tanks where they breed and killing them in houses." By deploying "measures suggested by science," they would prevent bites.[191] The commissioner formed a squad of twenty to twenty-five men divided into three groups. The first drained ponds. The second applied sheens of oil over water containers, while the last group disinfected houses of the sick and incinerated "large quantities of accumulated trash" where mosquitos might find stagnant water. The archival record yields little information about the interactions the third group had with local residents, but it is clear, more generally, that when zealous public health officials disinfected homes and inspected the afflicted, hygienic conditions, and water containers in them, residents' reactions ranged from collaborative to confrontational.

In 1914, the government allocated just 2.9 percent of its national budget to welfare; the military, by contrast, claimed 37.6 percent.[192] Small wonder, then, that a budget shortfall forced the public health department to withdraw personnel from Pomasqui after just three weeks of work, on June 16. Nevertheless, by July, Pomasqui had only a few convalescents, most of whom "imported it from malarial zones."[193] Although the mosquito breeding grounds "that multiply in the shore's river banks" had been cleared, Dr. Miño remained concerned that the cemetery was too close to town.[194] Dr. José Baquero, for his part, continued to work in Pomasqui even after the campaign was over. Despite his "poor health," he coordinated fumigating houses and draining swampy areas alongside the river "that threaten the population and may be the sole cause of ... malaria."[195] He also visited homes, requiring residents to keep their houses clean and to "remove by force those sick with malaria who refused medical care, a bad baseless belief."[196] Although Dr. Baquero's assertion that Pomasqui swamps caused malaria would eventually prove "baseless" itself, he and other public health officials in rural areas were regularly reminded that scientific medicine had made as many enemies as inroads in the highlands. When it was "impossible" for the sick to go to health clinics, doctors made house calls. Intended to bring medical science to reticent patients, those visits could be tense. Sometimes perceived as infringing upon private lives, some dwellers insulted, hid from, or fled providers whose class and often race differed from their own.

In Guayaquil, National Director of Public Health Dr. León Becerra felt the problems of inadequate finances too, noting the "grave economic difficulties" that prompted him to eliminate Guayaquil's mosquito control program in 1914.[197] Attributing good public health in the region "to the fight ... against mosquitos," he warned, "If service is suspended for too long, the damned diseases will return ... that is the worst ghost of foreigners who arrive or hope to arrive at our beaches."[198] But at least one other Guayaquil public health official was more optimistic, praising the city's successful campaigns against yellow fever, dysentery, and bubonic plague in 1914, and asserting that "malaria has fallen out of style and influenza [grippe] is annoyed to find itself alone."[199]

If malaria had fallen out of style, it quickly came back into fashion. Informed by Gorgas and other scientists, "antimalaria measures" in Guayaquil included "grass cutting, drainage, and oiling" (figure 22).[200] Since the rainy season had been "especially favorable to the development of ... Anopheles," a malaria epidemic erupted with a "very heavy" mortality rate by June 1919, as Dr. Becerra had predicted.[201] RF representatives advocated drainage, ditching, and filling low-lying areas to prevent puddles, as evident in photographs of Guayaquil's public squares, streets, and private patios filled with water during the rainy season (figures 23 and 24).[202] Ecuadorian public health officials embraced but were not constricted by RF antimalaria strategies.

When an "urgent antimalarial campaign in all towns in the Republic where the disease existed" began in 1924, the Ecuadorian government sold four lots of land to pay for the initiative.[203] Without state finances or a significant RF presence (like in Mexico and Brazil) to support large-scale environmental sanitation projects or mass quininization, the Ecuadorian government deployed resources at their disposal on a smaller scale. In addition to spreading oil on pools and ditches, Ecuadorian public health officials used salt, particularly in latrines and patios, to destroy and disinfect mosquito breeding grounds.[204] They also used the pesticide Kreso—derived from coal tar—to

Drainage ditch, Guayaquil.

FIGURE 22. "Drainage ditch, Guayaquil." Photograph by M. E. Connor, 1920. Rockefeller Foundation Photographs. Courtesy of Rockefeller Archive Center.

One of the main streets in Guayaquil.

FIGURE 23. Stagnant water in Guayaquil. Photograph by M.E. Connor, 1920. Rockefeller Foundation Photographs. Courtesy of Rockefeller Archive Center.

sanitize homes and public buildings.[205] Innovation and experimentation drove their malaria control campaigns, and national research informed Ecuador's multivariate strategies.[206] In September 1929, for example, Francisco Campos Po from the University of Guayaquil natural sciences department published a study demonstrating how to use "'Chara' to destroy the anopheles larvae that were agents of malaria."[207]

Ecuadorian officials drained and dried swamps and ponds, and dredged and cleaned canals and drains to eliminate mosquito breeding grounds.[208] When the Tahuando River where people bathed and washed clothes began forming pools where it should have been draining in December 1930, officials extended channels to empty stagnant water that "favors the propagation of anopheles that maintained malaria in Ibarra."[209] Public support—whether sincere or coerced—was paramount to success. As an engineer led public draining and cleaning work in Ibarra in 1936,[210] the city council threatened to fine landowners who did not drain standing water and clean canals and irrigation aqueducts on their property.[211] Addressing standing water could be contentious.[212] As in Pomasqui, the Ibarra antimalarial campaigns were

Filling a square, near center of city, Guayaquil.

FIGURE 24. A flooded plaza in Guayaquil. Photograph by M. E. Connor, 1920. Rockefeller Foundation Photographs. Courtesy of Rockefeller Archive Center.

based on incomplete knowledge of malaria etiology. Draining stagnant water was standard procedure, but unnecessary in a city some 2400 meters above sea level as malarial mosquitos do not live at that altitude.

Ecuadorian officials regularly distributed quinine for those suffering from malaria and as a prophylactic for those living amidst malarial epidemics.[213] With an "urgent antimalarial campaign" throughout the Republic in 1936, officials hoped they could "provide sufficient quantities of quinine."[214] Often they could not. In 1936, 50 percent of the population in Ibarra was suffering from malaria, "all of whom had to be cared for because they were people of true insolvency," and "not enough quinine was sent from Tumbabiro to cure them."[215] With limited budgets, public health officials advanced multivariate plans that tapped into the efforts and resources of private individuals. Such was the case in 1936, when Dr. Espinosa compelled landowners to "immediately drain pools and swamps and clean wastewater canals" and ordered "plasmoquilina or something similar to cure the sick, Chimba insecticide to destroy adult anopheles and . . . quinine. And models for new mosquito-proof construction model [houses]."[216] With proven methods grounded in (contemporary) science, he felt confident the antimalaria campaign would be successful.

In regions where malaria was endemic, officials like Dr. Espinosa encouraged mosquito-proof housing with RF support. Houses constructed with adobe or mud walls and straw or zinc roofs with little ventilation "favored anopheles attacks and malarial infection," particularly in the late afternoons when families gathered.[217] Although few rural Ecuadorians could afford new construction, some national officials and RF representatives tried to make it obligatory. Local authorities in places like Otavalo requested housing models so they could "obligate inhabitants in the parishes" to construct them.[218] With an eye toward the range of socioeconomic situations, at least two mosquito housing models were available.[219] One crucial component was screening.[220] Some authorities mandated that new construction meet mosquito housing codes.[221] This was likely wasted effort, however, as those who contracted malaria most likely did so during coastal migrations, since a city 2532 meters above sea level was unlikely to harbor malarial vectors.[222]

With dense collections of children, schools could become centers of contagion, and student illnesses could be harbingers of larger health problems lurking in communities. For those reasons, public health officials were particularly attuned to the public health of schools and reported malaria cases immediately.[223] When the teacher and occupant-owner of the house where the Mista de Chespi school operated fell ill with fever in 1939, Ecuador's General Director of School Hygiene considered it a "serious threat for the school, many students had been infected and others out of fear did not attend classes."[224] A few years later in January 1942, Puellaro was "invaded by malaria and the harm that continues developing in alarming form."[225] Of the 105 boys and 105 girls matriculated, 45 and 80 respectively had fallen ill, along with four teachers and four other adults at the school. Ten months later in Mindo, the infection rate was nearly 100 percent: by November 5, only two people in the town had not fallen ill. Because so many children were sick, attendance was down 20 to 50 percent. Despite the outbreak, teachers were making a "great effort not to stop classes."[226] In an already beleaguered rural education system, malaria could devastate schools.

Into the 1940s, Ecuadorian officials maintained a multifaceted "constant systemic campaign to combat" malaria.[227] Asking for a hundred vials of quinine to treat eighty-five patients in September 1942, public health officials declared malaria endemic in the indigenous *cantón* of San Miguel de Urcuqui and its parish Tumbabiro.[228] At 2592 and 2172 meters above sea level respectively, neither place likely hosted malarial vectors, but returning migrants may have contracted malaria frequently enough on the coast that their presence made malaria appear endemic. Sitting 2418 meters above sea level, Cotacachi seldom had malaria. When people who "had never left the town center" contracted malaria, the municipal medical official attributed it to the "growing abundance day by day of anopheles and mosquitos."[229] He feared that Cotacachi would become a "distinctly malarial zone." Owing to malaria, *antiquilostomiasis* (intestinal infection), dysentery, and an earthquake in May 1943, "everyone in the region has had to live out in the open and subject to many privations."[230] He encouraged national authorities "to take advantage of the last months of summer because . . . it would be impossible to verify any work due to the difficulties of getting to that parish during the winter." In addition to draining stagnant water and "petrolizing some areas," he planned to administer quinine to those who were sick, provide a preventative dose to the healthy, and advise everyone to use mosquito nets.[231]

As science advanced, scapegoating thrived. In 1939, Director of Health Dr. Leopoldo Izquieta Pérez mandated that airplanes originating from Cali be disinfected because they carried "a large quantity of mosquitos that constitute a real threat of . . . malaria worsening."[232] Dating to early-nineteenth-century independence movements, fears about germs jumping borders exacerbated historical tensions between Ecuador and Colombia (and other Latin American nations).[233] When malaria appeared in Pomasqui in 1947, authorities claimed a Colombian had introduced the "danger of contagion."[234]

Into the late 1940s, budget cuts regularly threatened to "return clean zones to infected ones" in Ecuador.[235] Underscoring the importance of continued funding, the Ecuadorian Minister of Social *Previsión* (Welfare) and Health argued, "The creation of sanitary units obviously demands expenses, but they will be very well rewarded, as one can see in countries more advanced than ours."[236] Absent rich coffers, Ecuador pragmatically pursued multivariate approaches that best addressed what local circumstances necessitated.

CONCLUSION

Malaria's ongoing presence in Guatemala and Ecuador can make it seem intractable. As late as 2004, malaria infected more than 57,000 Guatemalans, comprising more than 40 percent of all cases in Mesoamerica. But malaria's history offers a lens through which to mark the ways science, medicine, and social relations shaped each other over time.[237] As it traveled in indigenous bodies from coastal plantations to highland villages, malaria marked the ways poverty, geography, and ethnicity made some people more susceptible to tropical diseases than others. Social conditions determined morbidity.[238] Patterns of treatment—ranging from providing a few US scientists prophylactics to subjecting scores of migrant indigenous workers to malaria's maladies without adequate housing, mosquito nets, or nutritious meals—reveal social hierarchies.[239] Neither Ecuador nor Guatemala instituted fundamental structural change that could have curtailed malaria.[240] As much as public health campaigns increasingly accessed expanding scientific knowledge, tight budgets regularly compelled officials to deploy their least expensive resource: labor.

Instead of a universal approach, Ecuadorian and Guatemalan authorities adjusted strategies depending on local conditions, evolving science, national resources, and leaders' convictions. Informed by international research about antimalaria strategies and science, Guatemala and Ecuador charted antimalaria campaigns that involved combinations of environmental sanitation, drug distribution, larvae-eating fish, window and door screens, mosquito nets, and specific housing. Scant resources and varied ecologies and populations drove innovation and improvisation. Although campaigns were not always successful, they pioneered paths to malaria control in developing countries. Ecuador independently pursued malaria control while Guatemala often collaborated with the RF to develop and maintain antimalarial projects. Far more frequent and persistent in Guatemala than Ecuador, RF antimalaria interventions never matched the success of their early-twentieth-century yellow fever campaigns in both countries.[241] Elusive eradication mitigated the RF's influence on Guatemalan officials who seldom surrendered their unique approaches to combating malaria when resources and political stability afforded opportunities to do so on their own terms.

Malaria was more than an ailment: it was also a rhetorical tool. Local residents deployed it to attract government resources, and national officials used it to validate domestic interventions. In Guatemala, such justifications could legitimize corvée labor. Antimalarial campaigns often dovetailed nicely with other public health initiatives. Efforts to provide potable water and lavatories to rural communities frequently mentioned antimalarial campaigns as justification for such work. As problematic as malaria was, it could advance agendas.

Officials in both nations also suggested that highland malaria explained poverty, when in fact, malaria was just a symptom. To obscure vastly unequal land distribution (particularly in Guatemala where by 1950, some 2 percent of the population controlled 72 percent of arable land, whereas 88 percent of the population controlled 14 percent of the land) that catalyzed labor migration and contributed to health problems, officials made claims of highland malaria transmission at altitudes where that was not possible.[242] Rather than addressing the root causes of poverty and underdevelopment, officials targeted the disease.

Indigeneity, Racist Thought, and Modern Medicine

THE GUATEMALAN REVOLUTION (1944–54) spurred widespread labor organizing, agrarian reform, and extended social services to the poor, including medical care.[1] But medical professionals continued to discount certain practitioners and patients, to the point where some doctors used the latter as involuntary research subjects. From 1946 to 1948, USPHS doctors on contract with the PASB, on whom the USPHS had considerable influence, infected indígenas and other Guatemalans with syphilis, gonorrhea, and chancroid. PASB targeted the most vulnerable Guatemalans as research subjects: prisoners, mental hospital inmates, military conscripts, indígenas, sex workers, and orphans. Associations between criminality and indigenous culture meant indígenas were particularly vulnerable to imprisonment and confinement. Instead of informing research subjects that they were being infected with syphilis, let alone seeking their consent, researchers enticed individuals to participate by offering cigarettes and soap.[2] US and Guatemalan medical professionals and authorities approached those groups as if they had no rights, and thus prior consent was assumed not to matter.

The experiments were led by the US doctor John C. Cutler, with assistance from Dr. Luis Galich and another Guatemalan, Dr. Juan Funes, who had been trained on a USPHS fellowship. Cutler, Galich, and Funes did a series of experiments in which they paid female sex workers who had contracted syphilis and gonorrhea to have intercourse with uninfected male subjects drawn from the population of vulnerable Guatemalans (particularly soldiers). When those sexual relations failed to yield statistically significant infection rates, Cutler employed a more direct, invasive, and painful methodology, this time working on inmates at the National Mental Health Hospital. Doctors abraded each subject's penis with a hypodermic needle, and then dripped a syphilitic emulsion onto a cotton pad on the abraded area for one to two hours.[3] Aware that mental health patients could not give consent, some senior USPHS researchers were uncomfortable with those experiments. At least one pushed Cutler to terminate them. Instead, Cutler largely conducted them in secret.[4]

Cutler and other USPHS and PASB researchers believed indígenas were ideal test subjects, both because they were already marginalized, and because, as Cutler saw it, experimenting on "pure Indians" would allow for the practice of "pure science." His notion of pure science entailed "shoot[ing] living germs into human bodies" (like US researchers did with rabbits in laboratories) as part of the experiment, as opposed to studying previously infected individuals like the African American men in the 1932–72 USPHS study in Tuskegee, Alabama.[5] In turn, he wanted "pure" indigenous subjects to disprove his boss US Surgeon General Thomas Parran's theory that syphilis was "biologically different" in "negros," Mesoamerican "Indians," and whites.[6] Assistant chief of the USPHS Venereal Disease Division and PASB Caribbean sector chief Dr. Joseph Spotto secured indigenous subjects and advised Cutler not to confuse the "Indians" by offering them explanations.[7] Since some subjects only spoke indigenous languages, they would not have understood US and Guatemalan doctors even had they tried to explain their research.[8]

Among Guatemalan researchers, debates had circulated in the 1930s and 1940s over whether indigenous Guatemalans had acquired immunity to syphilis.[9] The longstanding myth that indigenous people of the Americas had given syphilis to Spanish conquistadores influenced these disputes. For his part, Funes rejected these notions and encouraged the government to extend venereal disease control measures to highland communities. He also advocated using indigenous languages in such public health campaigns.[10] Reflecting the assimilationist and interventionist bent of political leaders during the Guatemalan Revolution, Funes argued that these public health campaigns would "civilize" indígenas and uplift the nation.[11]

As the experiments progressed and they encountered problems with the accuracy of diagnostic tests for syphilis, Cutler and his team became more focused on questions of race. They sought to study whether factors in the population, tropical environment, or presence of malaria confounded study results. Ultimately, Cutler concluded indígenas had no "racial immunity" to syphilis.[12] Contravening Dr. Quintana's efforts to dispel racist notions that "Indians" were "uncooperative" and "superstitious," Cutler complained, "The

Indians had ... very widespread prejudices against frequent withdrawals of blood ... [and were] uneducated and superstitious."[13]

Medical experimentation on marginalized people has a long history. During and after slavery in the United States, medical professionals and authorities experimented on people of African descent. For example, James Marion Sims, considered the founder of modern gynecology, callously operated on enslaved Black women to learn how to treat vesico-vaginal fistulae. Assuming they experienced little or no pain, he (like many of his colleagues) denied them anesthesia during operations even when their agony was apparent.[14] Those cruel practices set the stage for the USPHS Tuskegee trials, in which some of the African American men infected with syphilis were denied treatment (without being told) so that medical researchers—including Cutler—could observe the disease as it progressed.[15] Although USPHS researchers had injected otherwise healthy prisoners with syphilis in Indiana in 1943, in pursuit of less oversight and cheaper research labor, the USPHS targeted a nation well within the US political, economic, and—thanks largely to the RF—medical orbits of power.[16] Shortly after news of the USPHS experiments came to light in 2010, the US government formally apologized.

Similarly, malaria research presaged unethical medical conduct in Guatemala. Women in their first months of pregnancy who attended an urban clinic served as a control group in a 1945 malaria study. "The objective has been to get the average normal values in women in Guatemala City at 4850 feet above sea level," explained the head of the antimalaria campaign.[17] By 1945, infant mortality was linked to malaria, but his report makes no mention of obtaining consent before drawing patients' blood.[18] Few Guatemalan or US researchers at the time concerned themselves with securing consent. Although blood draws may not have interfered with appropriate healthcare delivery, instead of concentrating on infant and maternal health, the clinic was a contact zone where medical professionals advanced their malaria expertise and patients unwittingly became objects of research. Some Guatemalan medical professionals approached treatment as research.[19] Part of Guatemala's nastier legacies, such blurred lines between providing healthcare and conducting research were erased altogether the following year.

Overcrowded and underresourced, institutions like Guatemala City's Central Penitentiary, National Mental Health Hospital, and national orphanage were ill-prepared to refuse the inducements offered by the USPHS, which included donated drugs, refrigerators, and a movie projector.[20] Yet the targeting of indigenous subjects cannot simply be explained in terms of economic pressure. The military, for example, enjoyed robust budgets. But it had a long history of coercively conscripting young indigenous men in the highlands, whom anti-indigenous racism had long cast as expendable in the views of ladinos and Creoles.[21]

That such blatant human rights violations came during Arévalo's democratic administration, which vowed to free people from fascist oppression and exploitation, and at a time when medical professionals like Funes were becoming more attuned to the needs of indígenas, speaks to the insidiousness and pervasiveness of anti-indigenous racism. The state perceived indigenous Guatemalans not as citizens, but as charges, or worse still, burdens.[22] As the preceding chapters have demonstrated, the Guatemalan government and Ministry of Health had been using scientific medicine to marginalize indigenous healthcare practices and epistemologies for decades—and by extension, indigenous communities, histories, and worldviews. Small wonder, then, that Guatemalan officials were receptive to US medical advances.

Like the RF, the US government had approached Guatemala as a "workshop" where it could experiment with programs before pursuing them at home or on the world stage.[23] While Guatemalan officials and intellectuals expressed outrage when the USPHS experiments came to light, they generally failed to reflect upon their own nation's responsibility, or on the fact that, a year before the syphilis experiments, Guatemalan researchers had conducted malaria experiments on pregnant women at a prenatal clinic. Guatemalan President Álvaro Colom (2008–12) asked Guatemalan archivists and academics to research and write an in-depth historical account and analysis of the syphilis experiments, but it remains largely unread. Although the authors recognize Guatemala's complicity, they emphasize the US role in the experiments. Tellingly, the report's cover has an image of US experiments on African American prisoners rather than the Guatemalan trials.[24]

The USPHS Guatemalan syphilis experiments provide another window into the transnational influences and comparative distinctions between Guatemala and Ecuador. A shared distrust of social medicine and disparagement of indígenas facilitated the conditions whereby US and Guatemalan medical professionals approached marginalized Guatemalans first as test subjects and second, if at all, as patients. But in Ecuador, absent a shared cynicism toward social medicine, and with much less virulent racism among medical professionals, a culture of experimentation on marginalized people never emerged. With eugenics that emphasized a national rather than ethnic *raza* and a medical culture that at least accepted (albeit without endorsing) indigenous healing and occasionally exalted indigenous approaches to public health and responses to epidemics, Ecuador ensured indígenas would more likely become participants and even collaborators, rather than subjects, in public health initiatives.

The distinct trajectories of race relations in Guatemala and Ecuador shaped and were shaped by the dynamic relationships between indigenous and scientific medicines and their practitioners, as well as by outside influences. Without demanding assimilation, Ecuadorians celebrated indígenas who incorporated learned medicine. This stance was remarkable in a region where Latin American nations decried dirty "indios" for catalyzing epidemics, restricted citizenship to educated people who maintained good hygiene, and privileged scientific medicine.[25] Although efficacious RF public health programs lent legitimacy to Guatemalan and Ecuadorian governments that collaborated with them, the costs of international public health interventions often outweighed the benefits. Whereas Ecuador's relative autonomy kept the more deleterious effects of foreign public health interventions at bay, Guatemala's firm position in the US sphere of influence could undermine its public health.[26]

Public health is not always the unproblematic good it seems. Whether in extreme forms like the syphilis experiments, or in the subtler forms of control it took throughout the first half of the twentieth century, scientific medicine was put to work delegitimizing indigenous practices, self-determination, and connections to history. Yet it seldom dominated popular or hybrid healing altogether. The same public health initiatives that expanded state authority provided indígenas opportunities to deflect state overtures and advance their healing practices and knowledge. When we examine the ways indígenas collaborated with, adapted to, redeployed, ignored, and contested public health initiatives, we get a fuller picture of the ways that many actors—not just international and national advocates, but also curanderos, empíricos, and their patients—have shaped the practice, delivery, and experience of modern medicine in Latin America. The success of many public health initiatives was determined as much by indígenas' responses to them as by officials who crafted and implemented them.

Indigenous midwives and curanderos who demonstrated the relevance of their knowledge and effectiveness of their practices could also mitigate medical professionals' and public health officials' denigration of indígenas. Healers, patients, and medical professionals who made concessions demonstrated that efficacy trumped ideology. Such concessions fostered hybrid healthcare and syncretic medical discourse.[27]

As was true elsewhere in the Americas, marginalized people subject to state power redeployed popular notions about the health and welfare of the nation to claim their place in it.[28] Indígenas resisted mandates they considered detrimental: in Ecuador, for example, they continued to keep the domestic animals on which they depended in their courtyards, even after authorities prohibited them. But they also adopted what served them, sometimes integrating it with their own practices. Sigchos indígenas used live vaccine inoculation alongside their traditional healing practices. Faced with epidemics, Ecuadorian indígenas adapted learned medical methods that, though they undercut longstanding tradition, were crucial to survival, such as replicating vaccination campaigns and burning infected homes and corpses. Kaqchikel patients traveled to Guatemala City to consult medical doctors after hinterland healing methods failed. Indígenas' adoption of such strategies and methods speaks both to the urgency of the problems they faced and to a degree of trust in the government.

In turn, some officials advanced vernacular medicine that incorporated scientific and traditional knowledge. Blanco-mestizo public health officials lauded indigenous vaccination campaigns, and ladino doctors explained disease etiology in ways that resonated with indigenous notions of illness.[29] Some medical professionals incorporated aspects of indigenous midwifery, and judicial officials recognized susto as a medical condition, contravening elite discourse about the inferiority of indigenous medicine.[30]

The capacity of indigenous and other marginalized populations to advance their interests and to influence national and imperial overtures shaped public health campaigns. As manifestations of how local ideas and concerns influenced public health initiatives, indigenous leaders facilitated public health campaigns, indigenous empíricos administered vaccines, and indígenas served on municipal public health committees.[31] Local appropriation and adaptation of public health campaigns were crucial to their success.[32] In 1944, municipal empíricos identified and treated typhus patients in Guatemalan neighborhoods who family members might have otherwise hid.[33] As part of a broader effort to tilt the balance of power from highland hacendados to indigenous huasipungueros, Ecuadorian national officials made concessions to incorporate indígenas. As shown in the extent to which public health initiatives in each country incorporated and valued indígenas, Ecuadorian indígenas established more autonomy and political power than their Guatemalan counterparts. In Guatemala and Ecuador, the politics of indigeneity—particularly the level to which the state included, defended, ignored, or exploited indígenas—was as consequential for public health as scientific developments.

Public health interventions into people's private lives altered local social relations and cultural norms. Ecuadorian and Guatemalan officials vilified both untrained midwives and ignorant mothers as threats to public health, blaming women for their countries' high infant mortality rates. Yet officials recognized that their nations desperately needed midwives' services, particularly in rural areas where medical professionals were lacking. With experiential and formal knowledge, women who worked as nurses and midwives, whether trained or untrained, continued to support mothers and facilitate reproduction. Indigenous curanderos and midwives who survive in the archival record offer evidence that indigenous healing thrived despite international and national efforts to establish scientific medicine as the only legitimate option. Female providers dominated natal care. Unlicensed midwives in Guatemala and university-educated midwives in Ecuador cared for many more poor and working-class women than did male doctors. Midwives also articulated proposals, highlighted inequalities, and shaped solutions to high infant mortality rates that adhered to local realities and experiences. Ecuadorian natal care outreach clinics demonstrate that medical professionals' exchanges with local populations largely determined the efficacy of reproductive health initiatives. As part of their outreach to pregnant women and new mothers, Ecuadorian midwives expanded their autonomy by confronting or eluding doctors who supervised them. They freed up their time for their patients and themselves by gradually reducing their written reports to distant superiors (much to this historian's chagrin). Pursued by Guatemalan authorities, indigenous midwives there similarly deployed evasion, even as they provided critical healthcare.

As efforts to reinforce the supposed inferiority of women and indígenas remind us, public health initiatives were intimately tied to the state's disciplinary power, but this hegemony was not watertight. Indigenous curanderos and other empíricos countervailed medical professionals', public health officials', RF representatives', and government authorities' efforts to establish a medical monopoly on healthcare.[34] Both nations promoted hygiene partly to instill notions of citizenship that included self-control, acquiescence, and good health, but each state's capacity to enforce public health mandates was attenuated, particularly in rural regions. The RF similarly fell short of its goal "to remake civilization along American lines" through "a full transfer of technology."[35] Indígenas and their healers shaped rural healthcare and public health initiatives in ways that neither RF representatives nor government agents could have predicted.

RACISM AND SCIENCE

Broadly speaking, historians of medicine maintain an elevated status for science in their analyses and narratives. But while science drove the study and practice of medicine in both Guatemala and Ecuador, it was not the only or even necessarily the most salient factor in public health initiatives or health-care outcomes. Other factors included race, gender, class, politics, elite machinations, topography, climate, language, culture, indigenous and traditional healing, and authorities', officials', indígenas', curanderos', midwives', public health representatives', patients', and medical professionals' perceptions—including, importantly, what Alan Kraut calls the "medicalization of preexisting prejudices."[36]

To the extent that racism can be measured, the medicalization of prejudices was more persistent and pernicious in Guatemala than Ecuador. Both countries had their faults. When poverty undermined the ability of rural indígenas to keep their bodies and homes clean, for example, authorities and officials portrayed them as dirty, diseased retrogrades. But in Ecuador, indigenous hygiene was not criminalized, and—thanks to better recourses (for example, appeals to the Junta Central de Asistencia Pública) and engagement (such as public health messaging directed at them in their language)—Ecuadorian indígenas were less likely to be stigmatized as vectors of disease than their Guatemalan counterparts. Ecuadorian officials were also more likely to attribute ill health to poverty and insufficient potable water and sewage systems, rather than indigenous rituals. In Guatemala, the medicalization of racism was more malevolent: elites, authorities, and journalists frequently blamed indígenas for their own ill health, and RF representatives there generally followed suit.

Consider, for example, the work of Ecuadorian Dr. Pablo Arturo Suárez (1888–1945), the general director of the Servicio de Sanidad from 1926 to 1929.[37] Unlike many of his contemporaries, whose lives and work centered around Guayaquil, Suárez was raised in Ambato and its environs, and thus was familiar with Andean indigenous culture. His writings on indigenous life in the 1930s reveal empathy and understanding that many of his predecessors and contemporaries lacked.[38] Suárez's compassionate portrayal of indígenas distinguished him from Guatemalan Nobel Laureate Miguel Angel

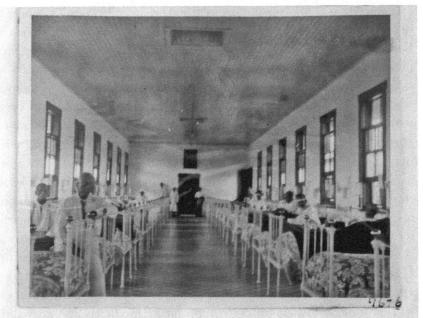

Interior of one of the new public wards. Note colored bedspreads, and brass knobs on beds – reflecting Indian influence

FIGURE 25. "Colored bedspreads, and brass knobs ... reflecting Indian influence."
Photograph by Dr. Robert Lambert (?), 1922. Rockefeller Foundation Photographs. Courtesy
of Rockefeller Archive Center.

Asturias, who disparaged indigenous culture and proposed miscegenation
and acculturation to improve indígenas' and the nation's lot. Mitigated racist
thought helped Ecuadorian officials facilitate more efficacious public health
campaigns than their Guatemalan counterparts.

Yet a 1922 RF photograph suggests that Guatemalan and RF officials
attempted to make at least some overtures toward accommodating ethnic
difference (figure 25). Emphasizing a Guatemalan hospital's attempt to incorporate indigenous culture, the caption reads, "Interior of one of new public
wards. Note colored bedspreads and brass knobs on beds—reflecting Indian
influence."[39] The effect of such interior designs is difficult to discern, but—
given that public hospitals were generally sites that repressed indigenous
healing practices—the ward's design can be understood as an attempt to
combine indigeneity and modernity.

However, the assertion that colorful blankets and brass knobs reflected
"Indian influence" betrays a superficial understanding of indigenous

cultures, where symbols and colors were more than efforts to enliven outfits or spaces. In Comalapa, for example, the red stripes along the shoulders of Kaqchikel women's *huipiles* (hand-woven blouses) represented the violence (either blood or fire depending on the weaver and wearer) of Spanish invasions. The black-and-white photograph makes it hard to say much about whether the colors chosen by this Hispanic institution would have been inviting for indigenous patients. The brass knobs are even more difficult to relate to indigenous culture. Perhaps the designers were thinking of the staffs indigenous leaders carried to denote their authority, or, more generally, associating the knobs' shine with images of colorful indigenous residents. Viewed from these perspectives, the public ward's designs may have been a kind of microcosm for the way the RF was, more broadly, unable to see the complexity and completeness of indigenous cultures in Guatemala.

RF representatives steeped in US racism found familiar ground in Guatemala, where ladinos and Creoles regularly disparaged, exploited, and abused indígenas. Where racism had deep and broad roots, its medicalization was apparent and insidious. Even exceptional RF officials who arrived in Guatemala with open minds quickly cemented their connections with Creole and ladino medical professionals whose families often owned plantations where indígenas toiled under miserable conditions for negligible wages. As a result, public health campaigns seldom addressed indígenas' specific needs, concerns, or interests. A dialectical tension developed between RF representatives and Guatemalan officials over the extent to which each party emphasized class and material conditions. Some RF representatives highlighted how poverty undermined indigenous health, whereas their Guatemalan colleagues attributed illnesses to indigeneity.

RF engagement in Ecuador largely skirted indigenous interaction altogether, because the RF tended to work in Guayaquil where few indígenas lived. The Ecuadorian state did not comprehensively exploit indígenas. With eugenics focused on improving the nation rather than reducing indigeneity, Ecuadorian officials included indígenas in the march toward progress. Knowledge of relations with, discourse about, and status of indígenas in Ecuador likely attenuated RF representatives' racial thinking there.

RF staff provide a bellwether for the intensity and ubiquity of racism in each country. Ecuadorian indígenas enjoyed some ethnic immunity to the stigmas that so readily attached themselves to their Guatemalan counterparts. Partly attributable to their differential engagement with indígenas in each country, RF representatives' perceptions of Kichwas in Ecuador were less strident than their portrayals of Mayas in Guatemala. To his credit, Nelson Rockefeller understood how charged ethnic relations were, noting, "anything done in relation to Indians might offend the powers that be in many Latin American countries."[40] The foundation's distinct engagement with and perceptions of indígenas in Guatemala and Ecuador demonstrates how an interactive matrix of different types of racism shaped and were shaped by foreign public health and medical professionals in national contexts.

Even as the RF offered aid, countries saw public health as an effort not to serve imperial agendas but to improve national well-being without disrupting the socioeconomic status quo. Governments expected indígenas to transition to scientific medicine, but offered few resources to facilitate this. As was true of Latin America more broadly, rural poor Guatemalan and Ecuadorian indígenas lacked adequate health services.[41] Because neither nation had the resources to extirpate empiricism, these Janus-faced states concurrently vilified and condoned indigenous and other unlicensed healers. Portraying indígenas as anti-modern even as they embraced aspects of learned medicine set the stage for pitting scientific against indigenous medicine. With limited budgets, each nation's allocation of public health resources fell along racial (nonindigenous over indigenous) and geographic (urban rather than rural) lines. Political and economic priorities determined public health initiatives.[42] Ultimately, Ecuadorian and Guatemalan medical professionals were too few in number and their tools too blunt to purge unlicensed practitioners or to liberate indígenas from disease.[43] Indicating how the intertwined relationship between geography and ethnicity shaped each state's provision of healthcare, the combination of indigeneity and rurality meant states often left highland indígenas to their own devices.[44]

Although some indígenas rejected public health overtures and avoided healthcare institutions, few doubted their right to healthcare and public health services. Unlike Mexican indígenas who considered public health a limited resource controlled by authorities, Ecuadorian and Guatemalan indígenas considered healthcare a right even when accessing it was difficult.[45] They maintained a sense of medical citizenship, which varied across place, race, class, gender, and other factors. In a pattern evident throughout Latin American court records from the colonial to republican eras, they tended not to decry their exclusion, but instead to demonstrate their vulnerability and make claims to care,[46] placing themselves at the center of state concern.

Public health initiatives and scientific medicine were intertwined with national belonging, which in turn dictated who had access to those resources.

Nations such as Mexico sought to transform rural residents into citizens through public health campaigns (hookworm in the 1920s; malaria in the 1950s), hygiene expectations (using latrines and wearing shoes), and scientific medicine (submitting to physicians).[47] In Guatemala and Ecuador, healthcare personnel and public health officials similarly shaped who was included in (those who embraced scientific medicine) and who was excluded from (poor indígenas who propagated disease, indigenous vendors who wore rebozos, urban unlicensed curanderos) the national collective. At the 1938 Pan American Conference in Lima, Peru, delegates recognized indígenas as citizens, though Guatemala (like Peru and Mexico) struggled to define them. Even as Guatemalan IING scholars advocated redistributing resources to indígenas, they distinguished between "premodern, underdeveloped" indígenas and "modern, fully developed" citizens.[48] Indígenas had to accept some level of state-sanctioned medicine to enjoy Guatemalan citizenship. Framed differently in Ecuador, citizenship was tied to literacy until the 1979 constitution removed that requirement, thereby enfranchising many indígenas. Despite not being citizens, illiterate indígenas forged paths to public health and medical care.

1944–PRESENT

The sexually transmitted infections experiments notwithstanding, Arévalo's administration made public health inroads with indígenas by disseminating information about health campaigns in indigenous communities. Thereafter, many Kaqchikel appreciated Arévalo's plan to distribute vaccinations and eradicate vector insects.[49] When he dispatched health brigades to rural areas, indígenas did not consider it intrusive because he made the problem and goals explicit. Where resistance persisted, Arévalo sent doctors or local indigenous commissions to explain the situation to residents.[50] Despite Guatemala's strides in the first half of the twentieth century, the World Bank was unimpressed, observing in 1951, that "malaria ... malnutrition and unsanitary dwellings are still sapping the energy of vast numbers of Guatemalans."[51]

Intending to address such social injustices while growing Guatemala's economy, President Jacobo Arbenz (1951–54) expropriated and redistributed idle arable land (much of which belonged to UFCO). In contrast, the "pro-imperialist" administrations of Galo Plaza Lasso (1949–52) and Velasco

Ibarra (1952–56) facilitated Ecuador's expanding capitalist development.[52] By the early 1950s, the RF recognized that social medicine—and specifically, addressing malnutrition and famine—was as important as science in improving individual and public health. As their efforts to increase agricultural production ramped up, their international public health interventions faded.[53]

By the mid-twentieth century, Kichwas and Mayas were on the cusp of dramatically different realities despite experiencing similar stigmas, illnesses, and poverty. Ecuador included Kichwas and their healing practices in the creation of its healthcare policies, an ethos that helped facilitate an indigenous rights movement that grew into one of Latin America's strongest. Guatemala, however, persecuted Mayas. The US Central Intelligence Agency engineered a coup in Guatemala that ended Arbenz's democratically-elected administration and facilitated the military's control of the government; during the subsequent civil war (1960–96), indígenas comprised the overwhelming majority of victims. The military government's persecution of Mayas turned genocidal after 1980, when state security forces systematically raped, tortured, and killed indígenas and razed indigenous communities.[54] Even at their lowest points, indigenous-state relations never devolved into genocide in Ecuador.

Despite the two nations' increasingly divergent political and medical trajectories, some elements of Guatemalan health in the second half of the twentieth century began to mirror the combination of respect for indigenous healing practices and social medicine in Ecuador. When US doctor Carroll Behrhorst founded a health clinic in Chimaltenango (Guatemala) in 1962, he knew that social and economic injustice shaped his clientele's health. To improve public health in the surrounding areas, he trained indigenous leaders and curanderos in scientific healthcare and also initiated potable water projects, literacy and agricultural extension programs, vaccination campaigns, and family planning workshops. Many veterans of his program, who had both Kaqchikel language skills and understanding of local culture, established successful health clinics in remote rural communities. As one Kaqchikel nurse noted, "In the country and in the homes, the cause of the problems can be seen more directly. Here in the clinic, merely the diseases are seen."[55] Behrhorst insisted public health initiatives would have little long-term impact without furnishing "the structure and tools to build an equitable society."[56] Rural health promoter supervisor Carlos Xoquic concurred: "Curing diseases without touching their origins is an error, a mistake. A sick and malnourished person might recover well at the hospital, but confronted with same situation at home will soon get sick again. The most important thing is prevention of disease. . . . If the cause is contaminated water or a lack of hygiene, it is fairly easy to advise a patient, but one should not tell every malnourished patient to feed himself better, for that person might not have the money to buy better food."[57]

As Behrhorst knew, advocating for social and economic reforms in Central America could be perilous. When empowered rural residents in neighboring Costa Rica vocalized how unemployment and poverty impeded their ability to maintain good health, officials there considered community participation subversive and disenfranchised participants from health policy decision-making.[58] Such activism (or unwelcome dissent) could be fatal under Guatemala's military government. Yet attention to social and economic conditions helped Guatemala nearly halve its death rate from 28.5 deaths per thousand in 1940–44 to 15 deaths per thousand in 1965–70. (Those gains notwithstanding, chronic malnutrition continued to plague indigenous communities.)[59]

Scientific, indigenous, Afro-descendant, folk, and Hispanic medicines increasingly interconnected into the late twentieth century, but some practitioners and patients sought to distinguish their knowledge base. By tapping into scientific medical resources available through private and nongovernmental healthcare organizations, indigenous midwives expanded their social capital in ways that legitimized their traditional knowledge and practices.[60] Remarkably, during a civil war that disproportionately terrorized Mayas, the Center for Mesoamerican Studies on Appropriate Technology (CEMAT) initiated field and lab work in 1976 to identify, understand, and produce medicinal plants for primary healthcare. Indigenous knowledge of plants' medicinal uses was crucial to that project and the FARMAYA natural products laboratories that emerged some fifteen years later.[61] Yet among indigenous healthcare practitioners with some medical training, critiques of curanderos could be fierce. Empírica Margarita Salpor Chalí sharply distinguished her work from that of rural healers: "I am not a doctor, [but] I treat them all. One cannot send them away when they are so sick and in pain, and just let them die. . . . They all used to go to brujos before, and some people still do. There are many brujos here in the mountains. They have their tables—tables of stone with crosses on them, as many as seven crosses for different gods. But the brujos are of the devil and don't help the people, so the people come to me for medicine and continue to come."[62] Even as she denigrated traditional healing, Salpor Chalí recognized that many of her contemporaries continued to consult it. In a testament to how strongly Mayas defended indigenous medicine, many criticized K'iche Maya Nobel Peace Prize laureate Rigoberta Menchu for using a doctor to deliver her baby. Some Maya salespeople even attached their own cautionary messages to pharmaceutical labels, hoping to undermine scientific medicine with its own techniques.[63]

Today, the challenges of integrating indigenous cosmologies, worldviews, and health practices into national health systems remain. Ecuador has progressed further along that path than Guatemala. Recognizing the nation as pluricultural and multiethnic, the 1998 Ecuadorian constitution officially validated traditional medicine practitioners. The following year, the Ecuadorian Ministry of Health founded the National Department of Health of Indigenous Peoples. Throughout Latin America, governments created official processes to license traditional medicine. Enjoying significant political power, Ecuadorian indigenous groups ensured their interests and needs remained on national agendas during times of political turmoil. After indigenous protests fueled the 2005 overthrow of President Lucio Gutiérrez (2003–05), legislators drafted an intercultural constitution that incorporated *Sumak Kawsay*—the indigenous principle of living in harmony with nature.[64] Part of a larger trend toward intercultural health in twenty-first-century Latin America motivated by a resurgence of curanderos, midwives, empíricos, bonesetters, herbalists, and other traditional healers, Sumak Kawsay and other accommodations in the 2008 constitution speak to indigenous medicine's vibrancy and relevance in a nation that has a rich history of scientific medical breakthroughs. Medical pluralism continues to mark healing and well-being in twenty-first century Ecuador, where people are increasingly embracing Sumak Kawsay or a *buen vivir* (living well) philosophy that advances community-centric, ecologically-balanced, and culturally-sensitive approaches to development and social coexistence rooted in a Kichwa cosmovision.[65]

Such developments reflect ongoing efforts to build social trust between indígenas and officials. Without that trust, the outcomes for public health tend to be bleak. Political scientist Francis Fukuyama found that from 2019–22, the nations who best weathered the coronavirus pandemic were those whose governments enjoyed broad trust. Governments need to respond to crises with culturally-sensitive forms of outreach, and they need to build that sensitivity even before crisis arises.

Writing this book during a pandemic has brought into focus the patterns that connect past and present, including the underlying racist inequities that make some people more vulnerable to disease than others. In the early twentieth century, rather than build crucial infrastructure like piped water and sewer systems, Guatemalan and Ecuadoran officials blamed poor and indigenous people for illnesses that, absent such infrastructure, spread quickly. Similarly, US public health responses to COVID-19 called for social distancing, but did not initially provide sufficient personal protective equipment or facilitate other safety measures for exposed front-line workers who could not afford to isolate themselves. Poor and working-class people of color had higher morbidity and mortality rates than their wealthy and middle-class light-skinned counterparts.[66]

Even before the period I examine here in this book, Latin American indígenas have been disproportionately devastated by disease, beginning with the arrival of Europeans in the Americas. Prior to the sixteenth century, Ecuadorian and Guatemalan indigenous populations numbered as many as 1.6 and 2 million, respectively. But they had no immunities to the European diseases of smallpox, typhus, and measles brought by Spanish invaders, and by the early seventeenth century, indigenous populations had plummeted by some 90 percent.[67] The 1918–20 influenza pandemic disproportionately harmed indígenas, and the COVID-19 pandemic appears to be doing so too. Latin America has been the region hit hardest by coronavirus, known in Kaqchikel as *itzel yab'il* (bad/ugly/evil virus/illness) and *nimyab'il* (big virus/disease). By September 2020, the ten countries with the highest coronavirus death toll were all in Latin America or the Caribbean, and those numbers were likely undercounted.[68] Guatemala and Ecuador have not released statistics about death, infection, and indigeneity, but numbers from other Latin American countries do not bode well: in Brazil, indigenous people were six times more likely to be infected by COVID-19 than white Brazilians.[69] To counteract that trend in Guatemala, officials, communities, and NGOs disseminated public health materials that were translated into indigenous languages and incorporated local contexts.[70] Although such materials are a good start, more must be done to eliminate barriers indigenous populations face. The historical legacy of Guatemalan medical practitioners' and authorities' (and RF representatives') inability to accommodate indigenous healing practices and knowledge, establish a trustworthy presence in indigenous communities, or speak indigenous languages continues to undermine public health projects and healthcare.

That lack of interest, care, and respect for others harms public health efforts not just within nations, but across them. Consider, for example, the fact that in just two weeks in December 2018, two indigenous Guatemalan children died in US Customs and Border Patrol custody. Jakelin Amei Rosmery Caal Maquin, a seven-year-old K'ekchi Maya girl, died of dehydration. Felipe Gómez Alonso, an eight-year-old Chuj Maya boy, died from influenza B. Their deaths are grim reminders of inequity not just within the borders of Guatemala, but globally, as the Global North continues to exploit the Global South, resulting in an ongoing refugee crisis.[71] Like tens of thousands of other Guatemalans, these children were fleeing poverty, gang violence, and the effects of climate change in Guatemala, all of which can be traced, in meaningful ways, to US foreign policy, trade, and consumption. Their deaths remind us that public health is not just about, say, distributing medicine—though that matters too, and certainly, had these children received adequate care from the United States, they would be alive today. But poverty, violence, and climate change all contribute to rising mortality and morbidity rates around the globe, particularly for those suffering from economic and racial inequalities. Unless we treat these problems, too, as public health crises, our collective losses will continue to mount.

NOTES

ABBREVIATIONS USED IN THE NOTES

AGCA	Archivo General de Centroamérica
AMP	Archivo Municipal de Patzicía
ANE	Archivo Nacional Ecuador
AP	Asistencia Pública collection, MM
BNG	Biblioteca Nacional de Guatemala
CIRMA	Centro de Investigaciones Regionales de Mesoamérica
DC	Dieseldorff Collection, TULAL
DGE	Dirección General de Estadística
DGS	Director General de Sanidad
DHG	Director de Hospital General
FLA	Fondo de Libros Antiguos, BNG
HNG	Hemeroteca Nacional de Guatemala
INE	Instituto Nacional de Estadística
JP-C	Jefetura Política de Chimaltenango records
JP-S	Jefetura Política de Sacatepéquez records
LNDLSC	Loyola-Notre Dame Library Special Collections
MGJ	*Memoria de las labores del ejecutivo en el ramo de Gobernación y Justicia*
MM	Museo de Medicina
MPN	*Memoria de la Dirección General de la Policía Nacional* (1926–30); *Memoria de los trabajos realizados por la dirección general de la Policía Nacional* (1932–40)
MSGJ	*Memoria de la Secretaría de Gobernación y Justicia*

MSP	*Memoria de los labores [trabajos] realizados por la dirección general de Sanidad Pública y sus dependencias*
RAC	Rockefeller Archive Center
SA	Sanidad collection, MM
SP	Índices de Salud Pública
TULAL	Tulane University, Latin American Library

A NOTE ON SOURCES, METHODOLOGY, AND EVIDENCE

1. Crosby, "Past," 1177; Crosby, *America's Forgotten Pandemic*.

2. Cueto and Palmer, *Medicine*, 12, 16.

3. Alexander Yarza de los Ríos argues that indigenous languages are connected to "ancestral medicinal processes." See Yarza de los Ríos, "Abya Yala's Disability."

4. Few, *For All*; Gómez, *Experiential Caribbean*; Warren, *Medicine*; Greene and Podolsky, "Keeping."

5. Obregón, *Batallas*; Cueto, *Return*.

6. Rosenberg, *Cholera Years*.

7. Gómez, *Experiential Caribbean*, 7 (quote); Few, *For All*.

8. For a notable exception, see Zulawski, *Unequal Cures*.

9. Historian Deirdre Cooper Owens similarly demonstrates how racial science contradicted assumptions about black people's inferiority; see *Medical Bondage*.

10. MM, SA, 0643, Reglamento Especial sobre aprovisionamento y venta de leches ca. 1926–1927, article 15; Reglamento especial de carnicerias (Tercenas) ca. 1926–1927, article 15; and Reglamento de panaderias ca. 1926–1927, article 23.

11. For studies that consider learned medicine's engagement with popular medicine, see Palmer, *Popular Medicine*; Gómez, *Experiential Caribbean*. For studies of distinct versions of biomedicines and "biomedical uncertainty," see Street, *Biomedicine*; Berg and Mol, *Differences*; Mol, *Body*; Livingston, *Improvising*.

12. In an exception to this rule, historian Ronn Pineo researched and analyzed disease data for early twentieth-century Guayaquil; see "Misery." Working on Puerto Rico and Colonial Africa respectively, historians Ann Zulawski and Helen Tilley also found statistics to be elusive. See Zulawski, "Environment"; Tilley, "Ecologies," 24. Not until the 1890s did statistician-bureaucrat Jacque Bertillon and his French colleagues develop a scientific classification of disease for death certificates; see Birn, "Revolution," 158.

13. Pineo, "Misery," 615; McNeill, *Mosquito Empires*, 52.

14. Carlos A. Miño, "Informe de la Subdirección de Sanidad de la provincial de Pichincha al Ministro de Sanidad y al Director del Servicio de Sanidad Pública," appendix to Peñaherrera, *Informe* (1914), 442.

15. León Becerra, "Informe del Director de Sanidad," in Peñaherrera, *Informe* (1915), 505–7.

16. Clark, *Conjuring*.

17. Palmer, *Launching*, 132.

18. Ibid., 217.

19. *MSP*, 1933, 339–40. Mal de ojo (evil eye) is a curse conveyed by a malevolent glare that many indigenous and Hispanic cultures believed could cause illness.

20. *MSP*, 1945, 135–36.

21. *MSP*, 1944, 363.

22. *MSP*, 1945, 135–36.

23. Ibid., 137.

24. Palmer, *Launching*, 139.

INTRODUCTION

1. AGCA, SP, expediente (ex.) 23224, 1942, correspondencia, Cipriano Chovix Chalí to DHG, August 31, 1942.

2. AGCA, SP, ex. 23224, 1942, correspondencia, Alberto Calí Cuzal to DHG, August 31, 1942.

3. Crandon-Malamud, *Fat of Our Souls*; Feierman and Janzen, "Introduction," 5.

4. Hines, "Power and Ethics," 228–29; Gibbings, *Our Time*.

5. Bunzel, *Chichicastenango*; Lipp, "Comparative Analysis," 110–11; R. Adams, *Análisis*, 37–38; Sellers-García, "Plaga occulta."

6. Esquit, *Superación*; Esquit, *Otros poderes*; Grandin, *Blood*; Clark and Becker, *Highland Indians*.

7. Marc Becker, "Limits," 50.

8. Espejo, *Voto*; Paredes, *Oro*.

9. A. Sáenz and Palacios, "Dimension demografica," 151–61; Iturralde, "Nacionalidades Indígenas." Since Ecuador did not conduct a national census until 1950, determining the indigenous and rural populations before then is difficult.

10. MM, SA, 0734, comunicaciones enviadas, Gualsaqui, Otavalo, Inspector Garcés, June 10, 1945. Whereas disease refers to a (often socially constructed) biological pathology, illness refers to a human experience. See Kleinman, *Writing*, for explorations of how bodily and social conditions interchanged.

11. Bell, *Frontiers*, 7; Mitman, "Search," 192.

12. Harrar, "Draft."

13. Indígenas sought to maintain a balance between corporeal, community (society), natural, and supernatural forces. See Bautista-Valarezo, et. al., "Towards an Indigenous Definition"; Harvey, "Maya Mobile Medicine," 48; Silverblatt, *Sun*, 173; Kimball, *Open Secret*; Cueto and Palmer, *Medicine*, 14.

14. In both Ecuador and Guatemala, racism differed by region, especially on the coasts where it was directed at African descendants. This book focuses on anti-indigenous racism. Although Afro-Ecuadorians, like Afro-Guatemalans, contributed to and experienced health care and public health in diverse ways, a study of their rich healing traditions and engagement in each nation's medical history is beyond the scope of this book.

15. Earle, *Return*, 163.

16. Medical science's hegemony was easier to assert than to achieve. See Stern, "Buildings," 74; H. Tilley, *Africa*, 182; Sobrado Botey, "La epidemica," 350; D. Rodríguez, *Right*, 100–1; Gomez, *Silver Veins*, 166.

17. Historian Beatrix Hoffman recognizes a similar phenomenon, which she calls "rights consciousness," whereby people demanded access to health services without necessarily using a language of rights (*Health Care*, xii). When James Paulin posed the idea of medical citizens in 1947, he referred to general practitioners or family doctors who help "to guide the affairs of the family and of the community along safe and sane lines" ("Medical Citizenship," 448). In many Guatemalan and Ecuadorian highland communities, *curanderos* and *comadronas* (midwives) rather than physicians pursued those goals. My framing of medical citizenship is based on more recent scholarship that conceptualizes the term as an individual's right and ability to access medical resources. See Wailoo, et al., *Death Retold*; Rodríguez, *Right*; Oosterhuis and Huisman, "Politics"; Nguyen, *Republic*; Rose, *Politics*, 24–25, 131–37, 140–44.

18. Lane, *Quito*, 167.

19. Clifford, *Predicament*.

20. Prieto, *Liberalismo*, 45.

21. Marc Becker, *¡Pachakutik!*, 3–5; Clark and Becker, "Indigenous Peoples," 12.

22. Chávez, *Mestizaje*, 77–79. Of course, some free Africans and Afro-Ecuadorians climbed the social ladder.

23. Sánchez Parga, *Etnia*, 95–99.

24. Ospina Peralta, *Aleación*, 428, 433.

25. Satter, *"Indígena o Ciudadano?"*

26. Maloney, "Negro"; de la Torre Espinosa, *Afroquiteños*; Prieto, *Liberalismo*, 74n20; Benítez and Garcés, *Culturas*; Clark and Becker, "Indigenous Peoples," 7, 10, 12; Marc Becker, *¡Pachakutik!*, 149, 189; Lucero, "Locating."

27. L. Rodriguez, *Search*, 24. Although Marcos Cueto points to social medicine's "heterodox European current," Espejo and other Andean physicians attest to social medicine's deep roots in Latin America. See Cueto, "Social Medicine"; Paz Soldán, *Medicina*; Lerner, "Crecimiento"; Waitzkin et al., "Social Medicine"; Knipper, "Antropología"; Ewig, "Health Policies."

28. Asselbergs, *Conquered Conquistadors*; Gudmundson, "Negotiating Rights"; Lokken, "Marriage"; Restall and Lutz, "Wolves"; Herrera, *Natives*; Komisaruk, *Labor*. The term ladino dates to the late seventeenth century and was first used to describe persons of mixed descent (mestizos, mulattos, *castas*). Some indigenous "Mexicanos" in Guatemala identified themselves as ladino to distinguish themselves as more civilized (and thus more deserving of privileges) than other indigenous groups. After Guatemalan independence in 1821, ladinos were increasingly disassociated from mestizos. Instead, they took pains to identify themselves with European or Spanish culture. Although culture is paramount in identifying ladinos, blood stricture is still important on a personal level, at least ideologically if not biologically. Most ladinos have some indigenous blood, but choose not to recognize or represent these cultural, social, or historical aspects of their identity. They are the minority in

Guatemala but enjoy political and economic power. Even poor ladinos often hold themselves to be superior to indígenas. Thus political, economic, social, and cultural structures are predicated on racist views that are at best paternalistic and at worst ethnocidal. The indígena-ladino binary reveals the construction of socio-racial categories in Guatemala but belies the complex concatenations of ethnic, gender, racial, and class identities. See Casaus Arzú, *Guatemala*, 119–26; Lutz, *Santiago*; Grandin, *Blood*, 83–85, 239; Matthew, *Memories*; C. Smith, "Origins," 86–87; C. Smith, "Race-Class-Gender Ideology," 734–35; K. Warren, *Symbolism*.

29. Gibbings, "Mestizaje."

30. According to two Guatemalan intellectuals who bookended the twentieth century, *indígenas* comprised more than 70 percent of the population. See Jorge García Salas, "Comentarios a la Iniciativa del Club 'Freedom of the Indian,'" *Diario de Centro-América*, May 1, 1920; Tzian, *Kajab'aliil Maya'iib'*. Keeping in mind the political (and at times corrupted) nature of census data in Guatemala, the 2002 census reported that 41.03 percent of Guatemalans identified as indigenous. See INE, *Censos nacionales XI*, 30–31.

31. DGE, *Sexto censo* 1, 239; Adams and Bastos, *Relaciones*, 36, 44; Casaus Arzú, "Metamorphosis."

32. Taracena Arriola, ed., *Etnicidad*; Esquit, *Superación*; Esquit, *Otros poderes*; Grandin, *Blood*.

33. AGCA, Indice 116, Chimaltenango 1918, legajo (leg.) 19a, expediente (ex.) 42.

34. Grandin, *Blood*; Sieder, "Paz," 292; Jonas, *Battle*, 23; Forster, *Time*, 2.

35. DGE, *Sexto censo*, 1, 239; Adams and Bastos, *Relaciones*, 36, 44; Casaus Arzú, "Metamorphosis."

36. Clark, *Conjuring*.

37. Zulawski, "Environment," 509.

38. Chomsky, *West Indian Workers*, 130, 137.

39. Zulawski, *Unequal Cures*, 36.

40. Reverby, "Normal Exposure."

41. RF's first forays into hookworm campaigns often buttressed state power. See Palmer, *Launching*; Palmer, *Popular Medicine*, 155–82; Birn, "Revolution," 178; Packard, *History*. By the 1930s, Mexican public health officials sought to spread scientific medicine to rural areas; see Cueto, *Cold War*, 10.

42. H. Tilley, *Africa*, 13; Mitman, "Search," 195; Guy, *White Slavery*, 130.

43. Like colonial officials and medics in Africa, Latin American authorities deployed science to embolden doctors and denigrate healers. See Bell, *Frontiers*, 6; Flint, *Healing*, x, 5, 93–95, 126, 135–156, 179–80; Osseo-Asare, "Writing," 71–72, 78–79; Osseo-Asare, *Bitter Roots*, 1, 10–13.

44. Gibbings, *Our Time*.

45. Abbott, *System*, 112–83.

46. A similar phenomenon unfolded in parts of Africa where patients consulted traditional healers even after authorities criminalized popular medicine. See H. Tilley, "History," 744, 749; Feierman and Janzen, "Introduction," 16–17. Although its exploration falls beyond the scope of this book, East Asian historiography of

medicine, particularly studies of traditional Chinese medicine and the rise of scientific medicine in China also complicate assumptions about the ascendancy of scientific medicine. See Rogaski, *Hygienic Modernity*; Lei, *Neither Donkey Nor Horse*.

47. BNG, FLA, indice Valenzuela I, 2377, Dr. Luis Toledo Herrarte, "Profilaxia del paludismo Conferencia dada en honor del Sr. Presidente de la República licenciado don Manuel Estrada Cabrera con motivo de la inauguración de su segunda periodo constitucional en el Salón de Actos de la Escuela de Medicina y Farmacia, el día 16 de Marzo de 1905."

48. *La Gaceta*, March 9, 1941; Peña Torres, *Historia*, 25; Morgan, *Community Participation*, 19; Martínez García, "Michel Foucault"; Cueto and Palmer, *Medicine*, 88; Sowell, *Tale*; Palmer, *Popular Medicine*; Cueto, *Salud*; Cueto, *Saberes andinos*; Cueto, *Regreso*.

49. AGCA, JP-S, 1928, letter from Santiago Zamora municipality signed DSO, May 12, 1928.

50. *MSGJ*, 1911, 6.

51. *MSP*, 1933, 7.

52. J. Romeo de León, "Paludismo de altura en Guatemala," *Boletin Sanitario de Guatemala* 7, no. 44 (1936): 67–79.

53. BNG, FLA, Valenzuela I, 2371, Secretaria de Gobernación y Justicia, *Informe para reprodulo commisión médica que fue al departamento de Baja Verapaz a combatir la epidemia de paludismo en diciembre 1904* (Guatemala City: Tipografía Nacional, 1905), 10.

54. *Diario de Centroamérica*, March 17, 1910.

55. SADINOEL, "Año nuevo," *El Impulso*, January 1, 1919, 1–2.

56. "Causas de la enfermedad en la clase indígena," *Diario de Centro América*, January 25, 1919, 7.

57. Cueto, *Return*, 20–21; Clark, *Conjuring*.

58. Clark, *Conjuring*.

59. L. F. Cornejo Gómez, "Informe del Delegado del Ecuador a la V Conferencia Sanitaria Internacional de las Repúblicas Americanas," appendix to Ayora, *Informe*, 348. German climate therapy advocated cold mountainous climates for convalescence; see Cueto and Palmer, *Medicine*.

60. Pineo, "Misery."

61. A. Adams and Giraudo, "Pack," 179–83, 182 (quotes).

62. W. Anderson, *Colonial Pathologies*; Stepan, *Hour*; Few, *For All*; Peard, *Race*; Montoya, *Making*; Green, "Doctoring"; Foucault, *Power/Knowledge*; Palacios, *Raza*; Vasconcelos, *Raza*. Medical racism manifests when medical professionals alter diagnostic or therapeutic care because of a patient's race or when public health officials alter responses based on assumptions about a community's or group's racial makeup.

63. Carter, "Social Medicine."

64. J. Rodríguez, *Civilizing*.

65. Espinosa, *Epidemic*; Palmer, *Launching*, 41–42, 46; Birn "Revolution."

66. Nugent, *Encrypted State*; Nugent, *Modernity*; Pineo, *Social*.

67. Stepan, "National," 501; Cueto, "Introduction," xi–xiv; Cueto and Palmer, *Medicine*, 141.

68. Morgan, *Community Participation*, 10–12, 18–19; Clark, *Conjuring*. The RF's public health school at Johns Hopkins University was decidedly wedded to scientific medicine and research; see Stepan, "National," 500.

69. R. Brown, "Public Health"; Cueto, *Cold War*, 18; Palmer, *Launching*, 218; Birn, "Revolution."

70. RAC, RF, RF Photographs, series 317, box 85, folder 1701, Dr. Rowan note, December 31, 1915.

71. RAC, RF, RF Photographs, series 317, box 85, folder 1701, photographs of Madura foot, 1919.

72. Espinosa, *Epidemic*.

73. Pineo, *Ecuador*.

74. Tworek, "Communicable Disease," 818–19.

75. RF, RG5, IHB/D, series 1, correspondence subseries 2_317 projects, box 79, folder 1121, letter from Dirección de Sanidad, servicio fiebre amarillo, February 4, 1919, Dr. Rose; All America Cables, Vía Colón, Guayaquil, February 5, 1919; letter, International Health Board, New York, March 10, 1919, Guayaquil, Dr. Rose from Connor.

76. Clark, *Redemptive Work*, 196.

77. Administración del señor general don Jorge Ubico, *Dos lustrous*, 9.

78. Packard, *History of Global Health*; Birn, "National-International Nexus"; Espinosa, "Globalizing"; Carter, "Social Medicine"; Birn and Necochea López, "Footprints," 519; Stepan, "National"; Borowy, *Coming*.

79. Briggs, McCormack, and Way, "Transnationalism"; Rosemblatt, "Other Americas." Also see Olsson, *Agrarian Crossings*, which "is not a comparative history but rather a history of comparisons, a study of interactions and exchanges" (4).

80. Saldaña-Portillo, *Indian*.

81. Palmer, *Launching*, 58.

82. Tuck, "Suspending"; Tuhiwai Smith, *Decolonizing*, 1; Tuhiwai Smith, Tuck, and Yang, *Indigenous*. For further analysis of indigenous peoples in the Americas, see Mallon, *Decolonizing*; Santoro and Langer, *Hemispheric Indigeneities*; Mallon, *Courage*; Gibbings, *Our Time*; Larson, *Trials*. Although medical anthropologists continue to dominate the field of indigenous peoples and medicine (Bastien, *Healers* immediately comes to mind), historians are increasingly looking at how indigenous people have shaped and have been shaped by medicine and science. See Zulawski, *Unequal Cures*; Dent and Santos, "'Unusual'"; Pribilsky, "Development."

83. Vizenor, *Survivance*.

84. Vizenor, *Fugitive Poses*, 93; Vizenor, *Manifest Manners*, vii.

85. Fuentes, *Dispossessed Lives*, 5–9, 7 (quote); Helton et al., "Question"; Rushforth, "*Gauolet* Uprising," 81–82, 109–10; Cooper Owens, *Medical Bondage*; Trouillot, *Silencing*.

86. Stern, "Buildings"; Hogarth, *Making*; O'Brien, "Pelvimetry"; Mckiernan-González, *Fevered Measures*; Cooper Owens, *Medical Bondage*; L. Briggs, *Reproducing*; Leavitt, *Typhoid Mary*; Fausto-Sterling, *Myths*.

87. H. Tilley, "History," 743, 746; Osseo-Asare, *Bitter Roots*, 23–28. For a critique of colonial histories and historians' tendency to craft narratives that adhere to

European chronology and theories rather than non-Western epistemologies and experiences, see Chakrabarty, "Postcoloniality."

88. Bell, *Frontiers*, 6; Flint, *Healing*, x, 5, 93–95, 126, 135–156, 179–80; Osseo-Asare, "Writing Medical Authority," 71–72, 78–79; Osseo-Asare, *Bitter Roots*, 1, 10–13.

89. Stepan, "National"; Soto Laveaga, "Bringing"; Rosemblatt, "Other Americas"; Espinosa, "Globalizing"; Birn and Necochea López, "Footprints."

90. W. Anderson, *Colonial Pathologies*; Lefler, ed., *Under the Rattlesnake*; Stoler, *Race*; David Arnold, *Colonizing*; Bell, *Frontiers*; Stern, "Buildings."

91. Stepan, *"Hour"*; Stern, *Eugenic Nation*; Stern, "Responsible Mothers."

92. Armus, *Ciudad*; Alexander, "Fever"; Bliss, "Science"; E. Abel, "From Exclusion."

93. Zulawski, *Unequal Cures*; Few, *For All*; Gómez, *Experiential Caribbean*; Mckiernan-González, *Fevered Measures*.

94. Dent and Santos, "Unusual"; Pribilsky, "Development"; Ventura Santos, Coimbra, and Radin, "Why Did They Die?"; de Moura Pontes and Santos, "Health Reform"; Suárez-Díaz, "Indigenous Populations." Scholars of the United States and Australia have delved deeply into the intersections of indigenous peoples and health care. See Greene, Braitberg, and Bernadett, "Innovation"; John, "Violence"; Radin, "Digital Natives"; Lanzarotta, "Ethics in Retrospect."

95. Soto Laveaga, *Jungle Laboratories*; Palmer, *Popular Medicine*; Sowell, *Tale*.

96. Jaffray, *Reproduction*.

97. See Mallon, ed., *Decolonizing*; Santoro and Langer, *Hemispheric Indigeneities*; Larson, *Trials*.

98. Esquit, *Superación*; Esquit, *Otros poderes*; Grandin, *Blood*; Clark and Becker, *Highland Indians*; Marc Becker, *Indians*.

99. For histories of medicine that address Guatemala, see Sigerist, "Medical History"; Cur, *Historia*; Martínez Durán, *Ciencias médicas*; Orellana, *Indian Medicine*; Few, *For All*; Few, "Curing."

100. Rodas Chaves, *Revolucion*; Clark, *Gender*; Miles, *Living*; Roberts, *God's Laboratory*; Alchon, *Native Society*.

101. For an exploration of these waves, from the 1950s to the 2000s, see Stepan, "National." For other examples from the third wave, see Birn, "Wa(i)ves"; C. Abel, "External Philanthropy."

102. Cueto, *Cold War*; Palmer, *Launching*, 154–55; Packard, *History*; Birn, *Marriage*.

103. Palmer, *Launching*, 4 (quote), 39.

104. Packard, *Making*; Rosenberg, *Cholera Years*.

CHAPTER ONE

1. RAC, RF, Photographs, series 317, box 85, folder 1709, "Typical hookworm subject on El Pacayal," Dr. Rowan, 12–31–15.

2. Palmer, *Launching*.

3. Bunzel, *Chichicastenango*; Lipp, "Comparative Analysis," 110–11; Wisdom, *Chorti Indians*, 354n25; R. Adams, *Análisis*, 84; Oakes, *Two Crosses*, 166; Paul and McMahon, "Mesoamerican Bonesetters," 244–45, 250–51, 254–55, 259.

4. Historian Pablo Gómez similarly examines seventeenth-century Afro-Caribbean healers on their own merits in *Experiential Caribbean*.

5. Urioste, "Sickness."

6. Colson and de Armellada, "Amerindian Derivation."

7. Bastien, *Healers*; Bastien, "Qollahuaya-Andean Body"; Bastien, "Differences"; Alchon, *Native Society*, 27.

8. Alchon, "Tradiciones," 19–20; Alchon, *Native Society*, 28.

9. Alchon, "Tradiciones," 20.

10. Sosa and Durán, "Familia," 181.

11. Guáman Poma, *Nueva crónica*, I, 89. While Kichwa is the spelling used in modern Ecuador, in Peru and particularly during the colonial period, Quechua was the standard spelling.

12. Alchon, "Tradiciones," 19–20; Alchon, *Native Society*, 28.

13. Rubio Orbe, *Indios ecuatorianos*, 135–39; Bautista-Valarezo, "Towards an Indigenous Definition"; Alchon, "Tradiciones médicas," 20.

14. Cueto and Palmer, *Medicine*, 35 (quote); Bastien, *Healers*; Bastien, "Qolla-huaya-Andean Body"; Bastien, "Differences"; Alchon, *Native Society*, 27.

15. Alchon, "Tradiciones," 22–23; Alchon, *Native Society*, 30.

16. Newson, *Life*, 88–89; Alchon, "Tradiciones," 20–21.

17. Alchon, *Native Society*, 73; Harvey, "Maya Mobile Medicine," 51.

18. Bastien, *Healers*; Huber and Sandstrom, *Mesoamerican Healers*; Orellana, *Indian Medicine*; Rohloff and Sotz Mux, *Tiq'aqomaj Qi'*; Sharon, *Wizard*.

19. Bastien, *Healers*; Bastien, "Qollahuaya-Andean Body"; Bastien, "Differences"; Alchon, *Native Society*, 27; Newson, *Life*, 89.

20. Amazonian Quijos similarly sought to distinguish themselves from Inkas who imposed Kichwa even as they considered them "unworthy of being conquered." See Archivo de historia oral ecuatoriana, Lourdes Jipa, oral history interview, April 27, 2019, https://stgibson.wixsite.com/ahoe/ahoe-20190022-jipa-lourdes; Gibson, Newman, and Carcelen-Estrada, "Indigeneity and Disabilities."

21. R. Adams, *Análisis*, 43–45; Thompson, *Rise*, 287; Wisdom, *Chorti Indians*, 308.

22. Icú Perén, "Revival," 4, 10, 12; Guerra, "Maya Medicine."

23. Concern for reproductive health among Mayas is evident in the remedies such as *Juanislama* plant leaves to treat blood flow (after a miscarriage) and encourage menstruation. See Garcia-Kutzbach, "Medicine," 939; de Landa, *Maya*, 117; Ximénez, *Historia*, 246–48; Few, "Curing," 33.

24. Tedlock, *Popol Vuh*, 92.

25. Wisdom, *Chorti Indians*, 334–35.

26. Guerra, "Maya Medicine"; Whitlock, *Everyday Life*, 76.

27. Messer, "Hot"; R. Adams, *Análisis*, 48–49; Garcia-Kutzbach, "Medicine," 938.

28. Few, "Healing," 26–28, 36; Wisdom, *Chorti Indians*, 357–58, 346–49; R. Adams, *Análisis*, 47–55; Icú Perén, "Revival," 6; A. Warren, "Dorotea," 58–59.

29. Wisdom, *Chorti Indians*, 359–60.

30. R. Adams, *Análisis*, 50–64.

31. Ximénez, *Historia*, 246–48; Few, "Healing," 33.

32. Few, "Curing," 31.

33. Few, "Curing," 30; Warren, "Dorotea."

34. Alchon, "Tradiciones médicas," 24, 34.

35. A. Warren, "Dorotea," 57, 59; Few, "Healing," 32.

36. Hernández-Sáenz and Foster, "Curers," 40–44; Lipp, "Comparative Analysis"; Mckiernan-González, *Fevered Measures*; Crandon-Malamud, *Fat of Our Souls*; Cueto and Palmer, *Medicine*, 30.

37. Newson, *Making*; Alchon, *Native Society*, 90–92.

38. Hernández-Sáenz and Foster, "Curers," 40–44; Lipp, "Comparative Analysis."

39. R. Adams, *Análisis*, 38, 69.

40. Ibid., 95–97, 98; Gillin, *Culture*, 107–8.

41. Viesca Treviño, "*Curanderismo*," 47.

42. Huber, "Introduction," 16; de Landa, *Maya*; Few, "Healing," 28

43. Alchon, *Native Society*, 106–7.

44. Ibid., 108; Lanning, *Royal Protomedicato*; Malavassi Aguilar, *Marginalidad social*.

45. Malavassi Aguilar, "Análisis," 356; Palmer, *Popular Medicine*, 53–54; Few, "Circulating."

46. Cueto and Palmer, *Medicine*, 40, 48. Espejo also staunchly defended his profession, decrying the many deaths caused by the "inexperience of those who have the temerity to call themselves Medical professors" (Alchon, *Native Society*, 104–5).

47. Alchon, "Tradiciones," 25–28; Few, "Healing," 27; Warren, "Dorotea," 59.

48. Few, "Healing," 30.

49. Solomon, "Shamanism"; Solomon, "Fury," 88; Alchon, "Tradiciones," 30, 34; Alchon, *Native Society*, 100, 123, 128.

50. Cueto and Palmer, *Medicine*, 54–55, 92; Necochea López, *History*, 24, 25, 30; Sowell, *Tale*.

51. Sosa and Durán, "Familia," 182.

52. Vásquez, "Familia," 220.

53. Peña Torres and Palmer, "Rockefeller Foundation," 59; Palmer, *Launching*, 149, 177.

54. Palmer, *Popular Medicine*, 183–216; Hernández Sáenz and Foster, "Curers," 40–44; Lipp, "Comparative Analysis."

55. Palmer, *Launching*, 143, 152.

56. Sosa and Durán, "Familia," 181.

57. R. Adams, *Análisis*, 37–38.

58. Wisdom, *Chorti Indians*, 307–8, 332–34.

59. ANE, Exp. 21, legajo 5, Babahoyo September 30, 1902; leg. 2, June 30, 1902; leg. 3, Julio 31, 1902.

60. Briggs and Mantini-Briggs, *Tell Me Why*; Crandon-Malamud, *Fat of Our Souls*.

61. Chaves et al., "Implementação da política."

62. McCreery, *Rural Guatemala*, 195; McCreery, *Sweat*, 107–44; Larson, *Trials*; de la Cadena, *Indigenous Mestizos*.

63. The 1940 Guatemalan census counted 3,283, 209 people, of whom 1,498,745 were identified as speaking an indigenous language. See DGE, *Quinto censo*, 10, 15; Saunders, *People*. The 1950 Ecuadorian census counted 3,202,757 people. A 1942 study estimated that Ecuador's population was 40 percent indigenous, 40 percent mestizo, 10 percent white, and 5 percent each black and mulatto. See Dirección Nacional de Estadisticas, *Ecuador*, 55; Clark and Becker, "Indigenous Peoples," 10; Marc Becker, *¡Pachakutik!*; Cueto and Palmer, *Medicine*, 41–42.

64. Confederación de Nacionalidades Indígenas del Ecuador (CNIE), *Nacionalidades indigenas*, especially chapter 1; González Suárez, *Historia general*; Clark and Becker, "Indigenous Peoples," 3, 10; Alchon, *Native Society*.

65. O'Connor, "Helpless Children?"; Williams, "Making," 218, 222–23.

66. Cevallos, *Resumen*, 13–14.

67. Ospina Peralta, *Aleación inestable*, 30, 40, 428, 432, 436; Iturralde, "Nacionalidades."

68. Baldwin, *Contagion*.

69. Alfaro, "Presidential Address," 281–82.

70. Peñaherrera, *Informe*, xlvii; Clark, *Conjuring*; Cueto, *Cold War*, 72; Cueto and Palmer, *Medicine*, 107.

71. Puga, *Informe*; Clark, *Conjuring*.

72. Ayora, *Informe*, xlvii.

73. Dawson, *South American Republics*, 341.

74. Daniel Alarcón, "City of the Dead," *New Yorker*, March 14, 2002, 48.

75. Clark and Becker, "Indigenous Peoples"; Clark, *Conjuring*.

76. Baud, "Liberalism"; Marc Becker, *Indians*, 8–9; Clark, *Redemptive Work*; Clark, "Racial Ideologies," 374, 376–77, 390; Clark, "Indians," 50–51, 56, 68–69.

77. McCook, *States*, 103.

78. Jaramillo Alvarado, *Indio*, 150.

79. Marc Becker, *Indians*, xiv-xv, 19–20.

80. CNIE, *Nacionalidades Indígenas*, especially chapter 1.

81. Iturralde, "Nacionalidades," 12.

82. Rubio Orbe, *Indios*, 135–39.

83. Iturralde, "Nacionalidades," 12.

84. Ospina Peralta, *Aleación*, 26 (quote), 429; Bustos Lozano, *Culto*; Tribunal Supremo Electoral de Ecuador, *Elecciones*, 56; Marc Becker, *Indians*, 18–22; McCook, *States*, 10.

85. F. P. Farar, "A Physician Who is a President," *New York Times*, March 4, 1928; Rodas Chaves, *Revolución*; Clark, *Conjuring*; Capello, *City*, 21. Previously *Sanidad* had been under the Ministry of the Interior, which had a larger group of divisions that fell under its responsibilities and competed for its attention and resources.

86. Lloyd, "Pan American Sanitary Bureau," 928–29.

87. Pineo, "Misery," 622; D. Rodríguez, *Right*, 187; Clark, *Conjuring*. When physicians from Ramon Grau San Martín in Cuba (1933–34, 1944–48) to Salvador Allende in Chile (1970–73) became national leaders, politics were charged with a focus on well-being.

88. Farar, "Physician"; Rodas Chaves, *Pensamiento*; Clark, *Conjuring*.

89. Pineo, "Misery," 624; Clark, *Conjuring*.

90. Clark, "Race," 193, 208n26; Ospina Peralta, *Aleación*, 21–22, 430.

91. Lucero, "Locating," 27–29; Marc Becker, *Indians*, xvi, 72, 78–80.

92. Maiguashca and North, "Origenes"; Maiguascha, "Sectores subalternos"; Marchán Romero, "Crisis"; Clark, "Racial Ideologies," 375–76, 381.

93. L. Rodríguez, *Search*, 224–26.

94. Ospina Peralta, *Aleación*, 435.

95. Clark, "Racial Ideologies," 393.

96. Guerrero, "Desintegración."

97. Almeida, "Nuevo movimiento"; CNIE, *Nacionalidades*; Marc Becker, *Indians*, 77–104; Clark, "Race"; Clark, "Racial Ideologies"; Prieto, *Liberalismo*; Marc Becker, "Limits," 57; Clark, *Gender*, 7, 12; Capello, *City*, 21, 204, 259n58; Marc Becker, *¡Pachakutik!*, 84, 204, 210n4.

98. Ospina Peralta, *Aleación*, 37, 40, 431, 440–41.

99. MM, AP records; Arcos and Marchán, "Apuntes"; Estrada Ycaza, *Regionalismo*, 265; Pineo, "Misery," 611, 636; Clark, *Conjuring*; Becker and Tutillo, *Historia*.

100. CNIE, *Nacionalidades*.

101. Ibid.

102. MM, AP 1188, Correspondencia recibida de Moyurco, cartas de Anibal Maldonado, Hacienda Muyurco, October 10 and 15, 1946; CNIE, *Nacionalidades*.

103. MM, AP 1188, Correspondencia recibida de Moyurco, carta de Anibal Maldonado, Hacienda Muyurco, October 10, 1946.

104. MM, AP 1196, Felipe Campues to Director de Junta Central Asistencia Pública, May 25, 1949.

105. Ibid.

106. MM, AP 1196, Andres Chihuano (de Jose María), huasipunguero to Director de Junta Central Asistencia Pública, ca. July 1949.

107. MM, AP 1196, Joaquín Catucuamba to Director de Junta Central Asistencia Pública, August 18, 1949.

108. Ibid.

109. MM, AP, 1101, 1925; MM, AP1104, 1947 (hacienda records); Becker and Tutillo, *Historia*.

110. Clark, *Redemptive Work*, 76–83; Clark and Becker, "Indigenous Peoples."

111. Capello, *City*, 81, 114, 179–209.

112. MM, SA 0695, 1942, Northeast Military Health Services to Gonzalo Fabara, January 10, 1942.

113. Birn, "National-International Nexus," 700 (quote); Carter, "Social Medicine"; Waitzkin, et al., "Social Medicine"; Van Reenen, "What Is Social Medicine?"; Anderson, Smith, and Sidel, "What Is Social Medicine?"; Pieper Mooney, "Cold War Pressures"; Granados, "Social Medicine"; Packard, *Making*, 91–96, 138–39.

114. Löwly, "Historiography"; Packard, *History*.

115. Striffler, *Shadows*, 33, 40, 47, 216n5; Clark, *Conjuring*. In 1962, Ecuadorian workers invaded UFCO's Tenguel plantation.

116. Maxwell and Hill, *Kaqchikel Chronicles*, 307–8.

117. Taracena Arriola, *Invención*; McCreery, *Rural Guatemala*, 23, 56, 148–149; Woodward, *Rafael*, 54, 60–83; Oliver, "Cólera."

118. Gudmonson and Lindo-Fuentes, *Central America*; Thoresen, "Rebellion," 382; Ospina Peralta, *Aleación*, 25, 430–31; Palmer, *Launching*, 18, 98.

119. *Despacho de Gobernación*, 6.

120. AGCA, Guatemala City, B81.3 leg. 1092, exp. 23945, Municipalid de la capital, 1899, Informe por doctores sobre la inconveniencia de la existencia de la presa del rio de "Las Vacas," July 4, 1899.

121. Kirkpatrick, "Consumer Culture"; Kirkpatrick, "Phantoms."

122. *MGJ*, 1908, 1909.

123. Palmer, *Launching*, 10 (quote), 19–20; H. C. Clark, "The Field Parasite Rate for Malaria in Banana Divisions (Mainland CA)," UFCO-MD, *Annual Report* 1928, 71; Espinosa, *Epidemic*.

124. Gillick, "Life," 130, 213; Aliano, "Curing"; Handy, "Violence," 289; Chomsky, *West Indian Workers*, 100–1, 108–9.

125. Chomsky, *West Indian Workers*, 12, 96; Soluri, *Banana Cultures*.

126. Esquit, *Superación*; Esquit, *Otros poderes*; Gibbings, *"Mestizaje"*; Grandin, *Blood*. During a few brief periods in the 1920s, the *Generación 20* sought to reform Guatemalan society.

127. Gibbings, *Our Time*.

128. Carey, "Cautionary Tale."

129. Gudmundson and Lindo-Fuentes, *Central America*; McCreery, *Rural Guatemala*; Guerrero, "Desintegración"; Guerrero, "Imagen"; Clark, *Redemptive Work*, 76–83; Clark and Becker, "Indigenous Peoples."

130. Administración, *Dos lustrous*, 9.

131. Palmer, *Launching*, 190–91.

132. Administración, *Dos lustrous*, 10.

133. Ibid., 9.

134. Ibid., 7.

135. Ibid., 7.

136. Ibid., 7.

137. Ibid., 7.

138. Gleijeses, *Shattered Hope*, 28; R. Adams, "Ethnic Images," 144–45; Handy, "Sea."

139. de León Aragón, *Caída*; Handy, *Revolution*, 23; Forster, *Time*, 33–34; Carey, "Democracy."

140. The estimates of indigenous deaths vary greatly, but two independent studies indicate that somewhere between four and nine hundred Kaqchikels were killed during the three-day massacre. See Rodas and Esquit, *Élite Ladina*, 195; R. Adams, "Masacres," 16–18, 23.

141. Taracena Arriola, *Etnicidad*; Casaús Arzú, *Guatemala*.

142. *Diario de Centro América*, May 18, 1945.

143. Sieder, "Paz," 292; Jonas, *Battle*, 23; Forster, *Time*, 2.

144. Foss, "Obra," 207–8, 212.

145. Antonio Goubaud Carrera, "Conferencia del Director del Instituto, Licenciado Antonio Goubaud Carrera," *Boletín del Instituto Indigenista Nacional de Guatemala* 1:1 (oct.-dic. 1945): 22.

146. Gibbings and Vrana, *Out of the Shadow*; Chary and Rohloff, *Privatization*, xiii.

147. Crafts, "Mining"; Reverby, "'Normal Exposure'"; Palmer, "Caminos"; Cueto and Palmer, *Medicine*, 127.

148. Gibbings, *Our Time*; Asturias, *Sociologia*, 99.

149. AGCA, Inventario 1884–1924 índice, leg. 23097, Dirección del hospital general, November 26, 1922.

150. AGCA, Inventario 1884–1924 índice, Leg. 23107, American College of Surgeons to Dirección del hospital general, February 10, 1924.

151. AGCA, índice de salud, leg. 23225, 1942 correspondencia, Sanidad Pública to DHG, July 25, 1942; Reggiani, "De rastacueros a expertos"; Hochman, "Autonomy"; Vieira de Campos, *Políticas*.

152. Espinosa, *Epidemic Invasions*.

153. Carrillo and Birn, "Neighbors"; Ross, "Mexico's Superior Health Council."

154. de Almeida, "Circuito aberto"; Löwy, *Virus*; Birn, "O Nexo Nacional-Internacional."

155. Lloyd, "Pan American Sanitary Bureau," 925.

156. H. Tilley, *Africa*, 28–29; McNeill, *Something*, 198; Cueto, *Cold War*, 18; Palmer, *Launching*, 58, 62–63, 79.

157. Palmer, *Launching*, 62, 215; R. Brown, "Public Health," 900; Morgan, *Community Participation*, 18–19, 83; Palmer, *Popular Medicine*, 168; McNeill, *Something New*, 195–98.

158. Espinosa, *Epidemic Invasions*; Palmer, *Launching*, 41–42, 46; Cueto and Palmer, *Medicine*, 112; Birn, "Revolution."

159. Palmer, *Launching*, 89–114.

160. Palmer, *Popular Medicine*, 171.

161. Peña Torres and Palmer, "Rockefeller Foundation," 44, 49, 51, 57, 58, 63–64, 65; I. Molina, "Clase."

162. Cueto and Palmer, *Medicine*, 109, 112, 118.

163. Palmer, *Popular Medicine*, 155–57, 177–78; Palmer, *Launching*, 103, 113.

164. Peña Torres, *Historia*; Peña Torres, "Curanderos."

165. Centro de Ivestigaciones Regionales de Mesoamérica (CIRMA) TA/ATA no. 8, "Algo sobre parasitismo intestinal en los niños en Guatemala," *La Juventud Médica*, 10–11, no. 12–13 (1909): 194–95.

166. Ibid., 196.

167. Palmer, *Launching*, 20.

168. Ibid., 107.

169. RAC, RF Photographs, series 317, box 85, folder 1709.

170. Palmer, *Launching*, 89, 94–5, 102, 104.

171. RAC, RF Photographs, series 319, box 85, folder 1714, "Ethnology Section: Linguistic Map of Guatemala, Indians depicted in typical dress"; Palmer, *Launching*, 86, 90, 94–95, 103–4, 107, 126.

172. Palmer, *Launching*, 104.

173. RAC, RF Photographs, series 317, box 85, folder 1709, "Type of '*excusado*' being built on finca Las Mercedes," Dr. Rowan, 9–7–15.

174. Birn, "Revolution," 166.

175. Anderson, *Colonial Pathologies*, 104–29.

176. Palmer, *Launching*, 137.

177. RAC, RF Photographs, series 317, box 85, folder 1709, "Indian, age 26, weight 75 lbs. Note dropsical condition," 12–31–15, Dr. Rowan; Palmer, *Launching*, 70.

178. RAC, RF Photographs, series 317, box 85, folder 1709, "Typical hookworm subject on El Pacayal," Dr. Rowan, 12–31–15.

179. RAC, RF Photographs, series 317, box 85, folder 1709, "Indian in Native Dress," 4.20./21, Elmendorf; folder 1701, "View of site on Ancient Maya city of Quirigua," ca. 1939. See also folders 1714 and 1716 for evidence of RF interest in indigenous languages and artisanship.

180. Palmer, *Launching*, 186.

181. A similar phenomenon unfolded during the US New Deal when RF agents and Mexican agrarian populists developed networks that informed each nation's land reform projects in the 1940s. See Olsson, *Agrarian Crossings*.

182. Palmer, *Launching*, 185.

183. Asturias, *Sociología*, 99.

184. Ibid., 105–6.

185. Gibbings, "*Mestizaje*."

186. Turn-of-the-century sanitary officers along the US-Mexican border similarly used discourse about dirt and filth to distance Mexicans from U.S. citizens. See Stern, "Buildings," 64, 77.

187. Ibid., 67.

188. Palmer, *Launching*, 186–87.

189. Ibid., 190, 209–10; Stepan, "National," 500–1.

190. Palmer, *Launching*, 191–92.

191. McCreery, "Guatemala City."

192. Carey, *Our Elders*, 118–29.

193. Carey, "Cautionary Tale"; Palmer, *Launching*, 86.

194. Palmer, *Launching*, 86.

195. RF, RG5, IHB/D, series 1, correspondence subseries 2_317 projects, box 79, folder 1121, Heiser to Connor, July 24, 1919.

196. Schneider, "Model American," 165.

197. Cueto, "Introduction," xi-xiv; Cueto and Palmer, *Medicine*, 106, 141; Palmer, "Central American Encounters"; Palmer, *Launching*; Peña Torres and Palmer, "Rockefeller Foundation," 62; Cueto, *Cold War*; McCrea, *Diseased Relations*.

198. Palmer, *Launching*, 86.

199. Palmer, *Launching*, 208–10.

200. LNDLSC, GC, Box 22, folder Salubridad 1829–1933, Director del Fundación Rockefeller Commissión Internacional de Sanidad to Jefatura Política de Sacatepéquez, November 15, 1922.

201. Carey, *Our Elders*, 129–35; Palmer, "Central American Encounters," 326.

202. Palmer, "Central American Encounters," 326; Palmer, *Popular Medicine*; Palmer, *Launching*; Birn, "Going"; Birn, *Marriage*; Cueto, *Cold War*; David Arnold, *Warm Climates*; David Arnold, *Colonizing*; Anderson, "Postcolonial Histories"; McCrea, *Diseased Relations*.

203. RAC, RF, RG5, IHB/D, series 1, correspondence subseries 2_317 projects, box 79, folder 1123, Burres to Heiser, October 27, 1919.

204. RAC, RF, RG5, IHB/D, series 1, correspondence subseries 2_317 projects, box 79, folder 1123, Burres to Heiser, October 28, 1919. Similarly in Ecuador, RF agents were more likely to disparage than encourage indigenous healers, but they did not insist on employing medical professionals. See RAC, RF, RG 1.1 Projects, series 317, box 1, folder 4, Tennant, RF IHD Nov 8 1943, Brackett.

205. Siebenga, "Colonial," 447–49; Alavi, *Islam*, 225.

206. RAC, RF, RG5, IHB/D, series 1, correspondence subseries 2_317 projects, box 79, folder 1123, Burres to Heiser, October 28, 1919.

207. RAC, RG5, series 2, box 25, folder 53, Wycliffe Rose, "Observations on the Public Health Situation and Work of the International Health Board of Brazil," October 25, 1920, 8, 10, 13.

208. Birn, "Revolution," 166.

209. Palmer, *Launching*, 208.

210. RAC, RF, RG5, IHB/D, series 1, correspondence subseries 2_317 projects, box 79, folder 1123, Heiser to Burres, October 9, 1919.

211. RAC, RF, RG5, IHB/D, series 1, correspondence subseries 2_317 projects, box 79, folder 1123, Burres to Heiser, August 30, 1919.

212. RAC, RF, RG5, IHB/D, series 1, correspondence subseries 2_317 projects, box 79, folder 1123, Burres to Heiser, October 28, 1919. To overcome perceived limits of local health care providers in colonial Africa, medical professionals similarly advocated medically training locals. See H. Tilley, *Africa*, 214.

213. Juárez Muñoz, *Indio*, 159.

214. Gibbings, *Our Time*.

215. RAC, RF, RG5, IHB/D, series 1, correspondence subseries 2_317 projects, box 79, folder 1123, Burres to Heiser, October 28, 1919.

216. Palmer, *Launching*, 94–95.

217. RAC, RF, RG5, IHB/D, series 1, correspondence subseries 2_317 projects, box 79, folder 1123, Burres to Heiser, October 28, 1919.

218. Palmer, *Launching*, 100.

219. Ibid., 186.

220. RAC, RF, RG5, IHB/D, series 1, correspondence subseries 2_317 projects, box 79, folder 1123, Burres to Heiser, October 28, 1919.

221. Palmer, *Launching*, 185.

222. RAC, RF, RG5, IHB/D, series 1, correspondence subseries 2_317 projects, box 79, folder 1123, Heiser to Burres, November 25, 1919. Seven years earlier, a German planter from Guatemala wrote to RF director Wycliffe Rose for advice on how to keep indigenous laborers from reinfecting themselves with hookworm. See Palmer, *Launching*, 55.

223. Palmer, *Launching*, 85.

224. RAC, RF, RG 2–1930 (General Correspondence), series 319, box 41, folder 335, Molloy to Russell, December 19, 1930.

225. Stepan, "National."

226. RAC, RF, RG 1.1 Projects, series 317, box 1, folder 5, Foley to Tennant, August 26, 1944.

227. RAC, RF, RG 1.1 Projects, series 317, box 1, folder 5, Foley to Tennant, August 26, 1944.

228. RAC, RF, RG 1.1 Projects, series 317, box 1, folder 4, Brackett to Tennant, RF IHD November 8, 1943.

229. Reeves, *Ladinos*; Clark, *Redemptive Work*, 76–83; Carey, *Our Elders*; Clark and Becker, "Indigenous Peoples."

230. León Trujillo, "Sistema"; León Trujillo, "Política," 211–13; Thoresen, "Rebellion"; Ospina Peralta, *Aleación*, 22–27, 30, 37–38.

CHAPTER TWO

1. Paul and McMahon, "Mesoamerican Bonesetters," 244–45, 250–51, 254–55, 259; Wisdom, *Chorti Indians*, 343; Tedlock, *Time*, 57, 74; Hinojosa, *In This Body*. Similarly, despite his anti-clericalism and campaign against so-called ignorance and fanaticism, Mexican President Plutarco Elias Calles (1924–28) visited miraculous curandero Niño Fidencio in the late 1920s; see Agostini, "Ofertas."

2. *La Gaceta*, April 26, 1942.

3. Gillin, *Culture*, 32.

4. Gibbings, *Our Time*. If the lack of archival evidence thereafter is any indication, few if any were either sent or cultivated for export.

5. Earle, *Return*, 163.

6. Abbott, *System*; Clark, *Gender*, 112–83.

7. Unlike in Ecuador, social medicine only slowly evolved in Guatemala, where government discourse of social medicine did not develop until the 1944 revolution. See Carter, "Social Medicine." Unlike responses to Abraham Flexner's 1910 report that called for licensing all providers and standardizing medical school curricula and training, the strong medical modernizing push in the United States that

resulted in a dramatic drop in popular healers (particularly from 1915–45) never materialized in Latin America. See Flexner, *Medical Education*.

8. Tworek, "Communicable Disease," 816, 820, 829, 830–32.

9. Cueto, *Value*; Cueto, *Missionaries*; Palmer, "Central American Encounters"; Cueto and Palmer, *Medicine*, 126, 128–29; Palmer, *Launching*.

10. Bell, *Frontiers*, 6.

11. *MPN*, 1937, 15.

12. H. Tilley, *Africa*, 16.

13. Palmer, *Launching*, 218.

14. Nelson, *Who Counts?*, 153.

15. AGCA indice 116, 1915, leg 16c, ex 39; MM, SA0692, memo de Reglas Higi-enicas para el ninõ, DGS.

16. AMP, paq. 107, Libro de Sentencias Economicas 1945–1947, August 22, 1947.

17. AMP, paq. 126, letter to el jefe político Manuel Juárez Monasterio, December 8, 1944.

18. Baer, et al., "Enfermedades," 141–42; de Castañeda Martín, *Tratado*.

19. MM, SA0692, memo de Reglas Higienicas para el ninõ, DGS, 1935. Although the director did not specify his rationale, perhaps lemon juice served the same purpose as antibiotic drops meant to protect infants from blindness if the mother has gonorrhea.

20. George M. Foster notes the absence of susto or any similar syndrome in Spain's history ("Relationships").

21. R. Adams, *Análisis*; R. Adams and Rubel, "Sickness"; Rubel, "Epidemiology."

22. Sal y Rosas, "El mito"; Tschopik, "Aymara," 202, 211–12, 282–83; Rubel, "Epidemiology," 271.

23. Gillin, "Magical Fright," 348; Rubel, "Epidemiology," 270, 278.

24. Kimball, *Open Secret*, 180–81. For astute analysis of the connections Andean women make between emotions and conceptions of health, particularly pregnancy, see Tapia, *Embodied Protests*.

25. Botey Sobrado, "Epidémica," 357; Palmer, *Popular Medicine*, 67–70.

26. Secretaría de Gobernación y Justicia, Publicaciones de sanidad, *Influenza*.

27. CIRMA, E1/S4 no. 124, "Guatemala en la hora de America, nuestra riqueza agrícola: explotación de las plantas medicinales," *El Imparcial*, May 24–26; Carey, *Engendering*, 31–60; Hendrickson, *Border Medicine*; Cueto and Palmer, *Medicine*, 92–95.

28. Cueto and Palmer, *Medicine*, 104–5; Palmer, *Popular Medicine*, 25.

29. Palmer, *Popular Medicine*, 127, 130, 199; Carey, *I Ask*, 132–33.

30. MM, ANE, SA0892, letter to DGS, Dr. Alfonso "Alfonsito" Mosquera Narváez from Dr. J. M. Espinoso J., Ibarra, January 25, 1933. For tensions among nineteenth-century medical practitioners in British Guiana, see de Barros, "Dispensers."

31. Abbott, *System*.

32. Cueto, "Visions," 16–17; Palmer, *Popular Medicine*, 115.

33. AGCA, B82.3, leg. 1101, ex. 24405, Municipalidad de la capital, Guatemala, 1924, Sobre reapurtura de la oficina municipal de vacuna, 1924.

34. Estrada and Márquez Valderrama, "Recognition," 127; Palmer, *Launching*, 147.

35. AGCA, índice 116, Chimaltenango, leg. 19a, ex. 42, carta de German Medina, 1918.

36. *MSP*, 1933, 458.

37. "Reglamento para el ejercicio de la Medicina y demás profesiones conexas," Casa de Gobierno, Guatemala, April 16, 1935, article 67, *La Gaceta*, May 5, 1935, p. 1099.

38. Ibid., 1100.

39. Ibid., 1100–1.

40. *MSP*, 1933, 425–26.

41. MM, AP 1120, 1911, Dr. Villavicencio informe sobre Lazareto Pifo, March 2, 1911; Few, "'Monster'"; Jaffray, *Reproduction*, 141–73; Warren, *Medicine*. For many indigenous and other poor and working-class Guatemalans, *brujos* had the power to heal and sicken. Even a few authorities recognized that power. Andeans too understood that curanderos could both heal and harm (and even kill) patients; see Alchon, "Tradiciones," 221–22.

42. Wisdom, *Chorti Indians*, 346–47.

43. Ibid., 334.

44. In his study of African and Afro-Brazilian healers, too, historian James Sweet found, "Medicines and poisons are really one and the same" (*Domingo*, 124).

45. Tedlock, *Time*, 84–85; Bunzel, *Chichicastenango*; Carlsen and Prechtel, "Walking"; Wisdom, *Chorti Indians*, 343; León, *Llorona's Children*, 127–62; Hendrickson, "Restoring"; Hendrickson, "New Contexts"; Hendrickson, "Neoshamans"; Silverblatt, *Sun*, 174; Lambe, *Madhouse*, 94.

46. Paul and McMahon, "Mesoamerican Bonesetters," 244–45, 250–51, 254–55, 259.

47. R. Adams, *Análisis*, 31, 47–48.

48. Lipp, "Comparative Analysis," 112; de Córdova y Quesada, *Locura* 74.

49. Paul and McMahon, "Mesoamerican Bonesetters," 244–45, 250–51, 254–55, 259.

50. Ibid., 244–45, 250–51, 254–55, 259; Wisdom, *Chorti Indians*, 343; Tedlock, *Time*, 57, 74; Hinojosa, *In This Body*.

51. "Reglamento para el ejercicio de la Medicina," 1099.

52. "Brujos y curanderos a falta de médicos en los departamentos," *Liberal Progresista*, republished in *La Gaceta*, May 5, 1935, 1064.

53. Quotes in this paragraph are from "Brujos y curanderos a falta de médicos en los departamentos," *Liberal Progresista*, republished in *La Gaceta*, May 5, 1935, 1064–68.

54. Quotes in this paragraph are from Hernan Martínez Sobral, "Ideas religiosas de los indígenas: paganism, supersticiones, el chuch, kajau, el Itzinel," *Boletín Sanitario de Guatemala* 6, no. 42 (1935): 1091–92.

55. As in this case, even as twentieth-century African healers were marginalized, Africans' collective knowledge was not necessarily dismissed. See H. Tilley, *Africa*, 215–16.

56. Quotes in this paragraph are from Jose Pacheco Molina, "Fuentes medicinales de Quezaltenango: aguas amargas—fuentes Georginas," *Boletín Sanitario de Guatemala* 6, no. 42 (1935), 1101–4.

57. A decade later further north in Huehuetenango, public health officials similarly inspected a "fuente de aguas medicinales." See *MSP*, 1945, 550.

58. Bunzel, *Chichicastenango*; Lipp, "Comparative Analysis," 110–111; R. Adams, *Análisis*, 37–38.

59. AGCA, índice de salud pública, leg. 23206, correspondencia 1939, Tecpán to DHG, November 3, 1940.

60. AGCA, índice de salud pública, leg. 23225, correspondencia 1942, Santa Apolonia to DHG, May 16, 1942.

61. Carey, *I Ask*.

62. AGCA, Descripción índice, ex. 23234 (1943 correspondencia), 23231 1943 correspondencia, Chuarrachancho, March 12, report to DHG; Ruta military de emergencia, Barberena, February 12, 1943, report to DHG.

63. AGCA, Descripción índice, ex. 23227, 1942 correspondencia, Intendencia municipal de San Martín Jilotepeque report, October 17, 1942.

64. AGCA, Descripción índice, ex. 23227, 1942 correspondencia, Intendencia municipal y juzgado de paz report, Nueva Santa Rosa, October 18, 1942.

65. AGCA, Descripción índice, ex. 23231, 1943, Intendencia Municipal y Juzgado de Paz, Barberena, Departamento Santa Rosa to DHG, February 6, 1943.

66. Borges, "Healing," 181, 185; Carrillo, "Nacimiento"; Otovo, *Progressive Mothers*; O'Brien, "'If They Are Useful,'" 418, 423, 432, 439; Carrillo, "Profesionales."

67. *MPN*, 1933, 21. Contemporary Cuban medical professionals similarly sought to eradicate "fake doctors"; see Lambe, *Madhouse*, 92–93 (quote), 147. Unlike contemporary Mexico, little evidence exists of Guatemalan communities punishing charlatans, healers or brujos who did not deliver expected results. See Koppe-Santamaría, *Vortex*, 97–107.

68. *MPN*, 1935, 35. For medical opinions against curanderos, see "Clame Contra el Curanderismo en el Congreso Sanitario," *Boletín Sanitaria* 46 (1938): 530–31.

69. *La Gaceta*, May 5, 1935, 1066–67.

70. *MPN*, 1935, 35.

71. Carey, *I Ask*, 56–89.

72. *MPN*, 1935, 26.

73. *La Gaceta*, March 19, 1933.

74. *La Gaceta*, November 10, 1935.

75. *MSP*, 1939, 240.

76. *La Gaceta*, February 23, 1933.

77. *La Gaceta*, May 5, 1935, 1073.

78. Blier, *African Vodun*, 215.

79. Marjorie Becker, *Setting*.

80. Carey, *I Ask*, 56–89.

81. Quotes in this paragraph are from *La Gaceta*, May 5, 1935, 1069.

82. *La Gaceta*, May 5, 1935, 1069–1070, 1076.

83. *La Gaceta*, May 5, 1935, 1069.

84. *La Gaceta*, February 14, 1943.

85. Quotes in this paragraph are from *La Gaceta*, February 14, 1943, 1071–74.

86. *La Gaceta*, May 5, 1935, 1075. In colonial Ecuador, a shaman similarly exercised power from jail. See Alchon, *Native Society*, 128.

87. Quotes in this paragraph are from *MPN*, 1937, 14–15. That the Director of National Police had the same surname as a notorious "witch, midwife, and healer" suggests how closely intertwined the lives of authorities and *curanderos* were.

88. *MPN*, 1938, 40.

89. *La Gaceta*, March 26, 1933; *MPN*, 1934, 35; *MPN*, 1935, 26; *MPN*, 1929, 18.

90. *MPN*, 1938, 40.

91. Ibid.

92. *MPN*, 1939, 240.

93. *La Gaceta*, January 19, 1941.

94. *La Gaceta*, May 5, 1935, 1075–76.

95. Ibid., 1076.

96. Ibid., 1076.

97. AGCA, MG 1941 B L31889, No. 49, Fidel Torres to Jefe Político de Altaverapaz, October 16, 1941.

98. Grieb, *Guatemalan Caudillo*; Gibbings, *Our Time*, 314–15.

99. Gibbings, "*Mestizaje*."

100. AGCA, MG 1941 B L31889, No. 49, Fidel Torres to Jefe Político de Altaverapaz, October 16, 1941.

101. TULAL, DC; Gibbings, "Their Debts."

102. Asturias, *Guatemalan Sociology*, 101–3; Gibbings, "*Mestizaje*."

103. Cueto and Palmer, *Medicine*, 89; Cueto, *Cold War*, 4–5.

104. Estrada and Márquez Valderrama, "Recognition"; Cueto and Palmer, *Medicine*, 89–90. For German association with homeopathy beginning in mid-nineteenth-century Latin America, see Cueto and Palmer, *Medicine*, 57.

105. Dieseldorff, *Plantas*; Gibbings, *Our Time*, 290–92. Germans were regularly fascinated with indigenous peoples; see Rosier, *Serving*, 73–84.

106. Gibbings, *Our Time*, 291–92.

107. Selis Lope, *Secretos*; Gibbings, *Our Time*, 288–89. Emilio Rosales Ponce wrote with a pseudonym both in the press and in his book.

108. TULAL, DC, Maya Papers Box 148, Domingo Caal to Erwin Paul Dieseldorff, December 27, 1926; Gibbings, *Our Time*.

109. Kirkpatrick, "Consumer Culture."

110. *La Gaceta*, January 12, 1941.

111. *La Gaceta*, July 19, 1942. For an example of such documentation, see AGCA, índice de salud pública, hospitalization order for "el indígena" Pablo Matzar from Sanidad Pública, Sololá, May 30, 1942.

112. Meyer, "Madness," 206; Estrada and Márquez Valderrama, "Recognition," 136; Boyer, *Political Landscapes*, 80.

113. Quotes in this paragraph are from *La Gaceta*, May 9, 1943.

114. British East African authorities similarly outlawed witchcraft but permitted indigenous healers to offer their own "systems of therapeutics" within their communities. Also reflecting Guatemala, British East African officials struggled to enforce such laws. See H. Tilley, *Africa*, 182–83.

115. Alchon, *Native Society*, 66–67, 74–75, 104–5.

116. Vásquez, "Familia," 220.

117. Clark, *Conjuring*.

118. Clark, *Conjuring*; Clark, *Gender*, 112–83.

119. Estrada and Márquez Valderrama, "Recognition," 135–37; Clark, *Conjuring*.

120. Clark, *Conjuring*.

121. Necochea López, *History*, 69.

122. Cueto, *Return*.

123. Núñez Butrón, "Qué es el Rijchardismo?"

124. MM, SA 0746, Delegación sanidad de León, Latacunga, to Director de Sanidad, April 15, 1930.

125. Ibid.

126. Warren, *Medicine*; Few, *For All*; Few, "Circulating"; Cueto and Palmer, *Medicine*, 46–49; Palmer, *Popular Medicine*, 21–22; Fenner et al., *Smallpox*; Few, "Epidemics."

127. Cueto, *Return*; Cueto and Palmer, *Medicine*, 85.

128. Cueto and Palmer, *Medicine*, 90. In another example of how indigenous people coopted public health practices into their own customs and traditions, Kaqchikels in Tecpán still immediately wash all the clothes of the deceased in a tradition informed by authorities' mandates to do so when someone died of typhoid.

129. Sweet, *Domingo*, 233.

130. Palmer, *Popular Medicine*, 9.

131. MM, SA0887, report by Delegación de Sanidad Chimborazo y Bolivia in Riobamba, January 16, 1928.

132. Ibid.

133. *Boletín Sanitaria* 46 (1938): 90–92.

134. Cueto and Palmer, *Medicine*, 85.

135. MM, SA0692, Augusto Salvador to Head of Pharmacy and Medical Profession Inspection, October 25, 1946.

136. MM, SA0692, Carlos Fabara to Dr. Abel Alvear, October 24, 1946.

137. Ibid.

138. MM, SA0692, Tabacundo, October 25, 1946.

139. MM, SA0692, Carlos Fabara to Dr. Abel Alvear, October 24, 1946.

140. Ibid.

141. MM, SA0692, Dr. Abel Alvear to Servicio Sanitario Pichincha de Quito, December 18, 1946.

142. MM, SA0692, Decreta Jefatura de farmacias y profesiones médicas, Quito, November 1, 1946.

143. MM, SA0692, Decreta, Servico Sanitario Nacional, Pichincha, Quito November 28, 1946.

144. MM, SA0692, Dr. Abel Alvear to Servicio Sanitario Pichincha de Quito, December 18, 1946.

145. MM, SA0692, Carlos Fabara to Dr. Abel Alvear, October 24, 1946.

146. Even in Costa Rica, where medical professionalization undergirded state-building, authorities subverted scientific medicine's authority by certifying curanderos and other unlicensed practitioners. See Palmer, *Popular Medicine*, 5, 10.

147. Clark, *Conjuring*.

148. Quotes in this paragraph are from MM, SA 0793, 1947, report from E. Herdoíza enclosed in letter from Dr. José Gómez de la Torres to Abel Alvear, Jefe de control de Farmacias y Profesiones Médicas, October 13, 1947. Until the mid to late 1940s in Ecuador, a hospital nurse was akin to a domestic servant rather than someone with formal nursing training. See Clark, *Gender*.

149. MM, SA 0793, 1947, Dr. José Gómez de la Torres to Abel Alvear, Jefe de control de Farmacias y Profesiones Médicas, October 13, 1947.

150. Meyer, "Madness," 206.

151. Oral history interview with Ixki'ch, San Juan Comalapa, 6/28/01.

152. Carey, *Engendering*, 31–60.

CHAPTER THREE

1. Quotes in this paragraph are from MM, SA 0793, Dr. José Gómez de la Torre "Informe global" to Ministerio de Prevision Social y Sanidad, July 15, 1947.

2. Clark, *Gender*, 33–77.

3. Birn, "No More Surprising," 21; Necochea López, *History*, 20. Long before European contact, indigenous populations prioritized maternal and infant health. European diseases that increased indigenous infant mortality thereafter in Mesoamerica and the Andes were particularly devastating for Aztecs, Mayas, and other indígenas who considered children a good omen. See Shein, *Niño*; Alchon, *Native Society*, 87; Birn, "No More Surprising?"

4. Birn, "No More Surprising?," 24, 27–28, 37.

5. Ibid., 17–19, 24, 37. It did not do so in earnest until the 1940s (18).

6. AGCA, Dirección del Hospital General, 1923, leg. 23100, Ejemplar del Boletín de la Unión Panamericana, June 25, 1923.

7. Birn, "No More Surprising?," 26–27, 38.

8. Ibid., 31–32. As part of larger efforts to reduce infant mortality in the 1930s, Latin American governments passed laws and established programs to advance neonatal maternal practices that had their origins in late nineteenth-century *Gota de Leche* (Drop of Milk) clinics, which were informed by public hygiene and dietary science. Yet even after Uruguay instituted mandatory breastfeeding, infant

mortality remained high, suggesting poverty, hygiene, potable water, and other social issues were major parts of the problem. Latin American officials identified causes ranging from poverty and malnutrition to rural culture; they proposed solutions that included sanitation education, school health services, maternal and infant care clinics, and establishing milk stations and dining halls for pregnant women. Brazil established milk depots, breastfeeding incentives, infant hygiene clinics, "little mother" training programs, and robust baby contests. In Costa Rica, trained midwives visited new and expectant mothers' homes, and Mexican visiting nurses taught rural women infant nutrition and hygiene principles. See Pohl-Valero, "Raza," 471; Palmer, *Launching*, 200; Cueto and Palmer, *Medicine*, 70; Birn, "Doctors"; Wolfe, *Watering*, 152, 160; Otovo, *Progressive Mothers*; Palmer, *Popular Medicine*, 223, 226, 234–35; Clark, *Gender*, 33–77.

9. AGCA, JP-S 1928, carta de Guatemala to Jefe Político de Sacatepéquez, June 23, 1928.

10. *Boletín Sanitario de Guatemala*, IX, no. 46 (1938), 246–48; *Imparcial*, November 19, 1937.

11. Hurtado and Sáenz de Tejada, "Relations," 216.

12. Peña Torres, *Historia*, 30. As was true elsewhere, scientific medicine was a decidedly male field in Latin America. The Guatemalan female doctor who practiced as early as 1916, and Ecuador's first female physician who graduated in 1921, were exceptions in those nations even as Latin America was increasingly producing female doctors. See AGCA, B82.3, leg. 1101, ex. 24398 (Higiene Vacuna 1916), alcalde to Director, February 19, 1916; AGCA, descripcion indice de salud, leg. 23259, 1945–1947 correspondencia, Dr. Mario Antonio Cabrera to DGH, March 31, 1947; Clark, *Gender*, 3–5.

13. *MPN*, 1933, 21. For studies of the tension between obstetric and popular medicine in the United States and Europe see Furst, *Climbing*; Muscucci, *Science*; Wertz and Wertz, *Lying-in*.

14. Few, "'Monster'," 163; Leavitt, *Brought*. Scholars have demonstrated how conflict over human reproduction often emanated from such cultural and political tensions. See Turner, *Contested Bodies*; Fissell, *Vernacular Bodies*; Muscucci, *Science*; Jaffray, *Reproduction*.

15. Socolow, *Women*, 165–77; Webre, "Wet Nurses," 196; Martínez Paláez, *Patria*, 196.

16. O'Brien, "Pelvimetry"; Rivera-Garza, "Criminalization," 156, 171; D. Rodríguez, *Right*, 129–30. Whereas Brazilian experts enlisted elite women to promote scientific motherhood, Argentinian certified midwives served as "gynecopolice" to favor male over female knowledge and access. See Otovo, *Progressive Mothers*; Ruggiero, "Honor."

17. Cited in Palmer, *Popular Medicine*, 138.

18. Clark, *Gender*, 125.

19. Hurtado and Sáenz de Tejada, "Relations," 238.

20. Clark, *Gender*, 126.

21. AMP, paq. 126, Cayetana Aju solicitud para licencia de comadrona, September 23, 1941; "Reglamento para el ejercicio de la Medicina y demás profesiones

conexas," Casa de Gobierno, Guatemala, April 16, 1935, article 67, *La Gaceta*, May 5, 1935, 1099; Kimball, *Open Secret*; Cueto and Palmer, *Medicine*, 92–93; A. Warren, "Foreign." In Mexico, indigenous midwives embraced government training to engage more fully in national conversations about reproductive health (Gabriela Soto Laveaga, personal communication, January 2021).

22. AGCA, leg. 23176, Secretaria de Educación Pública, Guatemala, June 12, 1937; April 1937.

23. RAC, RF, RG 1.1 Projects, series 317, box 1, folder 2, Dr. Juan A. Montalván to Mary Elizabeth Tennant, November 13, 1941.

24. Birn, "No More Surprising," 29.

25. D. Rodríguez, *Right*, 144–45.

26. Dr. Manuel Hernández Jurado, "Breves consideraciones sobre la importancia de los institutos de eugensia y protección a la infancia en Central America," *Boletín Sanitario de Guatemala*, 7, no. 44, (enero-diciembre 1936): 135. In Guatemala, the difference between comadronas and parteras was subtle. Often listed as synonyms along with matrona in Guatemalan reference works, comadrona was understood as a vocation while partera was associated with an avocation and generally carried less respect than comadrona. In Ecuador, partera denoted an untrained midwife.

27. Ibid.

28. AGCA, descripción índice de salud, leg. 23259, 1945–1947 correspondencia, Director General de AS to DHG, August 19, 1946.

29. Carey, "Heroines."

30. Oral history interview with Ixmana, Comalapa, 7/4/01.

31. Departmento de publicidad de Gubernamental, "Defensa de la vida y la salud del Niño Guatemalteco," *Informaciones Nacionales* 2 (1 de mayo 1946), 6.

32. Ibid., 6.

33. Hinojosa, *Body*, 60.

34. Abercrombie, *Pathways*, 113.

35. Abbott, *System*; Clark, *Gender*, 112–83.

36. Carrillo, *Matilde*, 63–64.

37. Jaffary, *Reproduction*.

38. Sosa and Durán, "Familia," 182. In a slowly evolving process during the nineteenth century, certified midwives contracted to work at hospitals and other health care institutions. Formal midwifery training dated to at least 1835; see Clark, *Gender*, 114.

39. Landázuri Camacho, *Juana*; Clark, *Gender*, 115.

40. Pineo, "Misery," 624, 629 (quote); Clark, *Conjuring*.

41. MM, SA0837, Director de ingresos, Quito, August 20, 1929.

42. Roth, *Miscarriage*; Cooper-Owens, *Medical Bondage*; Jaffray, *Reproduction*.

43. Clark, *Gender*, 116–24, 119 (quotes).

44. Clark, *Gender*, 137–39; Clark, *Conjuring*.

45. Not until a woman enrolled in the Faculty of Law in 1936 were female students admitted to other areas of study; see Clark, *Gender*, 116.

46. Clark, *Gender*, 116.

47. Arnold and Yapita, *Wawas*; Kimball, *Open Secret*, 150; Gallien, "Delivering"; Zulawski, *Unequal Cures*, 120, 136–41.

48. MM, SA0692, letter, Tabacundo, October 25, 1946.

49. Clark, *Gender*, 112–16.

50. Goetschel, *Historias*; Clark, *Conjuring*; Clark, *Gender*, 137–39. Contemporary Peruvian midwives performed abortions to support themselves; see Necochea López, *History*, 23.

51. Clark, *Gender*, 120; Clark, *Conjuring*.

52. MM, SA0692, AVISO, Obra de Protección Infantil, Riobamba, June 12, 1935; Clark, *Gender*, 118–19, 121, 124.

53. Clark, *Gender*.

54. MM, SA0692, Esther García to DGS, November 27, 1935 (quote); MM, SA0692, Esther García to DGS, May 22, 1935.

55. MM, SA0692, Esther García to DGS, November 27, 1935.

56. MM, SA0692, Obra de Protección Infantil, Riobamba, June 12, 1935.

57. MM, SA0692, Eduardo Rosero M. to DGS, 1935.

58. MM, SA0692, letter, Riobamba, June 26, 1935.

59. MM, SA0692, Consuelo Rueda Saénz to Dr. Velasco, July 3, 1935.

60. Clark, *Conjuring*.

61. MM, SA0692, María Hermilidad to Dr. Don Carlos Velasco.

62. Ibid.

63. MM, SA0692, Consuelo Rueda Saénz to Dr. Alfonso Mosquera, November 1, 1935.

64. Lippke quotes are from MM, SA0806, report to Dr. Federica Alvear, jefe de departamento de materno infantil, Servicio Sanitario Nacional, Quito, April 2, 1946.

65. MM, SA0806, Servicio Sanitario Nacional, Pichincha, servicio materno-infantil, Quito, Dr. Alvear Pérez to Luis León, March 25, 1946.

66. Clark, *Gender*, 133–34.

67. MM, SA0806, Servicio Sanitario Nacional, Pichincha, Dr. Alvear Pérez to servicio materno-infantil, c. 1946.

68. Clark, *Gender*, 132.

69. L. Rodríguez, *Search*, 226.

70. MM, SA0692, Severa Urresta to DGS, October 10, 1935.

71. MM, SA0692, Dr. E. R. Rickard to Dr. Alfonso Mosquera Narváez, DGS, January 5, 1935.

72. MM, SA0692, Rafael Quevedo Coronel to DGS, October 10, 1935.

73. MM, SA0692, Utiles necesarios para la Protección Infantil de Ambato, Ambato, November 5, 1935; MM SA0692, Provincia de Tungurahua, Ambato to Dr. Luis Rodríguez, Jefe de la Campaña Prenatal, November 20, 1935 (emphasis in original).

74. MM SA0692, Provincia de Tungurahua, Ambato to Dr. Luis Rodríguez, Jefe de la Campaña Prenatal, Quito, November 20, 1935.

75. MM, SA0692, Dr. Pilliariz to Dr. Luis Rodríguez, Jefe de la Campaña Pre-natal, November 22, 1935.

76. Ibid.

77. MM, SA0692, DGS de Judith Granda to R, Obstetriz de Sanidad, Enfemia Cadena, Visitadora de Sanidad, November 18, 1935.

78. MM, SA0850, DGS to Obstetrica de Sanidad, April 4, 1940.

79. Necochea López, *History*, 60; Clark, *Gender*.

80. Clark, *Gender*, 133–35.

81. MM, SA0692, Leopoldina Padilla Cos to Alfonso Mosquera, November 15, 1935.

82. Ibid. Conflicts similarly rose in neighboring Peru where supervising physi-cians imposed strict performance standards on midwives. See Necochea López, *History*, 23.

83. MM, SA0806, Servicio Sanitario Nacional, Pichincha, to Servicio maternal infantil, Quito, May 4, 1946.

84. Ruggiero, "Honor," 368–70; Zulawski, *Unequal Cures*, 118–56; Palmer, *Popular Medicine*, 139–54; Clark, *Gender*, 136–37.

85. Clark, *Gender*, 131–32.

86. MM, SA0692, Consuelo Rueda Saénz to Alfonso Mosquera, October 1, 1935.

87. MM, SA0692, Consuelo Rueda Saénz to Alfonso Mosquera, November 1, 1935.

88. Ibid.

89. MM, SA0692, Leopoldina Padilla Cos to Alfonso Mosquera, November 15, 1935.

90. MM, SA0692, Consuelo Rueda Saénz to Alfonso Mosquera, November 1, 1935.

91. MM, SA0692, Consuelo Rueda Saénz to Alfonso Mosquera, October 1, 1935.

92. MM, SA0887, Delegación de Sanidad Chimborazo, May 4, 1928.

93. Clark, *Gender*, 127.

94. MM, SA0692, report from Severa Urrestra, Cayambe, October 1, 1935.

95. Clark, *Gender*, 128–29.

96. MM, SA0692, Consuelo Rueda Saénz to Alfonso Mosquera, October 1, 1935. The scathing language in the flyers and Rueda Sáenz's reports about untrained midwives was akin to US efforts to stamp out popular healers, including African American midwives, in the south, where states criminalized their practices. See Frazier, *African American Midwifery*.

97. MM, SA0692, Consuelo Rueda Saénz to Dr. Velasco, July 3, 1935.

98. Clark, *Gender*, 129.

99. MM, SA0692, letter from Riobamba, June 26, 1935.

100. MM, SA0692, Consuelo Rueda Saénz to Dr. C. Velasco, July 31, 1935.

101. Necochea López, *History*, 72.

102. MM, SA0692, Consuelo Rueda Saénz to Dr. C. Velasco, July 31, 1935.

103. Ibid.

104. Sal y Rosas, "Mito," 177–84; Rubel, "Epidemiology," 277. Depending on the properties of the leaves (antibacterial, antifungal, disinflammatory), the herb bath may have been therapeutic in ways recognized by medical science.

105. Alchon, "Tradiciones," 22. Rueda Sáenz also noticed everyone raised pigs but no one had corrals, which meant illnesses spread quickly from swine to humans. The health inspector's "energetic campaign" to build a corral in the town center stalled. See MM, SA0692, Consuelo Rueda Saénz to Dr. C. Velasco, July 31, 1935. While the "seasoning" ritual was customary, roaming pigs had as much to do with poverty as culture.

106. MM, SA0806, Servicio Sanitario Nacional, Pichincha, servicio materno-infantil, María de Hirsh-Mamroth to Luis León, March 9, 1956 (1946?).

107. Clark, *Gender*, 128.

108. Lippke quotes are from MM, SA0806, report to Dr. Federica Alvear, jefe de departamento de materno infantil, Servicio Sanitario Nacional, Quito, April 2, 1946.

109. Clark, *Conjuring*; Clark, *Gender*, 130–32.

110. MM, SA0692, memo de Reglas Higienicas para el ninõ, DGS, 1935. Medical science has documented how alcohol consumption by pregnant women can undermine fetal development and infant health.

111. Birn, "No More Surprising," 30.

112. AGCA, inventario 1884–1924, leg. 22785, Dirección del Hospital General 1871–1879.

113. Quotes in this paragraph are from Dr. Luis Gaitán, "J. Rufino Barrios y la Sanidad Pública de Guatemala," *Boletín Sanitario de Guatemala*, 6, no. 42 (1935), 951–52.

114. Wisdom, *Chortí Indians*, 285–307, 354, 343; R. Adams, *Análisis*, 38.

115. Palmer, *Popular Medicine*, 143; Viesca Trevino, "*Curanderismo*," 63.

116. Palmer, *Popular Medicine*, 153.

117. Hinojosa, *Body*, 102.

118. José Marín, "Curanderos"; Paul and McMahon, "Mesoamerican Bonesetters," 244–45, 250–51, 254–55, 259; Carey, *Engendering*, 31–60.

119. Oral history interviews: Ixchali', Comalapa (Ixch'onïk), 7/2/01; Ixmana', Comalapa, 7/4/01. O. Lewis, *Life*; Finkler, *Women*; Birn, "Skirting"; Michel, et al., "Ethnomedical Research."

120. LNDLSC, Guatemala Collection, box 22 folder 2, Salubridad 1829–1933, AGCA, JP-S 1930, Nómina de las parteras en esta ciudad, Antigua, Guatemala, 23 de noviembre 1931.

121. AGCA, JP-S 1930, Nómina de las comadronas que existen en al departamento de Sacatepéquez, August 27, 1932.

122. Carey, *Engendering*, 31–60.

123. AGCA, B81.3 leg 1092, ex. 23968, Higiene Pública to Jefe Político, Guatemala, August 23, 1911.

124. Quotes in this paragraph are from *MSGJ*, 1912, 9–12.

125. *MSGJ*, 1915, 14.

126. Quotes in this paragraph are from AGCA, índice de Salud Pública, leg. 23305, año 1931–1946, *Plan de Estudios de la escuela dental, reglamento y plan de estudios de la escuela de parteras y plan de estudios y programa de enfermeras* (Guatemala City: Tipografía Nacional, 1923).

127. Carrillo, "Nacimiento"; Zárate, *Dar*; Necochea López, *History*, 25; Clark, *Gender*.

128. AGCA, leg. 23176, Secretaria de Educacion Pública, Guatemala, June 12, 1937 and April 1937; AGCA, índice de Salud Pública, leg. 23211, 1940 corresondencia, Policía Nacional de Guatemala to Dr. Gaitán, DHG de Ordóñez, May 2, 1940; AGCA, leg. 23240, Dr. Victor Giordani to Hospital General y sus dependencias, May 16, 1940; AGCA, índice de Salud Pública, leg. 23225, 1942 correspondencia, Sanidad Pública de Guatemala to DHG, March 25, 1942.

129. AGCA, inventario 1884–1924, leg. 23070, presidential decree, December 23, 1913.

130. *MSGJ*, 1913, 7.

131. *Revista de la Cruz Roja Guatemalteca* 12 (1936): 12.

132. AGCA, descripción índice de salud, leg. 23259, 1945–1947 correspondencia, Dr. Victor Giordani, DHG, December 22, 1945.

133. AGCA, descripción índice de salud, leg. 23259, 1945–1947 correspondencia, Dr. Victor Giordani, DHG, to Alma Marina Chavez, February 26, 1946; AGCA, descripción índice de salud, leg. 23256, 1946 correspondencia, Ministry of Public Health and Social Assistance to DHG, February 18, 1946.

134. AGCA, Leg. 23305, 10-a-b.

135. AGCA, Leg. 23305, letter to Ministerio de Gobernación y Justicia, 1926; Palmer, *Popular Medicine*, 140.

136. AGCA, índice 140, leg. 23141, 1930, Universidad Nacional facultad de ciencias médicas to DHG, Guatemala City, June 16, 1930.

137. *MSP*, 1932, 45.

138. "Reglamento para el ejercicio de la medicina," 1099.

139. AGCA, Leg. 23305, 24, 24.

140. AGCA, Leg. 23305, 18.

141. AGCA, Leg. 23305, 17a-b, 15a-b.

142. AGCA, Leg. 23305, 25, 36a-b; Clark, *Gender*, 122–24.

143. AGCA, Leg. 23305, 16. As Estrada Cabrera's 1913 sponsorship of two British midwives demonstrates, foreigners held a special allure for Guatemalan authorities and medical professionals.

144. Hurtado and Sáenz de Tejada, "Relations," 216–17.

145. Governmental Decree April 16, 1935, articles 98 and 99, Mendez, *Recopilación*, 896; Greenberg, "Midwife Training," 1604–5; Acevedo and Hurtado, "Midwives," 275.

146. *MSP*, 1944, 292.

147. *MSP*, 1945, 523–34.

148. *MSP*, 1945, 471.

149. *MSP*, 1945, 406, 585–86.

150. *MSP*, 1951, Memoria labores unidad sanitaria departamento de Chimaltenango.

151. Córdova, *Pushing*; Palmer, *Popular Medicine*, 139–40; L. Briggs, *Reproducing*, 15.

152. *MSGJ*, 1909, 12.

153. Ibid., 12.

154. D. Rodríguez, *Right*, 118.

155. Dirección General de Sanidad Pública de Guatemala, *Reglamento*, 15.

156. *MGJ*, 1929, 372.

157. Ibid., 366.

158. Ibid.

159. Luis Gaitán and Julio Roberto Herrera, "Aporte al studio del problema de la mortalidad infantile en Guatemala," *Boletín Sanitario de Guatemala*, 12, no. 49 (1941), 49.

160. *Boletín Sanitario de Guatemala*, IX, no. 46 (1938), 246–48; *Imparcial*, November 19, 1937.

161. *Imparcial*, November 19, 1937.

162. *MSGJ*, 1928, 263–64.

163. Quotes in this paragraph are from Alvaro Idigoras, "Protección a la infancia," *Boletín Sanitario de Guatemala* 6, no. 42 (1935): 1123–29.

164. Carey, *I Ask*, 191–224.

165. Pohl-Valero, "Raza," 474–75, 80; Cueto and Palmer, *Medicine*, 70, 167; Vrana, "Imperative"; O'Brien, *Spiritual Surgery*; Necochea López, *History*, 5.

166. Carey, *I Ask*, 118–52.

167. Dr. David Escalantes, untitled article in *Boletín Sanitario de Guatemala* IX, no. 46 (1938): 269 (emphasis in original).

168. Ibid., 273. When participants at the first Central American Health Congress met in Guatemala City in 1937, the organizers sponsored a day trip to Antigua with lunch, marimba music, dancing, site seeing, and souvenirs. The Guatemalan daily *El Imparcial*, November 19, 1937, reported, "At eleven in the morning, in 20 automobiles, the distinguished guests left the capital, with a great number of women and young ladies in tow." Six young ladies from Antigua society bearing flowers and gifts greeted the guests. The reporter captured well perceptions of women's role in scientific medical research and scholarship: they could celebrate but not conduct those studies. See also *Boletín Sanitario de Guatemala* IX, no. 46 (1938): 246–48.

169. *Boletín Sanitario de Guatemala* IX, no. 46 (1938): 24.

170. Ibid.

171. Hernández Jurado, "Breves consideraciones," 133.

172. Ibid., 139 (emphasis in original).

173. TULAL, DC, Personal Correspondence, box 9, letter to Sr. Fidel Torres, jefe político departamental, February 8, 1942; Box 9, Sociedad Protectora del Niño, June 8, 1942; box 9, folder 9, Sociedad Protector del Niño to Guillermo Dieseldorff, September 19, 1942.

174. TULAL, DC, box 9, Dieseldorff to Senores Miembros de la Sociedad Protectora del Niño, June 15, 1942.

175. TULAL, DC, box 9, folder 11, "Sala de maternidad inaugurada en Cobán," *Nuestro Diario* November 10, 1942; *La Gaceta*, August 2, 1942.

176. TULAL, DC, box 9, folder 10, Hospital Nacional Central de Zona, Cobán, Alta Verapaz, October 20, 1942.

177. TULAL, DC, box 9, folder 7, Fabrica de camas, "Ideal," Guatemala, July 15, 1942, W. E. Dieseldorff, Coban.

178. Gibbings, "Progressive Mothers."

179. TULAL, DC, Personal Correspondence, box 9, folder 14, Guillermo Dieseldorff to Senores presidente y secretario del club Deportivo "Tohil" Carcha, January 13, 1943.

180. TULAL, DC, box 9, folder 11, "Sala de maternidad inaugurada en Cobán," *Nuestro Diario*, November 10, 1942.

181. TULAL, DC, box 9, folder 10, *Norte*, October 25, 1942.

182. TULAL, DC, box 9, folder 11, "Aires Cobaneros," *Norte*, November 14, 1942.

183. Ibid.

184. TULAL, DC, box 9, folder 17, "Dieseldorf acude a otra obra de caridad: cheque que pusó en manos del Dr. Ortega para contribuir a las reformas del Hospital San José, *Nuestro Diario*.

185. LNDLSC, GC, box 22, folder 2, Salubridad 1829–1933, AGCA, JP-S 1930, Dirección del Hospital "Pedro de Bethancourt" to Jefe Político, June 2, 1930.

186. Wolfe, *Watering*, 192; Capello, *City*, 212, 214.

187. Epanimondas Quintana, "En alimentación infantile el analysis químico de la leche de madre u nodriza, tal como se hace aquí, es inútil," *Boletín Sanitario de Guatemala*, 12, no. 49 (1941): 146–48 (quote 148).

188. Adams and Giraudo, "Pack," 187.

189. LNDLSC, GC, box 22, folder 2, Salubridad 1829–1933, AGCA, JP-S 1930, Dirección del Hospital "Pedro de Bethancourt" to Jefe Político, May 25, 1930. Cuban contemporaries similarly vilified women, particularly the "lethal ignorance of mothers" and their "truly criminal indifference" to infant mortality. D. Rodríguez, *Right*, 60 (quotes), 129. In turn, Mexican doctor Pilar Hernández-Lira argued untrained midwives were problematic; see Guy, *White Slavery*, 47.

190. LNDLSC, GC, box 22, folder 2, Salubridad 1829–1933, AGCA, JP-S 1930, Dirección del Hospital "Pedro de Bethancourt" to Jefe Político, May 25, 1930.

191. Quotes in this paragraph are from LNDLSC, GC, box 22, folder 2, Salubridad 1829–1933, AGCA, JP-S 1930, Dirección del Hospital "Pedro de Bethancourt" to Jefe Político, June 2, 1930 (emphasis in original).

192. In contrast to the director's portrayal of indígenas, historian Anne-Emanuelle Birn asserts, "Concern over the health of mothers and children was rooted in the region's indigenous cultures" ("No More Surprising," 37). Throughout Latin America, eugenic discourse suggested how race complicated medical modernization. See Peard, *Race*; Montoya, *Making*; Green, "Doctoring."

193. *MSP*, 1933, 532–33.

194. Ibid., 533.

195. Quotes in this paragraph are from *La Gaceta*, May 5, 1935, 1069–75.

196. The use of forceps by a "brujo, partero, and curandero" is particularly intriguing since his clientele was primarily indigenous. In nineteenth-century Mexico, obstetricians frequently used forceps with indigenous women because of eugenic assumptions about their reproductive anatomical inferiority; see Cházaro, "Pariendo"; O'Brien, "If They Are Useful," 22–23, 25–26.

197. Dr. Luis Gaitán, "La enfermera sanitaria visitadora que se necesita en Centroamérica," *Boletín Sanitario de Guatemala*, 7, no. 44 (1936), 90.

198. Ibid., 90.

199. *Revista de la Cruz Roja Guatemalteca* 5, vol. 2 (1936): 1–3.

200. Carey, *Engendering*, 31–60.

201. AGCA, índice 116, Chimaltenango 1900, Leg. 1a, ex. 25.

202. AGCA, índice 116 1914, leg 15c, ex 45.

203. AGCA, índice 116, 1915, leg 16c, ex 39.

204. Ibid.

205. AGCA, índice 116, Chimaltenango, 1914, leg. 15d, ex. 58.

206. Findlay, "Courtroom Tales," 217.

207. AGCA, índice 116, 1915, leg 16c, ex 39; AGCA, indice 116, 1915, leg 18, ex 13; AMP, ramo civil II, Manuel de la Cruz contra Angela Morales por insultos, July 5, 1927.

208. AGCA índice 116, 1915, leg 16c, ex 39.

209. AGCA, inventario 1884–1924, leg. 22733, solicitud de doña Amelia Lanuza de Samasoya, April 30, 1919.

210. In her study of childbirth in Zaire, Nancy Rose Hunt similarly noticed that distinctions between precolonial and modern practices were opaque; see *Colonial Lexicon*.

211. *La Gaceta*, May 5, 1935, 1068.

212. "Reglamento para el ejercicio de la Medicina," 1102.

213. Ibid.; AMP, paq. 126, Cayetana Aju solicitud para licencia de comadrona, September 23, 1941.

214. AGCA, JP-C 1944, Francisca Tacen obtener licencia como comadrona empírica, August 12, 1943.

215. AGCA, descripción índice de salud, leg. 232345, 1944–1946 correspondencia, Hospital Amatitlán to DHG, August 6, 1945.

216. AGCA, descripción índice de salud, leg. 23259, 1945–1947 correspondencia, Director General de Asistencia Social to DHG, August 19, 1946.

217. Ibid.

218. *MSP*, 1944, 417.

219. Ibid., 420.

220. Ibid., 421; *MSP*, 1945, 481 (quote), 485.

221. *MSP*, 1945, 13.

222. Cueto, *Cold War*, 36.

223. *Estudio Demografico*, 1–2, 18. Peru similarly enjoyed decreased infant mortality rates in the 1950s, thanks to antibiotics and DDT; see Necochea López, *History*, 103.

224. *MSP*, 1951, Memoria Annual de las labores de la oficina central de la sanidad municipal y sus dependencias December 1950–November 1951.

225. LNDLSC, GC, Box 8, Salubridad, Convenio de la dirección general de sanidad pública con las municipalidades para establecimiento y funcionamento de los municipalidades de dispensatorio de sanidad pública, July 1950.

226. Ibid.

227. Clark, *Gender*, 119–20.

228. Although it has no data for Ecuador, B. R. Mitchell's *International Historical Statistics* provides infant mortality rates in Guatemala from 1900–49, which ranged from 116 to 155 "per 1000 population," but those numbers excluded "the live-born who died immediately" 84, 89 (quote). From a high of 155 deaths per 1000 from 1900–04, the rate decreased to 123 from 1925–29, and then rose to 128 from 1935–39 before falling to 116 from 1950–54. Into the twenty-first century, infant and maternal mortality remained problematic for *indígenas*. See Cueto and Palmer, *Medicine*, 253.

229. AGCA, inventario 1884–1924, leg. 23234, presidential decree, May 4, 1943.

230. Grandin, *Blood*; Fischer, *Modernity*, 22; Gluck, "End," 687; Butler, "Restaging," 40–41; Mallon, *Peasant*; Guardino, *Peasants*; Williams, *Marxism*.

231. Mallon, *Courage*.

232. AGCA, JP-S 1928, letter to Jefe Politíco de Sacatepéquez, June 23, 1928.

233. AGCA, índice de Salud Pública, leg. 23225, 1942 correspondencia, Sanidad Pública de Guatemala to DHG, March 25, 1942.

CHAPTER FOUR

1. MM, SA0699, DGS, Servicio Sanitatorio Nacional, Quito, December 23, 1939.

2. MM, SA0876, Gobierno de Ecuador, Ibarra, July 8, 1936.

3. Zulawski, "Environment"; D. Rodríguez, *Right*, 6.

4. The RF and the United States similarly sought to bring Mexico, the Caribbean, and Central America into a US orbit of public health and healthcare with malaria and hookworm campaigns. Mexico, in turn, used antimalaria campaigns to fold the state of Chiapas and its indigenous populations into the nation by providing indispensable public health services. Meanwhile, US public health experts in the Philippines facilitated US occupation through quarantines and sanitation projects. See Cueto, *Cold War*; Cueto, "Introduction," xiii; W. Anderson, *Colonial Pathologies*.

5. Pineo, *Ecuador*.

6. MM, SA 0695, Comisario Nacional de Santo Domingo de los Colorados to director de Sanidad, May 9, 1942 (quote); H. Tilley, *Africa*, 174–75.

7. Cueto, *Cold War*, 120; Palmer, *Launching*; Birn, *Marriage*.

8. Carter, "Malaria"; Alvarez, "Malaria"; Zulawski, *Unequal Cures*; Cueto, "Tifo"; Armus, *Ciudad impura*; Blake, "Medicalization"; Obregon, "Building"; Di Liscia, "Viruela"; Kapeluz-Poppi, "Rural Health."

9. Espejo, *Reflexiones*, 53, 64; Alchon, *Native Society*, 104.

10. W. Anderson, "Colonial Medicine," 144.

11. López-Durán, *Eugenics*; Borges, "Puffy"; Dávila, *Diploma*; Armus, *Ciudad*; Hunt, *Colonial Lexicon*; Margaret Anderson, "Creating French Settlements"; Clark, "Género." Eighteenth-century French naturalist Jean-Baptiste Lamarck argued that species could be improved by characteristics inherited from ancestors and parents. Twentieth-century Latin American neo-Lamarckians asserted the environment did more than heredity to improve people. See Stepan, *"Hour."* Analyzed through the lens of sterilization, eugenics in Latin America was far less consequential than in the United States and Germany, where 90,000 and 400,000 individuals were sterilized, respectively. See Proctor, *Racial Hygiene*.

12. Vasconcelos, *Raza*; Stutzman, "Mestizaje"; Clark, "Race," 203–4; Clark, "Racial Ideologies," 386–88; Reeves, *Ladinos*; Taracena Arriola, *Invención*; Casaús Arzú, *Guatemala*; de la Cadena, *Indigenous Mestizos*. Informed by racial typing associated with culture, medical racialization in Ecuador and Guatemala differed from that in the United States where a biologized framework predominated. See Cooper Owens, *Medical Bondage*; Pernick, *Calculus*; Pernick, *Black Stork*. Concerned about "pathological *patrias*," many Latin American authorities deemed those regularly or incurably ill devoid of citizenship. See Hochman, et al., *Patologías*; Stepan, *"Hour"*; Martínez García, "Michel Foucault," 9, 11.

13. Carey, *Engendering*, 31–60.

14. Clark, "Medida"; Gibbings, *Our Time*, 134–35.

15. Foss, *Our Own Terms*, 21–49.

16. Marc Becker, "Limits," 52.

17. Foss, *"Obra,"* 212–13.

18. Oliver, "Cólera."

19. Woodward, *Rafael Carrera*, 54, 60–83; Oliver, "Cólera"; Williford, "Luces," 37–40; Tobar Cruz, *Montañeses*, 54–7; McCreery, *Rural Guatemala*, 23, 56, 148–9; Carey, *Our Elders*, 117–18.

20. Oral history interview with Kab'lajuj Tijax, Comalapa, 4/6/98.

21. Oral history interview with Ixsamaj, Comalapa, 9/6/98.

22. Carey, *Our Elders*, 118–29.

23. *Memoria de la Secretaria de Gobernación y Justicia*, 1919, 57–58.

24. "El estado sanitario de los departamentos," *Diario de Centro América*, January 8, 1919, 2.

25. In a 1946 government study, Guatemalan observers described rural housing ranging from primitive and humble to deteriorating and overcrowded. See Departmento de publicidad de Gubernamental, "Consideraciones sobre la vivienda rural," *Informaciones Nacionales*, no. 2, Guatemala (1946): 3–6. For (failed) efforts to

improve indigenous housing in Nahualá by removing wood-burning stoves from sleeping quarters in the early 1940s, see Foss, *Our Own Terms*, 21–49.

26. McCreery, "Coffee," 200.

27. Oral history interview with Ix'ajmaq, Poaquil, 7/1/01; *MSGJ*, 1931, 100; AGCA, Instituto General de Trabajo, Correspondencia, October 1948, leg. 48762 (actual no. leg. 69), letter from Labor Inspector, December 16, 1947; Bunzel, *Chichicastenango*, 143.

28. RAC, RF Photographs, series 317, box 85, folder 1709, "A typical Indian 'ranchito,'" Dr. Rowan, 12–31–15; "Typical native hut in eastern lowlands between Puerto Barrios and Guatemala City. Trip November 11-December 13, 1915," Dr. Rowan.

29. RAC, RF Photographs, series 317, box 85, folder 1709, "An Indian vapor bath," Dr. Rowan, 12–31–15.

30. Cueto and Palmer, *Medicine*,14, 22.

31. RAC, RF Photographs, series 317, box 85, folder 1709, "Dome-shaped mud bathhouse," Dr. Rowan, 1915.

32. RAC, RF Photographs, series 317, box 85, folder 1709, "An Indian vapor bath," Dr. Rowan, 12–31–15.

33. Stern, "Buildings," 67.

34. Palmer, *Launching*, 154–55.

35. Termer, *Ethnología*, 49.

36. Lipp, "Comparative Analysis," 96. Such myopia dated to late eighteenth-century officials who outlawed and periodically destroyed indigenous sweat baths and colonial doctors who considered sweat baths typhus propagators. See Few, "Epidemics"; Few, *For All*, 71.

37. *MSP*, 1933, 425.

38. *MSP*, 1933, 425.

39. *MSP*, 1933, 568.

40. *MSP*, 1933, 424.

41. *MPN*, 1926, 114.

42. *MSP*, 1933, 348.

43. *MSP*, 1933, 397.

44. Juárez Muñoz, *Indio*, 143–44.

45. A. Adams and Giraudo, "Pack," 183–84.

46. C. Briggs with Mantini-Briggs, *Stories*, 9.

47. Wisdom, *Chorti Indians*, 360–61; R. Adams, *Análisis*, 84.

48. Foss, *"Obra,"* 214; A. Adams and Giraudo, "Pack," 190.

49. Wisdom, *Chorti Indians*, 367–68.

50. Wagley, "Social," 76.

51. R. Adams, *Análisis*, 39, 69–71.

52. DGE, *Censo General de la República de Guatemala*, 1880, 26, 69–73.

53. DGE, *Censo General de la República de Guatemala*, 1893, 40.

54. "Reglamento interior del Instituto Agrícola de Indígenas," in Mendez, *Recopilación*, Tomo 12, 554–72.

55. Esquit, *Superación*; Esquit, *Otros poderes*; Grandin, *Blood*.

56. Asturias, *Guatemalan Sociology*, 99–103, 105–6; Gibbings, *Our Time*, 29–30, 252–56; Gibbings, *"Mestizaje."*

57. Pitti, "Jorge Ubico," 217.

58. Casaús Arzú, "Gran debate"; V. Tilley, *"Mestizaje."*

59. Gould, "Indigenista Dictators," 188–212; Gotkowitz, *Revolution*, 44; S. Lewis, *Rethinking*. In the 1930s, Peru developed what historian Marcos Cueto termed medical indigenism (*Return*, 63).

60. Giraudo and Martín-Sánchez, *Ambivalente historia*; Giraudo and Martín-Sánchez, "Rethinking Indigenismo."

61. Foss, *Our Own Terms*.

62. Casaús Arzú, "Generación"; Gibbings, *Our Time*, 251–52.

63. Juárez Muñoz, *Indio*, 117–18.

64. Carey, *I Ask*.

65. Gibbings, *Our Time*, 307; Carey, *I Ask*; Carey, "Drunks."

66. Stepan, *"Hour,"* 17.

67. Carey, "Rethinking."

68. Foss, *Our Own Terms*; Marc Becker, "Limits," 46, 49–50, 54, 57.

69. Oral history interview with K'ayb'il B'alam, 10/5/97, Tecpán.

70. Carey, "Mayan Soldier-Citizens." While Walter Little offers incisive analysis of Ubico's national fairs ("Visual Political Economy"), no one has examined closely the model villages, particularly as they relate to public health. Warwick Anderson and Randall Packard offer two possible frameworks. In Anderson's study of the Philippines, model villages demonstrated US approaches to medicine and public health and desecrated indigenous health practices (*Colonial Pathologies*). In contrast, Packard reveals how model villages in Nigeria were developed from the ground up and thereby allowed space for indigenous practices (*History*). This became a model village for mental health that officials sought to export to Mexico—a sharp contrast to the Philippine model village that was based on importing US strategies around public health.

71. Hernández de León, *Viajes presidenciales*, vol. II, 60.

72. Lokken, "Challenge," 112; Carey, *I Ask*.

73. *Diario de Centro América*, January 23, 1933.

74. *MSP*, 1939, 652.

75. *MSP*, 1945, 133.

76. *MSP*, 1933, 397.

77. *MSP*, 1933, 543.

78. AGCA, Descripción índice, ex. 23182, Intendencia Chichicastenango to DHG, about Jose Mejía and María Quino, January 13, 1938.

79. Ibid.

80. Palmer, *Popular Medicine*, 174, 178–80, 182. Insisting denizens maintain hygienic normative behaviors or alter or reconfigure their bodies to gain access to national belonging and state health care was common in other colonial and neocolonial states. See W. Anderson, *Colonial Pathologies*, 178; Bashford, *Imperial Hygiene*, 77–79

81. Gibbings, *Our Time*. Such depictions were common among US public health officials who portrayed Mexican immigrants as diseased even when they appeared healthy. See Stern, "Buildings," 77; A. Adams and Giraudo, "Pack," 184

82. Hernández Sandoval, *Guatemala's Catholic Revolution*, 32, 45, 110.

83. Martínez Sobral, "Ideas," 1091.

84. *MSP*, 1933, 342.

85. *MSP*, 1933, 349.

86. *MSP*, 1933, 349–50.

87. *MSP*, 1933, 346.

88. *MSP*, 1933, 350.

89. Administración, *Dos lustrous*, 13.

90. Stepan, *"Hour"*; Stern, "Responsible Mothers"; Schell, "Eugenics Policy"; O'Brien, "Pelvimetry," 21, 23, 24, 26–28; Few, *For All*; Pohl-Valero, "Raza," 457–58, 474–75; Noguera, *Medicina*; Urías Horcasitas, *Historias*; Urías Horcasitas, "Degeneracionismo"; L. Suárez, *Eugenesia*; Palacios, *Raza*; Vasconcelos, *Raza*; D. Rodríguez, *Right*, 141.

91. Stern, "Buildings," 64.

92. Administración, *Dos lustrous*, 13. In Central America, intellectuals similarly identified malnourishment as preventing individuals from fully participating in the nation. See Masferrer, *Mínimum vital*, 119.

93. Gibbings, *"Mestizaje."*

94. *MSP*, 1945, 150.

95. Pacino, "Liberating."

96. M. Foster, "Validating"; Stern, "Buildings," 74.

97. R. Adams, *Análisis*, 97.

98. Cueto and Palmer, *Medicine*, 112–14.

99. Wisdom, *Chorti Indians*, 309.

100. Crafts, "Mining," 222–23. Such an explanation was not unlike the conceptualizations of seventeenth-century microbiologists Robert Hooke and Antoni van Leeuwenhoek (who had no formal scientific training) that the latter dubbed animalcules.

101. Palmer, *Launching*, 50–51.

102. Peña Torres and Palmer, "Rockefeller Foundation," 51–53, 61 (quote); Palmer, *Launching*, 151.

103. Wisdom, *Chorti Indians*; R. Adams, *Análisis*, 93.

104. R. Adams, *Análisis*, 39.

105. R. Adams, *Análisis*, 93; Wisdom, *Chorti Indians*, 76.

106. Wisdom, *Chorti Indians*, 77.

107. R. Adams, *Análisis*, 70.

108. Bunzel, *Chichicastenango*; Lipp, "Comparative Analysis," 110–11.

109. Ixnal Ambrocia Cuma Chávez, personal communication, 2021.

110. *MSP*, 1945, 2. In Buganda, colonial officials similarly collaborated with local leaders to great effect to separate lakeside residents from infective flies. See Zeller, "Establishment," 162–78.

111. A. Adams and Giraudo, "Pack," 177.

112. *MSP*, 1945, 2.

113. *MSP*, 1945, 134.

114. Quotes in this paragraph are from *MSP*, 1945, 134.

115. Jaramillo Alvarado, *Indio*; Prieto, *Liberalismo*; Rubio Orbe, *Indios*; Marc Becker, "Limits"; M. Sáenz, *Indio*; Izcara, *Huasipungo*.

116. Capello, *City*, 89.

117. González Suárez, *Historia*, 226.

118. Capello, *City*, 100.

119. Vásquez, "Familia," 220.

120. MM, SA0836, Ministerio de Interior, February 25, 1916.

121. MM, SA Delegación de Chimborazo to DGS, Riobamba, July 13, 1926.

122. Clark, *Redemptive Work*, 187–98

123. MM, SA0837, Delegado de Sanidad de León, Latacunga, Quito, July 5, 1929.

124. MM, SA 0746, Delegación Sanidad Imbabura to DGS, March 26 1930.

125. Espejo, *Voto*; Paredes, *Oro*; A. Suárez, *Contribución al estudio*.

126. MM, SA0887, Alausí, October 8, 1928.

127. Stutzman, *"Mestizaje."*

128. Maiguashca and North, "Orígenes"; Maiguascha, "Sectores"; Marchán Romero, "Crisis"; Clark, "Racial Ideologies," 375–76, 381; Marc Becker, *Indians*.

129. A. Suárez, *Contribución al estudio*, 5. By the time he helped found the Ecuadorian Indigenist Institute in 1943, he recognized the importance of ethnicity.

130. A. Suárez, *Contribución al studio*. Bucking his Central American eugenic contemporaries, Salvadoran intellectual Alberto Masferrer similarly advocated transforming all individuals through self-improvement rather than targeting a group based on race, class, or gender (*Mínimum*).

131. Valarezo Galo, *Regreso*; Stutzman, "Mestizaje."

132. Clark, "Género," 203–6.

133. MM, SA 0695, Comisario Nacional de Santo Domingo de los Colorados to Director de Sanidad, May 9, 1942.

134. MM, SA 0332, Director de Sanidad to Comisario Nacional de Santo Domingo de los Colorados, May 19, 1942.

135. Rubio Orbe, *Indios*.

136. Ospina Peralta, *Aleación*, 431.

137. MM, SA 0822, Correspondencia recibida y despachada 1911–1912, Sección de Sanidad, Quito, May 3, 1911. In Ecuador, jefes políticos (political administrators) were national authorities in local areas; appointed by national governments, they had jurisdictions over *cantóns*.

138. MM, SA 0822, Correspondencia recibida y despachada 1911–1912, Sección de Sanidad, Quito, May 3, 1911.

139. MM, SA 0887, Alausí, July 22, 1928. Although most public health officials and employees in Ecuador and Guatemala were not indígenas, some municipal-level

health inspectors were indigenous. Such was the case with Claudio Sajché, who visited bakeries and other food stores in Quetzaltengo in 1933.

140. MM, SA 0887, Alausí, July 22, 1928.

141. MM, SA0887, Delegación de Sanidad Zona Austral, March 8, 1928.

142. MM, SA 0887, Delegación de Sanidad Chimborazo, Riobamba, April 11, 1928. For other evidence of indigenous uprisings during anti-plague campaigns, see Clark, *Conjuring.*

143. MM, SA 0892, Latacunga, February 8, 1933.

144. MM, SA 0891, Latacunga to Quito, January 20, 1933.

145. Ibid.

146. MM, SA 0892, Latacunga, February 8, 1933.

147. See for example, MM, SA0887, Delegación de Sanidad Chimborazo, Riobamba, May 4, 1928.

148. MM, SA 0892, Latacunga, February 8, 1933.

149. MM, SA0891, Latacunga, May 3, 1931.

150. Clark, *Conjuring.*

151. As anthropologist Lisa Stevenson demonstrates in her study of tuberculosis among Inuit and other Arctic region natives, some patients perceived public health interventions with good intentions as intrusive (*Life*). By juxtaposing the 1940s–1960s tuberculosis campaign that forcibly transferred rural ill to urban hospitals with the late-twentieth-century suicide prevention campaign that similarly removed suicide-susceptible indigenous people from their communities, Stevenson adeptly points to the gaps in historical archives that leave scholars surmising whether indigenous people feel marginalized or empowered by public health initiatives.

152. Cueto, *Cold War.*

153. Unlike in Argentina and Chile, for example, where the post-independence state launched extermination campaigns against indígenas.

154. MM, SA0767, Delegación de Sanidad Pública cantón Cotacachi, November 23, 1918.

155. Ibid.

156. MM, SA0692, República de Ecuador, Reglamento para inspectores de sanidad de la Provincia de Imbabura, ca. 1934; MM, SA0692, Informe presentado al municipio de Otavalo, Ibarra, December 10, 1934.

157. John D. Long, "La Campaña Antipestosa en Guayaquil," *Boletín de la Oficina Sanitaria Panamericana* 9, no. 8 (1930): 927.

158. John D. Long, "Bubonic Plague on the West Coast of South America in 1934," *Public Health Reports* 50, no. 29 (July 19, 1935): 923–32.

159. Clark, *Redemptive Work,* 152–53.

160. Ibid., 153.

161. MM, SA0643, Reglamento Especial sobre aprovisionamente y venta de leches, article 15, ca. 1926–1927.

162. Ibid.

163. Andean market women faced similar discrimination and racist policies in Bolivia and Peru. See de la Cadena, *Indigenous Mestizos*.

164. Cornelio Sáenz Vera, "Campaña antipestosa intensivo en la provincia de Chimborazo (Ecuador)," *Boletín de la Oficina Sanitaria Panamericana* 22, no. 10 (1943), 880; Morales, *Guinea Pig*; Clark, *Conjuring*.

165. Clark, *Redemptive Work*, 153. Mid-century Mexican anthropologists similarly defined sleeping on mats as part of indigenous lifestyles, see Cueto, *Cold Wars*, 124. Ecuadorian officials recognized that wealthy homes could have poor hygiene and sanitation with chickens wandering the hallways; see Clark, *Conjuring*.

166. Clark, *Conjuring*. If Guatemala was any indication, *indígenas* preferred sleeping in beds but could not afford them. See Instituto Indigenista Nacional de Guatemala, *San Bartolomé*, 10.

167. Clark, *Conjuring*.

168. MM, SA0891, Dr. Teran to DGS, March 22, 1933.

169. Victor Gabriel Garcés, "Cuestionario de la Oficina Internacional de Trabajo sobre situación de la raza indígena en el Ecuador," *Prevision Social* 8 (1941): 12–44.

170. MM, SA0891, Dr. Teran to DGS, March 22, 1933.

171. MM, SA 0887, Alausí, July 22, 1928.

172. Ibid.

173. Quotes in this paragraph are from MM, SA0692, Informe presentado al municipio de Otavalo, Ibarra, December 10, 1934.

174. Bautista-Valarezo, et al., "Indigenous Definition."

175. Quotes in this paragraph are from MM, SA 0695, 1942, Gonzalo Fabara to Northeast Military Health Services, January 10, 1942.

176. MM, SA0734, Charla Sanitaria versada sobre la Coquieluche, Radiodifundidad por "La voz de Imbabura," Ibarra, August 27, 1945.

177. Ibid.

178. Nading, "Love," 86.

179. MM, SA0734, Charla Sanitaria versada sobre la Coquieluche, Radiodifundidad por "La voz de Imbabura," Ibarra, August 27, 1945.

180. Quotes in this paragraph are from MM, SA0692, Dr. Abel Alvear to Servicio Sanitario Nacional, Pichincha, Quito, November 22, 1946.

181. Bautista-Valarezo, et al., "Indigenous Definition," 2. See also López-Cevallos and Chi, "Healthcare."

182. Carey, *I Ask*. Throughout Latin America, governments deployed scientific medicine to assimilate indígenas and promote modernization. See Sowell, *Medicine*; Cueto, *Cold War*, 10–11, 51, 103–5. A similar process unfolded in British colonies where authorities sought to Occidentalize non-European bodies as part of the development of public health infrastructure in India. British observers and intellectuals portrayed Indian Hindus as dirty, unruly threats to colonial order even when photographs of such Indian holy men as fakirs suggested otherwise. See Arnold, *Colonizing*; Siebenga, "Colonial"; Alavi, *Islam*. Colonial officials in Africa also consid-

ered popular medicine incompatible with modernization, see H. Tilley, *Africa*, 181–82.

183. Palmer, *Launching*, 48.

CHAPTER FIVE

1. MM, SA0876, Gobierno de Ecuador, letter to DGS from Dr. J.M. Espinosa, Ibarra, June 8, 1936.

2. Ibid.

3. Similarly, late nineteenth- and early twentieth-century Colombians portrayed leprosy as an indigenous disease. See Martínez Martín, *Lazareto*.

4. Dr. Carlos Catalán Prem, "El tifus exantemático en Chimaltenango," *Boletín Sanitario de Guatemala*, XI, no. 48 (1940), 138. Although much scholarship focuses on typhus as disease of war (McNeill, *Mosquito Empires*, 285, 295), typhus also ravaged peacetime communities.

5. MM, SA0734, Servicio Sanitario Nacional Cotopaxi, Latacunga, August 1, 1945. Early twentieth-century Mexican officials similarly associated poor *indígenas* with typhus. See Alexander, "Fever."

6. *MGJ*, 1917, 11–12.

7. MM, SA 0746, Delegación sanidad de León a DGS, Latacunga, 15 abril 1930.

8. *MSP*, 1933, 346.

9. Zulawski, *Unequal Cures*, 1, 38; Cueto, *Return*, 54; Sellers-García, "Plaga occulta"; LeBaron and Taylor, "Typhoid Fever."

10. LeBaron and Taylor, "Typhoid Fever"; Mckiernan-González, *Fevered Measures*, 167, 269; D. Rodríguez, *Right*, 201.

11. Zulawski, *Unequal Cures*, 41–43.

12. Vásquez Lapeyre, "Patologia"; Few, *For All*, 62–64; Zulawski, *Unequal Cures*, 75; Cueto, *Return*, 55; Gomez, *Silver Veins*, 19, 24, 160–62.

13. N. Molina, "Medicalizing," 28.

14. *MSGJ*, 1917, 101; Becerra, "Informe," 505.

15. Pineo, "Misery," 614; Clark, *Conjuring*.

16. Becerra, "Informe," 506.

17. MM, SA0678, carta de Subdirección de Pichincha a Ministro de Sanidad, February 11, 1914.

18. Ibid.

19. MM, SA0767, Delegación de Sanidad, Cantón de Otavalo, October 30, 1918.

20. Quotes in this paragraph are from MM, SA0767, Dirección General de Sanidad, Sangolquí, August 29, 1918.

21. Guatemalan prisoners too contracted typhoid while incarcerated; see AGCA, índice de Salud Pública, leg. 23187, 1938 correspondencia, Penitenciaría Central, Guatemala, July 8, 1938. Over time and across place, jails were known as "dens of infection"; see Sweet, *Domingo*, 150

22. MM, SA0767, Vecinos de parroquia Alfaro, December 6, 1918.

23. Ibid.

24. Cueto and Palmer, *Medicine*, 35–36, 40.

25. MM, SA0767, Vecinos de parroquia Alfaro, December 6, 1918.

26. Capello, *City*, 48, 53.

27. Carrión, *Quito*; Achig, *Proceso*.

28. MM, SA0767, Vecinos de parroquia Alfaro, December 6, 1918 (emphasis in the original).

29. Capello, *City*, 104.

30. Rodas Chaves, *Pensamiento*.

31. Pineo, "Misery," 635–36.

32. Quotes in this paragraph are from MM, SA0678, Subdirección de Pichincha to Ministro de Sanidad, February 11, 1914.

33. Clark, *Conjuring*.

34. Until 1925, the Ecuadorian congress rather than the executive controlled the national budget. See L. Rodríguez, *Search*, 97.

35. Clark, *Conjuring*.

36. Carey, *I Ask*, 92, 111, 115; Clark, *Conjuring*.

37. MM, SA 0746, Delegación sanidad de León to Director de Sanidad, April 15, 1930.

38. Transcription of May 10 letter enclosed in MM, SA 0746, to DS, May 14, 1930.

39. MM, SA 0746, R. Jeráud to DS, May 14, 1930.

40. MM, SA 0746, R. Jeráud to DS, May 17, 1930.

41. MM, SA 0746, R. Jeráud to DS, May 19, 1930.

42. MM, SA 0746, R. Jeráud to DS, May 22, 1930.

43. MM, SA 0746, DS, August 20, 1930.

44. MM, SA 0746, DS, September 6, 1930.

45. MM, SA 0746, Francisco Arrieta to DS, October 11, 1930.

46. MM, SA0887, Delegación de Sanidad Chimborazo, Riobamba, March 26, 1928.

47. MM, SA0692, Informe presentado al municipalidad de Otavalo, Ibarra de Sr. Presidente del Concejo cantonal, December 10, 1934, and Informe presentado al municipalidad de Cotacachi, Ibarra, de Sr. Presidente del Concejo cantonal, December 10, 1934.

48. MM, SA0692, Informe presentado al municipalidad de Otavalo, Ibarra de Sr. Presidente del Concejo cantonal, December 10, 1934, and Informe presentado al municipalidad de Cotacachi, Ibarra de Sr. Presidente del Concejo cantonal, December 10, 1934.

49. MM, SA0692, República de Ecuador, Reglamento para inspectores de sanidad de la Provincia de Imbabura, ca. 1934.

50. MM, SA0692, Informe presentado al municipalidad de Cotacachi, Ibarra de Sr. Presidente del Concejo cantonal December 10, 1934.

51. Ibid.

52. Ibid. Late nineteenth- and early-twentieth-century Mexico City authorities, similarly obsessed about decaying bodies, insisted on sealing coffins or dipping corpses in silver nitrate to neutralize decomposing bacteria. See Weber, *Death*.

53. MM, SA0692, Informe presentado al municipalidad de Cotacachi, Ibarra de Sr. Presidente del Concejo cantonal, December 10, 1934.

54. MM, SA0876, Direcciones General de Sanidad, Gobierno de Ecuador, Ibarra, June 8, 1936.

55. MM, SA0821, Comunicaciones recibidas, 1914, carta de Gobernación Pichincha, September 3, 1914, Subdirección de higiene y sanidad, and carta de Sociedad Funeraria Nacional, Quito, September 28, 1914.

56. MM, SA0678, Subdirección de Sanidad de Pichincha, 1914, Carlos Miño to Presidente de la Funeraria Nacional, September 16, 1914.

57. MM, SA0821, Comunicaciones recibidas, 1914, L. Becerra to Dirección Servicio de Sanidad, December 26, 1914.

58. MM, SA0678, CA Miño to Inspector General de Hospital Civil, Quito, February 6, 1914.

59. Ibid.

60. MM, SA0699, Subdirector provincial AP, Guaranda to DGS, February 23, 1939.

61. MM, SA0699, Viteri to DGS, December 23, 1939.

62. Ibid. Hiding the infirm was not uncommon in Latin America. See Zulawski, "Environment."

63. Quotes in this paragraph are from Cornelio Sáenz Vera, "Campaña antipestosa intensiva en la provincia de Chimborazo (Ecuador)," *Boletín de la Oficina Sanitaria Panamericana* 22, no. 10 (1943)," 881.

64. MM, SA0891, Estado Sanitario en las Diversas Provincias y las necesidades principales de Sanidad Pública, Alfonso Mosquera to DGS, March 4, 1931, pp. 3–4.

65. MM, SA0891, Latacunga, October 27, 1931.

66. MM, SA0850, Delegado Sanidad a Ministerio de Sanidad y Hygiene, Ambato, April 29, 1940.

67. MM, SA0891, Latacunga, October 27, 1931.

68. Quotes in this paragraph are from MM, SA0695, Previsión Social y Trabajo, Sanidad y Hygiene to DGS, May 1, 1942.

69. Quotes in this paragraph are from MM, SA 0734, comunicaciones enviadas, Gualsaqui, Otavalo, Inspector Garcés, June 10, 1945.

70. Some Mexican hospitals used worm larvae to close wounds (Elizabeth O'Brien, personal communication, August 2020).

71. On the other hand, many folk medicines (including those of Mesoamerica) associate worms entering the body with illness. In those instances, Garcés' rhetoric would have been detrimental. See Cattermole-Tally, "Intrusion"; Orellana, *Indian Medicine*, 109; Palmer, *Launching*, 142–43.

72. Alchon, *Native Society*, 20–22.

73. MM, SA0734, comunicaciones enviadas, Gualsaqui, Otavalo, Inspector Garcés, June 10, 1945.

74. Sáenz Vera, "Brote de Peste," 42.

75. Izcara, *Huasipungo*. Peruvian indígenas deloused people manually and then chewed lice because it allegedly increased immunity and improved blood. See Cueto, *Return*, 56.

76. MM, SA0734, comunicaciones enviadas, Gualsaqui, Otavalo, Inspector Garcés, June 10, 1945.

77. MM, SA 0792, letters to Dr. Luis León, Jefe Sanitario de Pichincha, August 13 and 20, 1947.

78. CIRMA, col. Doc 217, Mirano B. Padilla Matute, "Sobre el Tratamiento de Fiebre Tifoidea" (Guatemala City: Imprenta de la Paz, 1865), 8.

79. CIRMA, Col. Doc. 220, Dirección de Hospital General y sus dependencias informe y estados de 1888 (Guatemala City: Establecimiento Tipografico "La Union", 1889?), 3, 27.

80. RAC, RF Photographs, series 317, box 85, folder 1709, "El tambor—subject with severe case of hookworm, dirt-eater," Dr. Rowan, 1915.

81. Stern, "Buildings," 64, 67.

82. Ibid., 66.

83. AGCA, letter to Jefe Político de Sacatepéquez, July 26, 1927.

84. "Encontrose en la Laguna de San Antonio Aguascalientes una mina," *El Día, Diario Independiente*, May 20, 1927.

85. LNDLSC, GC, AGCA, Jefe Político de Chimaltenango to Jefe Político de Sacatepéquez, May 18, 1927.

86. *MSP*, 1933, 501.

87. *MSP*, 1933, 612.

88. *MGJ*, 1929, 5, 378.

89. *MGJ*, 1929, 390. Developed by Almroth Edward Wright, the first vaccine for typhoid was distributed for military use in 1896. See Y. Smith, "Typhoid Fever." In the late 1930s, Salvadoran doctor Salvador G. Aguilar experimented with a hydrochloric acid solution that enjoyed some success in treating typhoid. See *Boletín Sanitaria de Guatemala* 46 (1938): 343–45.

90. *MGJ*, 1929, 390.

91. *MSP*, 1933, 534.

92. Dirección General de Sanidad Pública de Guatemala, *Reglamento*, 3–11.

93. "Mortalidad por fiebre tifoidea in la República de Guatemala," *Boletín Sanitario de Guatemala*, 12, no. 49 (1941): 11.

94. Ibid., 11.

95. *Revista de la Cruz Roja Guatemalteca*, November 15, 1936, 1.

96. *MSP*, 1941, 234.

97. *MSP*, 1945, 11.

98. *MSP*, 1951, Mazatenango, December 1951.

99. Ibid.

100. *MSP*, 1941, 249; *MSP*, 1951, 8; *MSP*, 1945, 26, 37, 156, 158.

101. *MSP*, 1945, 469–71.

102. *MSP*, 1945, 133–34.

103. *MSP*, 1945, 133–34.

104. *MSP*, 1945, 133–34.

105. Crafts, "Mining Bodies."

106. DGE, *Censo General*, 1893, 39.

107. Ibid., 39–40.

108. Wagley, "Social," 76.

109. *MSGJ*, 1910, 10; *MSGJ*, 1913, 6.

110. *MSGJ*, 1915, 5.

111. Tworek, "Communicable Disease," 818–19.

112. *MSGJ*, 1923, 16.

113. Dirección General de Salubridad Pública (DSP), *Divulgación*, 4 (capital letters in original).

114. McNeill, *Mosquito Empires*, 79.

115. Remaining quotes in this paragraph are from DSP, *Divulgación*, 3–4 (emphasis in original).

116. Quotes in this paragraph are from DSP, *Divulgación*, 3–7.

117. Quotes in this paragraph are from *MSP*, 1933, 346–48.

118. *MSP*, 1933, 23, 31.

119. *MSP*, 1933, 24.

120. *MSP*, 1933, 375–76.

121. *MSP*, 1933, 533–34.

122. *MSP*, 1933, 532.

123. *MSP*, 1933, 32.

124. *MSP*, 1933, 3, 31 (quotes), 502.

125. *MSP*, 1933, 421–22.

126. *MSP*, 1933, 421–22.

127. Quotes in this paragraph are from Dr. Francisco Quintana, "Tratamiento del tifus exantemático por el absceso de foucher," *Boletín Sanitario de Guatemala*, 6, no. 42 (1935): 1115–16. Dr. Quintana also advocated Foucher's Abscess to treat typhus even though the treatment was old and long abandoned.

128. While it is unclear exactly what he meant by "toilet," context suggests general filth, or perhaps excrement.

129. *MSP*, 1933, 443–44.

130. *MSP*, 1933, 443–44.

131. Dr. José Bernard y Sarti A., "Nota interesante sobre tratamiento del tifus exantemático," *Boletín Sanitario de Guatemala*, 7, no. 44 (1936): 35.

132. Ibid., 36.

133. *MSP*, 1933, 542–43.

134. *MSP*, 1939, 652–60.

135. *MSP*, 1939, 660.

136. *MSP*, 1941, 165.

137. *MSP*, 1941, 237.

138. *MSP*, 1941, 237.

139. Epaminondas Quintana, "Estado sanitario de Centroamérica," *Boletín Indigenista* (March 1945); A. Adams and Giraudo, "Pack," 187, 195–96n61.

140. AGCA, Salud Pública, leg. 23240, 1944–1946 correspondencia, Informe relación con la epidemia de Tifus Exantemático que sufre el Asilo de Alienados, April 24, 1944.

141. Ibid.

142. *MSP*, 1951, 6.

143. *MSP*, 1945, 135.

144. *MSP*, 1945, 135–37.

145. *MSP*, 1945, 554.

146. *MSP*, 1945, 143.

147. *MSP*, 1945, 9–10.

148. *MSP*, 1945, 151, 455.

149. *MSP*, 1944, 98.

150. *MSP*, 1944, 117–118.

151. *MSP*, 1944, 337.

152. *MSP*, 1944, 13–14.

153. *MSP*, 1944, 416.

154. *Salubridad y Asistencia: orgáno del Ministerio de Salud Pública y Asistencia Social*, April 1951 (Guatemala, 1948–1951), 4: 7; *MSP*, 1951, Memoria de la sección control de tifo; Carey, *Our Elders*, 127–28; A. Adams and Giraudo, "Pack," 187.

155. RAC, RF, RG 5 Series 2_319 Projects, Box 31, Folder 187, W. H. Rowan, "Relief and Control of Uncinariasis in Guatemala," from March 20, 1915, to June 30, 1915.

156. Funes, "Plan General de acción de la lucha antivenérea," 11; Foss, *Our Own Terms*, 50–72.

157. Carey, *Our Elders*, 127–29; Carey, *Engendering*, 45; A. Adams and Giraudo, "Pack," 187.

158. Dr. Epaminondas Quintana, "Proyecto de educación sanitaria contra el Tifus Exantemático en Guatemala," *Gaceta Médica Centroamericana* vol 1 no. 2 (1943), 69.

159. Ibid., 69.

160. *MSP*, 1945, 162–63.

161. A. Adams and Giraudo, "Pack," 187–88.

162. Quintana, "Proyecto de educación," 69.

163. *MSP*, 1944, 350.

164. Carey, *Our Elders*, 127.

165. *MSP*, 1945, 149.

166. *MSP*, 1945, 149.

167. Quotes in this paragraph are from *MSP*, 1945, 590–91.

CHAPTER SIX

1. Since malaria survivors (of which there were many) showed no symptoms, they served as carriers, which made malaria more difficult to control than yellow fever. See McNeill, *Mosquito Empires*, 311.

2. *La Gaceta*, November 10, 1934, 2253.

3. MM, SA0793, Presidente de junta parroquial municipalidad de Sto. Domingo de los Colorados, July 21, 1947.

4. McNeill, *Mosquito Empires*, 52. Since those symptoms were difficult to distinguish from a host of other diseases, malaria was regularly misdiagnosed.

5. Becerra, "Informe," 505.

6. McNeill, *Mosquito Empires*, 53–54; Cueto, *Cold War*, 1.

7. MM, SA 0678, Subdirección de Sanidad de N. Baca, June 18, 1914. Since malaria parasite survival depends on close association of vertebrata and mosquitos, dense human populations are as much a contributor to malaria outbreaks as the water sources that sustain breeding sites.

8. While Europeans introduced *vivax*, Africans introduced *falciparum* to the Americas. See Newson, *Life*, 151–52.

9. J. Romeo de León, "Paludismo de altura en Guatemala," *Boletín Sanitario de Guatemala*, 7, no. 44 (1936), 72; Erwin Jacobsthal, "Los reticulocitos en la infección paludica," *Boletín Sanitario de Guatemala* 7, no. 44 (1936), 141; Ernesto Marroquín G., "Relación sucinta de los trabajos realizados desde 1931 a la fecha, por la sección de la lucha, antimalarica y sus dependencias," *Boletín Sanitario de Guatemala*, 7, no. 44 (1936): 156; Julio Roberto Herrera Solis, "Diez años de lucha antimalarica en Guatemala," *Boletín Sanitario de Guatemala*, 12, no. 49 (1941): 181–82; *MSP*, 1944, 49, 52; *MSP*, 1945, 65; Packard, *Making*; McNeill, *Mosquito Empires*, 54–57; J. Webb, *Humanity's Burden*, 162; Harris and Carter, "Muddying."

10. Bastien, *Healers*; Packard, *Making*, xi, 6–25; Honigsbaum, *Fever Trail*, 20–29, 114, 148, 273; Rocco, *Miraculous Fever Tree*, 21–23; Tagboto and Towson, "Antiparasitic Properties"; Caniato and Puricelli, "Review"; Cueto and Palmer, *Medicine*, 96; Crawford, *Andean Wonder Drug*; Steere, "Cinchona Bark."

11. Cueto, *Cold War*; Webb, *Humanity's Burden*, 148–50.

12. D. Rodríguez, *Right*, 201.

13. *MGJ*, 1930, 4–5.

14. AGCA, Descripción índice, ex. 23667, 1903–1922, Secretaria de Gobernación y Justicia, *Influenza*; Franco-Agudelo, "Rockefeller Foundation," 61.

15. Cueto, *Cold War*, 63, 74.

16. Sutter, "Nature's Agents," 752. Tropical medicine researchers and practitioners similarly inscribed racial difference into tropical pathology during the US colonization of the Philippines (1898–1946). See W. Anderson, *Colonial Pathologies*.

17. P. Brown, "Malaria"; Packard, *Making*.

18. Rocco, *Miraculous Fever Tree*, 60, 167; Cueto and Palmer, *Medicine*, 9, 23; McNeill, *Mosquito Empires*, 63, 86; Necochea López, *History*, 66.

19. Hipólito Ruíz and José Pavón, *Quinologia o Tratado del arbol de quina o cascarilla* (1792); Celestino Mutis, *Arcano de la Quina* (1828); both cited in Cueto and Palmer, *Medicine*, 43–44; Webb, *Humanity's Burden*, 95–101; Jarcho, *Quinine's Predecessor*. Nineteenth- and twentieth-century Spaniards also researched quinine and its multiple uses.

20. Honigsbaum, *Fever Trail*, 182.

21. Rocco, *Miraculous Fever Tree*, xvii-xviii, 248–49; Honigsbaum, *Fever Trail*, 68–70, 75–78, 150–51.

22. Honigsbaum, *Fever Trail*, 186.

23. Rocco, *Miraculous Fever Tree*, 111, 220, 223–25.

24. Luis M. Nuñez, "Apuntes sobre el paludismo en Guatemala," *Boletín Sanitario de Guatemala*, 6, no. 42 (1935), 1108; Webb, *Humanity's Burden*, 144.

25. MM, SA0767, Sanidad de Pichincha, Tenencia política perucho, November 20, 1918.

26. Ibid.

27. *Boletín Sanitario de Guatemala*, IX, no. 46 (1938), 155.

28. Nuñez, "Apuntes," 1107.

29. *MSP*, 1939, 1.3.

30. Morgan, *Community Participation*, 25.

31. *Diario de Centroamérica*, March 7, 1910 (quote); BNG, FLA, Valenzuela I, 2371, Secretaria de Gobernación y Justicia, *Informe*, 7.

32. *Diario de Centroamérica*, March 7, 1910.

33. *Diario de Centroamérica*, March 16, 1910.

34. Ibid.

35. Ibid.

36. Simmons, *Malaria*, 13, 96–98, 100, 117–20, 132–36, 234, 275–77; Cueto, *Cold War*, 2; McNeill, *Mosquito Empires*, 311–12. By 1935 Atabrine and Plasmochin had largely replaced quinine in malaria treatments in Panama; see Simmons, *Malaria*, 229; Webb, *Humanity's Burden*, 137.

37. Wisdom, *Chorti Indians*. Julio Roberto Herrera Solis suggests ancient Mayas lived with malaria; see "Diez años," 179.

38. R. Adams, *Análisis*, 43, 50.

39. *La Gaceta*, May 5, 1935, 1066.

40. Ibid., 1068–69.

41. AGCA, Descripción índice, ex. 23231, 1943 correspondencia, Chuarrachancho intendente municipal to DHG, March 12, 1943, and Mixco intendente municipal to DHG, March 22, 1943.

42. *MSP*, 1944, 363.

43. AGCA, Descripción índice, ex. 23124, 1927, Jefe Político de Izabal to DHG, March 5, 1927; AGCA, Descripción índice, ex. 23234, 1943 correspondencia, Municipalidad de Guatemala, Canal del norte y del sur, Puerto San José, March 23, 1943; AGCA, Descripción índice, ex. 23227, 1942 correspondencia, Hospital Nacional Escuintal to DHG, September 29, 1942.

44. AGCA, Descripción índice, ex. 23231, 1943 correspondencia, Tenedores to DHG, February 22, 1943.

45. AGCA, Descripción índice, ex. 23231, 1943 correspondencia, Santa Lucía Cotzumalguapa to DHG, July 5, 1943.

46. Rosenberg, "Foreword," vi; Packard, *Making*, 7–9; Mitman, "Search," 195.

47. LNDLSC, GC, Sacatepéquez, Agricultura, Box 29, Informe General al Ministro de Gobierno y Justicia, 1898.

48. Ibid.

49. BNG, FLA, índice Valenzuela I, 2377, Dr. Luis Toledo Herrarte, "Profilaxia del paludismo Conferencia dada en honor del Sr. Presidente de la República licenciado don Manuel Estrada Cabrera con motivo de la inauguración de su segunda periodo constitucional en el Salón de Actos de la Escuela de Medicina y Farmacia, el día 16 de Marzo de 1905."

50. *MGJ*, 1931, 6 (quote); *MPN*, 1932, 20, 68.

51. Sherchand, et al., "Preliminary Study."

52. Migration similarly spread diseases such as bubonic plague that indigenous migrants brought back to their highland communities; see Clark, *Conjuring*.

53. Gall, *Diccionario*, 3: 554.

54. LNDLSC, GC, Box 14, Agricultura, San Antonio Aguas Calientes alcalde to comisionado político, September 23, 1899. Colonial European references to fever-free mountainous areas in the Caribbean suggest those highlands were free of malaria; see McNeill, *Mosquito Empires*, 81, 284, 294.

55. Cueto and Palmer, *Medicine*, 193; Alchon, *Native Society*, 80–81. See also Packard, *Making*, 105–6; Bell, *Frontiers*, 19, 21; H. Tilley, "Medicine," 745.

56. AGCA, B81.3, leg. 1092, ex. 29367, Municipalidad de la capital, tenería de don Miguel Cloquell, 1910.

57. Ibid.

58. E. Castellanos Crocker, "La lucha contra el paludismo," *El Ideal*, October 1911, pp. 344–46.

59. AGCA, B81.3, leg. 1092, ex. 29367, Municipalidad de la capital, tenería de don Miguel Cloquell, 1910.

60. BNG, FLA, Valenzuela I, 2371, Secretaria de gobernación y justicia, *Informe para reprodulo comisión médica que fue al departamento de Baja Verapaz a combatir la epidemia de paludismo en diciembere 1904* (Guatemala City: Tipografía Nacional, 1905), 6, 7 (quote).

61. *MGJ*, 1910, 131. Three years later his successor similarly associated malaria with "the coasts." See *MGJ*, 1913, 6.

62. United Fruit Company Medical Department (UFCO-MD), *Annual Report*, 1914.

63. AGCA, Descripción índice, ex. 23124, 1927, letter to DHG from jefe político de Izabal, Puerto Barrios, March 5, 1927. UFCO laborers in Costa Rica preferred to use their own healers instead of UFCO medical facilities; see Chomsky, *West Indian Workers*, 12, 96, 137.

64. HC Clark, "The Field Parasite Rate for Malaria in Banana Divisions (Mainland CA)," UFCO-MD, *Annual Report* 1928, 71; Chomsky, *West Indian Workers*, 12, 96; Soluri, *Banana Cultures*.

65. Franco-Agudelo, "Rockefeller Foundation," 55.

66. Cueto and Palmer, *Medicine*, 95, 108.

67. RAC, Rockefeller Foundation, *Annual Report, 1915* (New York, 1915), 12.

68. Ibid., 12.

69. AGCA, Descripción índice, ex. 23667, 1903–1922, Secretaria de gobernación y justicia, *Influenza*.

70. Carey, "Cautionary Tale"; Packard, *Making*, 121; Franco-Agudelo, "Rockefeller," 63. Although they did not know it at the time, quinine could not cure vivax malaria—Guatemala's most common form—because of the latent liver phase of the parasite life-cycle.

71. RAC, Rockefeller Foundation, *Annual Report, 1926* (New York, 1926), 43–44.

72. RAC, Rockefeller Foundation, *Annual Report, 1932* (New York, 1932), 68. RF malaria expert Dr. Paul Russell insisted social medicine advocates undermined malaria eradication. See Franco-Agudelo, "Rockefeller Foundation," 65.

73. Palmer, *Launching*, 111.

74. RAC, RF, RG5, IHB/D, series 1, correspondence subseries 2_317 projects, box 79, folder 1123, RF, IHG, NY, Guatemala, Burres to Heiser, August 15, 1919.

75. RAC, RF, RG5, IHB/D, series 1, correspondence subseries 2_317 projects, box 79, folder 1123, Kirk to Burres, September 16, 1919; Palmer, *Launching*, 111.

76. Dirección General de Sanidad Publica, Sección de prevención contra la Malaria, *Nociones elementales*, 39 (emphasis in the original).

77. *MSP*, 1933, 376.

78. J. Romeo de León, "El anophelismo de alturas de Guatemala," *Boletín Sanitaria* 46 (1938): 67–79.

79. Ibid.

80. Ibid., 71.

81. *Revista de la Cruz Roja Guatemalteca* 9, no. 16 (December 1936).

82. RAC, RF, RG 1.1 Projects, series 319, box 1, folder 2: Escuintla (Malaria Control Demonstration) 1936, B. E. Washburn to Dr. Sawyer, July 30, 1936.

83. *MSP*, 1939, 616.

84. *MSP*, 1931, 116–17.

85. Packard, *Making*, 105.

86. *MSP*, 1939, 117–19.

87. AGCA, Descripción índice, ex. 23194, 1939 correspondencia, Subcomisario de Policía Nacional, Morales, to DHG, August 13, 1939.

88. Hooker, "Race."

89. Administración, *Dos lustrous*, 7.

90. Ibid., 7–8.

91. McNeill, *Something New*, 195–97.

92. McNeill, *Something New*, 197–98; Sutter, "Nature's Agents"; Espinosa, *Epidemic Invasions*; McCrea, *Diseased Relations*; Baldwin, *Contagion*; Carter, *Enemy*, 9, 102–4; J. Webb, *Long Struggle*; Packard, *Making*, 119; Zulawski, "Environment," 507–8, 513; Kapeluz-Poppi, "Rural Health"; Sufian, *Healing*; H. Tilley, *Africa*, 210–11; Radkau, *Nature*, 127–31; Corona, *Short Environmental History*, 69–75; Lovino, Cesaratti, and Past, *Italy*; Barca, "'Natural' Capitalism," 226; J. Webb, *Humanity's Burden*, 61–62, 145; Bevilacqua, et al., *Ambiente*, 123–26, 132–33, 159–66; Hall, "Thinking," 121; Hall, "Environmental Imperialism," 71.

93. LNDLSC, GC, Salubridad (box 7, folder 61), Pedro Townsend solicitud, April 11, 1924.

94. LNDLSC, GC, Salubridad (box 7, folder 61), SAAC municipalidad to jefe político, April 15, 1924.

95. LNDLSC, GC, Salubridad (box 7, folder 61), Pedro Townsend to jefe político, May 13, 1924.

96. LNDLSC, GC, Salubridad (box 7, folder 61), jefe político, August 20, 1924.

97. Rodríguez Rouaret, *Diccionario*, 166, 172–3; Carey, "Cautionary Tale."

98. Esquit, *Otros poderes*, 350; Mallon, "Indian Communities"; Carey, *Our Elders*, 132–37, 183; Diaz Romeu, "Régimen," 39–40; Dosal, *Power*, 54, 55, 58, 63–64; Gibbings, *Our Time*.

99. Taracena Arriola, "Marimba," 153; McCreery, *Rural Guatemala*; McNeill, *Something New*, 197.

100. AGCA, JP-S, jefe político de Sacatepéquez to Ministro de Fomento, January 6, 1927.

101. AGCA, JP-S, LC, Presidential Palace to jefe político de Sacatepéquez, July 21, 1927.

102. Such was true of nineteenth- and early twentieth-century Europeans whether they attributed epidemics to the environment or contagion (Baldwin, *Contagion*, 7–8). Doctors in Hong Kong and Calcutta similarly "blended the new germ theories with older miasmatic theories" (Sutphen, "Not What," 84).

103. Oral history interviews: Jun Ey, Aguascalientes, 11/12/97; Kablajuj Tz'i', Aguascalientes, 9/1/98; Waqxaqi' Kawoq, Aguascalientes, 11/8/97; Waqxaqi' Ajpu' by Jun Tojil, Barahona, 1998; B'eleje' Ajpu' by Jun Tojil, Barahona, 1998; Lajuj Aq'ab'al, Aguascalientes, 11/14/97; Wuqu' Imox, Aguascalientes, 11/12/97; Ixtojil by Jun Tojil, Barahona, 2/7/98; Jun Kej by Jun Tojil, Barahona, 1998; Waqxaqi' K'at, Aguascalientes, 11/8/97; Wuqu' Ajpu' by Jun Tojil, Barahona, 1998.

104. Oral history interview with Ka'i' Kawoq, Aguascalientes, 2/7/98.

105. Oral history interview with Kab'lajuj Kan, Barahona, 2/15/98.

106. *El Día, Diario Independiente*, May 20, 1927.

107. AGCA, JP-S, letter from San Antonio Aguascalientes to jefe político de Sacatepéquez, May 23, 1927.

108. AGCA, JP-S, 1927, Santiago Zamora, June 1, 1929; *MSP*, 1934, 372–3; Cueto, *Cold Wars*, 124, 139.

109. RAC, RF, RG 2–1930 (General Correspondence), series 319, box 41, folder 335, Molloy to Howard, September 29, 1930; Packard, *Making*, 6.

110. RAC, RF, RG 2–1930 (General Correspondence), series 319, box 41, folder 335, Molloy to Howard, September 29, 1930.

111. *MSP*, 1933, 30. At only 1186 meters above sea level, Lake Amatitlán too harbored malaria in 1933, which prompted an "active anti-larvae campaign along the lake's banks" (20). Malariologist Dr. Giaquinto Mira "devoted" that year to "cleaning the lake" (355).

112. RAC, RF, RG 2–1930 (General Correspondence), series 319, box 41, folder 335, Howard to Molloy, November 3, 1930.

113. Ibid. See also Cueto, *Cold War*, 17.

114. RAC, RF, RG 1.1 Projects, series 319, box 1, folder 2, B. E. Washburn to Dr. Sawyer, July 30, 1936.

115. *Boletín Sanitaria* 46 (1938): 405–7.

116. de León, "Anophelismo"; *El Liberal Progresista*, November 20, 1937.

117. In Guatemala, *A. albimanus*, *A. darlingi*, and *A. pseudopunctipennis* are the primary transmitters of malaria. See International Association of Medical Assistance for Travelers, "Guatemala."

118. *MSP*, 1933, 85.

119. Marroquín, "Relación sucinta," 193.

120. *MSP*, 1939, 116.

121. *MSP*, 1939, 10–14.

122. *MSP*, 1933, 529.

123. Simmons, *Malaria*, xiii.

124. RAC, Rockefeller Foundation, *Annual Report, 1944* (New York, 1944), 64.

125. *Boletín Sanitario de Guatemala*, IX, no. 46 (1938), 159.

126. Ibid., 246–48; *El Liberal Progresista*, November 20, 1937, 561. Other Latin American nations similarly deployed multifaceted approaches to malaria control. When Italians migrated to northwest Argentina in the late nineteenth century, the government established a multidimensional approach to protect immigrants from malaria. See J. Webb, *Humanity's Burden*, 146. The Mexican government also deployed an eclectic response during Lázaro Cárdenas's administration (1934–40). After World War II, his successors embraced medical approaches to antimalaria campaigns that resembled the more reductionist European and US models. See Kapeluz-Poppi, "Rural Health"; Cueto and Palmer, *Medicine*, 169. As part of a Cold War effort to gain loyalties, the United States funded antimalaria campaigns in Mexico, but without structural change—better diets and housing, potable water and sewerage systems, and accessible health care—malaria proved impossible to control. See Cueto, *Cold War*.

127. LNDLSC, GC, Sacatepéquez, Salubridad (box 7, folder 61), Disposiciones sanitarias presentadas a Jefe Político, 1933.

128. *MSP*, 1933, 530–31.

129. *MSP*, 1933, 355 (quote), 376.

130. RAC, Rockefeller Foundation, *Annual Report, 1932*, 68.

131. RAC, Rockefeller Foundation, *Annual Report, 1926*, 43–44.

132. RAC, RF, RG 1.1 Projects, series 319, box 1, folder 2, B. E. Washburn to Dr. Sawyer, July 30, 1936..

133. Nuñez, "Apuntes," 1107.

134. *Revista de la Cruz Roja Guatemalteca*, September 15, 1935.

135. Humphreys, *Malaria*; J. Webb, *Humanity's Burden*, 153–54.

136. *Revista de la Cruz Roja Guatemalteca*, May 1936, cover and p. 4.

137. RAC, RF, RG 1.1 Projects, series 319, box 1, folder 2, B. E. Washburn to Dr. Sawyer, July 30, 1936.

138. RAC, RF, RG 1.1 Projects, series 319, box 1, folder 2, Guatemala Malaria control demonstration, Escuintla, budget and designation, October 29, 1936 (emphasis added).

139. RAC, RF, RG 1.1 Projects, series 319, box 1, folder 2, B. E. Washburn to Dr. Sawyer, July 30, 1936.

140. RAC, RF, RG 1.1 Projects, series 319, box 1, folder 2, B. E. Washburn to Dr. Sawyer, October 1, 1936; Guatemala Malaria control demonstration, Escuintla, budget and designation, October, 29, 1936; Sawyer to Dr. Washburn, October 31, 1936.

141. Packard, *Making*, 119–21.

142. RAC, RF, RG 1.1 Projects, series 319, box 1, folder 2, B. E. Washburn to Dr. Sawyer, October 1, 1936.

143. RAC, RF, RG 1.1 Projects, series 319, box 1, folder 2, B. E. Washburn to Dr. Sawyer, October 31, 1936.

144. RAC, RF, RG 1.1 Projects, series 319, box 1, folder 2, B. E. Washburn to Dr. Sawyer, October 1, 1936; Packard, *Making*, 119.

145. *MSP*, 1939, 111, 113, 122.

146. Administración, *Dos lustrous*, 125.

147. Ibid., 125.

148. *MSP*, 1939, 111.

149. *Boletín Sanitaria* 46 (1938), 318–33. Concurrently, Sanitation Engineer Simeon Angel Alfaro in El Salvador was overseeing similar drainage projects.

150. *MSP*, 1932, 8.

151. *MSP*, 1939, 115.

152. AGCA, JP-S, Hacienda San Rafael Urías to jefe político de Sacatepéquez, December 9, 1927.

153. Administración, *Dos lustrous*, 125.

154. Administración, *Dos lustrous*, 125.

155. *MSP*, 1939, 114.

156. *MSP*, 1945, 143; *MSP*, 1944, 118.

157. *MSP*, 1951, 64.

158. Oral history interview with Iximnik'te', Tecpán, 5/30/98.

159. McCreery, *Rural Guatemala*, 267.

160. Oral history interview with Ixqa, Comalapa, 7/3/01.

161. Oral history interview with Ix'ajmaq, Poaquil, 7/1/01.

162. Bunzel, *Chichicastenango*, 143.

163. *MGJ*, 1931, 100.

164. AGCA, IGT-C, October 1948, leg. 48762, (actual no. leg. 69), letter from Labor Inspector, December 16, 1947.

165. AGCA, IGT-C, October 1948, leg. 48762, (actual no. leg. 69), letter to President of Guatemala, October 24, 1947.

166. Carter, *Enemy*, 2.

167. AGCA, índice 140, leg. 23178, Poder Judicial, Guatemala, October 25, 1937, Leocadio Paredes González; AGCA, índice 140, leg. 23141, Jefe de Guardia de Honor, December 9, 1930 (quote); AGCA, Descripción índice, ex. 23182, Fraijanes, intendente municipal, September 21, 1938, Carlos Arroyo.

168. AGCA, Descripción índice, ex. 23182, Juan Chinchilla, de Policía de Hacienda, March 6, 1938, Ecesodro Celada, San José Pinula, April 11, 1938, and Antonio Yspache y Magdalena Yspache, San José Pinula, April 19, 1938; AGCA, Descripción índice, ex. 23194, 1939 correspondencia, Villa Canales to DHG, November 21, 1939; AGCA, Descripción índice, ex. 23245, 1944–1946 correspondencia, Juan Mayorga Franco to DHG, March 7, 1945; AGCA, Descripción índice, ex. 23256, 1946 correspondencia, Rio Hondo to DHG, March 14, 1946; AGCA, Descripción índice, ex. 23245, 1944–1946, San Agustín Las Minas to DHG, December 3, 1945.

169. AGCA, Descripción índice, ex. 23182, Angel Blanco, Barberena, April 21, 1938.

170. AGCA, Descripción índice, ex. 23182, Herminio Saquil, El Jicaro, July 1, 1938.

171. Editorial, "La simplicidad campaña contra el tifo," *Boletín de la Oficina Sanitaria Panamericana* 25, No. 3 (1946), 265; *MSP*, 1944, 103; *MSP*, 1945, 2; Cueto and Palmer, *Medicine*, 133; Cueto, *Value*, 63.

172. AGCA, B101.1, leg. 3638, ex. 23240 (1944–1946 correspondencia), Manuel Samayoa to Manuel Gómez, December 27, 1944.

173. AGCA, Descripción índice, leg. 23050, 1904, Dirección del Hospital General, Consulado General Americano to DHG, October 11, 1904.

174. MM, SA0891, Tulcán to DGS, February 5, 1933.

175. MM, SA0876, Gobierno de Ecuador, Ibarra, to DGS, October 16, 1936. During the colonial period, Jesuits established sugar plantations worked by enslaved Africans in the Chota Valley. Thereafter the valley maintained a predominantly Afro-Ecuadorian population.

176. MM, SA0876, Gobierno de Ecuador, Ibarra, to DGS, November 16, 1936.

177. Ibid.

178. Brown, "Malaria"; Packard, *Making*.

179. MM, SA0876, Gobierno de Ecuador, Ibarra, to DGS, November 16, 1936.

180. Kipple, *Caribbean Slave*; Carl Zimmer, "'Global Greening' Sounds Good," *New York Times*, July 30, 2018.

181. Packard, *Making*, 113.

182. Espejo, *Voto*; Paredes, *Oro*; A. Suárez, *Contribución al estudio*.

183. MM, SA0876, Gobierno de Ecuador, Ibarra, to DGS, October 16, 1936.

184. Ibid. (emphasis in original).

185. MM, SA0695, Ministro de Previsión Social y Trabajo to DGS, October 7, 1942.

186. Ibid.

187. Ibid.

188. MM, SA0695, unsigned letter to DGS, October 21, 1942.

189. MM, SA0792, Dr. Roberto Nevárez Vásquez to DGS, July 4, 1947.

190. Quotes in this paragraph are from MM, SA0678, Intendente General de Policía, May 16, 1914; MM, SA0678, Sr. Aurelio Vaca Rosas, Jefe de Oficina de Vacuna, to Ministro de Sanidad, May 19, 1914.

191. Quotes in this paragraph are from MM, SA 0678, Subdirección de Sanidad de N. Baca, June 18, 1914.

192. Rodríguez, *Search*, 225.

193. MM, SA0678, C. A. Miño to Ministerio de Sanidad, July 7, 1914.

194. Ibid.

195. MM, SA0821, Dr. José Baquero to Carlos Miño, July 6, 1914.

196. Ibid.

197. MM, SA0821, Dr. León Becerra to Dr. Miño, September 20, 1914.

198. Ibid.

199. MM, SA0821, Sanidad Pública de Guayaquil to Dr. Miño, August 29, 1914.

200. RAC, RF, RG5, IHB/D, series 1, correspondence subseries 2_317 projects, box 79, folder 1121, May 30, 1919.

201. RAC, RF, RG5, IHB/D, series 1, correspondence subseries 2_317 projects, box 79, folder 1121, Connor to Rose, June 10, 1919.

202. RAC, RF, RF Photographs, series 317, box 84, Folder 1699, 1918–1920, and box 85, folder 1714.

203. MM, AP1292, Servicio Sanitario Nacional to Inspector Tecnico de Sanidad, March 7, 1924.

204. MM, SA 0821, Subalterno Esmeraldas to Sr. Director de Sanidad Pública, May 31, 1914; MM, SA 0821, Subdirector de Sanidad to Ministro de Interior, Ecuador (Sr. Ministro de Relaciones Exteriores, me dice), Quito, May 7, 1914.

205. MM, SA0822, Dr. León Becerra to Dr. Miño, February 8 and March 29, 1917.

206. MM, SA0695, Ministro de Educación, oriente, Departamento de Sanidad, November 13, 1942.

207. MM, SA0837, Ministerio Previsión Social y Sanidad, Quito, September 11, 1929.

208. MM, SA0876, Gobierno de Ecuador, Ibarra, Julio 8, 1936, asunto: se vuelve informar del estado sanitario de la parcialidad Zama del Cantón Otavalo, sobre campaña antipalúdica.

209. MM, SA0746, Delegación Sanidad de Imbabura, Ibarra, December 12, 1930.

210. MM, SA0876, Gobierno de Ecuador, Quito, August 4, 1936.

211. MM, SA0876, Concejo Cantonal de Ibarra, nd. 1936, and Gobierno de Ecuador, Ibarra, July 21, 1936. For a similar strategy in contemporary Otavalo, see MM, SA0876, Gobierno de Ecuador, Ibarra July 21, 1936.

212. Carey, "Cautionary Tale."

213. MM, SA0876, Gobierno Ecuador, Ibarra, November 6, 1936.

214. MM, SA0876, Gobierno Ecuador, Ibarra, May 26, 1936.

215. MM, SA0876, Gobierno Ecuador, Ibarra, to DGS, November 16, 1936.

216. MM, SA0876, to DGS from Dr. J. M. Espinosa, Ibarra, June 8, 1936.

217. *MSP*, 1939, 193.

218. MM, SA0876, Gobierno de Ecuador, Ibarra, July 8, 1936.

219. MM, SA0876, Gobierno de Ecuador, Quito, August 4, 1936.

220. Sutter, "Nature's Agents," 751; Packard, *Making*, 121.

221. MM, SA0876, Gobierno de Ecuador, Ibarra, to DGS, October 16, 1936.

222. Morgan, *Community Participation*, 30–31.

223. MM, SA0699, Escuela Fiscal de Niños, December 4, 1939.

224. MM, SA0699, Minsterio de Educación Pública, Higiene Escolar, Quito, May 31, 1939.

225. MM, SA0695, Minsterio de Educación Pública, Higiene Escolar to subdirector de Sanidad, Quito, January 9, 1942.

226. MM, SA0695, Ministerio de Educación, Oriente to DGS, November 5, 1942.

227. MM, SA0332, Ministro de Previsión Social y Sanidad, Quito, September 17, 1942.

228. Ibid.

229. MM, SA0695, Oficina Higiene Municipal, Cotacachi, to Alfonso Mosquera, September 21, 1942.

230. Ibid.

231. Ibid.

232. MM, SA0699, Servicio de Sanidad, DGS, Guayaquil, January 9, 1939.

233. Pacino, "Constructing," 39–40, 45.

234. MM, SA0793, Jaime Ribaneneira, August 22, 1947; SA0792, Dr. Luis León, Jefe Sanitario de Pichincha, August 22, 1947.

235. MM, SA0793, Ministro de Previsión Social y Sanidad, July 15, 1947.

236. Ibid.

237. Cueto, *Cold Wars*, 161.

238. Chomsky, *West Indian Workers*, 130, 136.

239. Carey, "Cautionary Tale."

240. Nor did mid-century Mexico; see Cueto, *Cold War*.

241. Carey, "Yellow Fever."

242. Trefzger, "Guatemala."

CONCLUSION

1. Gibbings and Vrana, *Out of the Shadow*; Gleijeses, *Shattered Hope*; Handy, *Revolution*; Harms, "God"; Forster, *Time*.

2. Crafts, "Mining Bodies"; A. Adams and Giraudo, "Pack"; Carey, *I Ask*.

3. Reverby, "'Normal Exposure'"; Palmer, "Caminos"; Cueto and Palmer, *Medicine*, 127; A. Adams and Giraudo, "Pack."

4. Lydia Crafts, personal correspondence, April 25, 2022.

5. Crafts, "Mining Bodies."

6. A. Adams and Giraudo, "Pack," 190.

7. Ibid., 190.

8. AGCA, Legajo 24120, Fondo de la Salud Pública, los expedientes de los pacientes del asilo.

9. Dr. Erwin Jacobsthal, "Sobre el problema del tratamiento de la sífilis en Centro América," *Boletín Sanitario de Guatemala*, no. 59 año xiii (1942): 125.

10. Funes, "Plan General de acción de la lucha antivenérea," 11; A. Adams and Giraudo, "Pack," 190; Foss, *Our Own Terms*, chapter 2.

11. Dr. Juan Funes, "Proyecto de nueva legislación antivenérea, Consideraciones Generales," *Salubridad y Asistencia: Organo del Ministerio de Salud Publica y Asistencia Social* II, no 3 (1949)," 3–4.

12. National Archives, Records of Dr. John C. Cutler, John C. Cutler, "Final Syphilis Report," February 24, 1955.

13. A. Adams and Giraudo, "Pack," 190.

14. Washington, *Medical Apartheid*; Cooper Owens, *Medical Bondage*.

15. Reverby, *Examining*.

16. Crafts, "Mining Bodies."

17. *MSP*, 1945, 113.

18. *MSP*, 1945, 113; Cueto, *Cold War*, 39.

19. Palmer, *Launching*, 210.

20. Carey, *Elders*, 177–94; Carey, "Mayan Soldier-Citizens."

21. Reverby, "'Normal Exposure'"; Cueto and Palmer, *Medicine*, 127.

22. Cueto and Palmer, *Medicine*, 127; Reverby, "'Normal Exposure'."

23. Grandin, *Empire's Workshop*; Gardiner Harris, "Concern over Foreign Trials for Drugs Sold in U.S.," *New York Times*, June 21, 2010, A14; Petryana, *When Experiments Travel*.

24. Informe de la Comisión Presidencial para el Esclarecimiento de los Experimentos Practicados con Humanos en Guatemala, "Consentir"; Hornblum, *Acres*, 154–55.

25. Buffington, *Criminal*; Cueto and Palmer, *Medicine*, 234.

26. A. Adams and Giraudo, "Pack," 187

27. Palmer, *Launching*, 166–67.

28. Bronfman, *Measures*, 95–106.

29. As further evidence of the constant give and take between indigenous and scientific medicine, the long-running debate about whether doctors should learn to diagnose and treat susto continues into the twenty-first century. See Rachel Nolan, "Language Barrier," *New Yorker*, January 6, 2020, 30.

30. Carey, "Heroines." In late colonial Mexico, enlightenment-era physicians experimented with indigenous treatments for rabies. See Hernández Sáenz, "Matters."

31. Stepan, "Only Serious Terror."

32. Cueto, *Cold War*, 14, 158, 165.

33. *MSP*, 1944, 416.

34. D. Rodríguez, *Right*.

35. Murard and Zylberman, "Seeds?" 463, 465.

36. Kraut, *Silent Travelers*, 2–4.

37. Vélez and Cifuentes, "Vida," 28.

38. A. Suárez, *Contribución al estudio*. For analyses of his writings, see Clark, "Race"; Prieto, *Liberalismo*.

39. RAC, RG 1.1 Projects, series 319, box 1, folder 1; RF Photographs, series 317, box 85, folder 1706.

40. RAC, RRP, Box 23, Folder 8, "Minutes of the Meeting of the Policy Board," February 4, 1942.

41. Cueto and Palmer, *Medicine*, 106.

42. Cueto, *Return*.

43. Vaughn, "Healing," 288; H. Tilley, *Africa*, 27; Bell, *Frontiers*.

44. MM, SA 0332 19 mayo, 1942, comisario nacional, Santo Domingo de los Colorados. In Africa, colonial Britain's insufficient funds (and medical staff) similarly led to the neglect of Africans' health. See H. Tilley, "History," 745–46, 749.

45. Cueto, *Cold War*, 156.

46. Premo, *Enlightenment*; Carey, *I Ask*.

47. Birn, "Revolution," 174–78; Cueto, *Cold War*; W. Anderson, *Colonial Pathologies*; Arnold, *Colonizing*.

48. Foss, "*Obra*," 203.

49. Oral history interviews with Jun Tz'i', Pamumus, Comalapa, 7/11/98; Ix'umül, Simaulew, Comalapa, 4/15/98; Wuqu' Iq', Xiquín Sanahí, Comalapa, 12/17/97; Ka'i' Aq'ab'al, Tecpán, 6/7/98; Wo'o' Iq', Panicuy, Comalapa, 12/2/97; Lajuj Kan, Pachitur, Comalapa, 10/16/97; Ixpo't, Poaquil, 11/17/97; Kaji' Imox, Comalapa, 8/2/98; Jun Kan, Comalapa, 8/19/98.

50. Carey, *Our Elders*, 267.

51. International Bank for Reconstruction and Development, *Economic Development*, 121.

52. Quintero and Silva, *Ecuador*, 9; Handy, *Revolution*.

53. Harrar, "Draft."

54. Oficina de Derechos Humanos del Arzobispado de Guatemala, *Memoria*; Comisión para el Esclarecimiento Histórico, *Guatemala*; Marc Becker, *¡Pachakutik!*

55. Steltzer, *Health*, 9.

56. Behrhorst, "Introduction," xxxiii.

57. Steltzer, *Health*, 24.

58. Morgan, "International Politics," 211, 216–18; Morgan, *Community Participation*, 1–2, 11–12, 14–15.

59. Alajajian, et al., "Patrones."

60. Chary and Rohloff, *Privatization*, xxv.

61. Caceres, *Plantas*, 4; Caceres, "Traditional Uses."

62. Steltzer, *Health*, 63.

63. Harvey, "Maya Mobile Medicine," 59.

64. José María León Cabrera and Clifford Krauss, "Deal Struck in Ecuador to Cancel Austerity Package and End Protests," *New York Times*, October 13, 2010; Cueto and Palmer, *Medicine*, 253.

65. Acosta and Martínez, *Buen vivir*; Kowii, "*Sumak Kawsay*."

66. Similarly, many contemporary international and private organizations have attempted to eliminate malaria with bednets permeated with pyrethroids instead of making (or advocating for) structural changes to mitigate underlying poverty.

67. Lovell, "Wake"; MacLeod, *Spanish Central America*.

68. Azam Ahmed, "In the Epicenter of Mexico's Epicenter, Feeling Like a 'Trapped Animal'," *New York Times*, September 23, 2020.

69. Julie Turkewitz and Manuela Andreoni, "The Amazon, Giver of Life, Unleashes a Pandemic," *New York Times*, July 25, 2020.

70. M. Webb and Cuj, "Guatemala's Public Health."

71. Maria Sacchetti, "Official: Guatemalan Boy Who Died in U.S. Custody Tested Positive for Influenza B, Final Cause of Death Remains Under Investigation," *Washington Post*, December 28, 2018; Dara Lind, "The Death of 7-Year-Old Jakelin Caal Maquin in Border Patrol Custody Isn't an Isolated Outrage," *Vox*, December 18, 2018.

BIBLIOGRAPHY

PRIMARY SOURCES

Archives

Academia de Geografía e Historia de Guatemala (AGHG), Guatemala City,
 Guatemala
Archivo General de Centroamérica (AGCA), Guatemala City, Guatemala
 Índice 116, Criminal Chimaltenango, 1900–1925. This index corresponds
  to the criminal records generated by the Juzgado de Primera Instancia
  de Chimaltenango. The documents to which the index refers are
  organized by year, *legajo* (file in the form of a bundle) and *expediente*
  (proceeding).
 Índices de Salud Pública (SP) (including índice 140 and Inventario
  1884–1924). These indexes correspond to public health records generated
  by the General Hospital in Guatemala City and other regional hospitals.
 Jefetura Política de Chimaltenango (JP-C), 1925–1944. District governor's
  records for Chimaltenango. These documents are catalogued by year,
  legajo, and *expediente*. Where appropriate and helpful, I further list a brief
  description of the document itself. The vast majority of these documents,
  if not all, pertain to San Martín Jilotepeque.
 Jefetura Política de Sacatepéquez (JP-S), 1924–1941. District governor's
  records for Sacatepéquez. These documents are arranged by *paquete* (pack-
  age) and year. I also delineate them by date and heading.
Archivo de Ministerio de Salud, Guatemala City, Guatemala
Archivo Nacional Ecuador (ANE), Quito, Ecuador
Archivo Municipal de Patzicía (AMP), Patzicía, Guatemala. These documents are
 identified by *paquete* number.
Biblioteca Nacional de Guatemala (BNG), Guatemala City, Guatemala
 Fondo de Libros Antiguos (FLA)
Centro de Investigaciones Regionales de Mesoamérica (CIRMA), Antigua,
 Guatemala

Hemeroteca Nacional de Guatemala (HNG), Guatemala City, Guatemala. Collection of national newspapers.

Loyola-Notre Dame Library Special Collections (LNDLSC), Baltimore, Maryland

Guatemala Collection (GC). These documents are identified by box and folder numbers.

Museo de Medicina (MM), Quito, Ecuador

Asistencia Pública (AP) (Public Assistance)

FEM collection of pamphlets, codigos, and other materials

Sanidad (SA) (Health Services)

National Archives, Atlanta, Georgia

Records of John C. Cutler

Rockefeller Archive Center (RAC), Rockefeller Foundation (RF), Sleepy Hollow, New York. These documents are identified by Record Group (RG), Photographs, and/or Series numbers as well as box and folder numbers.

Tulane University, Latin American Library (TULAL), Dieseldorff Collection (DC), New Orleans, Louisiana. These documents are identified by box and folder numbers.

Government Publications

Administración del señor general don Jorge Ubico. *Dos lustrous de obra sanitaria en la República de Guatemala*. Guatemala City: Publicaciones del partido liberal progresista, 1942.

Alfaro, Eloy. "Presidential Address to Congress, October 20, 1908." Translated in *Foreign Relations of the United States Diplomatic Papers, 1908: The American Republics*. Washington, DC: US Government Printing Office, 1908, 281–82.

Ayora, José María. *Informe que el Ministro de lo Interior, Policía, Obras Públicas, etc. presenta a la Nación en 1912*. Quito: Imprenta y Ecuadernación Nacionales, 1912.

Becerra, León. "Informe del Director de Sanidad." In *Informe que Modesto A. Peña-herrera, Ministro de lo Interior, Municipalidades, Policía, Obras Públicas, etc., presenta a la Nación en 1915*. Quito: Imprenta y Encuadernación Nacionales, 1915.

Boletín del Instituto Indigenista Nacional de Guatemala, 1945.

Boletín de la Oficina Sanitaria Panamericana, 1930–1946.

Boletín Sanitaria, 1938.

Boletín Sanitario de Guatemala, órgano de la Dirección General de Sanidad Pública de Guatemala, 1935–1942.

Confederación de Nacionalidades Indígenas del Ecuador (CNIE). *Las nacionali-dades indigenas en el Ecuador: nuestro proceso organizativo*. Quito: Ediciones Tinicui-Abya Yala, 1989.

Departamento de publicidad de Gubernamental. *Informaciones Nacionales*, 1946.

Despacho de Gobernación y Justicia presenta a la asamblea legislativa de la República de Guatemala en sus sesiones ordinarias de 1890. Guatemala City: Establecimiento Tipográfico de La Unión, ca. 1890.

Dirección General de Estadística (DGE). *Censo General de la República de Guatemala, levantado en el año de 1880.* Guatemala City: Establecimiento Tipografíco de *El Progreso*, 1881.

———. *Censo General de la República de Guatemala. Levantado en 26 de Febrero de 1893.* Guatemala City: Tipografía y Encuadernación "Nacional," 1894.

———. *Quinto censo general de población*, 7 de abril 1940. Guatemala: Secretaría de Hacienda y Credito Público, 1942.

———. *Sexto censo general de la población 1950.* Guatemala City: Oficina Permanente del Censo, 1953.

Dirección General de Sanidad Pública de Guatemala. *Divulgación sanitaria contra el tifus exantemático.* Guatemala City, 1928.

———. *Reglamento para la profilaxia de las enfermedades transmisibles.* Guatemala City: Tipografía Nacional, 1933.

———. Sección de prevención contra la Malaria. *Nociones elementales y prevenciones gráficas contra el Paludismo.* Guatemala: Tipografía Nacional, 1929.

Dirección Nacional de Estadisticas. *Ecuador en Cifras.* Quito, 1944.

Estudio Demográfico de la población del municipio de Amatitlán del departamento de Guatemala, practicada febrero y marzo 1949.

Funes, Juan. "Proyecto de nueva legislación antivenérea, Consideraciones Generales." *Salubridad y Asistencia: organo del Ministerio de Salud Pública y Asistencia Social* Tomo II, Número 3 (Marzo 1949), 3–4.

Gómez Cornejo, L. F. "Informe del Delegado del Ecuador a la V Conferencia Sanitaria Internacional de las Repúblicas Americanas." Appendix to José María Ayora, *Informe que el Ministro de lo Interior, Policía, Obras Públicas, etc. presenta a la Nación en 1912.* Quito: Imprenta y Encuadernación Nacionales, 1912.

Hernández de León, Federíco. *Viajes presidenciales: breves relatos de algunas expediciones administrativos del General D. Jorge Ubico, presidente de la República.* Guatemala City: Tipografía Nacional, 1940.

Informe de la Comisión Presidencial para el Esclarecimiento de los Experimentos Practicados con Humanos en Guatemala. "Consentir el daño: experimentos médicos de Estados Unidos en Guatemala, 1946–1948." Guatemala City, October 2011.

Instituto Indigenista Nacional de Guatemala. *San Bartolomé Milpas Altas: síntesis socio-economico de una comunidad indígena Guatemalteca.* Guatemala City: Ministerio de Educación Pública, 1949.

Instituto Nacional de Estadística (INE). *Censos nacionales XI de población y VI de habitaciones: características de la población y de los locales de habitación censados.* Guatemala City: Instituto Nacional de Estadística, 2003.

International Bank for Reconstruction and Development. *Economic Development of Guatemala (Economic Survey Mission).* Baltimore, MD: Johns Hopkins University Press, 1951.

Memoria de la Dirección General de la Policía Nacional (MPN). Guatemala City: Tipografía Nacional. Annually, 1926–1930.

Memoria de la Secretaría de Gobernación y Justicia (MSGJ). Guatemala City: Tipografía Nacional. Annually, 1908–1915.

Memoria de las labores del ejecutivo en el ramo de Gobernación y Justicia (*MGJ*). Guatemala City: Tipografía Nacional. Annually, 1929–1932.

Memoria de las labores [trabajos] realizados por la dirección general de Sanidad Pública y sus dependencias (*MSP*). Guatemala City: Tipografía Nacional. Annually, 1932–1952.

Memoria de los trabajos realizados por la dirección general de la Policía Nacional (*MPN*). Guatemala City: Tipografía Nacional. Annually, 1932–1940.

Mendez, Rosendo P., ed. *Recopilación de las leyes de la República de Guatemala, 1935–1936*, vol. LIV. Guatemala City: Tipografía Nacional, 1938.

Oficina de Derechos Humanos del Arzobispado de Guatemala. *La memoria tiene la palabra: sistemización del proyecto interdiocesano de recuperación de la memoria histórica*. Guatemala City: ODHAG, 2007.

Peñaherrera, Modesto A. *Informe que Modesto A. Peñaherrera, Ministro de lo Interior, Municipalidades, Policía, Obras Públicas, etc.* Quito: Impresa y Encuadernación Nacionales, 1914–1915.

Puga, Amalio. *Informe del Ministerio de lo Interior, Policía, Beneficencia, Obras Públicas, etc. a la Nación en 1908*. Quito: Imprenta Nacional, 1908.

Recopilación de la leyes de la República de Guatemala, 1893–1894, Tomo 12. Guatemala: Tipografía y Encuadernación Nacional, 1895.

Salubridad y Asistencia: orgáno del Ministerio de Salud Pública y Asistencia Social (Guatemala), 1948–1951.

Secretaría de Gobernación y Justicia, Publicaciones de sanidad. *La influenza (Grippe) medidas para combatirlo*. Guatemala City: Tipografía Nacional 1918.

———. *Informe para reprodulo comisión médica que fue al departamento de Baja Verapaz a combatir la epidemia de paludismo en diciembre 1904*. Guatemala City: Tipografía Nacional, 1905.

Tribunal Supremo Electoral de Ecuador. *Elecciones y democracia en el Ecuador* (1989). https://repositories.lib.utexas.edu/bitstream/handle/2152/17573/libro_18 .pdf?sequence=2, last accessed March 9, 2021.

United States Bureau of American Republics. *Ecuador: A Handbook*. Washington, DC: Government Printing Office, 1894.

Newspapers and Periodicals

El Día, Diario Independiente (Guatemala), 1927.

Diario de Centroamérica (Guatemala), 1910–1945.

Gaceta médica Centroamericana (Guatemala), 1943.

La Gaceta: revista de policía y variedades (Guatemala), 1933–1943.

El Ideal (Guatemala), 1911.

El Imparcial (Guatemala), 1937.

El Impulso (Guatemala), 1919.

El Liberal Progresista (Guatemala), 1935.

Medicina social, 1944.

Previsión Social, 1941.

Public Health Reports, 1935.
Revista de la Cruz Roja Guatemalteca (Guatemala), 1935–1936.
United Fruit Company Medical Department, Annual Report. Boston 1914, 1928.

Oral History Interviews

Due to the continued political volatility of Guatemala and recurrent human rights abuses, I have preserved the anonymity of my collaborators for their safety. I have used pseudonyms that derive from the Maya calendar. Female informants can be recognized by the "Ix" prefix to their one-word names. In contrast, male names have two words. When a research assistant performed the interview, they are listed by their Maya name. The author performed all other interviews. All interviews were conducted in Kaqchikel.

Name	Date	Town/Aldea	Interviewer
B'eleje' Ajpu'	1998	Barahona	Jun Tojil
Ix'ajmaq	7/1/01	Poaquil	Author
Ixchali'	7/2/01	Comalapa	Ixch'onïk
Iximnik'te'	5/30/98	Tecpán	Author
Ixki'ch	6/28/01	Comalapa	Author
Ixmana	7/4/01	Comalapa	Author
Ixpo't	11/17/97	Poaquil	Author
Ixsamaj	9/6/98	Comalapa	Author
Ixtojil	2/7/98	Barahona	Jun Tojil
Ixqa	7/3/01	Comalapa	Author
Ix'umül	4/15/98	Simaulew, Comalapa	Author
Jun Ey	11/12/97	Aguascalientes	Author
Jun Kan	8/19/98	Comalapa	Author
Jun Kej	1998	Barahona	Jun Tojil
Jun Tz'i'	7/11/98	Pamumus, Comalapa	Author
Kab'lajuj Kan	2/15/98	Barahona	Author
Kab'lajuj Tijax	4/6/98	Comalapa	Author
Kablajuj Tz'i'	9/1/98	Aguascalientes	Author
Ka'i' Aq'ab'al	6/7/98	Tecpán	Author
Ka'i' Kawoq	2/7/98	Aguascalientes	Author
Kaji' Imox	8/2/98	Comalapa	Author
K'ayb'il B'alam	10/5/97	Tecpán	Author
Lajuj Aq'ab'al	11/14/97	Aguascalientes	Author
Lajuj Kan	10/16/97	Pachitur, Comalapa	Author
Waqxaqi' Ajpu'	1998	Barahona	Jun Tojil

Waqxaqi' Kawoq	11/8/97	Aguascalientes	Author
Waqxaqi' K'at	11/8/97	Aguascalientes	Author
Wo'o' Iq'	12/2/97	Panicuy, Comalapa	Author
Wuqu' Ajpu'	1998	Barahona	Jun Tojil
Wuqu' Imox	11/12/97	Aguascalientes	Author
Wuqu' Iq'	12/17/97	Xiquín Sanahí, Comalapa	Author

Archivo de historia oral Ecuatoriana, Lourdes Jipa, oral history interview, April 27, 2019, https://stgibson.wixsite.com/ahoe/ahoe-20190022-jipa-lourdes.

SECONDARY SOURCES

Abbott, Andrew. *The System of Professions: An Essay on the Divisions of Expert Labor.* Chicago: University of Chicago Press, 1988.

Abercrombie, Alan Thomas. *Pathways of Memory and Power: Ethnography and History among an Andean People.* Madison: University of Wisconsin Press, 1998.

Abel, Christopher. "External Philanthropy and Domestic Change in Colombia Health Care: The Role of the Rockefeller Foundation, ca. 1920–1950." *Hispanic American Historical Review* 75, no. 3 (1995): 339–76.

Abel, Emily. "From Exclusion to Expulsion: Mexicans and Tuberculosis Control in Los Angeles, 1914–1940." *Bulletin of the History of Medicine* 77, no. 4 (Winter 2003): 823–49.

Acevedo, Dolores, and Elena Hurtado. "Midwives and Formal Providers in Prenatal Care, Delivery and Post-Partum Care in Four Communities in Rural Guatemala: Complementarity or Conflict?" In *Demographic Diversity and Change in Central American Isthmus,* edited by Anne Pebley and Luis Rosero-Bixby, 269–325. Santa Monica, CA: RAND, 1997.

Achig, Lucas. *El proceso urbano de Quito: ensayo de interpretación.* Quito: Centro de Investigaciones/CUIDAD, 1983.

Acosta, A., and E. Martínez, eds. *El buen vivir: una vía para el desarrollo.* Quito, Ecuador: Ediciones Abya-Yala, 2009.

Adams, Abigail E., and Laura Giraudo. "'A Pack of Cigarettes or Some Soap': 'Race,' Security, International Public Health, and Human Medical Experimentation during Guatemala's October Revolution." In *Out of the Shadow: Revisiting the Revolution from Post-Peace Guatemala,* edited by Julie Gibbings and Heather Vrana, 175–97. Austin: University of Texas Press, 2020.

Adams, Richard N. *Un análisis de las creencias y prácticas médicas en un pueblo indígena de Guatemala.* Instituto Indigenista Nacional, Publicaciones Especiales, no. 17. Guatemala City: Editorial del Ministerio de Educación Pública, 1952.

———. "Ethnic Images and Strategies in 1944." In *Guatemalan Indians and the State: 1540–1988,* edited by Carol Smith, 141–62. Austin: University of Texas Press, 1990.

———. "Las masacres de Patzicía de 1944." *Revista Winak Boletín Intercultural* (Guatemala: Universidad Mariano Gálvez), 7 (1–4) (1992): 3–40.

Adams, Richard, and Santiago Bastos. *Las relaciones étnicas en Guatemala, 1944–2000.* Antigua: CIRMA, 2003.

Adams, Richard N., and Arthur J. Rubel. "Sickness and Social Relations." In *Handbook of Middle-American Indians*, edited by Manning Nash and Robert Wauchope, chapter 17. Austin: University of Texas Press, 1967.

Agostini, Claudia. "Ofertas médicas, curanderos y la opinión pública: el Niño Fidencio en el México posrevolucionario." *ACHSC*, 45, no. 1 (enero-junio 2018): 215–43.

Alajajian, Stephen, et al. "Patrones alimentarios y agrícolas de hogares con niños desnutridos en dos comunidades indígenas con distinto nivel socioeconómico en Guatemala." *Estudios sociales: revista de alimentación contemporánea y desarrollo regional* 30, no. 55 (enero-junio 2020), https://doi.org/10.24836/es.v30i55.935.

Alavi, Seema. *Islam and Healing: Loss and Recovery of an Indo-Muslim Medical Tradition, 1600–1900.* New York: Palgrave Macmillan, 2008.

Alchon, Suzanne Austin. *Native Society and Disease in Colonial Ecuador.* Cambridge, UK: Cambridge University Press, 2002.

———. "Tradiciones médicas nativas y resistencia en el Ecuador Colonial." In *Saberes Andinos: ciencia y tecnología en Bolivia, Ecuador, y Perú*, edited by Marcos Cueto, 15–36. Lima: Instituto de Estudios Peruanos, 1995.

Alexander, Ryan M. "The Fever of War: Epidemic Typhus and Public Health in Revolutionary Mexico City, 1915–1917." *Hispanic American Historical Review* 100, no. 1 (Feb. 2020): 63–92.

Aliano, David. "Curing the Ills of Central America: The United Fruit Company's Medical Department and Corporate America's Mission to Civilize (1900–1940)." *Estudios Interdisciplinarios de América Latina y el Caribe*, 17, no. 2 (2006): 35–59.

Almeida, Ileana. "El nuevo movimiento político de los indios." In *Nueva historia del Ecuador, volumen 13. Ensayos generales II: nación, estado y sistema político*, edited by Enrique Ayala Mora, 42–46. Quito: Editorial Grijalbo Ecuatoriana/Corporación Editora Nacional, 1995.

Alvarez, Adriana. "Malaria and the Emergence of Rural Health in Argentina: An Analysis from the Perspective of International Interaction and Co-operation." *Canadian Bulletin of Medical History* 25, no. 1 (2008): 137–60.

Anderson, Margaret Cook. "Creating French Settlements Overseas: Pronatalism and Colonial Medicine in Madagascar." *French Historical Studies* 33, no. 3 (2010): 417–44.

Anderson, Matthew R., Lanny Smith, and V. W. Sidel. "What Is Social Medicine?" *Monthly Review*, January 1, 2005. http://www.monthlyreview.org/0105anderson.htm.

Anderson, Warwick. "The Colonial Medicine of Settler States: Comparing Histories of Indigenous Health." *Health and History*, 9, no. 2 (2007): 144–54.

———. *Colonial Pathologies: American Tropical Medicine, Race & Hygiene in the Philippines.* Durham, NC: Duke University Press, 2006.

———. "Postcolonial Histories of Medicine." In *Locating Medical History: The Stories and Their Meanings*, edited by Frank Huisman and John Harley Warner, 285–306. Baltimore: Johns Hopkins University Press, 2004.

Arcos, Carlos, and Carlos Marchán. "Apuntes para una discusión sobre los cambios en la estructura agraria serrana." *Revista Ciencias Sociales* 2, no. 5 (1978): 13–51.

Armus, Diego. *La ciudad impura: salud, tuberculosis y cultura en Buenos Aires, 1870–1950.* Buenos Aires: Edhasa, 2007.

Arnold, David. *Colonizing the Body: State Medicine and Epidemic Disease in Nineteenth Century India.* Berkeley: University of California Press, 1993.

———, ed. *Warm Climates and Western Medicine: The Emergence of Tropical Medicine, 1500–1900.* Amsterdam: Rodolphi, 1996.

Arnold, Denise Y., and Juan de Dio Yapita. *Las wawas del Inka: hacia la salud materna intercultural en algunas comunidades andinas.* La Paz: Instituto de Lengua y Cultura Aymara, 2002.

Asselbergs, Florine. *Conquered Conquistadors: The Lienzo de Quauhquechollan: A Nahua Vision of the Conquest of Guatemala.* Boulder: University Press of Colorado, 2004.

Asturias, Francisco. *Historia de la medicina in Guatemala.* Guatemala City: Tipografía Nacional, 1902.

Asturias, Miguel Angel. *Guatemalan Sociology: The Social Problem of the Indian.* Translated by Maureen Ahern. Tempe: Arizona State University Press, 1977.

———. *Hombres de Maíz.* Guatemala City: Losada, 1949.

———. *Sociología Guatemalteca: el problema social del indio.* Tempe: Arizona State University Press, 1977 [1923].

Baer, Roberta D., et al. "Las enfermedades populares en la cultura Española actual: un estudio comparado sobre el mal de ojo." *Revista de Dialetología y Tradiciones Populares*, LXI, no. 1 (January-June 2006): 139–56.

Baldwin, Peter. *Contagion & the State in Europe, 1830–1930.* Cambridge, UK: Cambridge University Press, 1999.

Baud, Michiel, "Liberalism, *Indigenismo*, and Social Mobilization in Late Nineteenth-Century Ecuador." In *Highland Indians and the State in Modern Ecuador*, edited by A. Kim Clark and Marc Becker, 72–88. Pittsburgh: University of Pittsburgh Press, 2007.

Bautista-Valarezo, Estefanía, et al. "Towards an Indigenous Definition of Health: An Explorative Study to Understand the Indigenous Ecuadorian People's Health and Illness Concepts." *International Journal for Equity in Health* 19, no. 101 (2020): 1–8.

Barca, Stefania, "A 'Natural' Capitalism: Water and the Making of the Italian Industrial Landscape." In *Nature and History in Modern Italy*, edited by Marco Armiero and Marcus Hall, 215–30. Athens: Ohio University Press, 2010.

Bastien, Joseph. "Differences between Kallawaya-Andean and Greek-European Humoral Theory." *Social Science and Medicine* 28 (1989): 45–51.

———. *Healers of the Andes: Kallawaya Herbalists and Their Medicinal Plants.* Salt Lake City: University of Utah Press, 1987.

———. "Qollahuaya-Andean Body Concepts: A Topographical-Hydraulic Model of Physiology." *American Anthropologist* 87 (1985): 595–611.

Bashford, Alison. *Imperial Hygiene: A Critical History of Colonialism, Nationalism, and Public Health*. New York: Palgrave MacMillan, 2007.

Becker, Marc. "The Limits of 'Indigenismo' in Ecuador." *Latin American Perspectives* 39, no. 5 (September 2012): 45–62.

———. *Indians and Leftists in the Making of Ecuador's Modern Indigenous Movements*. Durham, NC: Duke University Press, 2008.

———. *¡Pachakutik!: Indigenous Movements and Electoral Politics in Ecuador*. Lanham, MD: Rowman and Littlefield Publishers, 2010.

Becker, Marc, and Silvia Tutillo. *Historia agraria y social de Cayambe*. Quito: FLACSO, 2009.

Becker, Marjorie. *Setting the Virgin on Fire: Lázaro Cárdenas, Michoacán Peasants, and the Redemption of the Mexican Revolution*. Berkeley: University of California Press, 1995.

Behrhorst, Carroll. Introduction to Steltzer Ulli, *Health in the Guatemalan Highlands*, xii–xxxv. Vancouver: Douglas and McIntyre, 1983.

Bell, Heather. *Frontiers of Medicine in Anglo-Egyptian Sudan, 1899–1940*. New York: Oxford University Press, 1999.

Benítez, Lilyan, and Alicia Garcés. *Culturas ecuatorianas: ayer y hoy*. 7th ed. Quito: Ediciones Abya-Yala, 1993.

Berg, Marc, and Annemarie Mol. *Differences in Medicine: Unraveling Practices, Techniques, and Bodies*. Durham, NC: Duke University Press, 1998.

Bevilacqua, Piero, et al. *Ambiente e Risorse Nel Mezzogiorno Contemporaneo*. Corigliano Calabro, Italy: Meridiana Libri, 2000.

Birn, Anne-Emanuelle. "'No More Surprising Than a Broken Pitcher'? Maternal and Child Health in the Early Years of the Pan American Sanitary Bureau." *Canadian Bulletin of Medical History* 19 (2002): 17–46.

———. "Doctors on Record: Uruguay's Infant Mortality Stagnation and Its Remedies, 1895–1945." *Bulletin of the History of Medicine* 82, no. 2 (Summer 2008): 311–54.

———. "Going Global in Uruguay: Child Well-being and the Evolution of International Health." *American Journal of Public Health* 95, no. 9 (2005): 2–13.

———. *Marriage of Convenience: Rockefeller International Health and Revolutionary Mexico*. Rochester, NY: Rochester University Press, 2006.

———. "O Nexo Nacional-Internacional na Saúde Pública: O Uruguai e a Circulação das Políticas e Ideologias de Saúde Infantil, 1890–1940. The National-International Nexus in Public Health: Uruguay and the Circulation of Child Health and Welfare Policies." *História, Ciêcias, Saúde—Manguinbos* 13, no. 3 (2006): 675–708.

———. "Revolution, the Scatalogical Way: The Rockefeller Foundation's Hookworm Campaign in 1920s Mexico." In *Disease in the History of Modern Latin America: From Malaria to AIDS*, edited by Diego Armus, 158–81. Durham, NC: Duke University Press, 2003.

———. "Skirting the Issue: Women and international Health in Historical Perspectives." *American Journal of Public Health* 89 (1999): 399–407.

———. "Wa(i)ves of Influence: Rockefeller Public Health in Mexico, 1920–50." *Studies in the History and Philosophy of Biological and Biomedical Sciences* 31, no. 1 (2000): 381–95.

Birn, Anne-Emanuelle, and Raúl Necochea López. "Footprints on the Future: Looking Forward to the History of Health and Medicine in Latin America in the Twenty-First Century." *Hispanic American Historical Review* 91, no. 3 (2011): 503–27.

Blake, Stanley. "The Medicalization of Nordestinos: Public Health and Regional Identity in Northeastern Brazil, 1889–1930." *The Americas* 60, no 2 (2003): 217–48.

Blier, Suzanne Preston. *African Vodun: Art, Psychology, and Power.* Chicago: University of Chicago Press, 1995.

Bliss, Katherine. "The Science of Redemption: Syphilis, Sexual Promiscuity, and Reformism in Mexico City." *Hispanic American Historical Review* 79, no. 1 (February 1999): 1–40.

Borges, Dana, "Healing and Mischief: Witchcraft in Brazilian Law and Literature, 1890–1922." In *Crime and Punishment in Latin America: Law and Society Since Late Colonial Times,* edited by Ricardo D. Salvatore, Carlos Aguirre, and Gilbert M. Joseph, 181–210. Durham, NC: Duke University Press, 2001.

———. "Puffy, Ugly, Slothful and Inert: Degeneration in Brazilian Thought, 1880–1940." *Journal of Latin American Studies* 25, no. 2 (1993): 235–256.

Borowy, I. *Coming to Terms with World Health: The League of Nations Health Organisation, 1921–1946.* Frankfurt: Peter Lang, 2009.

Botey Sobrado, María Ana. "La epidemia del cólera (1856) en Costa Rica: una visión del largo plazo." *Diálogos Revista Electrónica de Historia* 9 (2008): 345–77.

Boyer, Chris. *Political Landscapes: Forests, Conservation, and Community in Mexico.* Durham, NC: Duke University Press, 2015.

Briggs, Charles L., with Clara Mantini-Briggs. *Stories in the Time of Cholera: Racial Profiling During a Medical Nightmare.* Berkeley: University of California Press, 2003.

Briggs, Charles L., and Clara Mantini-Briggs. *Tell Me Why My Children Died: Rabies, Indigenous Knowledge, and Communicative Justice.* Durham, NC: Duke University Press, 2016.

Briggs, Laura. *Reproducing Empire: Race, Sex, Science, and U.S. Imperialism in Puerto Rico.* Berkeley: University of California Press, 2003.

Briggs, Laura, Gladys McCormack, and J. T. Way. "Transnationalism: A Category of Analysis." *American Quarterly* 60, no. 3 (September 2008): 625–48.

Bronfman, Alejandra. *Measures of Equality: Social Science, Citizenship and Race in Cuba, 1902–1940.* Chapel Hill, NC: University of North Carolina Press, 2004.

Brown, Peter. "Malaria, *Miseria*, and Underpopulation in Sardinia: The 'Malaria Blocks Development' Cultural Model." *Medical Anthropology,* 17, no. 3 (1997): 239–54.

Brown, Richard E. "Public Health and Imperialism: Early Rockefeller Programs at Home and Abroad." *American Journal of Public Health* 66, no. 9 (September 1976).

Buffington, Robert. *Criminal and Citizen in Modern Mexico*. Lincoln: University of Nebraska Press, 2000.

Bunzel, Ruth. *Chichicastenango: A Guatemalan Village*. Seattle: University of Washington Press, 1967 [1952].

Bustos Lozano, Guillermo. *El culto a la nación. Escritura de la historia y rituals de la memoria en Ecuador, 1870–1950*. Quito: Fondo de Cultural Económica/Universidad Andina Simón Bolivar, 2017.

Butler, Judith. "Restaging the Universal: Hegemony and the Limits of Formalism." In *Contingency, Hegemony, Universality: Contemporary Dialogues on the Left*, edited by Judith Butler, et al., 11–43. New York: Verso, 2000.

Caceres, Armando. *Plantas de uso medicinal en Guatemala*. Guatemala City: Editorial Universitaria, 1999.

———. "From Traditional Uses of Mesoamerican Medicinal Plants to Modern Phytotherapy in Guatemala." *Planta Medica* 81, no. 16 (2015). https://www.researchgate.net/publication/284750535.

Caniato, R., and L. Puricelli. "Review: Natural Antimalarial Agents (1995–2001)." *Critical Reviews in Plant Sciences* 22, no. 1 (2003): 79–105.

Capello, Ernesto. *City at the Center of the World: Space, History, and Modernity in Quito*. Pittsburgh: University of Pittsburgh Press, 2011.

Carey, David Jr. "A Cautionary Tale of Environmental Management: Water Management, Land Reclamation, and Malaria in Twentieth-Century Guatemala." *Environmental History* 26, no. 3 (July 2021): 555–80.

———. "A Democracy Born in Violence: Maya Perceptions of the 1944 Patzicía Massacre and the 1954 Coup." In *After the Coup: An Ethnographic Reframing of Guatemala 1954*, edited by Timothy J. Smith and Abigail E. Adams, 73–98. Champaign: University of Illinois Press, 2011.

———. "Drunks and Dictators: Inebriation's Gendered, Ethnic, and Class Components in Guatemala, 1898–1944." In *Alcohol in Latin America: A Social and Cultural History*, edited by Gretchen Pierce and Áurea Toxqui, 131–57. Tucson: University of Arizona Press, 2014.

———. *Engendering Mayan History: Kaqchikel Women as Agents and Conduits of the Past, 1875–1970*. New York: Routledge, 2006.

———. "Guatemala since 1840." In *The Oxford Handbook of Central American History*, edited by Robert Holden, 485–517. New York: Oxford University Press, 2022.

———. "Heroines of Healthcare: Germana Catu and Maya Midwives." In *Faces of Resistance: Maya Heroes, Power, & Identity*, edited by Ashley Kistler, 137–56. Tuscaloosa: University of Alabama Press, 2018.

———. *I Ask for Justice: Maya Women, Dictators, and Crime in Guatemala, 1898–1944*. Austin: University of Texas Press, 2013.

———. "Mayan Soldier-Citizens: Ethnic Pride in the Guatemalan Military 1925–1945." In *Military Struggle and Identity Formation in Latin America: Race, Nation and Community 1850–1950*, edited by Nicola Foote and René D. Harder Horst, 136–56. Gainesville: University Press of Florida, 2010.

————. *Our Elders Teach Us: Maya-Kaqchikel Historical Perspectives. Xkib'ij kan qate' qatata'*. Tuscaloosa: University of Alabama Press, 2001.

————. "Rethinking Representation and Periodization in Guatemala's Democratic Experiment." In *Out of the Shadow: Revisiting the Revolution from Post-Peace Guatemala*, edited by Julie Gibbings and Heather Vrana, 145–72. Austin: University of Texas Press, 2020.

————. "Yellow Fever's Historical Lessons for COVID-19: International Interventions and Disease Control in Early Twentieth-Century Ecuador and Guatemala." *Journal of Developing Societies* (2021): 1–30.

Carlsen, S. Robert, and Martin Prechtel. "Walking on Two Legs: Shamanism in Santiago, Atitlán, Guatemala." In *Ancient Traditions: Shamanism in Central Asia and the Americas*, edited by Gary Seaman and Jane S. Day, 77–111. Niwot: University Press of Colorado, 1994.

Carrillo, Ana María. *Matilde Montoya, primera médica Mexicana*. Mexico City: DEMAC, 2002.

————. "Nacimiento y muerte de una profesión. Las parteras tituladas en México." *DYNAMIS* 19 (1999): 167–90.

————. "Profesionales sanitarias y lucha de poderes en el México del siglo XIX." *Asclepio. Revista de historia de la medicinas y de la ciencia* 1, no. 2. 1998: 149–66.

Carrillo, Ana María, and Anne-Emanuelle Birn. "Neighbors on Notice: National and Imperialistic Interests in the American Public Health Association, 1872–1921." *Canadian Bulletin of Medical History* 25, no. 1 (2008). https://doi .org/10.3138/cbmh.25.1.225.

Carrión, Fernando. *Quito: crisis y política urbana*. Quito: CUIDAD/Editorial el Conejo, 1987.

Carter, Eric C. "Social Medicine and International Expert Networks in Latin America, 1930–1945." *Global Public Health*, 14, nos. 6–7 (2019): 791–802.

————. *Enemy in the Blood: Malaria, Environment, and Development in Argentina*. Tuscaloosa: University of Alabama Press, 2012.

————. "Malaria, Landscape, and Society in Northwest Argentina in the Early Twentieth Century." *Journal of Latin American Geography* 7, no. 1 (2008): 7–38.

Casaús Arzú, Elena Marta. "La metamorfosis del racismo en la élite de poder en Guatemala." In *Racismo en Guatemala? Abriendo el debate sobre un tema tabú*, edited by Clara Arenas Bianchi et al., 45–109. Guatemala City: AVANCSO, 2004.

————. *Guatemala: Linaje y racismo*. Guatemala City: Facultad Latinoamericana de Ciencias Sociales, 1994.

————. "El gran debate historiográfico de 1937 en Guatemala." *Revista Complutense de Historia de América*, 34 (2008): 209–31.

————. "La generación del 20 en Guatemala y sus imaginarios de nación." In *Las redes intelectuales centroamericanas: un siglo de imaginarios nacionales 1820–1920*, edited by Marta Elena Casaús Arzú y Teresa García Giráldez, 253–90. Guatemala City: F&G Editores.

Cattermole-Tally, Frances. "The Intrusion of Animals into the Human Body: Fantasy and Reality." *Folklore* 106 (1995): 89–92.

Cevallos, Pedro Fermín. *Resumen de la historia del Ecuador*. Lima, 1870.

Chakrabarty, Dipesh. "Postcoloniality and the Artifice for History: Who Speaks for 'Indian' Pasts?" *Representations* 24, no. 1 (Winter 1992): 1–26.

Chary, Anita, and Peter Rohloff. *Privatization and the New Medical Pluralism: Shifting Healthcare and Landscapes in Maya Guatemala*. New York: Lexington Books, 2015.

Chaves, M., et al. "Implementação da política de saúde indígena no Pólo-base Angra dos Reis, Rio de Janeiro, Brasil: entraves e perspectivas." *Cadernos de Saúde Publica*. Rio de Janeiro, Brazil 22, no. 2 (2006): 295–305.

Chávez, Rodrigo. *El mestizaje y su influencia social en América*. Guayaquil: Imprenta Municipal, 1937.

Cházaro, Laura. "Pariendo instrumentos médicos: los forceps y pelvimetros entre los obstetras del siglo XIX en México." *DYNAMIS* 24 (2004): 27–51.

Chomsky, Avi. *West Indian Workers and the United Fruit Company in Costa Rica, 1870–1940*. Baton Rouge: Louisiana State University Press, 1996.

Clark, A. Kim *Conjuring the State: Public Health Encounters in Highland Ecuador, c. 1908–1940*. Pittsburgh: University of Pittsburgh Press, forthcoming.

———. *Gender, State, and Medicine in Highland Ecuador: Modernizing Women, Modernizing the State, 1895–1950*. Pittsburgh: University of Pittsburgh Press, 2012.

———. "Género, raza y nación: la protección a la infancia en el Ecuador (1910–1945). In *Antología de estudios de género*, edited by Gioconda Herrera Mosquera, 183–210. Quito: FLACSO, 2001.

———. "Indians, the State and Law: Public Works and the Struggle to Control Labor in Liberal Ecuador." *Journal of Historical Sociology* 7, no. 1 (March 1994): 49–72.

———. "La medida de la diferencia: las imágenes indigenistas de los indios serranos en el Ecuador (1920s a 1940s)." In *Ecuador racista: imágenes y identidades*, edited by Emma Cervone and V. Fredy Rivera, 111–26. Quito: FLACSO, Sede Ecuador, 1999.

———. "Race, 'Culture,' and Mestizaje: The Statistical Construction of the Ecuadorian Nation, 1930–1950." *Journal of Historical Sociology* 11, no. 2 (June 1998): 185–211.

———. "Racial Ideologies and the Quest for National Development: Debating the Agrarian Problem in Ecuador." *Journal of Latin American Studies* 30 (1998): 373–93.

———. *The Redemptive Work: Railway and Nation in Ecuador, 1895–1930*. Wilmington, DE: Scholarly Resources, 1998.

Clark, A. Kim, and Marc Becker, eds. *Highland Indians and the State in Modern Ecuador*. Pittsburgh, PA: University of Pittsburgh Press, 2007.

Clark, A. Kim, and Marc Becker. "Indigenous Peoples and State Formation in Modern Ecuador." In *Highland Indians and the State in Modern Ecuador*, ed. A. Kim Clark and Marc Becker, 1–21. Pittsburgh, PA: University of Pittsburgh Press, 2007.

Clifford, James. *The Predicament of Culture: Twentieth Century Ethnography, Literature, and Art*. Cambridge, MA: Harvard University Press, 1988.

Colson, Audrey Butt, and Cesareo de Armellada. "An Amerindian Derivation for Latin American Creole Illnesses and Their Treatment." *Social Science and Medicine* 17 (1983): 1229–1248.

Comisión para el Esclarecimiento Histórico (CEH). *Guatemala, memoria del silencio.* Guatemala City: CEH, 1999.

Cooper Owens, Deirdre. *Medical Bondage: Race, Gender, and the Origins of American Gynecology.* Athens: University of Georgia Press, 2017.

Córdova M., Isabel. *Pushing in Silence: Modernizing Puerto Rico and the Medicalization of Childbirth.* Austin: University of Texas Press, 2018.

Corona, Gabriella. *A Short Environmental History of Italy: Variety and Vulnerability.* Winwick, UK: The White Horse Press, 2017.

Crafts, Lydia. "Mining Bodies: Medical Experimentation and Ethics During the Guatemalan Spring, 1944–54." Ph.D. diss., University of Illinois at Urbana-Champaign, 2019.

Crawford, James Matthew. *The Andean Wonder Drug: Cinchona Bark and Imperial Science in the Spanish Atlantic, 1630–1800.* Durham, NC: Duke University Press, 2016.

Crandon-Malamud, Libbet. *From the Fat of Our Souls: Social Change, Political Process, and Medical Pluralism in Bolivia.* Berkeley: University of California Press, 1993.

Crosby, Alfred W. "Past and Present of Environmental History." *American Historical Review* 100, no. 4 (1995): 1177–89.

———. *America's Forgotten Pandemic: The Influenza of 1918.* Cambridge, UK: Cambridge University Press, 2003.

Cueto, Marcos. *Cold War, Deadly Fevers: Malaria Eradication in Mexico, 1955–1975.* Washington DC/Baltimore: Woodrow Wilson Center Press/Johns Hopkins University Press, 2014.

———. "Introduction." In *Missionaries of Science: The Rockefeller Foundation and Latin America,* edited by Marcos Cueto, ix–xx. Bloomington: University of Indiana Press, 1994.

———, ed. *Missionaries of Science: The Rockefeller Foundation and Latin America.* Bloomington: Indiana University Press, 1994.

———. *El regreso de las epidemias. Salud y sociedad en el Perú del siglo XX.* Lima: Instituto de Estudios Peruanos, 2000.

———. *Salud, cultura, y sociedad en América Latina.* Lima: Instituto de Estudios Peruanos, 1996.

———. "Social Medicine and Leprosy in the Peruvian Amazon." *Americas* 61, no. 1 (2004): 55–80.

———. *The Return of Epidemics: Health and Society in Peru during the Twentieth Century.* Aldershot, UK: Ashgate, 2001.

———. *Saberes andinos: ciencia y tecnología en Bolivia, Ecuador, y Perú.* Lima: Instituto de Estudios Peruanos, 1995.

———. *The Value of Health: A History of the Pan American Health Organization.* Washington, DC: Pan American Health Organization, 2007.

———. "Tifo, varíola, e indigenismo: Manuel Núñez Butrón e a medicina rural em Puno, Peru." In *Cuidar, controlar, curar: Ensaios históricos sobre saúde e doença na América Latina e Caribe*, edited by Gilberto Hochman and Diego Armus, 295–329. Rio de Janeiro: Editoria Fiocruz, 2004.

———. "Visions of Science and Development: The Rockefeller Foundation's Latin American Surveys of the 1920s." In *Missionaries of Science: The Rockefeller Foundation and Latin America*, edited by Marcos Cueto, 23–51. Bloomington: University of Indiana Press, 1994.

Cueto, Marcos, and Steven Palmer. *Medicine and Public Health in Latin America: A History*. Cambridge, UK: Cambridge University Press, 2015.

Dávila, Jerry. *Diploma of Whiteness: Race and Social Policy in Brazil, 1917–1945*. Durham, NC: Duke University Press, 2003.

Dawson, Thomas C. *The South American Republics, Part II: Peru, Chile, Bolivia, and Ecuador, Venezuela, Colombia, Panama*. New York: G. P. Putnam's Sons, 1904.

de Almeida, Marta. "Circuito aberto: Idéias e intercâmbios medico-científicos na América Latina nos primórdios do século XX." *História, Ciêcias, Saúde—Manguinbos* 13, no. 3 (2006): 733–57.

de Barros, Juanita. "Dispensers, Obeah, and Quackery: Medical Rivalries in Post-Slavery British Guiana." *Social History of Medicine* 20 (2007): 243–61.

de la Cadena, Marisol. *Indigenous Mestizos: The Politics of Race and Culture in Peru, 1919–1991*. Durham, NC: Duke University Press, 2000.

de Castañeda Martín, R. P. *Tratado de las supersticiones y hechicerías del R. P. Fray Marín de Castañeda*. Madrid: La Sociedad de Bibliófilos Españoles, 1946.

de Córdova y Quesada, Armando. *La locura en Cuba*. Havana: Seoane, Fernández y Cía., Impresores, 1940.

de Landa, Diego. *The Maya: Diego de Landa's Account of the Affairs of Yucatan*. Edited and translated by A. R. Pagden. Chicago: J. Philip O'Hara, Inc, 1975.

de León Aragón, Oscar. *Caída de un régimen: Jorge Ubico-Federico Ponce, 20 de Octubre 1944*. Guatemala City: Facultad Latinoamerica de Ciencias Sociales, 1995.

de Moura Pontes, Ana Lucia, and Ricardo Ventura Santos. "Health Reform and Indigenous Health Policy in Brazil: Contexts, Actors and Discourses." *Health Policy and Planning* 35 (2020): i107-i114.

de la Torre Espinosa, Carlos. *Afroquiteños, ciudadanía y racism*. Quito: CAAP, 2002.

Dent, Rosanna, and Ricardo Ventura Santos. "'An Unusual and Fast Disappearing Opportunity': Infectious Disease, Indigenous Populations, and New Biomedical Knowledge in Amazonia, 1960–1970." *Perspectives on Science* 25, no. 5 (2017): 585–605.

Di Liscia, María Silvia. "Viruela, vacunación e indígenas en la pampa Argentina del siglo XIX." In *Entre médicos y curanderos: cultura, historia y enfermedad en la América Latina moderna*, edited by Diego Armus, 27–69. Buenos Aires: Grupo Editorial Norma, 2002.

Dieseldorff, Erwin Paul. *Las plantas medicinales del Departamento de Alta Verapaz*. Guatemala City: Tipografía Nacional, 1977 [1940].

Dosal, Paul. *Power in Transition: The Rise of Guatemala's Industrial Oligarchy, 1871–1994*. Wesport, CT: Praeger, 1995.

Durán Martínez, Carlos. *Las ciencias médicas en Guatemala: origen y evolución*. Guatemala City: Editorial Universitaria, 1964.

Earle, Rebecca. *The Return of the Native: Indians and Myth-Making in Spanish America, 1810–1910*. Durham, NC: Duke University Press, 2007.

Espejo, Eugenio. *Voto de un Ministro Togado de la Audiencia de Quito*. Quito: Comisión Nacional de Conmemoraciones Cívicas, 1994.

———. *Reflexiones sobre la viruela*. Quito, 1785.

Espinosa, Mariola. "Globalizing the History of Disease, Medicine, and Public Health in Latin America." *Isis: A Journal of the History of Science Society* 104, no. 4 (2013): 798–806.

———. *Epidemic Invasions: Yellow Fever and the Limits of Cuban Independence, 1878–1930*. Chicago: University of Chicago Press, 2009.

Esquit, Edgar. *Otros poderes, nuevos desafíos: relaciones interétnicas en Tecpán y su entorno departamental (1871–1935)*. Guatemala City: Magna Terra Editores, 2002.

———. *La superación del indígena: la política de la modernización entre las élites indígenas de Comalapa, Siglo XX*. Guatemala City: Instituto de Estudios Interétnicos, Universidad de San Carlos, 2010.

Estrada, Victoria, and Jorge Márquez Valderrama. "Recognition without a Diploma: The Wanderings of the Healer Indio Rondín in Early Twentieth-Century Colombia." In *The Gray Zones of Medicine: Healers and History in Latin America*, edited by Diego Armus and Pablo F. Gómez, 123–37. Pittsburgh: University of Pittsburgh Press, 2021.

Estrada Ycaza, Julio. *Regionalismo y migración*. Guayaquil: Archivo Histórico del Guayas, 1977.

Ewig, Christina. "Health Policies and the Historical Reproduction of Class, Race and Gender Inequalities in Peru." In *Indelible Inequalities in Latin America: Insights from History, Politics, and Culture*, edited by Paul Gootenberg and Luis Reygadas, 52–80. Durham, NC: Duke University Press, 2010.

Fausto-Sterling, Anne. *Myths of Gender: Biological Theories of Women and Men*. New York: Basic Books, 1992.

Feierman, Steven, and John M. Janzen. "Introduction." In *The Social Basis of Health and Healing in Africa*, edited by Steven Feierman and John M. Janzen, 1–23. Berkeley: University of California Press, 1992.

Fenner, F., et al. *Smallpox and Its Eradication*. Geneva: World Health Organization, 1988.

Few, Martha. *For All of Humanity: Mesoamerican and Colonial Medicine in Enlightenment Guatemala*. Tucson: University of Arizona Press, 2015.

———. "Circulating Smallpox Knowledge: Guatemalan Doctors, Maya Indians and Designing Spain's Smallpox Vaccination Expedition, 1780–1803." *The British Journal for the History of Science* 43, no. 4 (December 2010): 519–37.

———. "The Curing World of María García, an Indigenous Healer in Eighteenth-Century Guatemala." In *The Gray Zones of Medicine: Healers and History in*

Latin America, edited by Diego Armus and Pablo F. Gómez, 26–39. Pittsburgh: University of Pittsburgh Press, 2021.

———. "Epidemics, Indigenous Communities, and Public Health in the COVID-19 Era: Views from Smallpox Inoculation Campaigns in Colonial Guatemala." *Journal of Global History* 15, no. 3 (fall 2020): 380–93.

———. "'That Monster of Nature': Gender, Sexuality, and the Medicalization of a 'Hermaphrodite' in Late Colonial Guatemala." *Ethnohistory* 54 (1) (Winter 2007): 159–76.

Findlay, Eileen J. "Courtroom Tales of Sex and Honor: *Rapto* and Rape in Late-Nineteenth-Century Puerto Rico." In *Honor, Status and Law in Modern Latin America*, edited by Sueann Caulfield et al., 201–22. Durham, NC: Duke University Press, 2005.

Finkler, Kaja. *Women in Pain: Gender and Morbidity in Mexico*. Philadelphia: University of Pennsylvania Press, 1994.

Fischer, Sibylle. *Modernity Disavowed: Haiti and the Cultures of Slavery in the Age of Revolution*. Durham, NC: Duke University Press, 2004.

Fissell, Mary E. *Vernacular Bodies: The Politics of Reproduction in Early Modern England*. New York: Oxford University Press, 2004.

Flexner, Abraham. *Medical Education in the United States and Canada: A Report to the Carnegie Foundation for the Advancement of Teaching*. Bulletin no. 4. New York: Carnegie Foundation for the Advancement of Teaching, 1910.

Flint, Karen E. *Healing Traditions: African Medicine, Cultural Exchange, and Competition in South Africa, 1820–1948*. Athens: Ohio University Press, 2008.

Forster, Cindy. *The Time of Freedom: Campesino Workers in Guatemala's October Revolution*. Pittsburgh: University of Pittsburgh Press, 2001.

Foucault, Michel. *Power/Knowledge: Selected Interviews & Other Writings, 1972–1977*. Edited by Colin Gordon. New York, Pantheon Press, 1980.

Foss, Sarah. *On Our Own Terms: Development and Indigeneity in Cold War Guatemala*. Chapel Hill: University of North Carolina Press, 2022.

———. "'Una obra revolucionaria': *Indigenismo* and the Guatemalan Revolution, 1944–1954." In *Out of the Shadow: Revisiting the Revolution from Post-Peace Guatemala*, edited by Julie Gibbings and Heather Vrana, 199–221. Austin: University of Texas Press, 2020.

Foster, M. George. "The Validating Role of Humoral Theory in Traditional Spanish-American Therapeutics." *American Ethnologist* 15, no. 1 (1988): 120–35.

———. "Relationships Between Sapnish and Spanish-American Folk Medicine." *Journal of American Folklore* 66 (1953): 201–47.

Franco-Agudelo, Saul. "The Rockefeller Foundation's Antimalarial Program in Latin America: Donating or Dominating?" *International Journal of Health Services* 13, no. 1 (1983): 51–67.

Frazier, Jacinta Gertrude. *African American Midwifery in the South: Dialogues of Birth, Race, and Memory*. Cambridge, MA: Harvard University Press, 1998.

Fuentes, Marisa. *Dispossessed Lives: Enslaved Women, Silence, and the Archive*. Philadelphia: University of Pennsylvania Press, 2016.

Furst, Lillian, ed. *Climbing a Long Hill: Women Healers and Physicians*. Lexington: University of Kentucky Press, 1997.

Gall, Francis, ed. *Diccionario Geográfico de Guatemala*. Vol. 3. Guatemala City: Tipografía Nacional, 1983.

Gallien, Kathryn. "Delivering the Nation, Raising the State: Gender, Childbirth, and the 'Indian Problem' in Bolivia's Obstetric Movement, 1900–1982." Ph.D. diss., University of Arizona, 2015.

Garcia-Kutzbach, A. "Medicine among the Ancient Maya." *Southern Medical Journal* 69, no. 7 (1976): 938–39.

Gibbings, Julie. "Mestizaje in the Age of Fascism: German and Q'echi' Maya Interracial Unions in Alta Verapaz, Guatemala." *German History* (2016): 214–36.

———. *Our Time is Now: Race and Modernity in Postcolonial Guatemala*. Cambridge, UK: Cambridge University Press, 2020.

———. "Progressive Mothers, Populist Politics: Eugenics, Race, and Progress during Jorge Ubico's Guatemala." Paper presented at Latin American Studies Association annual conference, Boston, MA, May 24–27, 2019.

———. "'Their Debts Follow Them into the Afterlife': German Settlers, Ethnographic Knowledge, and the Forging of Coffee Capitalism in Nineteenth-Century Guatemala." *Comparative Studies in Society and History* 62, no. 2 (2020): 380–420.

Gibbings, Julie, and Heather Vrana, eds. *Out of the Shadow: Revisiting the Revolution from Post-Peace Guatemala*. Austin: University of Texas Press, 2020.

Gibson, Thomas Scott, Sara Newman, and Antonia Carcelen-Estrada. "Indigeneity and Disabilities in the Ecuadorian Oral History Archives." *Disability Studies Quarterly* 41, no. 4 (Fall 2021): np. https://doi.org/10.18061/dsq.v41i4.8454.

Gillick, S. Stephen, "Life and Labor in a Banana Enclave: *Bananeros*, the United Fruit Company, and the Limits of Trade Unionism in Guatemala, 1906 to 1931." Ph.D. diss., Tulane University, 1994.

Gillin, John. "Magical Fright." *Psychiatry* 11, no. 4 (1948): 387–400.

———. *The Culture of Security in San Carlos*. New Orleans: Middle American Research Institute, Tulane University, 1951.

Giraudo, Laura, and Juan Martín-Sánchez, eds. *La ambivalente historia del indigenismo: campo interamericano y trayectorias nacionales, 1940–1970*. Lima: Instituto de Estudios Peruanos, 2011.

Giraudo, Laura, and Stephen Lewis, eds.. "Rethinking Indigenismo on the American Continent." Special issue, *Latin American Perspectives* 39, no. 5 (2012).

Gleijeses, Piero. *Shattered Hope: The Guatemalan Revolution and the United States, 1944–1954*. Princeton, NJ: Princeton University Press, 1991.

Gluck, Carol. "The End of Elsewhere: Writing Modernity Now." *American Historical Review* 116, no. 3 (2011): 676–87.

Goetschel, María Ana. *Historias de rebelión y castigo: el aborto en Ecuador en la primera mitad del siglo XX*. Quito: FLACSO, 2021.

Gómez, Pablo F. *The Experiential Caribbean: Creating Knowledge and Healing in the Early Modern Atlantic*. Chapel Hill: University of North Carolina Press, 2017.

Gomez, Rocio. *Silver Veins, Dusty Lungs: Mining, Water, and Public Health in Zacatecas, 1835–1946*. Lincoln: University of Nebraska Press, 2020.

González Suárez, Federico. *Historia general de la República de Ecuador*. Quito: Casa de la Cultura Ecuatoriana, 1969 [1890].

Gotkowitz, Laura. *A Revolution for Our Rights: Indigenous Struggles for Land and Justice in Bolivia, 1880–1952*. Durham, NC: Duke University Press, 2007.

Gould, Jeffrey L. "Indigenista Dictators and the Problematic Origins of Democracy in Central America." In *The Great Depression in Latin America*, edited by Paulo Drinot and Alan Knight, 188–212. Durham, NC: Duke University Press, 2014.

Grandin, Greg. *The Blood of Guatemala: A History of Race and Nation*. Durham, NC: Duke University Press, 2000.

———. *Empire's Workshop: Latin America, the United States, and the Rise of the New Imperialism*. New York: Metropolitan Books, 2006.

Granados, C. "Social Medicine, Sexuality and Health." 2008. http://digitalrepository.unm.edu/lasm_cucs_en/127.

Green, James N. "Doctoring the National Body: Gender, Race, Eugenics, and the 'Invert' in Urban Brazil, ca. 1920–1945." In *Gender, Sexuality, and Power in Latin America since Independence*, edited by William French and Kathleen Bliss, 187–211. New York: Rowman and Littlefield Publishers, 2007.

Greenberg, Linda. "Midwife Training Programs in Highland Guatemala." *Social Science & Medicine* 16 (1982): 1599–1609.

Greene, Jeremy A., Victor Braitberg, and Gabrielle Maya Bernadett. "Innovation on the Reservation: Information Technology and Health Systems Research among the Papago Tribe of Arizona, 1965–1980." *Isis* 111, no. 3 (2020): 443–70.

Greene, Jeremy A., and Scott H. Podolsky. "Keeping Modern in Medicine: Pharmaceutical Promotion and Physician Education in Postwar America." *Bulletin of the History of Medicine* 83, no. 2 (Summer 2009): 331–77.

Grieb, Kenneth. *Guatemalan Caudillo: The Regime of Jorge Ubico, Guatemala, 1931–1944*. Athens: Ohio University Press, 1979.

Guardino, Peter F. *Peasants, Politics, and the Formation of Mexico's National State: Guerrero, 1800–1857*. Stanford, CA: Stanford University Press, 1996.

Gudmundson, Lowell. "Negotiating Rights Under Slavery: The Slaves of San Geronimo (Baja Verapaz, Guatemala) Confront their Dominican Masters in 1810." *The Americas* 60, no. 1 (July 2003): 109–14.

———. "On Green Revolutions and Golden Beans: Memories and Metaphors of Costa Rican Coffee Co-op Founders." *Agricultural History* 88, no. 4 (Fall 2014): 538–65.

———. "Peasant, Farmer, Proletarian: Class Formation in a Smallholder Coffee Economy, 1850–1950." In *Coffee, Society, and Power in Latin America*, edited by William Roseberry, Lowell Gudmundson, and Mario Samper Kutschbach, 112–50. Baltimore: Johns Hopkins University Press, 1995.

Gudmundson, Lowell, and Hector Lindo-Fuentes. *Central America, 1821–1871: Liberalism before Liberal Reform*. Tuscaloosa: University of Alabama Press, 1995.

Guerra, Francisco. "Maya Medicine." *Medical History* 8 (1964): 35–38.

Guerrero, Andrés. "La desintegración de la administración étnica en el Ecuador." In *Sismo étnico en el Ecuador*, edited by José Almeida et al., 91–112. Quito: DED-IME, 1993.

———. "Una imagen ventrílocua: el discurso liberal de la 'desgraciada raza indígena' a fines del siglo XIX." In *Imágenes e imagineros: representaciones de los indígenas ecuatorianos, siglos XIX y XX*, edited by Blanca Muratorio, 197–253. Quito: FLACSO-Ecuador, 1994.

Guáman Poma, Felipe. *La nueva crónica y buen gobierno*. 3 vols. Lima: Editorial Cultura, Dirección de Cultura, Arqueología e Historia del Ministerio de Educación Pública del Perú, 1956.

Guy, Donna. *White Slavery and Mothers Alive and Dead: The Troubled Meeting of Sex, Gender, Public Health, and Progress in Latin America*. Lincoln: University of Nebraska Press, 2000.

Hall, Marcus. "Thinking Like a Parasite: Malaria, Plasmodium, and Sardinia's Extraordinary Longevity." In *Italy and the Environmental Humanities: Landscapes, Natures, Ecologies*, edited by Serenella Iovino, Enrico Cesaretti, and Elena Past. Charlottesville: University of Virginia Press, 2018.

———. "Environmental Imperialism in Sardinia: Pesticides and Politics in the Struggle against Malaria." In *Nature and History in Modern Italy*, edited by Marco Armiero and Marcus Hall, 70–88. Athens: Ohio University Press, 2010.

Handy, Jim. *Revolution in the Countryside: Rural Conflict and Agrarian Reform in Guatemala, 1944–1954*. Chapel Hill: University of North Carolina Press, 1994.

———. "'A Sea of Indians': Ethnic Conflict and the Guatemalan Revolution, 1944–1952." *The Americas* 46, no. 2 (1989): 189–204.

———. "The Violence of Dispossession: Guatemala in the Nineteenth and Twentieth Centuries." In *Politics and History of Violence and Crime in Central America*, edited by Sebastian Huhn and Hannes Warnecke-Berger, 281–323. New York: Palgrave Macmillan, 2017.

Harms, Patricia. "God Doesn't Like the Revolution: The Archbishop, the Market Women, and the Economy of Gender in Guatemala, 1944–1954." *Frontiers: A Journal of Women's Studies* 32, no. 2 (2011): 111–39.

Harrar, George J. "Draft of 'Agricultures and the Rockefeller Foundation.'" June 1, 1951. *100 Years: The Rockefeller Foundation*. Last accessed August 10, 2022. https://rockfound.rockarch.org/digital-library-listing/-/asset_publisher/yYxpQ-feI4W8N/content/draft-of-agriculture-and-the-rockefeller-foundation-.

Harris, M., and Eric D. Carter. "Muddying the Waters: A Political Ecology of Mosquito-Borne Disease in Rural Ecuador." *Health and Place* 57 (2019): 330–38.

Harvey, T. S. "Maya Mobile Medicine in Guatemala: The 'Other' Public Health." *Medical Anthropology Quarterly* 25, no. 1 (2011): 47–68.

Helton, Laura, et al. "The Question of Recovery: An Introduction." *Social Text* 33, no. 4 (2015): 1–18.

Hendrickson, Brett. *Border Medicine: A Transcultural History of Mexican-American Curanderismo*. New York: New York University Press, 2014.

———. "Neo-shamans, Curanderos, and Scholars: Metaphysical Blending in Contemporary Mexican American Folk Healing." *Nova Religio: The Journal of Alternative and Emergent Religions* 19, no. 1 (2015): 25–44.

———. "New Contexts for Curanderismo: Recasting Mexican American Folk Healing within American Metaphysical Religion." *Journal of the American Academy of Religion* 81, no. 3 (September 2013): 620–43.

———. "Restoring the People: Reclaiming Indigenous Spirituality in Contemporary Curanderismo." *Spiritus: A Journal of Christian Spirituality* 14, no. 1 (spring 2014): 76–83.

Hernández Sáenz, Luz María. "Matters of Life and Death: The Hospital of San Pedro in Puebla, 1790–1802." *Bulletin of the History of Medicine* 76, no. 4 (2002): 669–97.

Hernández Sáenz, Luz María, and George M. Foster. "Curers and their Cures in Colonial New Spain and Guatemala: The Spanish Component." In *Mesoamerican Healers*, edited by Brad R. Huber and Alan R. Sandstrom, 19–46. Austin: University of Texas Press, 2001.

Hernández Sandoval, L. Bonar. *Guatemala's Catholic Revolution: A History of Religious and Social Reform, 1920–1968*. Notre Dame, IN: University of Notre Dame Press, 2019.

Herrera, A. Robinson. *Natives, Europeans, and Africans in Sixteenth-Century Santiago de Guatemala*. Austin: University of Texas Press, 2003.

Hines, Sarah. "The Power and Ethics of Vernacular Modernism: The Misicuni Dam Project in Cochabamba, Bolivia, 1944–2017." *Hispanic American Historical Review* 98, no. 2 (2018): 223–56.

Hinojosa, Servando. *In this Body: Kaqchikel Maya and the Grounding of Spirit*. Albuquerque: University of New Mexico Press, 2015.

Hochman, Gilberto. "From Autonomy to Partial Alignment: National Malaria Programs in the Time of Global Eradication, Brazil, 1941–1961." *Canadian Bulletin of Medical History* 25, no. 1 (2008): 161–91.

Hochman, Gilberto, and Diego Armus. *Cuidar, controlar, curar: Ensaios históricos sobre saúde e doença na América Latina e Caribe*. Rio de Janeiro: Fiocruz, 2004.

Hochman, Gilberto, et al., eds. *Patologías de la patria. Enfermedades, enfermos y nación en América Latina*. Buenos Aires: Lugar Editorial, 2012.

Hoffman, Beatrix. *Health Care for Some: Rights and Rationing in the United States since 1930*. Chicago: University of Chicago Press, 2012.

Hogarth, Rana A. *Making Racial Difference in the Atlantic World, 1780–1840*. Chapel Hill: University of North Carolina Press, 2017.

Honigsbaum, Mark. *Fever Trail: In Search for the Cure for Malaria*. New York: Farrar, Straus and Giroux, 2001.

Hooker, Juliet. "Race and the Space of Citizenship: The Mosquito Coast and the Place of Blackness and Indigeneity in Nicaragua." In *Blacks and Blackness in Central America: Between Race and Place*, edited by Lowell Gudmundson and Justin Wolfe, 246–77. Durham, NC: Duke University Press, 2010.

Hornblum, A. M. *Acres of Skin: Human Experiments at Holmesburg Prison*. New York: Routledge, 1998.

Huber, Brad R. "Introduction." In *Mesoamerican Healers*, edited by Brad R. Huber and Alan R. Sandstrom. Austin: University of Texas Press, 2001.

Huber, Brad R., and Alan R. Sandstrom, eds. *Mesoamerican Healers*. Austin: University of Texas Press, 2001.

Humphreys, Margaret. *Malaria: Poverty, Race, and Public Health in the United States*. Baltimore: Johns Hopkins University Press, 2001.

Hunt, Nancy Rose. *A Colonial Lexicon: Of Birth Ritual, Medicalization, and Mobility in the Congo*. Durham, NC: Duke University Press, 1999.

Hurtado, Elena, and Eugenia Sáenz de Tejada. "Relations between Government Health Workers and Traditional Midwives in Guatemala." In *Mesoamerican Healers*, edited by Brad R. Huber and Alan R. Sandstrom, 211–42. Austin: University of Texas Press, 2001.

Icú Perén, Hugo. "Revival of Maya Medicine and Impact for Its Social and Political Recognition in Guatemala: A Case Study Commissioned by the Health Systems Knowledge Network." Unpublished manuscript, March 2007.

International Association of Medical Assistance for Travelers. "Guatemala General Health Risks: Malaria." Last accessed August 25, 2021. https://www.iamat.org /country/guatemala/risk/malaria.

Iovino, Serenella, Enrico Cesaretti, and Elena Past, eds. *Italy and the Environmental Humanities: Landscapes, Natures, Ecologies*. Charlottesville: University of Virginia Press, 2018.

Iturralde, Diego G. "Nacionalidades Indígenas y estado nacional en Ecuador." In *Nueva historia del Ecuador, volumen 12. Ensayos generals II: nación, estado y sistema político*, edited by Enrique Ayala Mora, 9–58. Quito: Editorial Grijalbo Ecuatoriana/Corporación Editora Nacional, 1995.

Izcara, Jorge. *Huasipungo*. Quito: Imprenta Nacional, 1936.

Jaffray, Nora. *Reproduction and Its Discontents in Mexico: Childbirth and Contraception from 1750–1905*. Chapel Hill: University of North Carolina Press, 2016.

Jaramillo Alvarado, Pio. *El indio ecuatoriano: contribución al estudio de la sociología indoamericana*. Quito: Editorial Casa de la Cultura Ecuatoriana, 1954 [1922].

Jarcho, Saul. *Quinine's Predecessor: Francesco Troti and the Early History of Cinchona*. Baltimore: Johns Hopkins University Press, 1993.

John, Maria. "The Violence of Abandonment: Urban Indigenous Health and the Settler Colonial Politics of Non-Recognition in the United States and Australia." *Native American and Indigenous Studies* 7, no. 1 (Spring 2020): 87–120.

Jonas, Susanne. *The Battle for Guatemala: Rebels, Death Squads, and U.S. Power*. Boulder, CO: Westview Press, 1991.

José Marín, Juan. "De curanderos a médicos. Una aproximación a la historia social de la medicina en Costa Rica: 1800–1949." *Revista de Historia* (Costa Rica) 32 (July-December 1995): 72–76.

Juárez Muñoz, Fernando. *El indio guatemalteco: ensayo de sociología nacionalista*. Guatemala City: Tipografía Latina, 1931.

Kapeluz-Poppi, Ana María. "Rural Health and State Construction in Post-Revolutionary Mexico: The Nicolaita Project for Rural Medical Services." *The Americas* 58, no. 2 (2001): 261–83.

Kimball, Natalie L. *An Open Secret: The History of Unwanted Pregnancy and Abortion in Modern Bolivia*. Newark, NJ: Rutgers University Press, 2020.

Kipple, Kenneth. *The Caribbean Slave: A Biological History*. Cambridge, UK: Cambridge University Press, 2002.

Kirkpatrick, Michael D. "Consumer Culture in Guatemala City During the 'Season of Luis Mazzantini', 1905: The Political Economy of Consumption." *Journal of Latin American Studies* 52, no. 4 (2020): 735–58.

———. "Phantoms of Modernity: The 1894 Anarchist Furor in the Making of Modern Guatemala City." *Urban History* 44, no. 2 (2017): 231–52.

Kleinman, Arthur. *Writing at the Margin: Discourse Between Anthropology and Medicine*. Berkeley: University of California Press, 1995.

Knipper, Michael. "Antropología y 'crisis de la medicina': el patólogo M. Kuczynski-Godard (1890–1967) y las poblaciónes nativas en Asia Central y Perú." *Dynamis* 29 (2009): 97–121.

Komisaruk, Catherine. *Labor and Love in Guatemala: The Eve of Independence*. Stanford, CA: Stanford University Press, 2013.

Koppe-Santamaría, Gema. *In the Vortex of Violence: Lynching, Extralegal Justice, and the State in Post-Revolutionary Mexico*. Berkeley: University of California Press, 2020.

Kowii, Ariruma. "El *Sumak Kawsay*." In *Antología del pensamiento crítico ecuatoriano contemporáneo*, edited by Gioconda Herrera Mosquera, et al., 437–44. Buenos Aires: Centro Latinoamericano de Ciencias Sociales, 2018.

Kraut, Alan M. *Silent Travelers: Germs, Genes, and the "Immigrant Menace."* Baltimore: Johns Hopkins University Press, 1994.

Lambe, Jennifer. *Madness: Psychiatry and Politics in Cuban History*. Chapel Hill: University of North Carolina Press, 2017.

Landázuri Camacho, Mariana. *Juana Miranda: fundadora de la maternidad en Quito*. Quito: Banco Central, 2004.

Lane, Kris. *Quito, 1599: City and Colony in Transition*. Albuquerque: University of New Mexico Press, 2002.

Lanning, John Tate. *The Royal Protomedicato: The Regulation of Medical Professions in the Spanish Empire*. Edited by John Jay TePaske. Durham, NC: Duke University Press, 1985.

Lanzarotta, Tess. "Ethics in Retrospect: Biomedical Research, Colonial Violence, and Iñupiat Sovereignty in the Alaskan Arctic." *Social Studies of Science* 50, no. 5 (2020): 778–801.

Larson, Brooke. *The Trials of Nation Making: Liberalism, Race, and Ethnicity in the Andes, 1810–1910*. Cambridge, UK: Cambridge University Press, 2004.

Leavitt, Judith Walzer. *Brought to Bed: Childbearing in America, 1750–1950*. New York: Oxford University Press, 1986.

———. *Typhoid Mary: Captive to the Public's Health*. Boston: Beacon Press, 1988.

LeBaron, Charles W., and David N. Taylor. "Typhoid Fever." In *Cambridge Historical Dictionary of Disease*, edited by Kenneth F. Kipple, 345–49. Cambridge: Cambridge University Press, 2003.

Lefler, Lisa, ed. *Under the Rattlesnake: Cherokee Health & Resiliency.* Tuscaloosa: University of Alabama Press, 2009.

Lei, Sean Hsiang-lin. *Neither Donkey Nor Horse: Medicine in the Struggle Over Chinese Medicine.* Chicago: University of Chicago Press, 2014.

León, Luis. *La Llorona's Children: Religion, Life, and Death in the U.S.-Mexican Borderlands.* Berkeley: University of California Press, 2004.

León Trujillo, Jorge G. "Un Sistema político regionalizado y su crisis." In *Ecuador en crisis. Estado, etnicidad y movimientos sociales en la era de la globalización*, 28–37. Barcelona: ICARIA, 2003.

———. "Política y movimientos sociales en el Ecuador de entre dos siglos." In *Estado del país. Informe Cero. Ecuador 1950–2010*, edited by FLACSO, et al., 207–29. Quito: Estado del País, 2011.

Lerner, Adrián. "Crecimiento urbano, salud pública y saneamiento en Iquitos (c. 1860–1980)." In *Salud pública en el Perú del siglo XX: paradigmas, discursos y políticas*, edited by Jorge Lossio and Eduardo Barriga, 19–45. Lima: Instituto Riva-Agüero, 2017.

Lewis, Oscar. *Life in a Mexican Village: Tepoztlán Revisited.* Urbana: University of Illinois Press, 1963.

Lewis, Stephen E. *Rethinking Mexican Indigenismo: The INI's Coordinating Center in Highland Chiapas and the Fate of a Utopian Project.* Albuquerque: University of New Mexico Press, 2018.

Little, Walter. "A Visual Political Economy of Maya Representations in Guatemala, 1931–1944." *Ethnohistory* 55, no. 4 (2008): 633–63.

Lipp, Frank. "A Comparative Analysis of Southern Mexican and Guatemalan Shamans." In *Mesoamerican Healers*, edited by Brad R. Huber and Alan R. Sandstrom, 95–143. Austin: University of Texas Press, 2001.

Livingston, Julie. *Improvising Medicine: An African Oncology Ward in an Emerging Cancer Epidemic.* Durham, NC: Duke University Press, 2012.

Lokken, Thomas Paul. "Marriage as Slave Emancipation in Seventeenth-Century Rural Guatemala." *The Americas* vol. 58, no. 2 (2001): 175–200.

———. "The Challenge of Reform: Pluralism and Repression in Guatemala, 1920–1944." Master's thesis, University of Saskatoon, 1989.

López-Cevallos, Daniel, and Chunhui Chi. "Healthcare Utilization in Ecuador: A Multilevel Analysis of Socio-Economic Determinants and Inequality Issues." *Health Policy Plan* 25, no. 3 (2010): 209–18. http://www.ncbi.nlm.nih.gov/pubmed/19917653.

López-Durán, Fabiola. *Eugenics in the Garden: Transatlantic Architecture and the Crafting of Modernity.* Austin: University of Texas Press, 2008.

Lovell, George W. "In the Wake of Columbus: Amerindian Antecedents to COVID-19." *Active History*, June 23, 2020. https://activehistory.ca/2020/06/in-the-wake-of-columbus-amerindian-antecedents-to-covid-19.

Löwy, Ilana. "Historiography of Biomedicine: 'Bio,' 'Medicine,' and In Between." *ISIS* 102, no. 1 (2011): 116–22.

———. *Virus, moustiques, et modernité: A fiévre jaune au Brésil entre sicence et politique*. Paris: Archives Contemporaines, 2001.

Lucero, José Antonio. "Locating the 'Indian Problem': Community, Nationality, and Contradiction in Ecuadorian Indigenous Politics." *Latin American Perspectives* 30, no. 1 (2003): 23–48.

Lutz, Christopher. *Santiago de Guatemala, 1541–1773*. Norman: University of Oklahoma Press, 1994.

MacLeod, Murdo J. *Spanish Central America: A Socioeconomic History, 1520–1720*. Berkeley: University of California Press, 1973.

Maiguascha, Juan. "Los sectores subalternos en los años 30 y el aparecimiento del velasquismo." In *Las crisis en el Ecuador: los treinta y ochenta*, edited by Rosemary Thorpe, 79–94. Quito: Corporación Editora Nacional, 1991.

Maiguashca, Juan, and Liisa North. "Origenes y significado del velasquismo: lucha de clases y participación politica en el Ecuador, 1920–1972." In *La cuestión regional y el poder*, edited by Rafael Quintero, 89–159. Quito: Corporación Editora Nacional, 1991.

Malavassi Aguilar, Ana Paulina. "Análisis sobre la inmunización contra las enfermedades prevenibles en Costa Rica y su impacto social, 1950–2000: una mirada crítica de las políticas públicas a través de las Memorias de Salud." In *Historia de las desigualdades sociales en América Central. Una visión interdisciplinaria. Siglos XVIII-XXI*, edited by Ronny J. Viales Hurtado and David Díaz Arias, 354–78. San José: CIHAC, 2016.

———. *Entre la marginalidad social y las orígenes de salud público*. San José: Editorial de la Universidad de Costa Rica, 2003.

Mallon, Florencia. *Courage Tastes of Blood: The Mapuche Community of Nicolás Ailío and the Chilean State, 1906–2001*. Durham, NC: Duke University Press, 2005.

———, ed. *Decolonizing Native Histories: Collaboration, Knowledge, and Language in the Americas*. Durham, NC: Duke University Press, 2011.

———. "Indian Communities, Political Cultures, and the State in Latin America, 1780–1990." *Journal of Latin American Studies* 24 (1992): 35–53.

———. *Peasant and Nation: The Making of Postcolonial Mexico and Peru*. Berkeley: University of California Press, 1995.

Maloney, Gerardo F. "El negro y la cuestión nacional." In *Nueva historia del Ecuador, volumen 12. Ensayos generals II: nación, estado y sistema político*, edited by Enrique Ayala Mora, 59–98. Quito: Editorial Grijalbo Ecuatoriana/Corporación Editora Nacional, 1995.

Marchán Romero, Carlos. "La crisis de los años treinta: differenciación social de sus efectos económicos." In *Las crisis en el Ecuador: los treinta y ochenta*, edited by Rosemary Thorpe, 31–60. Quito: Corporación Editora Nacional, 1991.

Martínez García, Yesenia. "Michel Foucault y su planteamiento teórico para estudiar los enfermos, las enfermedades y las politícas de salud en Honduras, 1880–1954." Unpublished manuscript, 2018.

Martínez Martín, Abel Fernando. *El Lazareto de Boyacá: lepra, medicina, iglesia y estado, 1869–1916*. Tunja: Universidad Pedagógica y Tecnológica de Colombia, 2006.

Martínez Paláez, Severo. *La Patria del Criollo: An Interpretation of Colonial Guatemala*. Edited by Christopher Lutz and George Lovell. Durham, NC: Duke University Press, 2009.

Masferrer, Alberto. *"El mínimum vital."* *Cultura: revista del Ministerio de Educación*, no. 47 (1968): 117–32.

Matthew, Laura E. *Memories of Conquest: Becoming Mexicano in Colonial Guatemala*. Chapel Hill: University of North Carolina Press, 2012.

Maxwell, Judith M., and Robert M. Hill III, trans. and exegesis. *Kaqchikel Chronicles: The Definitive Edition*. Austin: University of Texas Press, 2006.

McCrea, Heather. *Diseased Relations: Epidemics, Public Health, and State-Building in Yucatán, Mexico, 1847–1924*. Albuquerque: University of New Mexico Press, 2011.

McCook, George Stuart. *States of Nature: Science, Agriculture, and Environment in the Spanish Caribbean, 1760–1940*. Austin: University of Texas Press, 2002.

McCreery, David. "Coffee and Indigenous Labor in Guatemala, 1871–1980." In *The Global Coffee Economy in Africa, Asia, and Latin America, 1500–1989*, edited by William Gervase Clarence-Smith and Steven Topik, 206–31. Cambridge, UK: Cambridge University Press, 2003.

———. "Guatemala City." In *The 1918–1919 Pandemic Influenza: The Urban Impact in the Western World*, edited by Fred R. van Hartesveldt, 161–83. New York: The Edwin Mellen Press, 1992.

———. *Rural Guatemala, 1760–1940*. Stanford, CA: Stanford University Press, 1994.

———. *The Sweat of Their Brow: A History of Work in Latin America*. Armonk, NY: M. E. Sharpe, 2000.

Mckiernan-González, Raymond John. *Fevered Measures: Public Health and Race at the Texas-Mexico Border, 1848–1942*. Durham, NC: Duke University Press, 2012.

McNeill, John R. *Something New under the Sun: An Environmental History of the Twentieth-Century World*. New York: Norton, 2000.

———. *Mosquito Empires: Ecology and War in the Greater Caribbean, 1620–1914*. Cambridge, UK: Cambridge University Press, 2010.

Messer, Ellen. "The Hot and Cold in Mesoamerican Indigenous and Hispanicized Thought." *Social Science and Medicine* 25 (1987): 339–46.

Meyer, Manuella. "Madness and Psychiatry in Latin America's Long Nineteenth Century." In *The Routledge History of Madness and Mental Health*, edited by Greg Eghigian, 193–209. New York: Routledge, 2017.

Miles, Ann. *Living with Lupus: Women and Chronic Illness in Ecuador*. Austin: University of Texas Press, 2013.

Minich Avril, Julie. "Enabling Whom?: Critical Disability Studies Now." *Lateral* 5, no. 1 (2016), https://csalateral.org/issue/5-1/forum-alt-humanities-critical-disability-studies-now-minich.

Michel, Joanna, et al. "Ethnomedical Research and Review of Q'eqchi Maya Women's Reproductive Health in the Lake Izabal Region of Guatemala: Past, Present and Future Prospects." *Journal of Ethnopharmacology*, February 3, 2016. https://doi.org/10.1016/j.jep.2015.12.006.

Mitchell, B. R. *International Historical Statistics: The Americas, 1750–1988.* 2nd ed. New York: Stockton Press, 1993.

Mitman, Gregg. "In Search of Health: Landscape y Disease in American Environment History." *Environmental History* 10 no. 2 (April 2005): 184–210.

Mol, Annemarie. *The Body Multiple: Ontology in Medical Practice.* Durham, NC: Duke University Press, 1998.

Molina Jiménez, Iván. "Clase, género, y etnia van a la escuela. El alfabetismo en Costa Rica y Nicaragua (1880–1950)." In *Educando a Costa Rica. Alfabetización popular, formación docente y género (1880–1950),* edited by Iván Molina Jiménez and Steven Palmer, 19–55. San José: Editorial Porvenir, 2003.

Molina, Natalia. "Medicalizing the Mexican: Immigration, Race, and Disability in Early Twentieth-Century United States." *Radical History Review* 94 (Winter 2006): 22–37.

Montoya, Michael. *Making the Mexican Diabetic: Race, Science, and the Genetics of Inequality.* Berkeley: University of California Press, 2011.

Morales, Edmundo. *The Guinea Pig: Healing, Food, and Ritual in the Andes.* Tucson: University of Arizona Press, 1995.

Morgan, Lynn Marie. *Community Participation in Health: The Politics of Primary Care in Costa Rica.* Cambridge, UK: Cambridge University Press, 1993.

———. "International Politics and Primary Health Care in Costa Rica." *Social Science and Medicine* 30, no. 2 (1990): 211–19.

Murard, Lion, and Patrick Zylberman. "Seeds for French Health Care: Did the Rockefeller Foundation Plant the Seeds between the Two World Wars?" *Studies in the History and Philosophy of Biology and Biomedical Sciences* 31, no. 3 (2000): 463–75.

Muscucci, Orella. *The Science of Women: Gynecology and Gender in England, 1800–1929.* Cambridge, UK: Cambridge University Press, 1990.

Nading, Alex M. "'Love Isn't There in Your Stomach': A Moral Economy of Medical Citizenship among Nicaraguan Community Health Workers." *Medical Anthropology Quarterly* 27, no. 1 (2013): 84–102.

Nguyen, Vinh-Kim. *The Republic of Therapy: Triage and Sovereignty in West Africa's Time of AIDS.* Durham, NC: Duke University Press, 2010.

Necochea López, Raúl. *A History of Family Planning in Twentieth-Century Peru.* Chapel Hill: University of North Carolina Press, 2014.

Newson, A. Linda, *Life and Death in Early Colonial Ecuador.* Norman: University of Oklahoma Press, 1995, 88–89, 151–52.

———. *Making Medicines in Early Colonial Lima, Peru: Apothecaries, Science and Society.* Leiden: Brill, 2017.

Noguera, Carlos Ernesto. *Medicina y política: discurso médico y prácticas higiénicas durantes la primera mitad del siglo XX en Colombia.* Medellín: Fondo Editorial Universidad EAFIT, 2003.

Nelson, Diane M. *Who Counts? The Mathematics of Death and Life after Genocide.* Durham, NC: Duke University Press, 2015.

Nugent, David. *The Encrypted State: Delusion and Displacement in the Peruvian Andes.* Stanford, CA: Stanford University Press, 2019.

———. *Modernity at the Edge of Empire: State, Individual and Nation in the Northern Peruvian Andes, 1885–1935.* Stanford, CA: Stanford University Press, 1997.

Núñez Butrón, Manuel. "Qué es el Rijchardismo?" *Medicina social* 3 (1944).

Oakes, Maud. *The Two Crosses of Todos Santos.* New York: Series Bollingen XXVII, 1951.

Obregon, Diana. *Batallas contra la lepra: estado, medicina y ciencia en Colombia.* Medellín, Colombia: Banco de la República—Fondo Editorial Universidad EAFIT, 2002.

———. "Building National Medicine: Leprosy and Power in Colombia, 1870–1910." *Social History of Medicine* 15 (2002): 89–108.

O'Brien, Elizabeth. "'If They Are Useful, Why Expel Them?': Las Hermanas de la Caridad and Religious Medical Authority in Mexico City Hospitals, 1861–1874." *Mexican Studies/Estudios Mexicanos* 33, no. 3 (Fall 2017): 22, 23, 25–26, 417–42.

———. "Pelvimetry and the Persistence of Racial Sciences in Obstetrics." *Endeavor* 37, no. 1 (2012): 21–28.

———. *Spiritual Surgery: The Roots of Reproductive Injustice in Mexico (1770–1940).* Chapel Hill: University of North Carolina Press, 2023.

O'Connor, Erin. "Helpless Children or Undeserving Patriarchs? Gender Ideologies, the State and Indian Men in Late Nineteenth-Century Ecuador." In *Highland Indians and the State in Modern Ecuador,* edited by Kim Clark and Marc Becker, 56–71. Pittsburgh: University of Pittsburgh Press, 2007.

Oliver, Lilia V. "El cólera y los barrios de Guadalajara en 1833 y en 1850." In *Salud, cultura y sociedad en América Latina,* edited by Marcos Cueto, 87–100. Washington, DC: Organización Panamericana de la Salud—Instituto de Estudios Peruanos, 1996.

Olsson, Tore C. *Agrarian Crossings: Reformers and the Remaking of the US and Mexican Countryside.* Princeton, NJ: Princeton University Press, 2017.

Oosterhuis, Harry, and Frank Huisman. "The Politics of Health and Citizenship: Historical and Contemporary Perspectives." In *Health and Citizenship: Political Cultures of Health in Modern Europe,* edited by Frank Huisman and Harry Oosterhuis, 1–40. London: Pickering and Chatto Publishers, 2013.

Orellana, Sandra. *Indian Medicine in Highland Guatemala: The Prehispanic and Colonial Periods.* Albuquerque: University of New Mexico Press, 1987.

Ospina Peralta, Pablo. *La aleación inestable: origen y consolidación de un Estado transformista: Ecuador, 1920–1960.* Buenos Aires/Ecuador: Editorial Teseo/Universidad Andina Simón Bolívar, Sede Ecuador, 2020.

Osseo-Asare, Abena Dove. *Bitter Roots: The Search for Healing Plants in Africa.* Chicago: University of Chicago Press, 2014.

———. "Writing Medical Authority: The Rise of Literate Healers in Ghana, 1930–1970." *Journal of African History* 57, no. 1 (2016): 69–91.

Otovo, T. Okezi. *Progressive Mothers, Better Babies: Race, Public Health, and the State in Brazil, 1850–1945*. Austin: University of Texas Press, 2016.

Pacino, Nicole. "Constructing a New Bolivian Society: Public Health Reforms and the Consolidation of the Bolivian National Revolution." *The Latin Americanist* 57, no. 4 (2013): 25–55.

———. "Liberating the People From Their 'Loathsome Practices:' Public Health and 'Silent Racism' in Post-Revolutionary Bolivia." *História, Ciências, Saúde-Manguinhos* 24, no. 4 (October/December 2017). http://doi.org/10.1590/s0104-59702017000500014.

Packard, Randal. *A History of Global Health: Interventions into the Lives of Other Peoples*. Baltimore: Johns Hopkins University Press, 2016.

———. *The Making of a Tropical Disease: A Short History of Malaria*. Baltimore: Johns Hopkins University Press, 2007.

Paige, M. Jeffrey. *Coffee and Power: Revolution and the Rise of Democracy in Central America*. Cambridge, MA: Harvard University Press, 1997.

Palacios, Nicolás. *Raza Chilena*. NP: 1904.

Palmer, Steven. "Caminos transnacionales de la ciencia aplicada en Guatemala." *Mesoamérica* 32, no. 53 (2011): 1–6.

———. "Central American Encounters with Rockefeller Public Health, 1914–1921." In *Close Encounters of Empire*, edited by Gilbert M. Joseph, Catherine C. LeGrand, and Ricardo D. Salvatore, 311–32. Durham, NC: Duke University Press, 1998.

———. *Launching Global Health: The Caribbean Odyssey of the Rockefeller Foundation*. Ann Arbor: University of Michigan Press, 2010.

———. *From Popular Medicine to Medical Populism: Doctors, Healers, and Public Power in Costa Rica, 1800–1940*. Durham, NC: Duke University Press, 2003.

Paredes, Ricardo. *Oro y sangre en Portocavelo*. Quito: Editorial Artes Gráficas, 1938.

Paul, Benjamin D., and Clancy McMahon. "Mesoamerican Bonesetters." In *Mesoamerican Healers*, edited by Brad R. Huber and Alan R. Sandstrom, 243–69. Austin: University of Texas Press, 2001.

Paulin, James E. "Medical Citizenship." *The Georgia Review* 1, no. 4 (1947): 445–51.

Paz Soldán, Carlos Enrique. *La medicina social: ensayo de sistematización*. Lima: Imprenta SS CC, 1916.

Peard, Julyan. *Race, Place, and Medicine: The Idea of the Tropics in Nineteenth-Century Brazil*. Durham, NC: Duke University Press, 1999.

Peña Torres, María Ligia. *Historia de la salud pública en Nicaragua: del protomedicato a la Dirección General de Sanidad 1859–1956*. Managua: IHNCA-UCA, 2014.

———. "Entre curanderos y médicos: disputas por las prácticas curativas en Nicaragua 1915–1928." Paper presented at VI Congreso Centroamericano, Managua, July 11–13, 2017.

Peña Torres, María Ligia, and Steven Palmer. "A Rockefeller Foundation Health Primer for US-Occupied Nicaragua, 1914–1928." *CBMH/BCHM* 25, no. 1 (2008), 43–69.

Pernick, Martin S. *A Calculus of Suffering: Pain, Professionalism, and Anesthesia in Nineteenth Century America.* New York: Columbia University Press, 1985.

———. *The Black Stork: Eugenics and the Death of "Defective" Babies in American Medicine and Motion Pictures since 1915.* New York: Oxford University Press, 1996.

Petryana, Adriana. *When Experiments Travel: Clinical Trials and the Global Search for Human Subjects.* Princeton, NJ: Princeton University Press, 2009.

Pieper Mooney, Jadwiga E. "From Cold War Pressures to State Policy to People's Health: Social Medicine and Socialized Medical Care in Chile." In *Peripheral Nerve: Health and Medicine in Cold War Latin America*, edited by Anne-Emanuelle Birn and Raúl Necochea López, 187–210. Durham, NC: Duke University Press, 2020.

Pineo, Ronn. *Ecuador and the United States: Useful Strangers.* Athens: University of Georgia Press, 2007.

———. "Misery and Death in the Pearl of the Pacific: Health Care in Guayaquil, Ecuador, 1870–1925." *Hispanic American Historical Review* 70, no. 4 (1990): 609–37.

———. *Social and Economic Reform in Ecuador: Life and Work in Guayaquil.* Gainesville: University of Florida Press, 1996.

Pitti, Joseph. "Jorge Ubico and Guatemalan Politics in the 1920s." Ph.D. diss., University of New Mexico, 1975.

Pohl-Valero, Stefan. "'La raza entra por la boca': Energy, Diet, and Eugenics in Colombia, 1890–1940." *Hispanic American Historical Review* 94, no. 3 (2014): 455–86.

Premo, Bianca. *The Enlightenment on Trial: Ordinary Litigants and Colonialism in the Spanish Empire.* New York: Oxford University Press, 2017.

Prieto, Mercedes. *Liberalismo y temor: imaginando los sujetos indígenas en el Ecuador postcolonial, 1895–1950.* Quito: FLACSO/Ediciones Abya Yala, 2004.

Pribilsky, Jason. "Development and the 'Indian Problem' in the Cold War Andes: 'Indigenismo', Science, and Modernization in the Making of the Cornell-Peru Project at Vicos." *Diplomatic History* 33, no. 3 (2009): 405–26.

Proctor, Robert. *Racial Hygiene: Medicine Under the Nazis.* Cambridge, MA: Harvard University Press, 1988.

Quintero, Rafael, and Erika Silva. *Ecuador: una nación en ciernes.* Tomo II. Quito: FLACSO/Abya-Yala, 1991.

Radin, Joanna. "Digital Natives: How Medical and Indigenous Histories Matter for Big Data." *Osiris* 32, no. 1 (2017). http://doi.org/10.1086/693853.

Radkau, Joachim. *Nature and Power: A Global History of the Environment.* Cambridge, UK: Cambridge University Press, 2002.

Reeves, René. *Ladinos with Ladinos, Indians with Indians: Land, Labor, and Regional Ethnic Conflict in the Making of Guatemala.* Stanford, CA: Stanford University Press, 2006.

Reggiani, Andrés H. "De rastacueros a expertos: modernización, diplomacia cultura y circuitos académicos transnacionales, 1870–1940." In *Los lugares del saber:*

contextos locales y redes transnacionales en la formación del conocimiento moderno, edited by Ricardo Salvatore, 159–87. Rosario, Argentina: Beatriz Viterbo Editora, 2007.

Restall, Matthew, and Christopher Lutz. "Wolves and Sheep?: Black-Maya Relations in Colonial Guatemala and Yucatan." In *Beyond Black and Red: African-Native Relations in Colonial Latin America*, edited by Matthew Restall, 185–221. Albuquerque: University of New Mexico Press, 2005.

Reverby, Susan M. *Examining Tuskegee: The Infamous Syphilis Study and Its Legacy.* Chapel Hill: University of North Carolina Press, 2013.

————. "'Normal Exposure' and Inoculation Syphilis: A PHS 'Tuskegee' Doctor in Guatemala, 1946–1948." *The Journal of Policy History* 23, no. 1 (2011): 7–28.

Rivera-Garza, Cristina. "The Criminalization of the Syphilitic Body: Prostitutes, Health Crimes, and Society in Mexico City, 1867–1930." In *Crime and Punishment in Latin America: Law and Society Since Late Colonial Times*, edited by Ricardo D. Salvatore, Carlos Aguirre, and Gilbert M. Joseph, 147–80. Durham, NC: Duke University Press, 2001.

Roberts, Elizabeth F. S. *God's Laboratory: Assisted Reproduction in the Andes.* Berkeley: University of California Press, 2012.

Rodas, Isabel, and Edgar Esquit. *Élite ladina-vanguardia indígena: de tolerancia a la violencia, Patzicía 1944.* Guatemala City: CAUDAL, 1997.

Rodas Chaves, Germán, ed. *Revolución Juliana: y salud colectiva.* Quito: Universidad Andina Simón Bolívar/Corporación Editora Nacional, 2012.

————. *Pensamiento médico: el liberalismo radical y la Revolución Juliana: trazos de la figura de Isidro Ayora.* Quito: Universidad Andina Simón Bolívar, 2017.

Rodríguez, Linda Alexander. *The Search for Public Policy: Regional Politics and Government Finances in Ecuador, 1830–1940.* Berkeley: University of California Press, 1985.

Rodríguez, Daniel A. *The Right to Live in Health: Medical Politics in Postindependent Havana.* Chapel Hill: University of North Carolina Press, 2020.

Rodríguez, Julia. *Civilizing Argentina: Science, Medicine, and the Modern State.* Chapel Hill: University of North Carolina Press, 2006.

Rocco, Fiammetta. *The Miraculous Fever Tree: Malaria and the Quest for a Cure That Changed the World.* New York: Harper Collins, 2003.

Rogaski, Ruth. *Hygienic Modernity: Meanings of Health and Disease in Treaty-Port China.* Berkeley: University of California Press, 2014.

Rohloff, Peter, and Magda Sotz Mux. *Tiq'aqomaj Qi': plantas medicinales y enfermedades communes.* Bethel, VT: Editorial Wuqu' Kawoq, 2008.

Romeu Diaz, Guillermo. "Del Régimen de Carlos Herrera a la Elección de Jorge Ubico." In *Historia General de Guatemala, Tomo V Epoca Contemporánea: 1898–1944*, edited by Jorge Luján Muñoz (director general) and J. Daniel Contreras R. (director del tomo), 37–42. Guatemala City: Asociación de Amigos del País, Fundación para la Cultura y el Desarrollo, 1996.

Rose, Nikolas. *The Politics of Life Itself: Biomedicine, Power, and Subjectivity in the Twenty-First Century.* Princeton, NJ: Princeton University Press, 2006.

Rosemblatt, Karin Alejandra. "Other Americas: Transnationalism, Scholarship, and the Culture of Poverty in Mexico and the United States." *Hispanic American Historical Review* 89, no. 4 (2009): 603–41.

Rosenberg, Charles E. *Cholera Years: The United States in 1832, 1849, and 1866*. Chicago: University of Chicago Press, 1987.

——. Foreword to *The Making of a Tropical Disease: A Short History of Malaria*, by Randal Packard, vii–x. Baltimore: Johns Hopkins University Press, 2007.

Rosier, Paul C. *Serving Their Country: American Indian Politics and Patriotism in the Twentieth Century*. Cambridge, MA: Harvard University Press, 2009.

Ross, Paul. "Mexico's Superior Health Council and the American Public Health Association: The Transnational Archive of Porfirian Public Health, 1887–1910." *Hispanic American Historical Review* 89, no. 4 (2009): 573–602.

Roth, Cassia. *Miscarriage of Justice: Women's Reproductive Lives and the Law in Early Twentieth-Century Brazil*. Stanford, CA: Stanford University Press, 2020.

Rouaret Rodríguez, Francisco. *Diccionario Municipal de Guatemala*. Guatemala City: Instituto de Estudios y Capacitación Cívica, 1996.

Rubel, Arthur J. "The Epidemiology of a Folk Illness: Susto in Hispanic America." *Ethnology* 3, no. 3 (1964): 268–83.

Rubio Orbe, Gonzalo. *Los indios ecuatorianos: evolución histórica y políticas indigenistas*. Quito: Corporación Editora Nacional, 1987.

Ruggiero, Kristin. "Honor, Maternity, and the Disciplining of Women: Infanticide in Late Nineteenth-Century Buenos Aires." *Hispanic American Historical Review* 72, no. 3 (1992): 353–73.

Rushforth, Brett. "The *Gauolet* Uprising of 1710: Maroons, Rebels, and the Informal Exchange Economy of a Caribbean Sugar Island." *William and Mary Quarterly* 76, no. 1 (January 2019): 75–110.

Sáenz, Alvaro, and Diego Palacios. "La dimensión demográfica del a historia ecuatoriana." In *Nueva historia del Ecuador, volumen 12. Ensayos generals I: espacio, población, región*, edited by Enrique Ayala Mora, 135–74. Quito: Editorial Grijalbo Ecuatoriana/Corporacion Editora Nacional, 1992.

Sáenz, Moisés. *Sobre el indio ecuatoriano y su incorporación al medio nacional*. Mexico City: Publicaciones de la Secretaría de Educación Pública, 1933.

Sal y Rosas, F. "El mito del Jani o Susto de la medicina indígena del Peru." *Revista de la Sanidad de Policia* (Lima) 18 (1958): 167–210.

Saldaña-Portillo, Josefina María. *Indian Given: Racial Geographies across Mexico and the United States*. Durham, NC: Duke University Press, 2016.

Sánchez Parga, José. *Etnia, poder y diferencia en los Andes septentrionales*. Quito: Ediciones Abya Yala, 1990.

Santoro, Miléna, and Erick D. Langer, eds. *Hemispheric Indigeneities: Native Identity and Agency in Mesoamerica, the Andes, and Canada*. Lincoln: University of Nebraska Press, 2018.

Satter, Aleezé. "*Indígena o Ciudadano?* Republican Laws and Highland Indian Communities in Ecuador, 1820–1857." In *Highland Indians and the State in Mod-*

ern Ecuador, edited by A. Kim Clark and Marc Becker, 22–36. Pittsburgh, PA: University of Pittsburgh Press, 2007.

Saunders, John. *The People of Ecuador: A Demographic Analysis*. Gainesville: University of Florida Press, 1961.

Schell, Patience. "Eugenics Policy and Practice in Cuba, Puerto Rico, and Mexico." In *Oxford Handbook of Global Eugenics*, edited by Alison Bashford and Philippa Levine, 485–87. New York: Oxford University Press, 2011.

Schneider, William H. "The Model American Foundation Officer: Alan Gregg and the Rockefeller Foundation Medical Divisions." *Minerva* 41, no. 2 (2003): 155–66.

Selis Lope, Mario. *Secretos de la raza: creencias, costumbres, medicina y supersticiones de los indígenas de la Verapaz*. Cobán, A. V.: Tipografía "El Norte," 1931.

Sellers-García, Sylvia. "Una plaga occulta: violencia y salud pública en la cuidad de Guatemala durante la colonia." *Mesoamérica* 38, no. 59 (2017): 1–22.

Sharon, Douglas. *Wizard of the Four Winds*. New York: The Free Press, 1978.

Shein, Max. *El niño precolumbiano*. Mexico, DF: Editorial Villicaña S.A., 1986.

Sherchand, J. B., et al. "A Preliminary Study on the Field Trials with Insecticide-Treated Mosquito Nets for Malaria Control in Rural Endemic Communities of Nepal." *Journal of Nepal Medical Association* 33 (1995): 195–203.

Siebenga, Rianne. "Colonial India's 'Fanatical Fakirs' and Their Popular Representations." *History and Anthropology* 23, no. 4 (2012): 445–66.

Sieder, Rachel. "'Paz, progreso, justicia y honradez': Law and Citizenship in Alta Verapaz during the Regime of Jorge Ubico." *Bulletin of Latin American Research* 19, no. 3 (2000): 283–302.

Sigerist, Henry E. "Medical History in Central and South America." In *Bulletin of the History of Medicine* 9, no. 3 (1942): 342–60.

Silverblatt, Irene. *Sun, Moon, and Witches: Gender Ideologies and Class in Inca and Colonial Peru*. Princeton, NJ: Princeton University Press, 1987.

Simmons, James Stevens. *Malaria in Panama*. Baltimore: Johns Hopkins University Press, 1939.

Smith, Carol. "Origins of the National Question in Guatemala: A Hypothesis." In *Guatemalan Indians and the State: 1540–1988*, edited by Carol Smith, 72–95. Austin: University of Texas Press, 1990.

———. "Race-Class-Gender Ideology in Guatemala: Modern and Anti-Modern Forms." *Comparative Studies in Society and History* 37 (1995): 723–49.

Smith, Linda Tuhiwai. *Decolonizing Methodologies: Research and Indigenous Peoples*. New York: Zed Books, 1999.

Smith, Linda Tuhiwai, Eve Tuck, and K. Wayne Yang, eds. *Indigenous and Decolonizing Studies in Education: Mapping the Long View*. New York: Routledge, 2019.

Smith, Yolanda. "Typhoid Fever History." *Medical and Life Sciences News*, April 29, 2021. Last accessed May 23, 2022. https://www.news-medical.net/health/Typhoid-Fever-History.aspx.

Socolow, Susan Migden. *Women of Colonial Latin America*. Cambridge, UK: Cambridge University Press, 2000.

Solomon, Frank. "The Fury of Andrés Arévalo: Disease Bundles of a Colonial Andean Shaman." In *Political Anthropology in Ecuador: Perspectives from Indigenous Cultures*, edited by Jeffrey Ehrenreich, 83–105. Albany: State University of New York, 1985.

———. "Shamanism and Politics in Late-Colonial Ecuador." *American Ethnologist* 10 (1983): 413–28.

Soluri, John. *Banana Cultures: Agriculture, Consumption, and Environmental Change in Honduras and the United States.* Austin: University of Texas Press, 2005.

Sosa, Ximena, and Cecilia Durán. "Familia, ciudad y vida cotidiana en el siglo XIX." In *Nueva historia de Ecuador: época republicana II*, 157–91. Quito: Universidad Andina Simón Bolívar/Corporación Editora Nacional, 2018.

Soto Laveaga, Gabriela. "Bringing the Revolution to Medical Schools: Social Service and a Rural Health Emphasis in 1930s, Mexico." *Estudios Mexicanos/Mexican Studies* 29, no. 2 (Summer 2013): 397–427.

———. *Jungle Laboratories: Mexican Peasants, National Projects, and the Making of the Pill.* Durham, NC: Duke University Press, 2009.

Sowell, David. *Medicine on the Periphery: Public Health in the Yucatán, Mexico, 1870–1960.* Lanham, MD: Lexington Books, 2015.

———. *The Tale of Healer Miguel Perdomo Neira: Medicine, Ideologies, and Power in the Nineteenth-Century Andes.* Wilmington, DE: Scholarly Resources, 2001.

Steere, William Campbell. "The Cinchona Bark Industry of South America." *Scientific Monthly* 61, no. 2 (1945): 114–26.

Steltzer, Ulli. *Health in the Guatemalan Highlands.* Vancouver: Douglas and McIntyre, 1983.

Stepan, Nancy Leys. "The National and the International in Public Health: Carlos Chagas and the Rockefeller Foundation in Brazil, 1917–1930s." *Hispanic American Historical Review* 91, no. 3 (2011): 469–502.

———. *"The Hour of Eugenics": Race, Gender, and Nation in Latin America.* Ithaca, NY: Cornell University Press, 1991.

———. "The Only Serious Terror in these Regions: Malaria Control in the Brazilian Amazon." In *Disease in the History of Modern Latin America*, edited by Diego Armus, 25–50. Durham, NC: Duke University Press, 2003.

Stern, Alexandra Minna. "Buildings, Boundaries, and Blood: Medicalization and Nation-Building on the U.S.-Mexico Border, 1910–1930." *Hispanic American Historical Review* 79, no. 1 (February 1999): 41–81.

———. *Eugenic Nation: Faults and Frontiers of Better Breeding in Modern America.* Berkeley: University of California Press, 2015.

———. "Responsible Mothers and Normal Children: Eugenics, Nationalism, and Welfare in Postrevolutionary Mexico, 1920–1940." *Journal of Historical Sociology* 12, no. 4 (1999): 369–97.

Stevenson, Lisa. *Life Beside Itself: Imagining Care in the Canadian Arctic.* Berkeley: University of California Press, 2014.

Stoler, Ann. *Race and the Education of Desire: Foucault's History of Sexuality and the Colonial Order of Things*. Durham, NC: Duke University Press, 1995.

Street, Alice. *Biomedicine in an Unstable Place: Infrastructure and Personhood in a Papua New Guinean Hospital*. Durham, NC: Duke University Press, 2014.

Striffler, Steve. *In the Shadows of State and Capital: The United Fruit Company, Popular Struggle, and Agrarian Restructuring in Ecuador, 1900–1995*. Durham, NC: Duke University Press, 2001.

Stutzman, Ronald. "El Mestizaje: An All-Inclusive Ideology of Exclusion." In *Cultural Transformation and Ethnicity in Modern Ecuador*, edited by Norman Whitten, 45–94. Urbana: University of Illinois Press, 1981.

Suárez, Arturo Pablo. *Contribución al studio de la alimentación y nutrición del Indio de Otavalo*. Quito: Imprenta de la Universidad Central, 1943.

———. *Contribución al estudio de las realidades entre las clases obreras y campesinas*. Quito: Imprenta de la Universidad Central, 1934.

Suárez, Laura. *Eugenesia y racismo en México*. Mexico: Universidad Nacional Autonoma, 2005.

Suárez-Díaz, Edna. "Indigenous Populations in Mexico: Medical Anthropology in the Work of Ruben Lisker in the 1960s." *Studies in History and Philosophy of Biological Sciences* 47 (2014): 108–17.

Sufian, Sandra. *Healing the Land and the Nation: Malaria and the Zionist Project in Palestine, 1920–1947*. Chicago: University of Chicago Press, 2008.

Sutphen, Mary P. "Not What, but Where: Bubonic Plague and the Reception of Germ Theories in Hong Kong and Calcutta, 1894–97." *Journal of the History of Medicine and Allied Sciences* 52, no. 1 (1997): 81–113.

Sutter, Paul S. "Nature's Agents or Agents of Empire?: Entomological Workers and Environmental Change during the Construction of the Panama Canal." *Isis* 98, no. 4 (2007): 724–54.

Sweet, James. *Domingo Álvares, African Healing, and the Intellectual History of the Atlantic World*. Chapel Hill: University of North Carolina Press, 2011.

Tagboto, Senyo, and Simon Towson. "Antiparasitic Properties of Medicinal Plants and Other Naturally Occurring Products." *Advances in Parasitology* 50 (2001): 199–295.

Taracena Arriola, Arturo, ed. *Etnicidad, estado y nación en Guatemala. Vol. 1, 1808–1944*. Vol. II: 1944–1985. Antigua, Guatemala, 2002.

———. *Invención criolla, sueño ladino, pesadilla indígena: Los Altos de Guatemala, de región a estado, 1740–1850*. San José, Costa Rica: Editorial Porvenir/CIRMA/Delegación Regional de la Cooperación Técnica y Científica del Gobierno de Francia, 1997.

———. "Marimba." In *The Guatemala Reader*, edited by Greg Grandin, Deborah T. Levenson, and Elizabeth Oglesby, 150–55. Durham, NC: Duke University Press, 2011.

Tapia, Maria. *Embodied Protests: Emotions and Women's Health in Bolivia*. Champaign: University of Illinois Press, 2015.

Tedlock, Dennis, trans. *Popol Vuh: The Maya Book of the Dawn of Life*. New York: Simon & Schuster, 1996.

———. *Time and the Highland Maya*. Albuquerque: University of New Mexico Press, 1992.

Termer, Franz. *Ethnología y ethnografía de Guatemala*. Guatemala City: Editorial de Ministerio de Educación Pública, 1957.

Thompson, Eric. *The Rise and Fall of Maya Civilization*. 2nd ed. Durham, NC: Duke University Press, 1966.

Thoresen, Beate. "Rebellion without a Shot—Peaceful Conflict Management in Ecuador." *Conflict, Security & Development*, 9, no. 3 (2009): 361–85.

Tilley, Helen. *Africa as a Living Laboratory: Empire, Development, and the Problem of Scientific Knowledge, 1870–1950*. Chicago: University of Chicago Press, 2011.

———. "Ecologies of Complexity: Tropical Environments, African Trypanosomiasis and the Science of Disease Control in British Colonial Africa, 1900–1940." *Osiris* 19 (2004): 21–38.

———. "Medicine, Empires, and Ethics in Colonial Africa." *AMA Journal of Ethics* 18, no. 7 (July 2016): 743–53.

Tilley, Virginia Q. "*Mestizaje* and the 'Ethnicization' of Race in Latin America." In *Race and Nation: Ethnic Systems in the Modern World*, edited by Paul Spickard, 82–109. London: Routledge, 2005.

Tobar Cruz, Pedro. *Los Montañeses*. Guatemala City: Ministerio de Educación Pública, 1959.

Trefzger, Douglas W. "Guatemala's 1952 Agrarian Reform Law: A Critical Reassessment." *International Social Science Review* 77, no. 1/2 (2002): 32–46.

Trouillot, Rolph-Michel. *Silencing the Past: Power and Production of History*. Boston: Beacon Press, 1995.

Tschopik, H. "The Aymara of Chucuito, Peru: Magic." *Anthropological Papers of the American Museum of Natural History* 44 (1951): 133–308.

Tuck, Eve. "Suspending Damage: A Letter to Communities." *Harvard Educational Review* 79, no. 3 (2009): 409–27.

Turner, Sasha. *Contested Bodies: Pregnancy, Childrearing, and Slavery in Jamaica*. Philadelphia: University of Pennsylvania Press, 2017.

Tworek, Heidi J. S. "Communicable Disease: Information, Health, and Globalization in the Interwar Period." *American Historical Review* 124, no. 3 (2019): 813–42.

Tzian, Leopoldo. *Kajab'aliil Maya'iib' Xuq Mu'siib': Ri Ub'antajiik Iximulew/Mayas y ladinos en cifras: El caso de Guatemala*. Guatemala City: Cholsamaj, 1994.

Urías Horcasitas, Beatriz. *Historias secretas del racismo en México (1920–1950)*. México: Tusquets Editores México, 2007.

———. "Degeneracionismo e higiene mental en el México posrevolucionario (1920–1940)." *Frenia* 4, no. 2 (2004): 37–67.

Urioste, George L. "Sickness and Death in Preconquest Andean Cosmology: The Huarochiri Oral Tradition." In *Health in the Andes*, edited by John Bastien and John M. Donahue. Washington, DC: American Anthropological Association, 1981.

Valarezo Galo, Ramón. *El regreso de los runas:la potencialidad del proyecto indio en el Ecuador contemporáneo*. Quito: COMUNIDEC Fundación Interamericana, 1993.

Van Reenen, Johann. "What Is Social Medicine? The US-European Perspective." 2008. http://digitalrepository.unm.edu/lasm_cucs_en/138.

Vasconcelos, José. *La raza cósmica*. Mexico City: Espasa Calpe SA, 1948.

Vásquez, María Antonieta. "Familia, costumbre y vida cotidiana a principios del siglo XX." In *Nueva historia del Ecuador, volumen 8. Epoca Republicana III: cacao, capitalismo, y revolución*, edited by Manuel Chiriboga and Guillermo Bustos, 205–33. General editor, Enrique Ayala Mora. Quito: Editorial Grijalbo Ecuatoriana/Corporación Editora Nacional, 1990.

Vásquez Lapeyre, Luis. "Patología y población indígena del Peru." *Peru Indígena* 2 (1952): 48–55.

Vaughn, Megan. "Healing and Curing: Issues in the Social History and Anthropology of Medicine in Africa." *Social History of Medicine* 7 (1994): 283–95.

Vélez, Jorge Luis, and Paulina Cifuentes. "Vida y legado de Dr. Pablo Arturo Suárez a la medicina ecuatoriana." *Revista Médica Vozandes*, 29, no. 1 (2018): 25, 28, 31.

Ventura Santos, Ricardo, Carlos E. A. Coimbra Jr., and Joanna Radin. "Why Did They Die?' Biomedical Narratives of Epidemics and Mortality Among Amazonian Indigenous Populations in Sociohistorical and Anthropological Contexts." *Current Anthropology* 61, no. 4 (2020). http://doi.org/10.1086/710079.

Vieira de Campos, André Luiz. *Políticas internacionais de saúde na Era Vargas: O Servicio Especial de Saúde Pública, 1942–1960*. Rio de Janeiro: Fiocruz, 2006.

Viesca Treviño, Carlos. "*Curanderismo* in Mexico and Guatemala: Its Historical Evolution from the Sixteenth to the Nineteenth Century." In *Mesoamerican Healers*, edited by B. R. Huber and A. R. Sandstrom. Austin: University of Texas Press, 2001.

Vizenor, Gerald. *Survivance: Narratives of Native Presence*. Lincoln: University of Nebraska Press, 2009.

———. *Fugitive Poses: Native American Indians' Sense of Absence and Presence*. Lincoln: University of Nebraska Press, 1998.

———. *Manifest Manners: Post-Indian Warriors of Survivance*. Lincoln: University of Nebraska Press, 1999.

Vrana, Heather. "The Imperative of Developmental Natalism: Endemic Goiter and El Salvador's Battle Against *Cretinismo*." *American Historical Review*, forthcoming.

Wagley, Charles. *The Social and Religious Life of a Guatemalan Village*. Menasha, WI: American Anthropological Association, 1949.

Wailoo, Keith, et al. *A Death Retold: Jessica Santillan, the Bungled Transplant, and Paradoxes of Medical Citizenship*. Chapel Hill: University of North Carolina Press, 2006.

Waitzkin, Howard, et al. "Social Medicine Then and Now: Lessons from Latin America." *American Journal of Public Health* 91, no. 10 (October 2001): 1592–1601.

Warren, Adam. "Between the Foreign and the Local: French Midwifery, Traditional Healers, and Vernacular Knowledge about Childbirth in Lima, Peru." *História, Ciências, Saúde—Manguinhos* 22, no. 1 (2015): 179–200.

———. "Dorotea Salguero and the Gendered Persecution of Unlicensed Healers in Early Republican Peru." In *The Gray Zones of Medicine: Healers and History in Latin America*, edited by Diego Armus and Pablo F. Gómez, 55–73. Pittsburgh: University of Pittsburgh Press, 2021.

———. *Medicine and Politics in Colonial Peru: Population Growth and the Bourbon Reforms*. Pittsburgh: University of Pittsburgh Press, 2010.

Warren, Kay. *Symbolism of Subordination: Indian Identity in a Guatemalan Town*. Austin: University of Texas Press, 1978.

Washington, Harriet. *Medical Apartheid: The Dark History of Medical Experimentation on Black Americans from Colonial Times to the Present*. New York: Penguin Random House, 2008.

Webb, James Jr. *Humanity's Burden: A Global History of Malaria*. New York: Cambridge University Press, 2009.

———. *The Long Struggle Against Malaria in Tropical Africa*. Cambridge, UK: Cambridge University Press, 2014.

Webb, Meghan, and Miguel Cuj. "Guatemala's Public Health Messaging in Mayan Languages during the COVID-19 Pandemic." *Journal of Indigenous Social Development*, 9, no. 3 (2020): 103–9.

Weber, Jonathan M. *Death is All Around Us: Corpses, Chaos, and Public Health in Porfirian Mexico City*. Lincoln: University of Nebraska Press, 2019.

Weber, Max. *The Protestant Ethic and the Spirit of Capitalism*. London: Routledge, 2005.

Webre, Stephen. "The Wet Nurses of Jocotenango: Gender, Science, and Politics in Late-Colonial Guatemala." *Colonial Latin American Historical Review* 10 (Spring 2001): 173–97.

Wertz, Richard and Dorothy. *Lying-in: A History of Childbirth in America*. New Haven, CT: Yale University Press, 1989.

Whitlock, Ralph. *Everyday Life of the Maya*. New York: Hippocrene Books, 1987.

Williams, Derek. "The Making of Ecuador's *Pueblo Católico*, 1861–1875." In *Political Cultures in the Andes*, edited by Nils Jacobson and Cristóbal Alvojín de Losada, 207–29. Durham, NC: Duke University Press, 2005.

Williams, Raymond. *Marxism and Literature*. Oxford: Oxford University Press, 1977.

Williford, Miriam. "Las luces y la civilización: The Social Reforms of Mariano Gálvez." In *Applied Enlightenment 19th Century Liberalism*, edited by Mario Rodríguez, 37–40. New Orleans: Middle American Research Institute, Tulane University, 1972.

Wisdom, Charles. *The Chorti Indians of Guatemala*. Chicago: University of Chicago Press, 1940.

Wolfe, Mikael D. *Watering the Revolution: An Environmental and Technological History of Agrarian Reform in Mexico*. Durham, NC: Duke University Press, 2017.

Woodward, Ralph Lee, Jr. *Rafael Carrera and the Emergence of the Republic of Guatemala, 1821–1871*. Athens: University of Georgia Press, 1993.

Ximénez, Francisco. *Historia natural del reino de Guatemala*. Guatemala City: José Pineda Ibarra, 1967.

Yarza de los Ríos, Alexander. "Abya Yala's Disability: Weaving with the Thread and Breath of the Ancestors." *Disability Studies Quarterly* 41, no. 4 (Fall 2021), https://dsq-sds.org/article/view/8445/6300.

Zeller, Diane. "The Establishment of Western Medicine in Buganda." Ph.D. diss., Columbia University, 1971.

Zárate, María Soledad. *Dar a luz en Chile, siglo XIX: de la "ciencia de hembra" a la ciencia obstétrica*. Santiago, Chile: University de Alberto Hurtado, 2007.

Zulawski, Ann. "Environment, Urbanization, and Public Health: The Bubonic Plague Epidemic of 1912 in San Juan, Puerto Rico." *Latin American Research Review* 53, no. 3 (2018): 500–16.

———. *Unequal Cures: Public Health and Political Change in Bolivia, 1900–1950*. Durham, NC: Duke University Press, 2007.

INDEX

Note: Page numbers in *italics* denote photos and maps.

abbreviations: used in notes, 227–28; used in text, xxviii

abortion and abortifacients, 92, 252n50

achi'lib'al (companionship), 60

Africa: colonial collaboration with local leaders for public health interventions, 263n110; criminalization and persecution of healers, 248n114; and malaria, 177, 273n8; midwifery, 258n210; model villages (Nigeria), 262n70; traditional medicine denigrated by scientific medicine, 231–32nn43,46, 242n212. *See also* British East Africa

African Americans: medical experiments on, 211; midwives, 253n96

Africanist historiography of health, 17–18

Afro-Central Americans, racial medicalization of tropical diseases and, 11, *12*, 185–86, *186*

Afro-Ecuadorians: overview, 229n14; and malaria in the highlands, 197–99, 280n175; racism and the racial hierarchy and, 5–6, 229n14; slave labor of, 5, 280n175

Afro-Guatemalans: overview, 229n14; criminalization and persecution of healers, 73–74, *74*; Garífunas (African-Arawak), 6; racial medicalization and, 11, *12*; racism and the racial hierarchy and, 6, 229n14; traditional healing practices of, 66, 246n55

agro-export economy: cacao trade, and improvements in indígenas autonomy and mobility, 30, 31–33; conscription of indigenous labor, 2, 29–30; as dependent on migrant labor, 198; land dispossession and expansion of, 2, 29, 37, 55; quinine, 179–80. *See also* coffee plantations; land dispossession; poverty as a structural determinant of indigenous health disparities; United Fruit Company

Aguascalientes, Guatemala, 181–82, 187–90

Aguila, Rafael, 137

Aguilar, Salvador G., 270n89

Aimacana, Juan Pedro, 138–39

alcohol: corn-beer establishments (chicherías), 134, 158; during pregnancy, 254; funerary practices and, 152; moonshine, 66, 69–70, 128; stereotype of inebriation, 30, 134

Alfaro, Eloy, 31

Allende, Salvador, 238n87

Alvear, Abel, 82–84, 95, 99, 144

American College of Surgeons, 42

American Public Health Association, tainted with imperialism, 42

Anderson, Warwick, 45, 120–21, 262n70

Andrada, J. M. Reina, 165

Anopheles guatemalnesis, 185, 191

Anopheles hectoris, 185, 191

Anopheles pseudopunctipennis, 191

Anopheles xelopiensis, 185, 191
antibacterial medicines, 7
antibiotics, 7; as typhoid treatment, 149
Anzueto, C. Rodrico, 67–68
Arbenz Guzmán, Jacobo, 171, 220, 221
archives: Ecuador and Guatemala's indigenous populations as too large for erasure from, xix; hybrid healthcare as demonstrated in, xiii–xiv, xx–xxi, xxii; indígena as term in, xx, 5; indigenous midwives' absence from, 98, 102; material culture of, as conveying the hierarchies of power, xxiv; silences on intersections of indigeneity and medicine, generally, xix, xx, 17–18, 139–40, 265n151; sources for the text, xxi, xxii–xxiv; unreliability of data in, xxiv–xxv, 161, 181, 195, 228n12
Arévalo Bermejo, José: and association of indígenas with disease, 172; election of, as free and fair, 40, 128; expansion of indígenas healthcare access, 133, 220; and infant mortality, 115; involuntary medical research occurring during administration of, 41, 212; Kaqchikel massacre following election of, 40, 240n140; Kaqchikel Maya on the democratic government of, 128, 171, 220; literacy materials developed in indigenous languages, 171; and migrant worker conditions, 196; Social Security Law, 40, 41; suffrage expanded by, 40; and turn toward acknowledgment of the state's failure to provide for indígenas, 40–41; and typhus, 170–71, 172
Argentina: and malaria control, 278n126; midwife certification, 250n16; postcolonial extermination campaigns against indígenas, 265n153; racial medicalization in, 11
Asociación Médica de Quito, 33
Asturias, Miguel Angel, 48, 75, 127, 128, 216–17
Aymara, xii–xiii, 61. *See also* Bolivia
Ayora Cueva, Isidro Ramon Antonio, 33, 88, 155
Ayora, José María, 31
Aztecs, maternal and infant health, 249n3

Bacillus Calmette-Guérin (BCG), 95
banana plantations. *See* United Fruit Company
Bautista-Valarezo, Estefanía, 145
Bayer, 75
Becerra, León, 154, 157, 201
Bedón, Rocío, xxii
Behrhorst, Carroll, 221–22
Birn, Anne-Emanuelle, 257n192
blackwater fever, 11
blanco-mestizos (Ecuador), definition of, 5. *See also* race and racism; racial order
blood, in indigenous worldviews and healing traditions: bloodletting practice, 25, 26; and Mayan reproductive health, 235n23; as sacred and finite, and resistance to blood draws, 126; as symbol of colonial violence, on clothing, 218
Bolivia: clothing worn by market women, prohibitions on, 266n163; poverty and health disparities of indígenas in, xii–xiii; quinine production, 179; racist thought and, 132
bonesetters: in the hierarchical spectrum of curanderos, 64; Ubico consulting, 57. *See also* indigenous healing practices
Brazil: COVID-19 pandemic, indígenas as hardest hit by, 224; homeopathy endorsed and regulated by, 75; infant mortality programs, 249–50n8, 250n16; RF hookworm project in, 43; RF malaria project in, 13, 178, 201; RF racism and, 51; RF yellow fever project in, 13
Britain, and quinine, 179, 183
British East Africa, 179, 248n114, 266–67n182, 284n44
British Guiana, 44
British India, 179, 266–67n182
Brown, Peter, 178
brujas (social healers, witches): and competency of individual practitioners, 75; dolls and other effigies used by, 69; empírica critique of, 222–23; and the medicine/poison continuum, 64; midwifery combined with, 111; and the power to both heal and harm, 63, 69, 245n41. *See also* indigenous healing practices

brujería (witchcraft): as Catholic church framing of indigenous healers, condemnation and punishment of, 27; indigenistas condemning, 128; police conflation of fraudulence with, 67–68, 69, 73, 76, 77, 248n114

Buß, Gerhard Enno, 48

bubonic plague: conscription of labor as spreading, 135; criticism of local authorities for neglect of hygiene, 135–36; Ecuadorian public health campaign (rat hunters), and indigenous movement against, 137–40, 141, 264–65n139; Ecuador study by PASB, 33; fleas as transmitting, 135, 141; migration of labor as spreading, 275n52; racial medicalization of, 11, 135, 158; railroads transporting infected rats to the highlands, 135

Burres, William T., 50–53, 183

Cabrera, Isidro, xxv, 169

cacao trade, and improvements in indígenas autonomy and mobility, 30, 31–33

Cacuango, Dolores, 35

Callas, Plutarco Elias, 243n1

Campos Po, Francisco, 203

Cárdenas, Lázaro, 278n126

Caribbean: COVID-19 pandemic death toll, 224; malaria-free highlands in, 275n54

Carrera, Rafael, 37, 123

Carter, Eric, 196

Catholic church: framing and punishing indigenous healing as witchcraft (brujería), 27; the papacy and malaria, 187; quinine commercialization and, 179

—ECUADOR: colonial period sugar plantation with slave labor, 280n175; indígenas insurrection against church taxes, 30

—GUATEMALA: convincing indígenas the government was trying to poison them, 37, 122–23; indígenas characterized as superstitious and ignorant by, 130; Liberal attacks on, 40, 122–23

Catu, Germana, 85, 89

Central America: as network oriented by and toward the US, 44. See also Costa Rica; El Salvador; Guatemala; Nicaragua;

Panama; Rockefeller Foundation (RF); United States — imperialism

Central American Health Conference (1937), 256n168; infant mortality, 107–8; malaria control strategy, 191–92; malaria, racial medicalization of, 11, 12, 185–86, 186

certificates of good health, government issued, 163

Céspedes, Benjamín, 88

Chacón, Lázaro, 39, 188–89

Chávez, Rodrigo, 5

chenopodium, 28, 132–33

Chiapas, Maya communities of, xii–xiii, 178, 259n4

Chile: Allende as physician and focus on well-being in, 238n87; postcolonial extermination campaigns against indígenas, 265n153

Chimaltenango province (Guatemala): infant mortality in, 111; midwives in, 105; and typhus, 166

China: malaria in ancient China, 187; traditional medicine denigrated by scientific medicine, 231–32n46

cholera epidemic (1837), 37, 122–23

Ch'orti Maya: on causes of illness, 133; and hybrid healthcare, 28, 126; malaria remedies, 180; and the power to both heal and harm, 63–64; and resonances of scientific medicine with concepts of, 132

Chota Valley, Ecuador, 197–99, 280n175

citizenship. See medical citizenship; national belonging; voting rights of indígenas

Clark, A. Kim, 99, 140–41

class: Ecuadorian licensed midwives and tensions with clients, 99, 117; Ecuadorian turn to improvement of rural lives based on, 136; and employment opportunities for indígenas, 54; and Guatemalan denigration of indígenas, 51–52; malaria treatment and biases of, 38, 183, 196, 207; public health messaging framed with, 148, 151, 153; RF racism and, 51–52; UFCO providing healthcare to managers but not workers, 38. See also ethnicity; gender; poverty; race and racism clothing and appearance, indigenous: barefootedness, 46; *follón/centro*, traditional wide skirt of street and market vendors, xxi–xxii, 141; formal photograph (Guatemala), *16*; funerary practice of redistributing, 140; Guatemalan midwife requirement, as excluding indígenas, 104; hair cutting and head shaving in lice treatments, 166; symbols and colors used in, 217–18; Ubico encouragement of wearing in military parades, 129, 131; women market vendors, prohibitions on, xxi–xxii, 141, 266n163

coffee plantations (Guatemala): continued abuse of indigenous laborers facilitated by governments, 38–39, 188; infant mortality increasing during harvests, 106; and racist thought about indígenas, 52; RF hookworm campaigns and, 52–53; structural racism compelling indígenas labor migration to, 37. *See also* compulsory labor; land dispossession

Cold War, 278n126

Colom, Álvaro, 212

Colombia: homeopathy endorsed and regulated by, 75; international interventions in public health campaigns and, 42; quinine production, 179; racial medicalization of leprosy, 267n3; tensions with Ecuador about germs jumping borders, 206

colonialism and the colonial period: Andean indígena healing practices downplaying, 25, 235n20; Catholic church framing and punishing indigenous healing as witchcraft (brujería), 27; Catholic-owned sugar plantation with slave labor, 280n175; hybrid healthcare and, 27, 88, 283n30; indígenas blamed for their own ill health, 120–21; infant mortality increases due to European pathogens, 249n3; and introduction of European pathogens, 26–27, 37, 120–21, 210, 224, 249n3; mal de ojo as introduced by the Spanish, 60–61; midwifery and, 88; pre-contact population of indígenas, 224; structural racism

inhibiting indígenas' autonomy and agency, 29; violence of, as symbol on clothing, 217–18. *See also* United States— imperialism

comadronas. *See* midwifery and midwives

companionship (*achi'lib'al*), 60

complementary healthcare. *See* hybrid healthcare

compulsory labor of indígenas: bubonic plague spread through, 135; in the colonial period, 29; corvée labor, 162, 207; Ecuadorian system of, and reform, 30, 31–32, 135; epidemics and feigned illness to avoid, 9; Guatemalan system of, 29–30, 37, 38–39, 41, 55, 127, 162, 188, 207; malaria control projects using, 207; in the postcolonial period, 29; reinstatement under Orellana, 188; typhoid contracted through, 162. *See also* agro-export economy; migratory labor of indígenas; poverty as a structural determinant of indigenous health disparities

conventional medicine. *See* scientific medicine

corn-beer establishments (chicherías), 134, 158

Costa Rica: certification of traditional healers, 249n146; infant mortality laws and programs, 87, 107, 249–50n8; malaria control, 193; RF hookworm project in, 43–44; shutting down dissent, 222

COVID-19 pandemic, 223, 224

criminalization and persecution of indigenous healthcare and healers: as attack on indigenous worldviews and communities, 3; in British East Africa, 248n114; cities as focus of, 8, 77–78; deaths of patients and, 68; doctors enlisting authorities for, 28, 67; evasion of arrest by curanderos, 68; foreign healers, 73–75, 85; medical professionalization advanced through, 58–59, 67; medical school refusals to train indígenas, 28; of midwives, 67, 71–72, 73, 88, 89–90, 92, 98, 103, 104, 111, 215, 258n196; news coverage as generally focusing on, 57, 65, 68, 69, 70, 71, 72, 72, 74, 76, 77–78; police claims that fear of curanderos prevented denunciations, 71; police conflation of fraudulence with brujería and curanderismo, 67–68, 69, 73, 76, 77, 248n114; police differentiation between rogue and credible healers, 68, 75; police narratives of effectiveness of persecutions, 68, 72–73; police narratives of harms, 67–68, 73; political instability catalyzing actions, 62; racial thought as influencing, 77, 85; Ubico administration and, 57, 67–79. *See also* racial medicalization (linking illness and race)

Criollos (Creoles) (Guatemala), 6. *See also* race and racism; racial order

Cuba: criminalization and persecution of indigenous healthcare and healers, 246n67; discovery of mosquitoes as vectors, 13; Grau San Martín as physician and focus on well-being in, 238n87; international interventions in public health campaigns and, 42; mothers blamed for infant mortality, 257n189

Cueto, Marcos, xix, 81

culturalist model of disease, xi–xiv. *See also* poverty as a structural determinant of indigenous health disparities; professionalization of medicine; racial medicalization (linking illness and race)

Cumming, Hugh, 162

curanderismo, 59–60, 62, 71–72; criminalization and persecution of, 64, 67–68, 73, 75, 76, 128

curanderos (traditional healers): definition of, 1; empírico critiques of, 222–23; finca health clinics employing, 66; Guatemalan recognition of need for, where doctors were absent, 55; hierarchical spectrum of, 64; hospital position of curandero de establecimiento, 28–29, 57–58; malaria treatments by, 180; political leaders who conducted campaigns against indigenous healing as seeking out, 57, 243n1; and the power to both heal and harm, 63–64, 69, 133, 245n41; working alongside colonial

doctors, 27. *See also* brujas (social healers, witches); criminalization and persecution of indigenous healthcare and healers; empíricos; hybrid healthcare; indigenous healing practices; midwifery and midwives

Cutler, John C., 209

cuyes. *See* guinea pigs (cuyes)

Daquilema, Fernando, 30

data unreliability: in the archives, xxiv–xxv, 161, 181, 195, 228n12; corrupt statistics from Ubico era (Guatemala), 195. *See also* imperfect knowledge

Dawson, Thomas, 31

DDT, 133, 134

Deiseldorff, Guillermo "Willi," 108–9

de León, J. Romeo, 184, 191

Dieseldorff, Erwin Paul, 75–76

diet, indigenous: and guinea pigs (cuyes), importance in, 141; iron deficiencies in, and geophagy ("dirt-eaters"), 161–62, *161*; Kichwa healing practice of moderating, 25; the marketplace for, racialization of, xxi–xxii, 141, 143–44, *144*, 266n163; poverty and malnourishment, and susceptibility to disease, 198; public health campaigns to improve, 141–42

disabilities, people with: disability understood to be both a curse and a gift, 63–64; malaria as disabling condition, 191

disease and illness, defined and distinguished, 229n10

diseases, illnesses, and maladies: cholera epidemic (1837), 37, 122–23; COVID-19 pandemic, 223, 224; dog bite, 66; iron deficiencies, geophagy, 161–62; jigger (nigua), 13, 46; leprosy, 267n3; Madura foot, 13; measles, 120, 129, 168; pian (tropical skin infection), 11; river blindness (*Onchocerca volvulus*), 11; tetanus, 13. *See also* bubonic plague; hookworm; infant mortality; influenza pandemic (1918–1919); intestinal worms and parasites; malaria; mal de ojo (evil eye); sexually transmitted infections (STIs); smallpox; susto (fright); tuberculosis; typhoid fever; typhus; yellow fever

divination, 26, 64, 69, 101, 111
doctors. *See* scientific medical doctors
dog bite, 66

Eberth, Carl, 149
Ecuador: budget for public health, 34, 95,
  200; Central Assembly of Public Assistance (Junta Central de Asistenica
  Pública), 35–36; constitution (1896), 5;
  constitution (1906), 5; constitution
  (1929), 32–33; constitution (1945), 136;
  constitution (1979), 220; constitution
  (1998), traditional medicine practitioners recognized, 221, 223; constitution
  drafted to incorporate the indigenous
  principle of living in harmony with
  nature, 223; free healthcare mandate for
  municipalities (1913), 79; Glorious
  Revolution (1944), 34; international
  interventions as largely absent in, 36;
  Law of Civil Registry (of deaths, 1900),
  xxiv; Ley Boticas (Pharmacy Law, 1920),
  80; Ley de Comunas (Community Law,
  1937), 34; Liberal Revolution (1895), 30;
  map, *xxvi*; and the military, autonomy
  of, 136; pro-imperialist administrations,
  220–21; quinine (cinchona tree) protections, 179; Reforma de la Ley de Jornaleros (Day Laborers' Reform Law, 1918),
  32; representative form of government,
  2; Revolución Juliana (1925), 32–33. *See
  also* Ecuadorian Servicio de Sanidad
  (Health Service); indigenous healing
  practices— Kichwa; indigenous movements, Ecuador; Kichwas (Ecuador);
  social medicine
Ecuadorian National Department of
  Health of Indigenous Peoples, 223
Ecuadorian Servicio de Sanidad (Health
  Service): Ayora Cueva and reorganiza-
  tion and extension to rural areas, 33,
  237n85, 238n87; budget of, 34, 153–54;
  establishment of, 31; local-national
  government dynamics and, 82–84,
  135–36; recognition of the health benefits of the highlands, 11; resource
  allocation along racial and geographic
  lines, 34, 153–54, 219; and state recogni-

tion of the importance of public health,
  31, 33. *See also* public health
  campaigns— Ecuador
Elmendorff, John, 50
El Quiche province (Guatemala), and
  typhus, 166, 172
El Salvador: individual self-improvement
  vs. group characteristics, 264n130;
  infant mortality and, 107; international
  interventions in public health campaigns and, 42; malaria control, 193;
  malaria treatment by curandero, 180;
  RF hookworm project in, 43
empíricos: critiques of curanderos by,
  222–23; as crucial in anti-typhus campaigns, 170; definition of, 4; diversity
  among, 64; poverty of, and licensing
  fees as prohibitive, 63, 88, 104–5; state
  recognition as municipal empíricos,
  62–63, 67, 170. *See also* brujas (social
  healers, witches); criminalization and
  persecution of indigenous healthcare
  and healers; curanderos (traditional
  healers); hybrid healthcare; indigenous
  healing practices; midwifery and
  midwives
Enrique, Carlos, 167
environmental explanations for disease
  outbreaks in areas of nonindigenous
  majority population, 10, 162, 163, 166
Escalantes, David, 107
Eskey, C. R., 33
Espejo, Eugenio, 6, 28, 120, 236n46
Espinosa, J. M., 142, 147, 155–56, 158, 204–5
Estevez, Carlos, 193–94
Estrada Cabrera, Manuel: cozy relationship
  with RF, 14, 48–49, 52; foreign midwives hired by, 103, 255n143; infant
  mortality reductions under, 102; the
  influenza pandemic and overthrow of
  (1920), 123, 188; public health rhetoric
  not matched by action or allocation of
  resources, 38, 49; RF denigration of
  indígenas as pleasing to, 48; Ubico's
  medical authority removed under, 39
ethnicity: explanations for disease outbreaks involving nonindigenous regions
  and towns as avoiding reference to, 10,

162, 163, 166; shift away from pathologizing indígenas, 168–69, 172. *See also*
Ch'orti Maya; indígenas; indigenous
healing practices; Kaqchikel Maya;
K'iche' Maya; Kichwas (Ecuador); Mam
Maya; Mayas (Guatemala); Q'eqchi'
Maya; race and racism; racial medicalization (linking illness and race)
eugenics: national eugenics of integration
(Ecuador), 3–4, 79, 119, 121, 136, 212–13,
218. *See also* racial eugenics
Europe: infant mortality and, 86; malaria
and, 177, 178, 192, 273n8; quinine commercialization and, 179; typhus and,
165. *See also* colonialism and the colonial period; European traditional
healing practices
European traditional healing practices:
cold climates preferred for convalescence, 232n59; homeopathy, 75; humoral
view of health, 25, 27. *See also* miasma
theory
excremental colonialism, 45

Farmer, Paul, xii
Federación Ecuatoriana de Indios (FEI),
34, 136
Fermín Cevallos, Pedro, 30
Few, Martha, xxi
fincas (large, landed estates): health clinics
for workers employing curanderos, 66;
labor investments seldom made by, 195;
malaria control and, 194–95; RF hookworm campaigns on, 44, 45, *46*, 51,
52–53, 55, 243n222; typhus on, 168,
170–71. *See also* coffee plantations
fleas: bubonic plague transmission via, 135,
141; guinea pigs targeted for control due
to carrying, 141, 159–60; typhus transmission via, 159–60, 165
Flexner, Abraham, 243–44n7
flies, as vector, 112, *112*, 132, 163
Foley, Dorothy, 54
follón/centro, traditional wide skirt prohibited for street and market vendors,
xxi–xxii, 141
France: and infant mortality, 86; and
quinine commercialization, 180

Fuentes, Maria, 17
Fukuyama, Francis, 223
funerary practices, indigenous: alcohol
imbibing and, 152; as bubonic plague
risk, 140; cemetery siting, 152–53, 156;
cremation of loved ones to contain
public health risk, as sacrifice, 142;
nonindigenous practices as similar to,
157; typhoid and, 152–53, 156, 157;
typhus spreading due to crowded conditions at funerals, 150, 158; wakes as
unlikely transmission site for typhoid,
156; wakes, malaria as ending, 189;
wakes prohibited in some regions, 140,
156–57
Funes, Juan, 171, 209, 210, 212

Gaitán, Luis, 105–6, 107, 111–12, 195–96
Galich, Luis, 209
Gálvez, Maríano, 37, 123–24
Garcés, Enrique, speaking indigenous
language to convey public health messages, 2, 159–60, 173, 269n71
Garcés, Victor Gabriel, 141–42
García Moreno, Gabriel, 30
Garífunas (African-Arawak), 6. *See also*
Afro-Guatemalans
gender: blaming of women for infant
mortality, 106, 110, 111–12, *112*, 215,
257n189; female honor, 91, 100–101, 103,
106; female suffrage, 32–33, 40; femini-
zation (or lack thereof) of midwives and
curanderismo, 71–72; marketplace
racialization and, xxi–xxii, 141, 143–44,
144, 266n163; women's expected role in
research and scholarship, 256n168. *See
also* class; mothers; poverty; race and
racism
Generación del 20, 128
geophagy ("dirt-eaters"), 161–62, *161*
German planters: espousing Q'eqchi' ethics
of reciprocity and medicinal plants,
75–76; exoticizing indígenas healing,
76; exploitation of indigenous labor, 75;
and hookworm campaigns, 243n222;
philanthropic projects of, 108–9; racist
stereotyping of indígenas, 52; refusing
to collaborate with the RF, 52

guinea pigs (cuyes): dietary and cultural importance of, 141; public health campaigns to control, and resistance to, 141, 157–58, 159–60, 214; sleeping mats on the floor vs. beds, 141, 266n165–166; in susto treatment, 61

Gutiérrez, Lucio, 223

gynecology: medical experiments on enslaved women and founding of, 211; professionalization of medicine and transfer of authority and power from midwives to male doctors, 88–90, 91, 250n16, 253n96. *See also* hybrid healthcare; midwifery and midwives; scientific medicine

haciendas (highland Ecuador): García Moreno undercutting control over indigenous labor, 30; *huasipungo* system (work in exchange for plot of land to work), 35–36; liberal politics in opposition to, and improvement of standing of indígenas, 30, 31–33, 34, 35, 55; and malaria in the highlands, 197–99, 280n175. *See also* compulsory labor of indígenas; poverty as a structural determinant of indigenous health disparities

Hackett, Lewis, 53

Heiser, Victor, 49, 51

Herrera, Julio Roberto, 106, 168, 191–92

Hippocrates, 143

Hoffman, Beatrix, 230n17

homeopathy, 75

honor, female, 91, 100–101, 103, 106

Hooke, Robert, 263n100

hookworm: indigenous cure of *epazotl* (chenopodium), adopted by RF, 28, 132–33; symptoms of, 44. *See also* Rockefeller Foundation (RF), hookworm campaigns

hospitals: acceptance of care by indígenas, increases in, 155–56, 158; admittance document apparently misused as credential by a curandero, 76; class bias in workers' treatment in, 38, 183, 196, 207; curanderos employed in, 28–29, 57–58; infant mortality and modernization of,

108–9; involuntary and/or unethical medical experimentation in, 41, 209–12; isolation from family of rural indigenous patients sent to urban hospitals, 177, 196–97, 265n151; and local-national government dynamics, 82–84; lotteries in fundraising for, 153; malarial highlands patients sent for treatment to the capital (Guatemala City), 38, 177, 181, 196–97; malarial lowlands patients sent for treatment to the capital (Guatemala City), 181; maternity, and professionalization of medicine, 88, 102, 106, 109, 113–14; maternity, midwives employed in, 57, 103–4, 113–14, 116, 251n38 (*see also* midwifery and midwives); newspaper coverage contrasting modern environment against curanderos, 76; and nurses, status of, 249n148; quarantine facilities (lazaretos), 155, 166–67, 170; refusal of care by indígenas even when deathly ill, 158; RF photo of ward showing "Indian influence," as evidence of shallow understanding of indígenas, 217–18, *217. See also* hybrid healthcare; infant mortality; medical citizenship; midwifery and midwives; rural highlands, lack of professional healthcare in

housing, indigenous: architectural specifications issued, 141; bubonic plague controls on, 141; destruction of, as disinfectant, 141, 142; and poverty, 123–24, 141, 260–61n25; typhoid fever and disinfection of, 155; typhus spreading in crowded houses, 150; unnecessary mandate for mosquito-proof housing (due to altitude), 205. *See also* guinea pigs (cuyes)

housing, wealthy, poor hygiene and sanitation in, 266n165

Huehuetenango province (Guatemala), and typhus, 166, 167, 169, 172

humoral view of health: bacteriology as resonating with, 132; European practices, 25, 27; Kichwa practices, 24–25, 27 hybrid healthcare (medical pluralism): appropriation of indigenous practices by doctors and pharmacists, 28; the archives as demonstrating, xiii–xiv, xx–xxi, xxii; collective knowledge as basis of healing systems, 60; in the colonial period, 27, 88, 283n30; contestations of, 75–76; cooperation among practitioners, 27, 57–58, 61–62, 85, 213, 214, 214–15, 283nn29–30; diversity of patients seeking, 24, 57, 58, 76; effectiveness as most important to patients, 24, 57, 126, 133, 213; as hegemonic, 60; hookworm treatment with chenopodium, 28, 132–33; hospital employment of comadronas, 57, 103–4, 113–14, 116, 251n38; hospital employment of curanderos, 28–29, 57–58; as increasingly interconnected, xiv, 222; indígenas as embracing, 1–2, 28–29, 60, 66–67, 143; indigenous healing and cooptation of scientific medicine, 80–82, 85, 214, 248n128; and infant mortality, reduction of, 87; malaria treatment with quinine, 179–80; medical authorities prescribing indigenous treatments, 61, 244n19; midwifery and, 90, 99–100, 101, 111, 114, 117, 254n110, 258n210; no system had the capacity to eliminate another from the range of therapeutic possibilities, 4, 59–60, 62, 85, 87, 213, 219; packaged remedies as alluring to indígenas, 126; pharmacists filling medicinal plant prescriptions, 61; political leaders who conducted campaigns against indigenous healing as seeking out curanderos, 57, 243n1; pragmatism of approaches in, 57; state-sanctioned institutions and coexistence of modalities, 61–62, 269n70; and *Sumak Kawsay* or *buen vivir* (living well) philosophy as growing, 223; as syncretic care, xiv, 67, 100; trial and error as basis of healing systems, 60. *See also* indigenous healing practices; midwifery and midwives; scientific medicine; social medicine

Ibarra, Ecuador, 197–98, 201, 203–4
Ibarra, Velasco, 220–21

Idigoras, Alvaro, 106
illness, defined and distinguished, 229n10. *See also* diseases, illnesses, and maladies
Imbabura province (Ecuador), and malaria in the highlands, 197–99, 201, 203–4, 280n175
imperfect knowledge and public health campaigns: overview, 148–49; in Ecuador, 197, 200–201, 203–4, 205–6. *See also* data unreliability
imperialism. *See* United States— imperialism
indígenas (indigenous people): community and family, isolation of rural patients transferred to urban hospitals, 177, 196–97, 265n151; community and social welfare as ethic, and adaptation of public health mandates, 142; definition of and usage of term, xx, 5; diversity among, 5, 127; marginalization of, 146, 147; as percentage of population in Ecuador, 2, 30, 229n9, 237n63; as percentage of population in Guatemala, 6, 30, 231n30, 237n63. *See also* class; clothing and appearance, indigenous; diet, indigenous; funerary practices, indigenous; housing, indigenous; indigenous healing practices; indigenous languages; indigenous movements; poverty; race and racism; respect; rural highlands, lack of professional healthcare in; *and the specific peoples:* Ch'orti Maya; Kaqchikel Maya; K'iche' Maya; Kichwas (Ecuador); Mam Maya; Mayas (Guatemala); Q'eqchi' Maya
indigeneity: outward ethnic markers and, 5, 22, 46, 127; uncertainty of meanings in the archives, 5. *See also* ethnicity; racial medicalization; racial order
indigenistas: overview, 121, 127–28; antityphus print materials developed by, 171; assimilation advocacy as typical of, 128, 130; condemnation of indigenous activism, 128; condemnation of indigenous healing practices, 128; "Day of the Indian" events, 122; as disadvantaging indígenas, 34, 128; disparagement of indigenous hygiene and health, 126;

indigenous languages: as connected to ancestral medicinal processes, 228n3; indigenista disparagement of, 171–72; journalist disparagement of, 190; literacy materials in, democratic administrations and development of, 171; and medicine/poison continuum, 64, 245n44; RF's hookworm campaign as ignoring, 44–45, 170–71

—PUBLIC HEALTH MESSAGING DELIVERED IN: overview, 148, 210; antityphus materials, 171; disrespect of indígenas and failure of, 2–3, 159–60, 173; Ecuadorian commitment to, 14, 121, 122, 160, 174; indigenista activism for, 122; respectful cultural sensitivity and success of, 148, 173

indigenous movements, Ecuador: overview, 121; against bubonic plague public health mandates, 137–39; against eradication of guinea pigs (cuyes), 141, 157–58; against hacendado exploitation, 32, 33; as circumscribing UFCO's power, 36; and cultural sensitivity as policy, 2, 137, 139; few violent conflicts in postcolonial era, 30, 139; indigenous healers as mobilizing, 28; indigenous rights movement facilitated by healthcare policy inclusion of Kichwas, 221; insurrection against church and state taxes, 30; massacre of indígenas at Leito hacienda, 32; organizations of, 32, 34, 136; overthrow of Lucio Gutiérrez, 223; and smallpox, 137; social mobility and political influence due to organizing, 5–6, 34, 35–36, 136

indigenous movements, Guatemala: overview, 121; the cholera epidemic and revolt led by Carrera (1837–1838), 37, 122–23; indigenistas condemning, 128; the influenza epidemic (1918–1919) and overthrow of Estrada Cabrera, 123; Ponce Vaides support and land dispossession protests by, and ladino massacre of Kaqchikels, 40, 240n140

indio, difference in meaning in Guatemala vs. Ecuador, xx

infant mortality: budgets inadequate to reduce, 95–96; the Central American Health Congress and, 107–8; colonial period and increases due to European disease introductions, 249n3; as economic issue in Europe, 86; focus on education vs. reforms of living conditions, 89; gastrointestinal diseases as cause, 106, 111, 114–15; hybrid healthcare and reduction of, 87; indigenous cultural concern for, 249n3, 257n192; laws and programs established to reduce, 87, 89, 107, 249–50n8; malaria as cause, 106, 211; midwives blamed for, 110, 111–12, 257n189; as moral issue in Latin American nations, 86–87, 105; mothers blamed for, 106, 110, 111–12, *112*, 215, 257n189; persistence despite medical professionalization and expansion, 86, 87–88, 91; and potable water infrastructure, lack of, 86, 87, 105, 110, 111, 116, 249–50n8; poverty and persistence of, 87, 249–50n8; research on, 105–6, 110, 211; RF director's observation on the waste of, 47–48; and vaccines, lack of, 95–96. *See also* midwifery and midwives

—ECUADOR: budgetary difficulties, 95–96; lack of tuberculosis vaccine, 95–96; maternal-infant healthcare program established to address, 92, 93–97, *93*, 98, 117, 215; midwives as critical to address, 89; as moral crisis, 105; persistence despite medical professionalization and expansion, 86, 88, 91. *See also* midwifery and midwives— Ecuador

—GUATEMALA: and breastmilk, insufficient, 105, 110, 114–15; eugenics theories and, 106–8, *108*, 110–11, 257n192; gastrointestinal diseases as cause, 106, 111, 114–15; healthy (light-skinned) baby contests, 107; malaria as cause, 106, 211; midwifery as crucial to protection of infant health, 102, 106, 112–13, 114, 115–16, 215; midwives blamed for, 110, 111–12, 215; modernization and science, critiques of, 109–10, 116; and mothers, advocacy for, 107; mothers blamed for, 106, 110, 111–12, *112*, 215; newborn clinics and nutritional programs for prevention of, 105, 111, 115–16; PAHO study of, 87; philanthropic projects modernizing hospitals, 108–9; poverty rejected by officials as cause of, 111–12; puericulture theory, 107; reductions under Estrada Cabrera, 102; research concluding malaria and gastrointestinal diseases as leading causes of, 106; statistics on, 102, 106, 115, 259n228; UNICEF involvement in, 115. *See also* midwifery and midwives— Guatemala

influenza pandemic (1918–1919): Ecuador as avoiding, 86; Estrada Cabrera's overthrow in the wake of, 123, 188; in Guatemala, 49, 123–25; indígenas as disproportionately harmed by, 224; racial medicalization and, 10; sweat bath closures and destruction by Guatemalan authorities, 125, 126, 145–46

Inkas, 25, 235n20

insect vectors, as resonating with indigenous understandings, 132

Instituto Indigenista Nacional de Guatemala (National Indigenist Institute of Guatemala, IING), 40–41, 122, 220

Intag, Ecuador, 199

international interventions in public health campaigns: overview, 41–42; the ongoing refugee crisis and need to address its root causes, 225; scientific medicine alone assumed to have merit, 59; US imperialism as risk in, 14, 42, 50, 59, 213. *See also* Pan American Sanitary Bureau (PASB); Rockefeller Foundation (RF); United States Public Health Service (USPHS)

International Sanitary Bureau, 42. *See also* Pan American Health Organization (PAHO); Pan American Sanitary Bureau (PASB)

intestinal worms and parasites: practical indigenous healers sought for, 64; Ubico targeting, 40. *See also* hookworm

Inuit people, 265n151

iron deficiencies, geophagy, 161–62

Iturralde, Diego, 32

Izquieta Pérez, Leopoldo, 206

jails and prisons: brujas profit in, 72, 247n86; and criminalization and persecution of indigenous healers, 72, 73, 74, 83, 92, 112–13; as incubators of disease, 118, 152, 267n21; prisoners in the involuntary USPHS medical research, 41, 209, 211, 212; self-policing by comadronas and threat of, 89; typhoid in, 118, 152, 267n21

Jaramillo Alvarado, Pío, 32

jefe políticos, defined, xix, 264n137

Jeráud, R., 154–55

jigger (nigua), 13, 46

Joaquina Maternity Ward (Guatemala City), 102, 103, 113–14

Juárez Muñoz, J. Fernando, 51–52, 126, 128

Kaqchikel Maya: on Arévalo and democratic government, 128, 171, 220; on the cholera epidemic (1837), 123; and claiming their right to healthcare, 2; classification of illness and type of healer consulted, 64; and conflation of the highlands and indígenas as diseased places and populations, 10; and COVID-19 pandemic, 224; and funerary traditions, 189; health clinics established via Carroll Behrhorst training, 221–22; hybrid healthcare pursued by, 1–2, 28, 214, 248n128; and malaria, 181–82, 189, 195; malaria prevention, 180; and medicine/poison continuum, 64; and migrant labor to coastal plantations, 181, 195; observation of illnesses introduced by the Spanish, 37; and the power to both heal and harm, 133; public health materials in language of, 171, 174; skepticism toward scientific medicine, 126–27; soul loss (susto) and treatment, 61; support for Ponce Vaides and massacre by ladinos, 40, 240n140; symbols and colors used on clothing, 217–18; and typhus, 147, 165, 166, 170, 171. *See also* indigenous healing practices— Maya; indigenous movements, Guatemala

K'iche' Maya: anti-typhus materials in language of, 171; cleanliness of town as surprise to inspector, 130–31; smallpox deaths, 125

Kichwas (Ecuador): ethnic belonging as shared local cultural understandings, 22–23; public health messages communicated in Kichwa language, 121, 122, 159–60, 173, 174; RF perceptions of, 218–19; spelling of, 235n11. *See also* indigenous healing practices— Kichwa; indigenous movements, Ecuador

Klebs, Edwin, 149

Kraut, Alan, 216

labor rights, to complain, 196

labor unions, violent suppression of, 188

ladinos (Europeanized, nonindigenous people of Guatemala): definition as term, 6, 230–31n28; racial binary established by the Liberals, 6, 127, 146, 161. *See also* race and racism; racial order

Lake Amatitlán drainage project, 278n111

Lake Atitlán, 190

Lake Quinizilapa drainage project (1927), 162, 187–90, 193, 194

land dispossession: agro-export economic expansion and, 2, 29, 37, 55; Arbenz's expropriation and redistribution plan, 220; Kaqchikel protest of, and massacre by ladinos, 40; labor migration as catalyzed by, 176–77, 206; Lake Quinizilapa drainage project and redistribution of land to indígenas, 188, 189; statistics on, 207–8; as structural inequality, 148, 173, 175. *See also* poverty as a structural determinant of indigenous health disparities

language. *See* indigenous languages; Spanish language

Latin America: child and infant care legislation and programs, 87, 249–50n8; COVID-19 pandemic death toll, 224; infant mortality viewed as moral issue in, 86–87, 105; international interventions in public health campaigns and, 41–43, 59; international interventions in public health campaigns and risk of US imperialism, 14, 42, 50, 59, 213; licensing laws for traditional medicine, 223; persistence of racial eugenics discourse in, 11, 257n192; scientific

medicine deployed to assimilate indígenas and promote modernization, 266–67n182; and structural determinants of disparate indigenous health outcomes, 144–45. *See also* indigenistas; medical citizenship; *specific countries*

latrines/toilets, 45, 46, 86, 134–35

lazaretos (quarantine facilities), 155, 166–67, 170

League of Nations Health Organization (LNHO), 22, 59, 165

Ledger, Charles, 179

Leeuwenhoek, Antoni van, 263n100

leprosy, 267n3

lice. *See* typhus

literacy: literacy materials in indigenous languages, 171; and public health materials in indigenous languages, 170–71; voting rights and requirement for, 6–7, 32–33, 40, 220

Little, Walter, 262n70

Lloyd, Bolivar J., 43

Long, John, 33, 42

López, Mariano, 123

MacPhail, Neil, 106

Madura foot, 13

malaria: overview, 206–8; as curable, 177; and disease etiology, ethnic divides in reception of, 188–90, 277n102; and funerary traditions, 189; and the geography of disease, 9–10; and infant mortality, 106; as lowland disease, primarily, 176; misdiagnosis and overdiagnosis of, 181, 273n4; morbidity and mortality rates, 177, 181, 182–83, 191, 195, 206; mosquito bite transmission, 177; parasites causing illness (*Plasmodium vivax* and *Plasmodium falciparum*), 177, 184, 273nn7–8; racial medicalization of (international), 178, 185–86, 186, 273n16; racial stereotyping of (international), 178; RF control projects, 13, 178, 201; as a rhetorical tool, 9, 178, 182, 197–98, 207; survivors as symptomless carriers, 273n1; symptoms, 176. *See also* malaria in the highlands; malaria mosquitoes and mosquito vector control; malaria treatments

malaria mosquitoes and mosquito vector control *(continued)*
Plasmodium falciparum), 177, 184, 273nn7–8; RF and preference for solution of, 183, 184; universal, well-funded, long-term antimalaria campaigns, 177–78

malaria treatments: class bias in, 38, 183, 196, 207; hybrid healthcare, 62, 182; indigenous laborers sent to Guatemala City for treatment, 38, 177, 181, 196–97; indigenous practices (other than quinine), 26, 180, 182; scientific medicine (other than quinine), 274n36; UFCO not allowing workers to use their healthcare system for, 38

—QUININE: Andean indigenous discovery, development, and use of, 177, 179; as appropriate treatment for highland malaria vs. vector control measures, 197; cinchona trees and bark (*quina*), 177, 179; commercialization of, 179–80, 192, 274n19; Ecuador and, 179, 197, 204, 205; Guatemala and, 180, 183–84; improperly taken by patient, 182; patient intolerance or distaste for, 180; RF employees and, 183; in strategies for malaria control, 191–92; vivax malaria not curable with (latent liver phase), 177, 276n70

mal de ojo (evil eye): definition of, 229n19; in hybrid healthcare, 60, 61, 100, 244n19; Spanish colonizers as introducing, 60–61; and unreliability of archival statistics, xxv

Mamani, Manuel Incra, 179

Mam Maya: on causes of illness, 133, 165; public health materials in language of, 171; as skeptical of scientific medicine, 126, 133

marketplace racialization, xxi–xxii, 141, 143–44, *144*, 266n163

Martínez Sobral, Hernán, 130, 131

Martin, W. M., 124

Masferrer, Alberto, 264n130

massage practice, 26, 101, 111, 125

Mayas (Chiapas), xii–xiii, 178, 259n4

Mayas (Guatemala): ethnic belonging as shared local cultural understandings,

22–23; mass deaths and infant mortality due to Spanish colonization, 37, 224, 249n3; *nahual* concept, and lake drainage, 189–90; persecution and genocide in the civil war (1960–96), 221, 222. *See also* Ch'orti Maya; indigenous healing practices— Maya; indigenous movements, Guatemala; Kaqchikel Maya; K'iche' Maya; Mam Maya; Q'eqchi' Maya

measles, 120, 129, 168

medical anthropology, xii–xiii, 233n82

medical citizenship: definition of, 4, 230n17; indígenas and, 2, 66–67, 143, 219

medical pluralism. *See* hybrid healthcare

medical professionals: blamed for public health campaign shortcomings, 164; class status of, 196; as concentrated in cities, 7, 8, 62. *See also* scientific medicine doctors

medical racism, 11, 232n62, 258n196

medical schools, Ecuador: endorsement of medical students in areas without doctors, 79–80; midwifery training, 89, 91, 251n38; nursing school, and preference for nonindigenous students, 54, 89; slowness of producing doctors, 62

medical schools, Guatemala: medical students as technical assistants with RF, 52; midwifery schools, and preference for nonindigenous students, 100–101, 102–3; nursing schools preferring nonindigenous students, 89; refusal to admit men of color, 28; slowness of producing doctors, 62

Menchu, Rigoberta, 223

mestizaje (racial mixing), 6, 121, 127, 146, 260n12. *See also* racial order

methodology of the text: archival sources, xxi, xxii–xxiv; literature review, 17–19; multiple lenses employed, 18; positionality of the researcher and, xxi–xxii; research trips, xx; transnational analysis centered on indigenous voices and agency, 16–19, 233n82. *See also* archives

Mexico: and Chiapas, Maya communities of, xii, xiii, 178, 259n4; citizenship of indígenas, 220; eugenicist obstetrics in, 258n196; funerary practices, regulation of, 269n52; homeopathy endorsed and regulated by, 75; and hybrid healthcare, 243n1, 269n70, 283n30; and indigenismo, 127–28; infant mortality and, 249–50n8, 257n189; in-migration to, 4; malaria control, 178, 201, 259n4, 278n126; medical citizenship of indígenas, 219; midwife training, 250–51n21; model villages, 262n70; and national belonging, 220; RF denigration of indígenas resonating with government discourse, 51, 241nn181,186; RF projects in, 13, 178, 201; sleeping mats in houses, 266n165

miasma theory: and cemetery siting, 152–53; definition of, 8; germ theory replacing, 8; and malaria, 182, 188–89, 190, 277n102; as resonating with Maya ideas about mal aire (bad air), 27

microbiology, as resonating with indígenas, 132, 263n100

midwifery and midwives: abortion and abortifacients and, 92, 252n50; conflicts with physicians, 96–97, 215, 253n82; hybrid healthcare and, 88, 90, 99–100, 101, 111, 114, 117, 254n110, 258n210; knowledge of, as superior to scientific medicine, 90; male practitioners of, 71, 73, 111, 258n196; mandated home-visit programs, 249–50n8; as predominantly female field, 71, 90, 215; professionalization of medicine and transfer of authority and power to male doctors, 88–90, 91, 250n16, 253n96

—INDIGENOUS: expansion of social capital of, 222; lunar eclipses asserted to complicate births, 60, 113; percentage of births attended by, 88; poverty of, and licensing as prohibitive for, 88, 104, 105; practices of, 90, 98–99, 100, 101, 111, 254n104; scientific medical doctors as learning from, 4, 85, 90, 214; the sweat bath as place of healing work by, 125

—LICENSURE AND TRAINING: accoutrements of, 104; consolidation of male physicians' power as goal of, 89,

250–51nn16,21; nonindigenous students preferred, 89, 91, 100–101, 102–3; poverty of indigenous midwives as prohibitive of, 88, 104–5

—UNTRAINED (COMADRONAS EMPÍRICAS, PARTERAS): as calling, 251n26; criminalization and persecution of, 67, 71–72, 73, 88, 89–90, 92, 98, 103, 104, 111, 215, 258n196; as crucial to infant mortality reduction programs, 87, 89; elites consulting, 113–14; and "partera" as term, 251n26; poverty and need for, 98, 99; self-policing of, 89, 116–17

midwives in Ecuador: and abortion, 92; budgetary constraints, 95–96; conflicts with physicians, 96–97, 215; criminalization and persecution of untrained midwives, 92, 98; and hybrid healthcare, 99–100, 117; indigenous practices, 90, 98–99, 100, 254n104; licensed midwives and class tensions with clients, 99, 117; licensed midwives as critical of the untrained, 92, 98–99; licensed midwives, growth in number of births attended by, 99; poverty and need for untrained midwives, 98, 99; poverty in cities, maternal-infant healthcare program established to address, 93–97, 93, 98, 117, 215; reputations of, need to defend, 96; rural lack of healthcare, and tacit approval of unlicensed midwives, 92–93, 116–17; scientific midwives (obstetrices científicas), 90; training and licensing, 89, 91, 251n38; untrained or partially trained midwives, 91–93, 98–99

midwives in Guatemala: and abortion, 104; clothing requirement as excluding indígenas, 104; criminalization and persecution of untrained midwives, 67, 71–72, 73, 88, 89–90, 103, 104, 111, 215, 258n196; elites consulting, 113–14; foreign midwives, preference for, 103, 104, 255n143; hospital employment of, 104; and hybrid healthcare, 101, 111, 114, 117; indigenous practices, 101; and infant mortality, crucial role in prevention of, 102, 106, 112–13, 114, 115–16, 215;

midwives in Guatemala *(continued)*
 and infant mortality, midwives blamed
 for, 110, 111–12, 215; judicial record
 supports the excellence of, 112–13; pay
 received by, 114; proposal for a free
 obstetric clinic (1911), 102; rural lack of
 healthcare, and practice by comadronas
 empíricas, 101–2, 105, 114, 116–17;
 scholarships to Mexico's Infant Hospital, 103; status of nurses and midwives,
 103–4, 249n148; trained and certified
 midwives (comadrona tituladas), 90,
 100–101, 102, 103–4, 114, 115–16; training and registration of comadronas
 empíricas (mid-1940s), 104–5, 114, 115;
 training as excluding indígenas, 89,
 100–101, 102–3, 104–5
migratory labor of indígenas: bubonic
 plague spread through, 275n52; Ecuadorian elites encouraging, to disrupt social
 organizing, 30; extremely poor living
 and working conditions for, 195–96;
 Guatemalan forced labor mechanisms
 and, 29; land dispossession as catalyzing, 176–77, 206; malaria in the highlands and, 176–77, 181–82, 184–85,
 197–98, 200; railroad construction and,
 32; yellow fever in the highlands and,
 197. *See also* compulsory labor of indígenas; poverty as a structural determinant
 of indigenous health disparities
Miño, Carlos A.: and malaria, 179, 199,
 200; and typhoid, 151, 153–54, 155, 157;
 on unreliability of statistics, xxiv
Mira, Giaquinto, 192, 278n111
Molloy, Daniel M., 53, 133, 190
moonshine, 66, 69–70, 128. *See also* alcohol
Morales, Rogelio, xxv, 172
Mosquera Narváez, Alfonso, 95, 158
mosquitoes: discovery of mosquito as
 vector, 13; number of species that spread
 diseases to humans, 177; as vector,
 resonating with indigenous understandings, 132; yellow fever control projects,
 13, 180. *See also* malaria mosquitoes and
 mosquito vector control
mothers: advocacy for, 107; blamed for
 infant mortality, 106, 110, 111–12, *112*,

215, 257n189; blamed for typhus, 165;
 and iron-deficient diets (geophagy),
 161–62; unethical medical research on
 malaria and, 211, 212. *See also* infant
 mortality; midwifery and midwives
Murgueytio, Reynaldo, 122

Nading, Alex, 134
national belonging: acceptance of some
 level of state-sanctioned medicine to
 enjoy, 220; eugenics of, and education,
 131–32; indígenas recognized as citizens,
 220; normative hygiene as requirement
 of, 130, 215, 220, 262–63nn80–81; "pathological patrias" concerns excluding the
 sick or malnourished from, 260n12,
 263n92. *See also* medical citizenship;
 voting rights of indígenas
national eugenics of integration (Ecuador),
 3–4, 79, 119, 121, 136, 212–13, 218.
 See also public health campaigns—
 Ecuador
Native Americans, and RF biases, 54
native survivance, 17
neo-Lamarckian ideas, 107, 121, 260n11. *See
 also* racial eugenics
newspaper coverage: dismissing indigenous
 intellect, 129; environmental explanations for disease in areas of nonindigenous majority population, 10; general
 focus on persecuting healers and professionalization of medicine, 57, 65, 68, 69,
 70, 71, 72, *72*, *74*, 76, *77*–*78*; on indigenous housing, 123; on infant mortality,
 108, *108*, 109, 112, *112*; of international
 antimalaria research, 192, *193*; on lack of
 doctors in rural areas, 65; malaria, 192,
 193; natural therapies promoted in, 57;
 racial medicalization in areas where
 indígenas comprised a majority of the
 population, 10–11; racist denigration of
 indígenas, 189–90
Nicaragua, RF hookworm program in,
 43–44
Nigeria, model villages, 262n70
nigua (jigger), 13, 46
Nuñez, Luis, 192
Núñez, Solón, 43

poverty as a structural determinant of indigenous health disparities *(continued)* denying and ignoring, 111–12, 129–30, 131, 173–74; RF director Rowan's observations of, 22, *23*, 45–47, *47*, 145; social medicine and understanding of, xii, 135, 143, 151. *See also* class; land dispossession; malaria in the highlands— official focus on control as deflecting attention from structural economic disadvantages; potable water infrastructure; poverty of indígenas; sanitation; scapegoating of indígenas as masking government failures to remedy structural inequalities

poverty of indígenas: barefootedness and, 46–47; fees for state recognition of empíricos as prohibitive, 63; health as undermined by, 195–96; and housing, 123–24, 141, 260–61n25; and indigenous healers, access to, 65, 130; infant mortality rates and, 87, 249–50n8; isolation from family imposed by, 177, 196–97; midwife licensing fees as prohibitive, 88, 104–5; RF photographs conveying, 14, *15*, 45–47, *47*. *See also* compulsory labor of indígenas; migratory labor of indígenas; poverty as a structural determinant of indigenous health disparities

Prem, Catalán, 165

professionalization of medicine. *See* criminalization and persecution of indigenous healthcare and healers; hybrid healthcare; indigenous healing practices portrayed as retrograde and dangerous; medical schools; public health campaigns; scientific medicine

public health campaigns: overview, 118–20; allocation of limited resources, 34, 146, 153–54, 219, 268n34, 284n44; class deployed as frame for, 148, 151, 153; as contravening indigenous culture and practices, 125, 126, 156, 265n151; cultural sensitivity and success of, 2, 133–34, 137, 139, 148, 166; doctors blamed for failures of, 164; elite interests/hierarchies of power furthered by, 8–9, 166, 186–87; as global trend deploying scientific medicine to assimilate non-European bodies

and promote modernization, 266–67n182; and indígenas' acceptance of scientific medicine, 155–56, 158; the politics of indigeneity (inclusion vs. exclusion) as highly consequential to, 24; resistance to, 126, 137–39, 141, 156–58, 214, 269n62; respect conveyed in, and success of, 148, 173. *See also* criminalization and persecution of indigenous healthcare and healers; imperfect knowledge; indigenous healing practices portrayed as retrograde and dangerous; indigenous languages— public health messaging delivered in; infant mortality; malaria; malaria in the highlands— official focus on control as deflecting attention from structural economic disadvantages; racial medicalization (linking illness and race); scapegoating of indígenas as masking government failures to remedy structural inequalities; typhoid fever; typhus

—ECUADOR: bubonic plague, 137–40, 141, 201, 264–65n139; cultural sensitivity in, 2, 137, 139; greater freedom of choice for indígenas in, 24; guinea pigs (cuyes) controls, and resistance to, 141, 157–58, 159–60, 214; hygiene manuals, 135; indigenous adaptation of customs to guidelines, 142–43; indigenous interpreters and, 137; as integrationist project, 3–4, 14, 23–24, 140, 143, 145, 173, 212–13, 218; marketplace racialization, xxi–xxii, 141, 143–44, *144*, 266n163; and pattern of respect for indigenous health practices, 2, 119, 121, 139, 146, 174, 212–13; right to healthcare (medical citizenship), encouragement to claim, 143; sanitation, 134–35; shared ethnicity of inspectors no protection from enmity due to intrusion into indigenous homes, 138–40, 264–65n139; turning toward indigenous hygiene and away from building sanitation projects (1920s), 140–41. *See also* malaria in the highlands— Ecuadorian campaigns

—Guatemala: as assimilationist project, 3, 23–24, 119, 127, 145, 173; cultural sensitivity and success of, 133–34, 166; discontinuation of measures abhorred by indígenas, 133; indigenous interpreters in collaboration with, 133–34, 170; paternalistic and punitive attitudes conveyed in, 14, 172. *See also* malaria in the highlands— Guatamalan campaigns

Puerto Rico, 190

Q'eqchi' Maya: ethics of reciprocity, 75; German intermarriage with, 6, 48, 75, 127, 131; German valuation of medicinal plants, 75–76; public health materials in language of, 171

quarantine facilities (lazaretos), 155, 166–67, 170

Quechua, as spelling, 235n11. *See also* indigenous healing practices— Kichwa; Kichwas (Ecuador)

Quetzaltenango province (Guatemala): medicinal waters of, 66; midwives in, 105; and typhoid, 162; and typhus, 166, 167

Quevado Coronel, Rafael, 95–96

Quiacaín, Ventura, 57

Quijos, 235n20

quinine. *See* malaria treatments— quinine

Quintana, Epaminondas, 110, 167, 168, 171–72, 174, 210, 271nn127–128

Quito, Ecuador: in colonial period, 28–29; and highland malaria, 176; indígenas in, 11, 36, 134, 151–52; RF nursing school development project, 54, 89; sanitation in, 134–35; Servicio de Sanidad (Health Service) in, 31, 33, 151, 153–54, 199; and typhoid, 151–53

race and racism: anti-African racism, 229n14; marketplace racialization, xxi–xxii, 141, 143–44, 144, 266n163; as persisting despite cultural sensitivity in public health interventions, 133–34; RF representatives' expression of, as varying according to the country they were working in, 4, 44–45, 48, 51–52, 54,

241nn181,186; US anti-black and anti-brown racism, 48, 51, 54, 161–62, 218. *See also* class; ethnicity; gender; medical racism; poverty; racial eugenics; racial medicalization (linking illness and race); racial order; racial stereotyping of indígenas

racial eugenics: French, and emergence of puericulture, 107; neo-Lamarckian ideas, 107, 121, 260n11; obstetrics practices and, 258n196; persistence of discourse in Latin America, 11, 257n192; sterilization policies of the US and Germany, 260n11. *See also* medical racism; national eugenics of integration (Ecuador); racial medicalization (linking illness and race)

—Guatemala: assimilation demanded by eugenicists, 3, 48, 75, 121, 128, 131; and culture vs. phenotype to identify race, 107, 121; education of indígenas, 131–32; infant mortality theories, 106–8, 108, 110–11, 257n192; preventive eugenics, 128. *See also* indigenistas; public health campaigns— Guatemala

racial medicalization (linking illness and race): culture as basis of racial typing in Ecuador and Guatemala, distinguished from the biologized framework of the US, 260n12; definition of, 11, 148, 216; as foreclosing indigenous participation in public health initiatives, 145, 148, 173; and geography, 9–12, 12, 150–51, 166, 185–86, 186; geophagy ("dirt-eaters"), 161–62, 161; indígenas themselves framed as vectors of disease, 8, 13, 48, 119, 129–30, 145, 146, 147, 216; of infant mortality, 110–11, 257n192; leprosy, 267n3; malaria (international), 178, 185–86, 186, 273n16; map of Central America illustrating, 186; map of Guatemala illustrating, 11, 12; and marginalization of indígenas, 146, 147; resistance of officials to, 148; shift away from, 168–69, 172; trope of indígenas on the cusp of contagion and, 159; typhoid fever, 9–11, 147–48, 149, 150–51, 156, 157, 160–61, 162, 163; typhus, 9–11, 147–48,

racial medicalization *(continued)*
149, 150–51, 158–59, 165, 168, 169–70.
See also indigenous healing practices
portrayed as retrograde and dangerous;
malaria in the highlands—official focus
on vector control as rationalization of
poverty to deflect attention from its
root causes; racial stereotyping of
indígenas; scapegoating of indígenas as
masking government failures to remedy
structural inequalities

racial order: colonial period and, 29; culture as basis of racial typing, vs. pheno-
type/genetics, 107, 121, 260n12; Ecuadorian hierarchy, 5–6; ethnic markers used
in racial typing, 5, 22, 46, 127; Guatemalan binary, establishment and effects
of, 6, 127, 146, 161; Guatemalan hierarchy, 6–7, 131, 230–31n28; lighter-
skinned citizens enjoying more privilege
than their darker-skinned counterparts,
5, 29, 45, 107, 131, 224. *See also* clothing
and appearance, indigenous; indigenous
languages

racial stereotyping of indígenas: overview,
118–19; anti-hygiene, 10–11, 48, 49,
123–26, 129, 151–52, 158, 165, 168; back-
wardness/resistance to modernization,
51–52, 125–26, 130, 164–65, 169–70;
cleanliness as surprise to inspectors,
130–31; cleanliness noted in contemporary ethnographies, 168; excremental
colonialism, 45; ignorance/stupidity,
2–3, 10, 118, 130, 131–32, 142, 172, 190;
inebriation, 30, 134; insalubriousness as
common trope, 153; by rural indigenous
leaders, typhoid epidemics and, 151–52.
See also racial medicalization (linking
illness and race); scapegoating of indígenas as masking government failures to
remedy structural inequalities

railroads: dispensary rail car project, 191;
and migration of Ecuadorian labor, 32;
transporting bubonic-plague infected
rats to the highlands, 135; UFCO control of Guatemalan, 38

rats, as carrier of bubonic-plague fleas, 135,
141; Ecuador public health campaign by

caza-ratas (rat hunters), and indígenas
movement against, 137–40, 141,
264–65n139

reciprocity ethic, 75

Reforma de la Ley de Jornaleros (Day
Laborers' Reform Law, 1918), 32

reproductive health: Maya healing practices, 26, 235n23. *See also* gynecology;
infant mortality; midwifery and midwives; mothers; obstetrics

respect: Ecuador and pattern of respect for
indigenous health practices, 2, 119, 121,
139, 146, 174, 212–13; in public health
communication, and success of, 148,
173; public health communication
lacking, and failure of, 2–3, 159–60, 173;
public health practice making enemies
of scientific medicine, 201

Retalhulew province (Guatemala),
typhoid, 162

Revolución Juliana (1925), 32–33

Reyna Barrios, José María, 127

RF. *See* Rockefeller Foundation

river blindness (*Onchocerca volvulus*), 11

Robles Valverde, Rodolfo, 11

Rockefeller Foundation (RF): overview, 3,
13; archives of, xx, xxiv–xxv; Central
American countries' inability to pay for
their programs, 49–50; fellowships to
Latin Americans to study abroad, 13, 50;
focus on diseases that affected US
soldiers, workers, and other travelers, 13,
43; international interventions in public
health campaigns and, 41–42; LNHO
funded by, 59; malaria control projects,
13, 178, 201; malaria treatments for
employees of, 183; mission to "sanitize"
the tropics for US business and military
interests by curbing tropical diseases, 3,
13, 43, 49, 119, 215, 259n4; racist thought
exhibited by, as varying according to the
country they were working in, 4,
44–45, 48, 51–52, 54, 145–46, 218–19,
241nn181,186; scientific medicine as
focus of, 13, 233n68; social medicine
denigrated by, 183, 192, 276n72; social
medicine embraced by, 221; state
responsibility for abysmal living condi-

tions not highlighted by, 89; on typhus, 9; US anti-black and anti-brown racism as influence on, 48, 51, 54, 161–62, 218; viewed as an arm of US imperialism by Latin Americans, 14, 50, 59, 213; yellow fever control projects, 13, 14, 43, 49, 54, 207. *See also* Rockefeller Foundation (RF), hookworm campaigns
—IN ECUADOR: disparagement of indigenous healing practices, 242n204; focus on the medical elite in cities, 53–54; lack of engagement with indígenas or rural areas, 53–54, 218; malaria projects, 54, 178, 201, *202–4*, 205, 207; nursing school development project, 54, 89; and public distrust of US imperialism, 14, 213; racist thought exhibited by, as calibrated by Ecuadorian context, 4, 44, 51, 54, 218–19; yellow fever control project, 14, 54
—IN GUATEMALA: as arm of US imperialism, local suspicions of, 14; development shaped by, 38; Estrada Cabrera relationship of, 14, 48–49, 52; focus on particular diseases and diversion of resources from urgent local needs, 13; greater effect on public health than in Ecuador, 120; hookworm campaign, 22, *23*, 28, 43; hospital ward photo showing "Indian influence," as evidence of shallow understanding of indígenas, 217–18, *217*; malaria project, 178, 181, 183, 184, 190, 192, 193–94, 207, 276n72; racial medicalization (linking illness and race), 161–62, 216, 218; racist thought exhibited by, as calibrated by Guatemalan context, 4, 44–45, 48, 51–52, 145–46, 217–18; rural public health as promise of, 13, 41; scientific terms translated into sociocultural context by, 132; and Ubico, 39; yellow fever project, 49. *See also* Burres, William T.; Molloy, Daniel M.; Rowan, Walter (RF Guatemalan director); Struse, Alvin
Rockefeller Foundation (RF), hookworm campaigns, 22, *23*, 28, 43–48, *47*, 49, 50, 51, 52–53, 55; chenopodium used to treat, and hybrid healthcare, 28, 132–33;

Costa Rica's program used as model for, 43–44; denigration of indígenas healers, 45, 50–51, 52, 54–55; entrée into Guatemala via, 22, 44; excremental colonialism and, 45, *46*; illustrations used to convey information, 171; indigenous languages ignored in, 44–45, 170–71; as legitimizing interventions in Latin America, 43; and medical subterfuge of using unlicensed employees to detect and treat, 50–53, 55; not the top priority for the governments involved, 22, 43; racist thought exhibited by, as varying depending on the country they were in, 44–45, 48, 51–52; resistance to, 43–44, 48, 50; Walter Rowan's observations of poverty as root of poor health, 22, *23*, 45–47, *47*; training and endorsements of empíricos, 43–44
Rockefeller, Nelson, 219
Rome, ancient, malaria and, 187
Rosenberg, Charles, xxi
Rose, Wycliffe, 51, 243n222
Rowan, Walter (RF Guatemalan director): on "dirt-eaters" (geophagy), 161–62, *161*; highlighting indigenous hygiene of sweatbaths, 14, 124–25, *124*, 145–46; on infant mortality, 47; on neglect of local needs by the RF, 13; overtures to dictator Estrada Cabrera and struggle to placate the medical establishment, 14, 52; photos taken by, 14, *15*, *23*, 45–46, *47*; on poverty as underlying poor health, 22, *23*, 45–47, *47*, 145
Rueda Sáenz, Consuelo, 92, 94, 96–97, 98–99, 253n96, 254n105
Rufino Barrios, Justo, 180
rural highlands, lack of professional healthcare in: concentration of doctors in cities, 7, 8, 62, 65, 67; criminalization of indigenous healers pursued less frequently, 8, 77–78; racist denigration of indígenas despite acknowledgment of, 10–11; slowness of medical schools in graduating doctors, 62; state dependence on indigenous healers due to lack of physicians, 8; urban bias of healthcare, 98, 103, 146, 219

—Ecuador: desire to prevent untrained/unlicensed practitioners while simultaneously authorizing some to practice, 79–85; endorsement of indigenous healers and medical students, 79–80; national-local government dynamics and, 82–84, 135–36; paltry resources of doctors in rural practices, 80; smallpox variolation coopted by indigenous healers, 80–82; unlicensed drug prescribers allowed to practice, 80; unlicensed midwives given tacit approval, 92–93, 116–17

—Guatemala: overview, 62, 84–85; dispensary rail car project, 191; empíricos as crucial in anti-typhus campaigns, 170; empíricos permitted to practice where no doctors were within ten-km radius, 64–65; malaria patients sent to Guatemala City hospital, 38, 177, 181, 196–97; and midwife practices, 101–2, 105, 114, 116–17; and percentage of population in rural areas, 7; state recognition of municipal empíricos, 62–63, 67, 170; and typhus, 166, 170, 172; vaccination campaigns run by empíricos, 62–63. *See also* malaria in the highlands

Russell, Paul, 276n72

Russia, and typhus, 165

Sacatepéquez province (Guatemala): infant mortality and, 110; and malaria, 184, 188, 192; midwives in, 102; and typhoid, 162; and typhus, 166

Sáenz Vera, Cornelio, 158, 160

Salpor Chalí, Margarita, 222–23

Sandoval, Joaquín, 62

saneamiento (cleaning), 60

Sanidad. *See* Ecuadorian Servicio de Sanidad (Health Service)

sanitation: animal husbandry issues of, 254n105; anti-typhus printed materials for, 171; Ecuadorian policy shift away from public works projects to hygiene, 140–41; excremental colonialism, 45; malaria regulations, 192; municipalities as responsible for, 154; sewage, 134–35; spitting prohibitions, 126; toilets/

latrines, 45, *46*, 86. *See also* potable water infrastructure

San Marcos province (Guatemala): typhoid, 162; typhus, 166, 167

scapegoating of indígenas as masking government failures to remedy structural inequalities: overview, 20, 118–19, 173–75; COVID-19 pandemic and, 223–24; in the effort to shed Ecuador's reputation for poor hygiene and sanitation, 134; inclusion implied by, 146; influenza epidemic (1918), 49; malaria and, 285n66; persistence of effects of, 148–49, 168; typhoid fever and, 118–19, 148–49, 154–55, 162; typhus and, 148, 150, 172. *See also* racial medicalization (linking illness and race); racial stereotyping of indígenas

scientific medical doctors: blamed for public health campaign shortcomings, 164; as concentrated in cities, 7, 8, 62, 65, 67; in conflict with midwives, 96–97, 215, 253n82; as learning from indigenous midwives, 4, 85, 90, 214; professionalization of medicine and transfer of authority and power to male doctors, 88–90, 91, 250n16, 253n96. *See also* criminalization and persecution of indigenous healthcare and healers; hybrid healthcare; medical schools; rural highlands, lack of professional healthcare in; scientific medicine

scientific medicine: acceptance by indígenas, 66–67, 143, 155–56; early-twentieth-century struggle to prove competency, 7; Ecuadorian public health campaigns making enemies of, 201; international public health interventions assuming sole merit of, 59; medical experimentation, involuntary and/or unethical, 41, 209–12; and national belonging, 220; no system had the capacity to eliminate another from the range of possibilities, 4, 59–60, 62, 85, 87, 213, 219; as primarily male field, 90, 250n12; refusal by indígenas, even when deathly ill, 158; as resonating with indigenous concepts, 132, 159, 263n100, 269nn70–71; skepti-

cism of indígenas toward, 126–27,
132–33; in the United States, hegemony
of, 243–44n7. *See also* criminalization
and persecution of indigenous healthcare and healers; Ecuador medical
schools; Guatemala medical schools;
gynecology; hospitals; hybrid healthcare; imperfect knowledge; indigenous
healing practices portrayed as retrograde and dangerous; medical citizenship; obstetrics; public health campaigns; scientific medical doctors; social
medicine; vaccines
sexually transmitted infections (STIs):
involuntary medical experiments on
Guatemalan indígenas, 41, 209–10,
211–12; the sweat bath as killing pathogens of, 125; Tuskegee trials, 210, 211
Simmons, James Stevens, 191
Sims, James Marion, 211
smallpox: blamed on indígenas, 125; and
culturally sensitive public health in
Ecuador, 137; introduced by Europeans,
120
—VACCINATION: in hybrid healthcare, 27;
indigenous hybrid practice of variolation (Sigchos), 27, 80–82, 149, 154, 214;
scientific medical vaccines and campaigns, 27, 80, 81, *81*
social medicine: Paul Farmer on, xii; Guatemala and elite resistance to, 162,
174–75, 212; and Guatemala's democratic period, 243–44n7; infant mortality analyzed through lens of, 86, 87;
PASB and USPHS conveying distrust
of, 162, 212; RF denigrating, 183, 192,
276n72; RF embracing, 221
—ECUADOR: in colonial period, 28; and
continued growth of popular healing,
58; and etiological narrative of typhoid
fever among prisoners, 152; father of
(Eugenio Espejo), 6; in postcolonial era,
36; and poverty as structural determinant of disease, 135, 143, 151
Sololá province (Guatemala), midwives
in, 105
Spain: and quinine, 274n19. *See also* colonialism and the colonial period

Spanish language: differences of word
meanings between countries, xix–xx;
journalist's racist depiction of indígenas
speaking, 190. *See also* indigenous
languages
spiritual power, and the hierarchical spectrum of curanderos, 64
spitting, 126, 134
Spotto, Joseph, 210
Spruce, Richard, 179
Stepan, Nancy, 128
Stevenson, Lisa, 265n151
Struse, Alvin, xxiv, 39, 45, 52; and Estrada
Cabrera, 48–49
Suárez, Pablo Arturo, 136, 141, 216–17
Suchitepéquez province (Guatemala), and
typhoid, 162
sugar economy, 32, 280n175
susto (fright): indigenous practices to cure,
28, 61, 99; the judicial system as
acknowledging, 60, 113, 214; long-running debate about whether medical
doctors should learn to diagnose and
treat, 283n29; origins in the Americas,
61; symptoms of, 61
sweat bath (temascal, tuj): Guatemalan
authorities prohibiting use, and destruction of, 125, 126, 145–46, 168, 261n36; as
killing pathogenic microbes, 125; as
place of healing work, 125; as predating
European contact, 124; RF director as
highlighting hygiene of, 14, 124–25, *124*,
145–46
Sweet, James, 245n44
syncretism. *See* hybrid healthcare
syphilis. *See* sexually transmitted infections
(STIs)

temascal. *See* sweat bath
tetanus, 13
toilets/latrines, 45, *46*, 86; lack of, and open
sewers in the streets, 134–35
Totonicapán province (Guatemala):
infant mortality in, 114–15; and typhus,
166, 170
tourism: indigenous model villages for,
129, 262n70; mosquito control projects
and, 194

witchcraft. *See* brujería (witchcraft)
World Health Organization (WHO), xii
World War I, 179
World War II, 195, 278n126
Wright, Almroth Edward, 149, 270n89

Xibalba, 26
Xoquic, Carlos, 221

Yañez, Rogelio, 118
yellow fever: Ecuador and, 54, 86, 95,
176, 197, 201; Guatemala and, 39, 49,
163, 176, 183; mosquito control, 13,
180; Panama Canal project and, 180;
ports declared "clean" of, 13; RF
control projects, 13, 14, 43, 49,
54, 207